P9-APW-571

Date Due

Clinton	Clinton		
APN3			
Goderich			
Seaforth	JUL. ‾ 4 1984		
AUG 2 0 1984			
9C 2 Feb 85			
BC 4 8 0			

Paul Martin

A Very Public Life

VOLUME I FAR FROM HOME

DENEAU

Published by
Deneau Publishers
411 Queen Street
Ottawa, Ontario K1R 5A6

© Paul Martin

Printed in Canada
First printing
1983

Design by Ron Greene and Janet Riopelle

Canadian Cataloguing in Publication Data

Martin, Paul, 1903–
A Very Public Life

Includes index.
ISBN 0-88879-092 (v. 1)

1. Martin, Paul, 1903–   2. Cabinet ministers—
Canada—Biography*   I. Title.

FC621.M37A3 1983   971.064′3′0924   C83-090124-8
F1034.2.M37A3 1983

FOR NELL

CONTENTS

Preface

When I left Britain in the fall of 1979, I entered new and unexplored territory. To be sure, my retirement as Canada's high commissioner marked the formal conclusion of a public life that had begun forty-five years before. But I have never been a man who just lowers the tent flap and walks away. A few weeks before I left for Canada, someone exclaimed to me, "You've had such a full life!" and I thought to myself, "What does that mean — 'had'?"

And so, sitting in the library at 12 Upper Brook Street in London — surrounded by boxes packed full of my books — I took up a pencil. On a piece of scrap paper, I wrote what became the first paragraph of this book.

For me, this was a daring act. From my youth, I have been a constant reader of the lives of others — biographies and autobiographies that serve as public testimonies. John Morley's *Life of Gladstone* was the first book that I ever took home from a library, and John Henry Newman's *Apologia pro vita sua* moved me when I studied it at university. It moves me yet. My library shelves are full of many similar works and I have always reverenced the time, perseverance and reflection that they embody. Although I am not a patient man, I have been inspired by their example and I determined to set out some details of my own life. Now I am not sure which was more difficult — living my life or writing about it. The Book of Ecclesiastes expresses it so well:

> of making many books, there is no end; and much study is an affliction of the flesh.

The making of this book has provided me with some surprises. As I wrote about my very public life, I have had to reflect on some very private experiences. My early years in Pembroke with my family and my student days at Toronto, Harvard, Cambridge and Geneva have been dealt with at length — perhaps taking more space than in many similar books. But these years are written about with love and attention. Most of the themes that dominated my later life began quietly in my youth and young manhood. Early in life, my course was set and my vision directed towards helping to solve the problems that bedevilled mankind. The sometimes difficult economic circumstances of my family prompted me to try to understand the means for attaining social betterment; the idealism for world peace that dominated the universities after the Great War made me ever aware of the need for a stable international order.

My ultimate objective — a public life — was never in question. Quite naturally, therefore, my story unfolds from that perspective. Some of the greatest Canadian public figures of my lifetime have scarcely revealed themselves or been revealed. Louis St. Laurent, the prime minister that I most admired, has received little attention. James Ilsley, perhaps the ablest of my contemporaries and a dear friend, has passed completely from view. In latter days, public servants, especially diplomats who had to maintain a professional silence, have been talkative; those politicians one expected to have been garrulous have remained largely taciturn.

This reserve is a pity. Despite all that is written and said, I believe that a public life is an honourable life. This book, for me, is a debt to the fading memories of men who shared my vocation. I want it to set out as faithfully as I am able what we hoped to accomplish.

Throughout the past four years as I worked on my text, I have always kept in mind John Henry Newman's preface to his *Apologia*. "I mean to be simply personal and historical," he wrote, and

> am doing no more than explaining myself and my opinions and actions. I wish as far as I am able to state facts, whether they are ultimately determined to be for me or against me.... I may be accused of laying stress on little things, of being beside the mark, of going into impertinent or ridiculous details, of sounding my own praise, of giving scandal; but this is a case above all others, in which I am bound to follow my own lights and to speak out my own heart.*

I have striven for the greatest degree of factual and historical accuracy in the preparation of the text. This has involved extensive research in manuscript collections, my own in particular. But I did not want to produce a work laden with footnotes that would scare the reader with the threat of excessive pedantry. Accordingly, the references have been kept to a minimum. To help achieve this end, sources from my own papers have not been cited.

It is difficult to write acknowledgments, but few books — and this one is no exception — can be produced without incurring important debts. First and most importantly of all, I should like to thank William R. Young, historian, whose assistance on this project has been invaluable. My many hundreds of hand-written pages have been made more acceptable by his suggested refinements, based upon his remarkable knowledge of the events of my life and times. Bill's historical scholarship has always impressed me — he has kept me unreasonably honest — and his phlegmatic disposition was an inspiration whenever the going got tough.

Jonathan Williams, my editor, has given the work a touch of his poetic Welsh soul, helping me to pull up my grammatical socks

---

* Cardinal Newman, *Apologia pro vita sua*, The World's Classics (Oxford University Press), p. xxxii.

and vigilantly watching over the preparation of the final manuscript.

My friend, John English, of the University of Waterloo, patiently and with great care, has provided valuable advice throughout the writing of this volume. Both he and Jack Granatstein, of York University, read the drafts. Robert Bothwell, of the University of Toronto, encouraged me in the initial stages of this venture. All have mustered their gentlest bedside manner to help a neophyte and non-academic author through the birthpangs of writing a book.

Several others provided useful and timely advice. My son, Paul, served as a constant critic and revealed unknown literary talent. My animated daughter, Mary Anne, lent her moral support and vigorous arguments. My sisters, Lucille, Marie, Claire and Anita, ransacked their homes for photographs and added their own stock of family lore.

My friend, Dr. Francis Leddy, read the manuscript; the former senator, H. Carl Goldenberg, read the chapters on labour policy; both with the sagacity for which they are known. Father Armand Maurer and Dr. Maryellen MacGuigan reinvigorated my zeal for philosophy.

Others have eased the way for the production of the book. Ramona Quenneville gave unstintingly of her time and spent hours deciphering and transcribing my handwriting; Dr. Margaret Mattson and Carman Carroll of the Public Archives of Canada made certain that my papers were always accessible. Marc Gotlieb provided research assistance for two summers. Louise Adamson efficiently copy-edited the manuscript; Anne Marie Kelly calmly and competently helped out in Ottawa. In Montreal, Susan Marcoux, Dianna Ewart and Lucy Santoro produced the final copy. Diane Johnston, with cheerful good humour and the greatest attention to detail, managed this operation.

The Social Sciences and Humanities Research Councils and many interested friends have helped to make this book possible.

My publisher, Denis Deneau, has given the lie to Lord Byron's claim, "Now, Barabbas was a publisher."

Last, but far from least, I come to my dear wife Nell. She has been my inspiration since we met forty-seven years ago. No one could have provided more gaiety to my life, or this book, than she has — certainly not the author. Every evening she sat and listened to that day's laboriously reworded text and gave me, as always, wise counsel and good-humoured riposte. If there are any failings in my work, they are mine; if there is any merit, it is truly hers.

Windsor, Ontario
25 September 1983

I

The River and the Town

OUR OLD BRICK HOUSE, with its white, low-hung verandah, bordered the sidewalk on Moffat Street, opposite the bishop's palace in the Ottawa Valley town of Pembroke. My parents lived here after moving from Ottawa a few months following my birth on 23 June 1903, and this was the house in which I grew up.

Pembroke sits on the south bank of the Ottawa River, facing Desjardinsville and Chapeau in the province of Québec. From the town, the Laurentian hills are seen across the winding, picturesque river — as memorable a vista as any I know. Throughout my life, in or outside Canada, the serene beauty of the Ottawa has stayed with me. From our verandah, I could see it beyond the hill on Renfrew Street; and when I worked in the town's lumberyards during summer holidays, the river was close at hand during each eleven-hour day. As the Canadian Pacific Railway's noon train wound its way westwards, I often gazed at it from the top of a lumber pile, watching it pass along the river's bank in the town's outer reaches. In my youth, I sat many times on Pembroke's old wharf, glorying in the ancient Laurentians beyond Chapeau and the river's sandy and irregular shoreline. Whenever I walked along

Renfrew Street, past the cathedral, the old Presbyterian church and the Carnegie library, the Ottawa was ever on my left — a sustaining presence.

I have seen many of the world's great rivers but know that in my boyhood I lived by one of unsurpassed charm. It was always a part of my dreams about the future, further inspired by the train's daily procession from Canada's capital to my Ottawa Valley town and beyond to the faraway Pacific. Have not all of us a river, a lake or a mountain that seized our imagination when we were young? I, too, had a river that I recall as part of my rich and ample heritage.

Before my parents moved to Pembroke, they lived on Ottawa's LeBreton Street in one of a row of brick houses with long narrow stairways, near the corner of Somerset Street. Their first daughter, Anne Marie, was born on 18 December 1901; to their sorrow, she died nine months later. I was their second child, born at 63 LeBreton Street and baptized Joseph James Guillaume Paul in the nearby Church of St. Jean Baptiste.

My father, Joseph Philippe Ernest, carried the Martin surname of his Irish forefathers from County Mayo, but in culture he remained thoroughly French. From Ottawa, where he was born on 22 May 1876, the family moved to Thurso, Québec, where my father was brought up. In the predominantly English town of Pembroke, most people knew him as "Philip." My grandfather, James Martin, was the last child of a large Irish immigrant family and the only one born in Canada — in Beauharnois, Québec, on 28 March 1833; he died at Thurso on 1 June 1887, when my father was eleven. James Martin married a French girl, Emma Lemaire, on 19 October 1858. My grandmother was born in St. Benoît, Québec, on 13 November 1842 and died in Ottawa on 21 August 1927. She had striking black eyes and was a rather formal lady, insisting on being called Madame Martin. My father returned to Ottawa from Thurso about 1896 and worked as a clerk for various merchants in the city. After he and my mother, Lumina

Chouinard, married on 12 February 1901, he changed jobs often, collecting bills for J. D. LeBlanc, an upholsterer and furniture dealer, and working in dry goods stores until we moved to Pembroke.

The Chouinards, who had moved to Ottawa from Montreal, were a very close-knit family. My mother was born on 17 October 1880. Her mother, Albina Philion, came from a family long established in Ottawa, some of whom had become priests and lawyers. However, my immediate forebears were not well off and doubled up in their various rented households in the area between Concession Street (now Bronson Avenue) and Booth Street. Before they married, my mother and father had lived a block apart on Cambridge Street. When my parents first settled on LeBreton Street, they lived with my mother's parents and near her uncle, Charles Chouinard, and his family. Grandmother Chouinard, "mémère," as I called her, was a loveable but strong-willed woman; I never felt as close to her as I did to my grandfather, Guillaume Chouinard, who always carried a pair of scissors in his vest pocket — a symbol of his work in the dry goods business. He was the most delightfully gullible man. When I was a young lad, I remember him pulling out his timepiece and saying, "Well now, my watch tells me it's going to rain." My father teased him about this prediction, but, backed into a corner by his remarks, Grandfather became adamant. So Father went upstairs, fetched a big basin of water, and trickled it over the porch roof. My grandfather, who was sitting on the verandah, got all excited at this apparent divine justification of his prophecy and cried, "Voici! Voici! La pluie!"

At the turn of the century, Pembroke, like many Ontario towns, had a distinct social structure. The town had been founded in 1828 by Peter White, a British naval veteran, who had been lured north by the lumber trade. When we arrived, the heirs of the pioneer families still controlled the larger businesses and owned a great deal of property in the area. In 1885 they had set up a power company, which generated electricity for the local industries and provided some of the first street lighting in Canada. Pembroke's industries included two large sawmills, Pink's foundry, and three factories that made boxes, barrels and matches. The owners and managers of these factories lived in big gingerbread houses on the treelined streets of the upper town and in the east end.

The Irish and French Canadians had come to Pembroke in the 1840s to work in the lumber mills; later, they and their descendants laboured in the newer factories and small businesses, where they continually jostled for the same jobs. This led to a certain lack of amity between them. Most of the Irish and French did not rise very high on the social ladder, and both were less inclined to pursue material progress than another of the town's racial groups, the Germans.

Pembroke's sizeable German community had arrived during the 1880s and were a very hardworking lot. Our neighbours at one time included a German family whose head toiled in the box factory for ten hours a day and then, after supper, worked until late at night on the upkeep of his property. Like our neighbour, the town's German population provided an example of what the Irish and the French might accomplish if they applied themselves. Father would stop work at six o'clock, but my mother, more conscious of others, used to tell him to look at our neighbours: "*They* own their own home." The implication was that if my father had not gone to the ball diamond to umpire a baseball game, or to the rink to referee a hockey game, we could have had some of the more tangible possessions of the people next door.

Our family was never well off; I doubt whether my father earned more than twenty dollars a week in his whole life. That he had not prospered in Ottawa caused him to accept his sister Alzire's invitation to move to Pembroke to work for her husband, Isidore Martin, in his grocery store. Uncle Isidore, one of three brothers from Buckingham, Québec, was a second cousin of my father; other Martin relatives worked on the railway as trainmen and conductors. My Aunt Alzire, a beautiful and humorous woman, was very much a leading character in the clan.

The first four years of my life were happy ones for my family. My father and mother had rented a house from the bishop of Pembroke, Narcisse Zephirin Lorrain.[1] The house stood on a double corner lot, which also held a stable to house the bishop's horses and carriages. My parents, particularly my devout mother, felt so proud to live across from the bishop's palace and St. Columbkille's Cathedral — the centre of the diocese of Pembroke. As the family filled out, my brother, sisters and I put the stable and its commodious hayloft to productive use. We enacted our own make-believe parliament and staged productions in high-spirited imitation of our elders; the sheriff and the gun-slinging cowboy, whom we saw at the nickel cinema, were favourite dramatic subjects.

My father was a popular grocer, unfailingly friendly and obliging to his suppliers and customers. Isidore appreciated his brother-in-law's qualities, and he and my father grew very close. The business was a fairly successful one, and Isidore could soon afford to spend more time away from the store. In 1907 my Uncle Isidore was elected mayor of Pembroke. But he served for only a term and lost when he ran for office a second time in 1908. That same year, a fire destroyed a large part of Pembroke's business section, gutting a nearby foundry that was never rebuilt. My uncle's business suffered; within a year he gave up his shop and took a job as a commercial traveller, compelling my father to seek employment in another grocery store. This time he found work with J. B. Kemp in the east end of town, where the more affluent families shopped. I sometimes asked him, "Papa, why don't you own a store?" Yet even though my father had spent a little time at Rigaud College in Québec, in some kind of commercial course, he was not cut out for business.

1 Bishop Lorrain's early episcopal life had been spent as a pioneer, visiting every parish in his diocese, which stretched right up to Hudson Bay. In 1928, I found a copy of a book by a priest named Proulx in the Widener Library at Harvard University. Entitled *A la Baie d'Hudson ou Récit de la première visite pastorale de Mgr. N. Z. Lorrain*, it provoked me to comment in my diary that "our lives, after all, are not the test of character and worth that the existence of early settlement was."

My father was a much beloved individual. Although not a tall man, he was very athletic and a great sport. He was strong, which I am not, and loved outdoor games — baseball most of all. Long after his playing days were over, Father was the indispensable umpire in senior games at the local diamond. When he was not at the ball park after supper, he would go upstairs and put on a white shirt, his blue suit and his fedora; then, with a cigar in his mouth, he would stroll downtown to buy the *Ottawa Journal* — mainly for the sports pages — say hello to the "boys," and saunter back.

Essentially a man of peace, my father did not like disputes or rancour at home. He rarely quarrelled with my mother and could not bear squabbles between any of his children. Sometimes my younger brother, Emile,[2] and I would bicker, as all boys do; it upset my father, but I never remember him raising his hand. Father would be hurt if we disobeyed him, but it was my mother who scolded us more often. A man of some reticence, my father was reluctant to make a great play of his emotions and never once said to me, "You're doing well" or "You're doing badly." He used to comment diffidently, "I'm glad you got this" — never much more than that. But when he died, we went through his clothes and found his pockets full of newspaper clippings concerning the activities of his eldest child.

A strong Catholic, my father never flaunted his religion; but he gave his all, uncomplainingly and with a great sense of humour. In his day, most practising Catholics did not question theological doctrines. He was a good churchman and loved taking up the collection. When I first brought my wife-to-be, Nell, to meet my parents before our marriage, we went to mass together. As a prank, Nell and I surreptitiously dropped buttons in the collection plate. This really tickled my father, who flipped them into the air and caught them again on the plate.

My father died in October 1943, just before communion at a mission in Pembroke's cathedral. He collapsed right on the front

2 Emile was born on 31 October 1906.

steps. During the service, the priest simply said, "There will be no sermon. Philippe Martin has preached it."

My mother shared her husband's deep religious beliefs. Though a vivacious and demonstrative woman, she was truly saintly — hardly ever without a rosary, repeating her religious devotions to the Mother of God. With prayer, she believed, no problem was insurmountable. Occasionally, she was a little intolerant of those who did not share her unwavering faith. For her, everything was God's will; she was always saying "We'll ask our Lord to do this" and "We'll ask our Lord to do that."

Mother's faith grew even stronger after I became ill as a young boy. When I was four years old, I contracted spinal meningitis, a common affliction in the early years of the century. My mother left no stone unturned to achieve the best for her children, and she set about helping to cure my disease. I received excellent medical attention from two local physicians, Dr. Bédard and his colleague Dr. Dodd, and Bishop Lorrain visited our house frequently to help my parents through this very trying time. I have no great recollection of it all, but I do remember going with my mother on the train to Montreal when I was perhaps eight or nine to visit Brother André, who later founded St. Joseph's Oratory. In his humble and thinly furnished room, with its beige walls, we knelt and prayed together for my full recovery. Mother also took me to be healed at the famous shrine of Ste. Anne de Beaupré. Her faith was so fervent that she believed a miracle had happened when I eventually recovered but for a weakened muscular condition in my shoulders and left leg. Until I regained the strength in my legs, I was pulled about in a small wagon by my father and later by Emile.

My parents passed on their religious devotion to me and to my brother and five sisters. They both fasted during Lent and encouraged us to make sacrifices too; I denied myself by not eating candy and by telling fewer fibs than normally. Mother's keenest hope was that someday I should enter the priesthood. I was and still am extremely sensitive to the teachings of the Catholic Church; when I do not observe them, I am conscious of not having done so and feel quite guilty about it. For me, faith is a joyous thing, although I am not always free from doubt and sometimes find it difficult to pray.

But when I was young, association with the church was not reserved for Sundays; it was a part of our daily existence. Bishop Lorrain took me for my first automobile ride, and as soon as I could, I became one of his altar boys. On one of our rides, the auxiliary bishop, Patrick Thomas Ryan, came with us to look after the failing bishop and gently took him to task for his childish behaviour. For a long time I served the early morning mass, said by Bishop Ryan, at the Grey Nuns' Convent.[3] When Bishop Lorrain passed on, I served as an acolyte at his funeral. During the service, the congregation had to crane their necks to see the bishop laid out in his episcopal finery in the open coffin. The undertaker, hidden behind the catafalque and at the head of the bier, quietly lifted up the body and put a cushion behind it to give everyone a better view. This created consternation among the faithful, who thought momentarily that the resurrection of Bishop Lorrain was taking place before their very eyes.

Our family was keenly conscious of being Catholic, aware that not everyone in Pembroke shared our religious belief. As a boy, I used always to scurry past the Anglican church for fear of being contaminated. A large tree stood outside our home on Isabella Street, where we moved after the Great War. On the eve of the twelfth of July — the day on which Orangemen celebrate William's victory at the Boyne over the Catholic King James II— my mother used to hang a religious medal on this tree, and we would all gather around and pray that it would rain like hell the next day. Years later, at a dinner party given by Lord Beaverbrook, I told the assembled guests about our lighthearted bigotry. Our host rejoindered by reciting the following quatrain:

---

3 Patrick Thomas Ryan had been the first priest ordained in St. Columbkille's in 1887. He was consecrated auxiliary to Bishop Lorrain on 25 July 1912 in the presence of two archbishops and six bishops. Seven months after Bishop Lorrain's death in December 1915, his auxiliary succeeded him to the see of Pembroke, where he served until his death on 15 April 1937 at age seventy-three.

Up the long ladder
And down the short rope.
God bless King Billy
And to hell with the pope.

Beaverbrook greatly enjoyed quoting this verse because he had
been brought up the son of the manse with childhood prejudices
against what he called "Papists."

I suppose that life in all small Ontario towns was much the
same: families were singled out by their religion as well as by their
national origin and language. And yet our biases were not unre-
mitting. I played with Carl Landsky, son of one of the three
Lutheran ministers, and greatly admired the figure cut by Pastor
Schroeder as he walked past our house every day, attired in a long
black coat with silk lapels.

Certain Protestants and Catholics in the town made common
cause against the demon rum. At one time Pembroke had a
militant parish priest, the patriarchal Father P. S. Dowdall, whose
oratory both inspired and intimidated his flock. During one sermon, he ripped off his loose cuffs and flung them out of the pulpit.
Apart from his Sunday exhortations, Father Dowdall's crusading
zeal took him into the bars the night before, searching for wayward
parishioners. One of the local Protestant doctors used to go to the
tavern and get tight every Saturday night. His wife, knowing
about Father Dowdall's mission, would ask him to look for her
husband. And so the priest made a point of going into each bar to
inquire, "Is George in here?", eventually finding the errant doctor
and shepherding him home. Dowdall was a big, hulking man from
Eganville, and I guess the doctor did not have the wherewithal to
refuse to come along.

Lucille and Marie, my first set of twin sisters, were born on 9
May 1909. Surprisingly unalike physically, they both show strong
independence of mind and take great delight in tripping me up.
My parents had another daughter three years later, my sister
Aline, born on 5 December 1912. Charles Henri was born after
Aline, but he was a blue baby and died when he was just two
months old. He passed away at my Aunt Alzire's house, and

Mother, who had been invited to her sister-in-law's for dinner, wheeled her dead infant back to our Moffat Street home. I remember Emile standing outside the house the next day, inviting passersby to come and pay their respects to his brother, who was lying inside in his small coffin.

Anita and Claire, my parents' second set of twin daughters, were born on 30 November 1915. When I babysat them, I would tell them stories, tapping my feet on the floor to imitate the approach of impending ghosts. When my mother arrived home, it would take her some time to calm down the two little girls.

Like my other sisters, Claire and Anita were far less exposed than Emile and me to our family's French heritage. Mother's custom was to recite each decade of the rosary alternately in French and English. Because the youngest girls could not say all the responses in French, they sometimes would gabble the words. In the end, my mother gave in and family prayers were said in English only.

When I began school at about the age of six, I was predisposed to work hard because my mother had always impressed upon me how important it was to apply oneself — to study hard so that we could get ahead in life. Mother spoke French and English extremely well and had taught school for a time when she lived with her uncle, le curé, at Embrun, near Alfred, a small town east of Ottawa.

I remember my first day in grade one; the separate school where Emile and I went stood diagonally across from the end of our yard on Isabella Street. The teaching staff were four young ladies and seven Grey Nuns of the Immaculate Conception, whose members also taught at the convent in Pembroke's residential Catholic girls' school. I spent eight years there with the same classmates — Roy and Lloyd Ludgate, "N. B." and Joe Giroux, and John Stoqua, from the Indian reservation at Golden Lake. I can recall them all vividly — their faces, personalities, and their place in the classroom. I had a crush on one of my classmates, Vera Chaput, and was often tempted to embrace her and to touch her pretty brown dress. But I could never command the courage. She may well have been, without my knowing it, my first love. School interested me so much that when I had to miss classes from time to time because of my illness, I longed to get back to the books.[4] My recollection is that I did reasonably well at school, particularly in my final year, or, as we called it, the "entrance class," but examinations were a nightmare.

It was not the teachers, however, but Miss Alma Beatty, Pembroke's librarian, who instilled in me an abiding love of literature. As a boy, I knew little about books except school texts, although my mother had often spoken of their value. There was no bookish influence in our home; apart from the big family Bible, our "library" consisted of a four-shelf bookcase that contained certain classics and the *Boys' Own Annual,* brought home by my father. There were also one or two histories of Canada written in French, including the first "nationalist" history, by François-Xavier Garneau. Books were not much in evidence in most of my friends' homes, either; I suppose their parents, like mine, could not afford them.

Miss Beatty introduced me to an entirely different world. She used to buy groceries at J. B. Kemp's store. One day when I was about twelve, she said to my father, "Well, I see Paul is doing very well. You'd better tell him to come to the library to see me." Miss

---

4 But even when I was confined to home, I kept myself busy. During my time at Harvard in 1928, I was passing through New Haven, Connecticut. As I wrote in my diary, it reminded me that as a boy, I had a connection with the town. My parents had bought me a set of steel parts, then known as "Meccano," which were made in New Haven: "No game has ever given me as much pleasure. The things I made out of these parts are legion in number. Well do I remember my pride and boyish glee when I received a certificate making me a 'Gilbert Engineer,' for an original model of a 'Merry-Go-Round,' a toy which, at the period of construction, seemed as complex and as wonderful as the great machines of modern industry. Time has taught that, relatively, the 'Merry-Go-Round' was the essence of simplicity in construction, but time can never change the satisfaction from the creation of my own."

Beatty's request was not to be ignored lightly, for she was known as a woman with definite ideas. So, shortly afterwards, I ventured into Pembroke's new Carnegie library, which stood near the top of the hill, close to the town hall with its painted clock tower. I had never seen a bigger or more wonderful room, although when I think of it now I realize that it was quite small. Row upon row of volumes were set out in the stacks. Miss Beatty removed two of them. "These are books you should look at," she said. "Sit down right now and start to read them." They were the two-volume *Life of William Ewart Gladstone* by John Morley.

Alma Beatty always kept in touch with "her boys," those youngsters whom she had introduced to the joys of reading. Just before the Liberal Party lost the 1957 general election — I was minister of national health and welfare — I received a lecture from her about our policy on old-age pensions. She was eighty-two then ("way over my allotted span," as she wrote to me) but she still took me and the government to task for raising the pension by only six dollars a month, instead of the ten dollars she felt was right. Of course, Miss Beatty and her family were staunch Tories and it would have made little difference, but I still wish she could have known that I had fought in cabinet for the ten-dollar pension increase.

When I was a boy, Alma Beatty helped open my eyes to the world around me. For as long as I can remember, even at the separate school, I had an urge to advance myself in order to enjoy some of the advantages that education can bring. We were a happy family despite our sometimes straitened circumstances, but from my books and personal observations I grew aware that there was a way of life different from ours. Our neighbours across Isabella Street, the Munros, lived in a large house befitting one of the wealthiest families in Pembroke. When my brother and I used to play with the Munro boys in their home, we could not help drawing comparisons with our own more modest dwelling.

To help make ends meet, I began to do various jobs in the afternoons after school. As soon as I had mastered my bicycle, I used it to deliver shoes for James and Duncan Grieve. Somewhat later, when Dan Jones, the editor and publisher of the weekly Pembroke *Standard* and a prominent Liberal, suggested to my mother that I sell his newspaper, I accepted eagerly. Dan Jones was the finest writer I had ever read, and I knew the *Standard* was the best damn paper in the world. On Thursdays, I would go into the dining room of the Hotel Pembroke with the permission of the owner, Mr. J. B. Teevens, to importune the diners to buy the *Standard*, hot off the press. Many of the commercial travellers knew nothing of the paper. "You haven't heard of Dan Jones?" I would ask in amazement. "Why, he's the best writer.... Listen to this." And then I would turn to the editorial page and read the great man's immortal words to my dining room audience.[5]

But my boyhood was not all school and odd jobs. Our yard was very popular with friends and neighbours, and in the summer we played baseball — my father and brother, and our friends the Ludgates and the Giroux. I was not as skilful as the others because of my meningitis. But the disability in my shoulders and legs did not hamper my efforts as a southpaw. Some of the balls I pitched might have been batted over the fence with relative ease, but I played tenaciously and with all my strength. My team-mates took account of my impairment and always defended my shortcomings, even if it meant a loss for our side. In winter, Father flooded the yard to make a skating rink, and it became a favourite gathering place. It was a way of coping with the severe winter and gave hours of pleasure to our friends, who skated there as often as schoolwork permitted.

One of our neighbours, Frank Nighbor, became a popular Pembroke hero and was among the first professional hockey players in Canada. His poke check marked him as a star among stars — Canada's greatest man on ice. More than once, at the end of the hockey season, after his trips to Vancouver and Ottawa, Frank gave me the sweater he had worn.

---

5 After a while, emboldened by my success as a huckster, I also began to sell a cheap scandal sheet called *Jack Canuck*. Father Dowdall found out and told my mother that I should not be peddling such a rag. She stopped me at once.

There were some games we did not play. I remember seeing a friend, Bob Bromley, dressed in white ducks, ambling down to have a game of tennis in the court next to the Presbyterian church. People like me did not play tennis. It was a badge of social distinction, and unless your father happened to be an accountant, a doctor or a lawyer, was a sport you had no part of. When I was courting Nell — at her family's cottage on Lake Erie — I was intrigued to discover that they had their own tennis court and could all play the game well. My wife's parents were much better off than mine.

Our third house on Isabella Street was quite cramped: there were just two bedrooms for my parents and their seven children. In the room where my mother slept were three beds for her and my five sisters. When I was home, I shared a bed in the other room with my father, while Emile slept downstairs in the small living room. This situation lasted until after I was at university and some of the other children began to leave home.

The floors of the house were covered in worn oilcloth — never a carpet to take off the chill — and each of the tiny rooms had wooden wainscotting and papered walls. We had a piano in the dining room — a Heintzman upright. I took lessons for a while but did not have Emile's aptitude for music. My parents kept paying for the piano — for years, it seemed — at two dollars a month. The piano was one of our few amenities. We were still obliged to boil water when we wanted a hot bath. The house was heated by a wood stove in the hallway and a large Findlay range in the kitchen — the room where we always ate, despite the fact that there was a dining room. The kitchen was, and still is for a lot of French Canadian families, the place where everything took place — it was eating room, discussion room and playroom. In my mind's eye, I can still see my sisters' diapers stretched out on a line across the kitchen, and my father, just home from work, stripped to the waist and washing himself at the kitchen sink.

※—※

Even the Great War did not upset the relative tranquillity of our lives. My mother and father shared the pro-war sentiments, and I do not recall anyone in the town being against Canada joining the conflict. As an altar boy, I had grown friendly with the German-born sexton of the cathedral. After August 1914, I heard all kinds of stories about him: that he was a German spy, and that his carrying coal around at night to heat the cathedral was somehow connected with helping the fatherland. Even members of my own family asked, "What's he doing there so late at night? Maybe it's something to do with the war." In the end, the talk got so bad that the poor fellow had to leave his job. I remember wondering what in the world a German spy in Pembroke would do for the Kaiser.

During the first year of the war, the young men of the town lined up in uniform on the hill in front of the town hall. It was a great spectacle to see them leave to fight in what I then thought was a good cause. I remember going down to the recruiting centre in an old hardware store in the town where I would chat for hours with the recruiting agents and the new volunteers.

My father strongly supported the war but was ardently opposed to conscription. The first time I ever attended a political meeting was when I went with him to hear the prime minister, Sir Robert Borden, speak at Pembroke's O'Brien Opera House in November 1917, during the general election campaign. I knew nothing about the election except what I had heard from my father, who was a great supporter of Sir Wilfrid Laurier, Borden's opponent; but I soon learned that conscription was the campaign's burning issue. Naturally, I was influenced by my father and came to believe that Borden was wrong to have introduced conscription against the wishes of the French people and for leading a crusade against Laurier, who had become my idol.

A related dispute also exercised the townspeople of Pembroke about this time: the Ontario government's regulation 17, restricting the teaching of French in the province's schools. While the Irish Catholics approved of, and indeed agitated for, this curtailment of French education, Franco-Ontarians were very upset about it. The dissent in Pembroke did not match the animosity felt in Ottawa — where the French schools closed down and children marched in protest against the regulation — but it concerned us just the same, perhaps because of the deep involvement of Bishop Lorrain. Certain people rightfully strove to extend the teaching of French in the town. At our separate school, we were taught only in English, and there was just one French teacher, despite the fact that nearly half my classmates were of French descent.

My background and our proximity to Ottawa, the centre of the conflict, meant that I was exposed to the controversy over regulation 17; I also heard about it when I visited my grandparents in the capital. My grandmother Chouinard belonged to St. Jean Baptiste parish in Ottawa, but one Sunday she went to mass at St. Patrick's, the Irish church on Kent Street. As the priest was walking down the aisle, he recognized her as a French-speaking Catholic from another parish and asked her to leave. The newspaper *Le Droit*, founded in 1913, became required reading for those like our family who supported the French side. Our neighbour, M. Longpré, a great friend of my parents, consistently pressed for more French in the schools; he and my father were both quite militant on the language issue. The undercurrent that began in those years seems to have persisted throughout my life.

The elevation of Bishop Patrick Ryan to succeed Bishop Lorrain in 1916 did nothing to still the local tongues. We all thought the delay in his confirmation as the Pembroke incumbent was attributable to the opposition of the French clergy and laymen; it seemed to the French as though the Irish were taking over the diocese. Bishop Ryan should have been popular, for he was a Pembroke boy — the son of a laundress, he had come from what in those days was called "a poor family." In the end, he settled any doubt as to his position in an original way. One Sunday, he delivered his whole sermon in English; then, without pausing, he repeated it word-for-word in French. The congregation had to sit on the uncomfortable cathedral pews until he had finished. My father appreciated the bishop's point, but he could not help quipping, "Thank God he doesn't speak German."

❊❊

Not too long after this, Bishop Ryan came to play an extremely important part in my life. I had written my entrance examinations in the spring of 1918 and had graduated from public school. Some relatives already thought I should get a job; I remember hearing one aunt saying, "Isn't it a pity Paul spends so much time reading? He should find work." I suppose it would have been my lot to end up in one of the local factories, as my brother did later on, had not fate intervened. I had often thought of being at college but had never foreseen any possibility of furthering my studies. Where would I get the money? My father could not afford it. One morning in the summer of 1918, after I had served mass for the bishop, he turned to me and said, "I saw in the paper that you've got your entrance examination. Would you like to go to college?"[6] When I said that I would, the bishop told me to ask my mother to come to see him.

I rushed home. "Oh Mother, I have the most wonderful news. Bishop Ryan wants to see you tonight."

I can see her yet, holding up her hands as she cried out, "Thank God." Obviously she had been praying for something like this. Mother went that evening to see the bishop. It was decided somehow or other — I do not recall whether he asked her or whether it was just implied — that I was going to be a priest. And that, at the time, is what I wanted to be, although even then I struggled between my desire to be a priest and my longing to be like Laurier. I wondered if perhaps I could be both.

In any event, the bishop and my mother arranged that the following September I should begin my course of studies at St. Alexandre in Ironside, just north of Ottawa on the Gatineau River. Like other colleges of its type, St. Alexandre was designed to give boys with a possible vocation for the priesthood the advantage of a French-language classical education. The $200-a-year cost of my tuition, room and board was paid by Bishop Ryan, but I did not know at the time that the money came to him from

6 The word "college" should not be understood to be synonymous with "university." It was used to denote an institution that provided a classical French education.

M. J. O'Brien, a lumber baron from Renfrew and a good friend
of the bishop. When I was at university, my unknown benefactor,
who had been appointed to the Senate in 1919, was quoted as
making what I thought of as a rather platitudinous address. In one
of my regular letters to the bishop, I remarked on this, telling him
of my low opinion of the upper house. Bishop Ryan thought my
comments a disgrace and replied that I ought to respect my country's institutions and those who served in them, that I had made an
idle and silly criticism and was merely following the mob. He ended
his letter: "Well, you should know that some of the funds which
have made possible your education at St. Alexandre were provided
by this man on whom, as you say, 'chloroform would not have
much effect.'" I never forgot the bishop's admonition; it taught me
to be better informed and more prudent.

One sultry day in early September, my father and Emile took
me to the college at Ironside. From Ottawa, where we went first,
we drove in a rented carriage — as often happened on special
occasions when my father took the family for an outing. We had
covers over us to keep the dust off our clothes. Leaving Landre-
ville's livery stable in Ottawa's "Flats," we crossed the Chaudière
Bridge to Hull. Eventually we passed over the Gatineau River,
saw ahead the cultivated fields of the college farm, and heard the
powerful roar of the rapids (the college is built near the river at a
point where the rapids are strong and the waters wind their way
around the college island of Ile Marguerite).

As my father turned the horses onto the ascending path, our
gaze took in what would be my home for the next three years. The
brick buildings of the college and its central clock tower overlooked a playing field and were ranged on a hill from where, on a
clear day, it was possible to see the towers of the Parliament
Buildings in Ottawa.

It was very hard to say goodbye to my father; both of us were so
overcome. Not even the warm greeting of Father Burgsthaler, the
big and powerful Alsatian superior, could assuage my melancholy.
Many nights were to follow when, in the dormitory of the first
division, I cried myself to sleep, suffering the sadness of first

separation from my beloved parents, brother and sisters. I was just fifteen and felt far from home.

Under the auspices of some French citizens, the college had first opened its doors as an agricultural school, but it had not prospered. By my time, it had become a classical college, run by the Holy Ghost fathers from Alsace-Lorraine, although with a sprinkling of members of the same order from Blackrock College in Dublin. The college had degree-granting authority from Laval University in Québec City.

Like other colleges in Québec, St. Alexandre followed a very spartan regimen. We arose every morning before six, made our beds and then went to early morning mass in the chapel. By seven, we would breakfast on porridge, coarse bread and jam; each of us took a turn waiting at table. We used utensils brought from home and would wash them after each meal in the same dish of soapy water, wiping them with a napkin that we kept for a week. After breakfast, everyone went to the study hall for a half-hour before classes began. At half-past ten, there was a break for about twenty minutes. Once the mid-day meal was finished, a short period of recreation preceded a study period and classes until four o'clock. Before the evening meal, there was an hour break and another hour of study. Supper was pea soup, meat and pudding; sometimes the food was terrible, but at least it was filling. We never had any luxuries. On feast days — St. Patrick's, St. Jean Baptiste, and Corpus Christi — peanuts were passed out for dessert. After supper, we were given another hour of recreation, followed by study until bed at nine.

The prefect of discipline, Father Emile Knaebel, our rather gruff professor of Greek and philosophy, would walk up and down the dormitory, his coat over his shoulders to keep out the chill, saying his beads, giving the odd blow here and there, and repeating, "Go to bed. Go to sleep." The mighty roar of the Gatineau rapids kept me awake at first but later lulled me to sleep as the bell of the clock tower struck its faithful note.

Yet despite the strictness of the college rules, those priests cared about us a great deal. During my first winter, a number of students died in the Spanish flu epidemic. I caught it too and was very sick. The college bursar, Father Mueller, ministered to us; he was not a registered medical doctor but was devoted to his boys, praying with us and looking after our needs. It was a terrible experience, and the epidemic took a dreadful toll across the country.

In the first division, where I started, our major subjects were English, French, Latin, Greek, some mathematics and religious knowledge. Two fathers whom I greatly respected were Jean Vichard and Joseph Lynch. The lanky Vichard, a real disciplinarian, taught us French, while Father Lynch took the Greek class. I have never had teachers as able in the art of exposition. The fathers of the Holy Ghost may not all have been great scholars, but they certainly knew how to arouse their students' enthusiasm.

The following year, I was promoted into the second division; here, some students were pursuing high school subjects, while others were following university courses. We benefited from a slight relaxation of the rules, but one still could not easily leave the college grounds between September and the Christmas break. In my three years at St. Alexandre, I only once came to Ottawa with permission. I had mentioned some other reason for the trip to the fathers, but I could not pass up this, my first opportunity to see a professional hockey game. Frank Nighbor, my Pembroke hero, was the chief drawing card.

Emile joined me at the college in the fall of 1919, but he accepted the rigours of St. Alexandre less willingly than I did and flew in the face of the college's regime. Father Burgsthaler spoke to the students each Friday afternoon in the senior study hall and took advantage of the occasion to review the "state of the Union" and to discourse generally on religion and deportment. The custom of dipping one's fingers into the font of holy water as one entered the study hall stimulated Emile's sense of humour. One afternoon, just before we gathered for the weekly lecture, he poured good blue ink into the font so that each student coming into the hall made an imprint on his forehead. As the evidence of the prank was gradually revealed, we restlessly awaited the grand entrance — with the expected result. Father Burgsthaler, whom I looked up to as a great leader, plunged his fingers into the font with vigour and consequence. My brother had seen to it that all were treated alike — superior and student. Unfortunately, Father Burgsthaler did not appreciate the fun, and the incident led to Emile's dismissal.

When he left the college, my brother returned to Pembroke and got a job in the Steel Equipment Company. After a while he moved to northern Ontario, where he worked at odd jobs, including a stint in a sawmill. In Timiskaming, Emile met his future wife, and eventually they moved to San Francisco. But he did not like the city, so they went south to Los Angeles, where he took up work as a linotype operator.

When I began my studies at St. Alexandre, it was assumed that I would enter the priesthood, but the issue had not been firmly settled in my own mind. I had inherited a great attachment to politics and was particularly fascinated by Sir Wilfrid Laurier and the Liberal Party. My father told me rather emotionally one day that he had heard Laurier speak at the college in Rigaud before he became prime minister. While he was wrongly identified by the Church hierarchy in Québec with the anticlerical liberalism of Europe, Laurier nonetheless did fight openly against the unconscionable influence of the Church in politics. My father did not know a lot about politics, but he told me how impressed he had been by this man, relentlessly struggling for the people against the established order. When Laurier began his speech at Rigaud, he was booed, but his eloquence soon won over the audience, and they gave him a tremendous ovation at the end.

My attachment to Laurier gained strength as I listened to my Aunt Mimi's stories about him. Mimi, my mother's younger sister, worshipped Sir Wilfrid but had never met him, although she worked in the East Block as a filing clerk. She used to take me down to All Saints' Church, opposite his home on Laurier Avenue, and we would sit on the church lawn and wait for him to come out.

This was where I first saw the impressive figure I so much admired. The second time, he was sitting in an open Ottawa streetcar, clad in a gray silk hat and long gray coat.

Laurier's death on 17 February 1919 was received with universal sorrow. Brother Jean, the college engineer, knew what Laurier meant to me and came to tell me he was dead; I took the news as one would that about a close relative. Wanting to express my own sense of loss, I decided to go to the funeral in Ottawa. But permission to leave the college was so difficult to obtain that I decided to set off without it. I trudged the ten miles to the city in the bitter cold and went to my grandmother's house on LeBreton Street. Then Aunt Mimi and I lined up with thousands of others at the Victoria Museum, the temporary home of parliament after the fiery destruction of the Centre Block, to view the body of the former prime minister, lying in state in his Windsor uniform. His life had become my beacon and in a mysterious way had influenced what I wanted to do.

The following day I went to the Basilica and watched with keen interest as Canadians from across the country gathered for the funeral service. I could not get in, so I got boosted up a tree on the other side of Sussex Street and watched as the funeral procession came out. Sir Robert Borden was the only one I recognized as the cortège made its way to Notre Dame Cemetery. When it had passed, I walked to the main Ottawa post office, on what is now Confederation Square, asked for some stationery at the wicket, and then stood at a counter and wrote a long, effusive letter to Lady Laurier, expressing my sympathy and telling her I would revere her husband's memory.

Back at St. Alexandre, I went, with some trepidation, to see Father Burgsthaler. Although he was none too pleased, he said, "Laurier meant a lot to you, didn't he? Well, it must have been a great funeral." I quoted from the homily delivered at the service by Father John E. Burke that I had read in the Ottawa newspaper (Burke had spoken the English sermon; the French was given by Archbishop O. E. Mathieu of Regina): "To you distinguished sons of Canada who have been honoured by being chosen pallbearers

... Bear him away gently, oh so gently. He is our beloved one; the nation's beloved. When you have arrived at the grave, lay him down tenderly; for the sod seldom covered a nobler heart."

The funeral affected me greatly. Later that year, on 8 December, I gave a speech on Laurier's life to the St. Alexandre Literary and Dramatic Society. I had spent a great deal of time preparing my address for this college-wide contest and was proud and pleased to be awarded first prize. Laurier's example had indeed set a path for me to follow. "He found our country a colony," said Father Burke, "and left it a nation." And when the archbishop had stressed that he had made it "the goal of his life to work towards the welfare of his fellow man," I knew that I could do likewise.

It was during my third year at Ironside that I resolved not to join the priesthood but to pursue secular studies, become a lawyer, and eventually enter public life. I wrote frankly to Bishop Ryan about my intentions. While he must have felt some disappointment about my decision, he agreed with me about the importance of public office and that good men should take it up. The bishop dismissed my suggestion that he no longer finance my training at St. Alexandre, but I would not allow him to help me beyond that. I was loath to tell my mother of my decision, and when I did manage to summon up the courage, it was clear that she was very hurt. My father certainly must have had views on the subject, but he did not express them. Both of them had always known that I had been fascinated by public life from childhood, but it was still a terrific shock to them when I made up my mind not to enter the priesthood.

I have often met young people and asked them, "What are you going to be?" If a child wants to be a great architect or a celebrated scientist, why should he or she not say so? If others wish to enter public life and become prime minister, why should they be reluctant to speak openly of their hopes? As Oliver Wendell Holmes once said, "Nothing is so commonplace as to wish to be remarkable." Before I was ten, I wanted to go into public life; it seemed to me a noble calling. Wilfrid Laurier had deeply impressed me —

chiefly because of my father, who would read aloud from his speeches as they were set down in the Ottawa newspapers. Laurier wanted Canada to become strong and united; the more I heard of him, the more I wished to be like him. Yes, as a young schoolboy, I determined to strive to get into parliament some day and, like Laurier, aspired to be worthy of leading the Canadian people as prime minister. Theologians speak of vocations for the church; I believe there are vocations in public life as well.

My decision to study law and pursue a public career meant that I must leave St. Alexandre. At that time, two of my Pembroke friends were in their final year at St. Michael's College at the University of Toronto. Emulating their example, I decided to apply for a place there. Since I proposed to continue my education in Ontario, I began to gird myself to pass the province's matriculation examinations, for which the curriculum in my Québec college had not prepared me. Father Lynch offered to help me get ready for the exams, which normally took place after one had finished four years of secondary school; I wrote them at the close of my third year at Ironside. That I succeeded in getting my matriculation in this shorter time reflects the high level of teaching at St. Alexandre and especially Father Lynch's selfless endeavours. It has always mystified me that I passed the algebra examination; high marks in Latin, Greek, history and literature must have compensated for my abysmal ignorance of mathematics.

I left St. Alexandre in June 1921, sent off with an encouraging salute from Father Lynch as he cycled out of the grounds on his daily bike ride. I will always be grateful to the college for instilling in me prudence and a strong appreciation of authority and wisdom. Perhaps St. Alexandre did not prepare its students for the economic and material side of life, but it taught me that most important precept: there is always more to learn.

Many years later it pleased me to help my alma mater in a small way. In May 1954, the superior telephoned me to say that the college needed money to expand its buildings and library. He thought that as a government minister, I might be able to help. I had to tell him that the federal government could not give money directly and that education was a matter constitutionally reserved for the provinces. Nevertheless, I asked him to leave it to me, because while we were talking I had formed a vague idea of how I might provide indirect assistance. I had just participated in several federal-provincial conferences and had dealt directly with Maurice Duplessis, a bitter political opponent but one who I knew had a fairly good opinion of me. After reaching the Québec premier by phone, I told him that I was talking to him as a former student of St. Alexandre and asked him to consider assisting the college.

I heard nothing for months, despite several promptings. Duplessis kept telling me he was looking into the matter; I suspected he might be trying to fob me off. Finally he called me up one day and asked, "Do you read the *Montreal Gazette*? Well, look at tomorrow's edition." Sure enough, the next day there was an announcement of provincial grants to various institutions, and among them one to St. Alexandre. I took part in the ceremony when the new buildings were opened and naturally referred to the generous help given by Duplessis. Some of my cabinet colleagues were annoyed at the tribute to a man they regarded as a demagogue, but it was the decent thing to do.

Once I had left Ironside, my immediate need was for money to begin my studies at St. Michael's in September. Despite my physical handicap, I was taken on for the summer at the Pembroke Lumber Company. During those sweltering months I learned the meaning of hard physical work.

The organization of a sawmill fascinated me. Whenever I went back to Pembroke in the summer holidays, I would go down to watch the sawyer at work. He was the man who kept the mill going and therefore received the highest wages — twelve dollars a day. Otto Schroeder, the sawyer who worked in the mill that summer of 1921, was my first "great man." I can see him yet, standing there in his straw hat, covered with sawdust.

The logs were cut in the lumber camps during the winter, put into the river in the spring, arranged in booms and towed down-stream to the mill. Pulled from the water with grappling spikes and put onto a conveyer, the logs were then moved into the mill. They were piled up there, ten and twelve at a time, on each side of what resembled a sloping roof. Then the sawyer operated an instrument that grabbed the logs and put them onto a carriage, manned by two workers, which flew rapidly back and forth. The sawyer directed them to cut the logs into one-, two-, or three-inch lumber.

My first and most tedious job was working out of a trough, from which I pulled slab wood that I dumped into a second trough (the slab wood was eventually sold as fuel). The day began at seven and ended at six, with an hour off at noon; I earned a dollar and fifty cents a day. The lifting put quite a strain on my weak shoulder muscles, but it helped to build me up quite a bit over the summer. Another job I was given was to pile three-inch "deal" on the high stacks of lumber outside the mill; it was pleasant being outside, exposed to the sun. As I grew more experienced, I was made a tally boy — a much easier task. Before the lumber is shipped, it has to be graded; a grader goes around evaluating the quality of the lumber, and the tally boy marks down the assessment.

What I experienced in Pembroke's mills helped shape my politi-cal principles and outlook. It was here that I learned about the lot of the working man and the value of trade unions. I suppose that our one dollar fifty a day was standard, but it was nevertheless a pittance for such a long shift and contrasted starkly with what went into the owners' pockets.

One of the vice-presidents of the lumber company used to walk through the mill every morning, immaculately dressed in a wing collar and sporting a carnation in his lapel. I grew to form a keen dislike of what his appearance represented. Pembroke really belonged to five or six men who lived beside one another, sat on each other's boards, and called all the tunes. I became acutely aware that the town was essentially a closed society, providing limited opportunities for young men like me. To my parents' chagrin, I even attended a meeting called to test Pembroke's reaction to the One Big Union, for I knew there had to be a better way.

In the early 1970s, I went down to the old Colonial mill by the stone CPR railway station and found to my amazement that it had been dismantled. The property was now owned by Consolidated Bathurst, and redundancies had forced a cutback in output. Now, whenever I enter my study, I am reminded of my work in the mill by a piece of beam on which is inscribed "From the Pembroke Lumber Mill, employer of young Paul Martin in the early 1920s — presented to Hon. Paul Martin by his grandsons all — Christmas 1974."

But it was not just my work at the lumber mill that made me aware of the problems of the ordinary worker. About the time I began work there, my father lost his job. J. B. Kemp had sold his store, and business had fallen off under the new owner, who was forced to close by the large grocery chains. Father was unemployed for quite a while. That was such a difficult period for him because he felt he could not fulfil his responsibility as head of the household. Although he had little enough to spend, he allowed himself his White Owl cigar. He could not say "Owl" but instead pronounced it "Aaahl." One night my mother, who worried about the family situation, said, "Le voici, avec un cigare dans sa bouche!" My father turned around with a smile on his face and replied, "Well, where do you want me to put it? In my hass?"

While he was out of work, my father had borrowed some money but somehow misplaced it. He was very distressed. One evening he was downstairs in the cellar and came across the missing cash. Overburdened by his months without work, and so relieved to find the money, my poor father began to weep. I had never seen him cry before.

After several anxious months without any income, he did manage to find work, at the Steel Equipment Company owned by E. A. Dunlop. It was a far cry from the grocery business, and my father often had to carry steel desks and cabinets on his shoulders. Yet I never remember him complaining. I used to think of him hoisting those heavy desks while I was sitting studying. His job and his attitude were manifestations of the nobility of labour but also of its servility. When I visited Pembroke, I would go and meet him at the steel plant, where he continued to work until he died. After we had walked home together, I would sit with him as he ate his dinner, wielding his knife and fork with his big, strong hands. Watching my father shaped my resolve to do something about industrial wages and the lot of the ordinary worker. The conditions in Pembroke's factories spurred my ill-starred venture into politics seven years after I went to work in the mill and confirmed only too quickly what my eventual role in life would be.

II

A "Liberal" Education

D URING THE SUMMER of 1921, as I prepared to enter St.
Michael's College, it began to dawn on me how small my
world was. I loved Pembroke and would miss the Ottawa
River, but I knew I had to leave. Working in the mill, saving my
money, I wondered what might lie ahead. Once I got to the
university, I quickly realized that the world was a bigger place
than Pembroke, than Toronto, than Ontario, and perhaps might
even include more than the Catholic Church.

Arriving in Toronto on 25 September 1921 was one of the great
thrills of my life. I had taken the train with my Pembroke friend
Frank Deloughery, then in his graduating year at St. Michael's,
and we pulled into Union Station sometime during the early
evening. The city was a revelation; I'd read that it was almost as
large as Montreal, but what struck me was how thoroughly Anglo-
Saxon and predominantly Protestant everything was. Frank and I
took the streetcar up Yonge and passed the big Eaton's store. (How
often my brother, sisters and I had gathered around the kitchen
table with our mother to pore through the T. Eaton catalogue,
from which she selected things to order by mail.) A few blocks
north, we got off and walked over to St. Michael's — up the long

29

curving road, to enter the college that would have such an influence on my life.

From reading the university calendar, I already knew that St. Michael's had been founded by the Basilian order in 1852. Although it had affiliated with the University of Toronto in 1881 and, thirty years later, had become one of the fully integrated arts colleges, such changes did little to alter its firmly sectarian ethos. I quickly discovered that University College alone had an interdenominational character; Trinity, Victoria, Knox and "St. Mike's" attracted Anglicans, Methodists, Presbyterians and Catholics, respectively.

I checked into the residence and was assigned a place in the dormitory for first-year students. On the "Jews' flat," as it was called, I shared a study room with Bob Ferroni of Sault Ste. Marie, whose football gear gave the room an odour all its own.[1] A friendly professor, Father M. J. Oliver, was in charge of the freshmen. He and the college registrar, Father E. J. McCorkell — they were known affectionately by the students as Mike and Gus — were my close friends and counsellors for many years afterwards. Father McCorkell was an impressive and commanding personality, a skilled administrator with a number of scholarly interests. One of my contemporaries, the writer Morley Callaghan, rightly referred to him as "a noble and good man, who gave the college its essential character and role." Father McCorkell's passing in 1981 was a great loss.

After settling in, Frank and I explored the neighbourhood. Hart House's Gothic tower and the heavy neo-Romanesque architecture of the Ontario Legislature at Queen's Park impressed me greatly. Frank pointed out the homes of some distinguished Torontonians: Sir John Willison, author of a biography of Laurier, lived in a fine house on Elmsley Place, next door to St. Michael's; Sir Thomas White, minister of finance in Borden's government, also had a home nearby; and Sir Joseph Flavelle and Vincent Massey

---

1 From my second year, I lived on the "Irish flat," where there were private rooms.

owned mansions round about. As we passed Sir Thomas White's house, a beggar stopped us to ask for money; this was a new experience for me. Frank, more inured to city life, walked on, but I felt very sorry for the man and gave him two bits.

Fascinated with all I had seen, I looked forward to college life, little concerned about how it was all to be financed. No obstacle must prevent my participating in the wonders of this newly discovered world!

The next day I met Father McCorkell to register for my courses. My room and board, he told me, would cost $275 for the year and I must pay university fees of seventy dollars. All I had was forty dollars. He was aghast. "For the whole year? What are you going to do?" "I don't know," I replied; "I thought I'd discuss that with you." Young and self-confident, I was sure the problem could be solved. Shortly afterwards, I found a part-time job as a cashier at the Blue Bird Café, a Chinese restaurant near the college, where I worked for most of my first year. When money got short, I arranged credit with Father McCorkell and received a little help from home. When he was working, Emile would mail me the occasional five dollars. My sister Lucille, who had left school in 1924 at the age of fifteen to start work as a telephone operator in Pembroke, sent me what she could out of her small salary. I do not think that my attending university caused tension in the family; rather, it was a source of pride.

I enrolled in what was called pass arts. A senior matriculation certificate would have enabled me to go into an honours course — something I was able to do at the end of the first year when my grades warranted the advancement. Unfortunately, that first year I had to take mathematics, the subject I had disliked the most at St. Alexandre. That I survived this additional burden in the university examinations is as mysterious an achievement as my scraping through in mathematics in the junior matriculation tests a year earlier. My mathematics teachers at University College, Dr. Alfred Tennyson de Lury and Professor I. Pounder, expressed their amazement at my inadequacy in a humane and sympathetic manner. Because science had not been taught at Ironside, I took

Professor Burton's widely attended general physics lectures. Latin, also compulsory in my first year, proved as easy for me as Euclid's submissions were intransigently imponderable.

During those initial weeks, my surroundings seemed so alien. I was a French Canadian who had attended a classical college. Even though Laurier was my true hero, at St. Alexandre I had been exposed to the nationalism of Henri Bourassa. Like him, the students at Ironside were not separatists, but they were proud of their background and conscious of the need to preserve their French Canadian culture. When I went to Toronto, I shared their pride in the French language and tradition; I was against the empire and rabidly prejudiced against plummy-voiced Englishmen.

One day at a noon lecture in Hart House, Arthur Meighen, leader of the opposition in Ottawa, was introduced by the warden, Burgon Bickersteth, whose cultivated English accent seemed quite foreign to me. Greatly exercised about this, I said to my friends as we left the lecture hall, "The idea — that we should have these damned Englishmen here!" Bickersteth heard about my remark and invited me to his rooms in Hart House. They were furnished in what I imagined was an English fashion, enlivened by many paintings on the walls — something I had never seen before.

The warden was friendly but immediately came to the point: "I understand you do not like me." His candour took me aback, but I summoned up enough courage to reply, "I don't dislike you but I do not like Englishmen, and I don't see why they should run this country."

Bickersteth patiently spoke to me about the virtues of tolerance, and I left his rooms a wiser man. In time he became one of my closest friends and a great influence on my life. His old-world training, his experience of living in several parts of Canada, his zeal for education, and his acquaintanceship with many political figures in Britain and Canada were transmitted to me and to my fellow students in the manner of a great teacher. In the autumn of 1979, I read the lesson at Burgon Bickersteth's funeral in the crypt of Canterbury Cathedral, in the presence of the archbishop. I was representing the University of Toronto and its generations and recalled with regret my early crudeness towards this fine man, whose friendship and advice broadened my vistas and gave substance to my ideas on the nobility of public life.

In the 1922-23 academic year, I had to decide which honours course to pursue. Had I been at Victoria, Trinity, or even University College, I probably would have taken English and history. But at St. Michael's, the Thomistic tradition was strong and I opted to take philosophy. Maurice de Wulf, from the University of Louvain, and Sir Bertram Windle joined Father McCorkell and Father Henry Carr, the college superior, in promoting a revival of medieval philosophy; St. Michael's eventually achieved world eminence in this field. The 1920s were intellectually exciting years at the college because these professors were breaking new ground in thought and teaching.

St. Thomas Aquinas is considered to be the greatest of the medieval thinkers, and the philosophy curriculum at St. Mike's was imbued with the principles of his system. This did not mean, however, that other philosophical traditions were ignored. Unlike the courses in some universities at that time, honours philosophy at St. Michael's emphasized modern German thought, including the writings of Kant and Hegel. Benedetto Croce was not overlooked, and sociologists such as Durkheim and Lévy-Bruhl had their place in the program, as well as the English Idealists and Locke, Berkeley and Hume.

Father McCorkell's lectures on nineteenth-century thought formed the intellectual foundations of my political liberalism and enriched my inherited emotional attachment to Laurier by leading me to the philosophical thought of John Stuart Mill. I was particularly impressed by Mill's insistence, in *On Liberty*, on the value of the individual and his priority over the interests of the collectivity. This I had been taught to recognize as a dangerous and modern doctrine; nonetheless, my wider reading soon persuaded me of its truth, and even today it remains my profound conviction.

Mill's political philosophy led me into an intellectual sympathy with the Liberal Party, for I could never support the collectivism of doctrinaire socialism or even the milder infringements on the individual's liberty proposed by the Co-operative Commonwealth Federation in the 1930s. But I still considered myself a reformer because even at university it was my contention that the function of government is to bring about a better social structure for the individual citizen. My belief was that only in the name of preventing either conflict with infallibility or harm to others could freedom be denied. Of course, *On Liberty* was written in more innocent times, when civil disaffection on the current scale seemed unlikely. It is even more difficult today to reconcile unfettered free expression with the pressing values of a stable society, which may require some limitations on the individual's liberty.

I suppose my political philosophy became established about 1924, and it grew out of the thought of the English liberal reformers. One of the first things that I did when I arrived in England five years later was to go to the University of London to imbibe the atmosphere associated with John Stuart Mill and Jeremy Bentham. Whenever I try to analyze a political issue today, I invariably go back to Mill to see how it squares with his political philosophy.

My undergraduate course was a remarkably comprehensive one. From the origins of Greek thought, we moved through the systematic philosophers, such as Plato and Aristotle (a particular favourite of mine), and on to Plotinus, NeoPlatonism and the Church fathers, notably Augustine. We then delved into the medieval period, paying special attention to St. Thomas Aquinas; later on, we read Descartes, Spinoza and Leibnitz. Immanuel Kant interested me because he argued that although we cannot prove God's existence from our own experience (as St. Thomas believed), mankind has a compelling need to postulate His reality to give meaning and substance to the moral life, including political action.

In his lectures, Father Carr similarly contended that science does not provide the final key to understanding the world. He argued in favour of a personal interpretation based on spiritual requirements. I have always found this view difficult to come to

terms with. Does it mean anything more than John Henry Newman's belief in the reliance on faith as a guide to truth or
probability?

Professor Maurice de Wulf laid the foundations for my lifelong
interest in medieval philosophy when he spoke of the thirteenth
century as a witness to a new conglomeration of European states
and as an era of intense intellectual effort — the golden age of
theology and scholastic philosophy; it was a time, too, when the
natural sciences made remarkable advances. Philosophy developed prodigiously in the universities and among the religious
orders; Paris and Oxford became the privileged centres of philosophy and theology.

These lectures and my reading led me to believe that no one
should ignore the place of Thomism in the teaching of philosophy.
The Thomism instilled in me at St. Michael's did not involve a
return to the Middle Ages. Jacques Maritain, the great French
philosopher, who made his first North American tour in 1932,
insisted that Thomism was a valuable twentieth-century meta-
physical system. Unless a philosophy develops in error, its application is timeless. It is absurd to speak of a philosophy steeped in the
most ancient philosophical traditions, formed at the time of
Aristotle, and re-examined in the twelfth and succeeding centur-
ies, as being unreal and inappropriate for our own time. What
Aquinas did was to build on Aristotle. I disagree with those
scholars who deny him a place in modern philosophy.

The lectures by Father Bellisle on St. Augustine had a marked
philosophical relevance; nobody understood Plato better than
Augustine himself. It has always seemed to me that his *Confessions*
deserve the high praise given them by the late R. A. ("Rab")
Butler, but Rab was mistakenly tempted to place that great auto-
biographical work ahead of Newman's *Apologia pro vita sua*.[2] John

2 Rab Butler twice was a contender for the leadership of the British Conservative
   Party — in January 1957, when Harold Macmillan succeeded Anthony Eden;
   and in October 1963, when Sir Alec Douglas-Home took over from Macmillan.
   On his retirement from politics in 1965, Butler became master of Trinity
   College, Cambridge.

Henry Newman, whose ideas McCorkell spoke of in his course on nineteenth-century thought, was an inspiration, and we learned of the beauty of "The Second Spring," one of his parochial sermons, *The Idea of a University* and *A Grammar of Assent*. On my library shelves are many books by and about Newman that continue to uplift and delight me.

Thomism was but one aspect of the philosophy taught at St. Mike's. It struck me often during this first year that my professors' stimulating courses would be regarded as close to heresy at St. Alexandre because what they regarded as philosophy was no more than theology. I particularly enjoyed a course in social ethics given by an enthusiastic newcomer to the staff, Basil Sullivan. The subject had a good deal of interest for students like me who were determined to play an active part in public life: it gave us a standard against which to measure our political beliefs.

Father McCorkell's other course, on English poetry, was among the most stimulating offered at St. Michael's. The registrar enjoyed his lectures almost as much as his students, and his reading of the poets left a lasting impression. Later, when I sat under the portrait of Lord Byron in the hall of Trinity College, Cambridge, I inevitably heard echoes of McCorkell reading from "Childe Harold's Pilgrimage."

My zeal for public life grew not only as a result of McCorkell's intellectual stimulation; it was also fuelled by his frequently speaking of the importance of education in political life. The St. Michael's student parliament, which he helped devise, was designed to arouse student interest in public affairs. At its very first session, in January 1922, I held the post of foreign minister in the Liberal cabinet of Joe May. Shortly thereafter, when May withdrew, I assumed the premiership. The opposition was formed by the Independents, led by Joe McGahey, Morley Callaghan, and the future university heavyweight boxing champion, Joe Mahon. Morley's command of language made him a formidable adversary.

Our party retained power when the 1922-23 session began, but we got a little careless about attendance; so Father McCorkell, who acted as governor general, decided to teach us a lesson and urged some opposition members to watch for an opportunity to bring down the government. After one session, we left without obtaining a formal adjournment; the opposition waited until we had gone and then passed a motion of censure. At the next meeting, they demanded our resignation. I refused and an uproar ensued, but Father McCorkell gave us no support. We had to capitulate, and I recommended that Charles Lamphier, a member of my cabinet, form a new administration. He called an election, but the Liberals were defeated by Joe McGahey's Independent Party. Still, we put up such a vigorous fight that we were returned to power before too long. That year, Morley Callaghan won the prize as the best speaker at the student parliament, and I won the Gough trophy for my overall contribution.

The experience of the student parliament induced some of us at St. Mike's to establish a small discussion club of fifteen members; it was called, a little preciously, the Quindecim. We were arrogantly arbitrary in our selection of members: Joe McGahey became president, and Joe Mahon and Morley Callaghan also belonged. A stimulating array of outsiders was invited to participate in our discussions. Professor C. B.Sissons of Victoria College spoke to us about bilingual education and separate schools; Dean A. T. de Lury gave a talk on Anglo-Irish literature that precipitated a discussion on the currently contentious Irish question; and businessman and scholar W. H. Moore attended a session on relations between French and English Canada. Moore's two books, *The Clash: A Study in Nationalities* and *Polly Masson*, provided telling arguments for a strong and united country based on tolerance between the two founding peoples. The emergence of the United Farmers of Ontario and the burgeoning cooperative movement made the talk given to the club by the leading agrarian, J. J. Morrison, an important event.

Throughout this period, I followed the troubled political situation with great interest; both Liberals and Conservatives appeared to be in danger from new populist movements. In the province of Ontario, a brand-new party, the United Farmers of Ontario, had taken over the government from Sir William Hearst's Conservatives. Joe Mahon's brother had lost in Guelph in 1919 as a United Farmers candidate. Joe was therefore known to some of the government members at Queen's Park; so we called on them and I met Melville Warren, who had won for the United Farmers in my home constituency of North Renfrew. At the same time, I was introduced to important members of the government, including Manning Doherty, the minister of agriculture; W. E. Raney, the attorney general; and Nelson Parliament, a Liberal whom the United Farmers government had appointed speaker of the legislature.

My extracurricular interest included amateur theatricals. I have a vivid memory of appearing in a stage adaptation of *Silas Marner* and of playing the red-nosed drunkard, Bardolph, in Shakespeare's *Henry IV*. One of my last appearances at St. Michael's Dramatic Society, in *The Regiment of Two*, was in an altogether different vein. As Ira Wilton, I had to convince my wife to allow me the freedom to go fishing. *The Varsity* commented tersely that I was "very adept at creating excuses."

Throughout my undergraduate years, my horizons widened. I remained loyal to St. Michael's because I thought there was great value in each college's individuality. Nonetheless, it became more apparent that I needed and wanted the outlook that comes from the university community as a whole. I had been going to hear public addresses outside the college ever since my first year, when I attended the Marfleet lectures given by Sir Robert Borden in the university's plush Convocation Hall. After his retirement as prime minister in 1920, Borden did all he could to explain Canada's developing international status and its membership in the League of Nations, emphasizing the importance of the government's adherence to the Treaty of Versailles. Later that year, Newton Rowell, vice-president of the League of Nations Society in Canada and a former minister in Borden's Union government, gave the

Burwash lectures; he spoke of the need for the League and stressed the importance of an international order. David Lloyd George, Britain's prime minister until 1922, spoke at Massey Hall in a triumph of oratory that brought the crowd roaring to its feet. His central theme — the empire's war record — concluded with a warning that "the world had better know that what the British Empire has done once she can do again — and she will... if freedom is imperilled." We heard this speech at the university on a sound-broadcasting system set up by the engineering students.

Listening to these and other speakers made me reflect on how my earlier prejudices were being softened. Despite his imperialism, I thought highly of Lloyd George. At Borden's lectures, I remembered his speech in Pembroke's opera house in 1917 and my father's and my hostility towards him. Now I was beginning to realize that there were many different points of view and that life was charged with problems to be solved. Progress was slow, but discovery and achievement were ever within reach.

My broadened outlook led me to take part in numerous inter-varsity and intercollegiate events. Many of these fell under the aegis of Hart House, which had been opened in 1919 by Vincent Massey to generate a university spirit among the students of the heterogeneous colleges. Hart House had equipment for every sport and contained a lecture room, a library, a music room, a sketch room, a darkroom for the camera club, several common rooms, and a huge, high-ceilinged dining hall. Some excellent amateur drama took place in the little theatre in the basement. Faculty, students and alumni organized and participated in these extra-curricular pursuits.

But my keenest interest was the debates, which were modelled on those at the Oxford and the Cambridge Unions, where students and leading public figures took issue on the major topics of the day. In November 1923, I began my debating career in the intervarsity series: Morley Callaghan and I took the negative against Eric Beecroft and Ernest Livermore of Victoria College on the question of whether the United States should cancel the Allies' war debt. Ever the moralist, I argued that the Allies should reimburse the

United States on ethical grounds. The adjudicators — former provincial attorney general W. E. Raney,[3] W. H. Moore, and Vincent Bladen, the economist — awarded Morley and me the victory because of our "more eloquent and rhetorical manner of delivery."[4]

At the beginning of my final year at St. Mike's, I spoke in a high-spirited debate that opened the Hart House season. W. E. Raney and I proposed the motion that "in the opinion of this House, there has now arisen a pressing need for a revision of the Constitution of Canada." Jim Endicott of Victoria College, about to leave for China as a missionary, and Maurice Cody, son of the Conservative minister of education, Canon H. J. Cody, spoke for the negative. As the audience came in, they divided into those supporting us — including Manning Doherty, Professor C. B. Sissons, and Arthur Roebuck — on one side of the room and our antagonists, Warden Bickersteth, H. J. Cody, W. F. Nickle, the Ontario attorney general, and Norman Endicott, Jim's brother — on the other side of the room. In the middle of the debate, Morley Callaghan discovered, to his mock chagrin, that he was sitting in the wrong section — the Conservative side — and he made a great show of moving seats. Throughout the speeches, the audience continually passed remarks — usually ironic, good-natured jibes at the various speakers.

As the lead speaker for the affirmative, I pointed out that the history of Canada was in essence a preparation for the final, logical step of revising the constitution to provide for complete nationhood. Catching the mood of the occasion, and as provocation to my opponents, I argued that the governor general, who represented the monarch "in a capacity as useless as it is prominent," should hold office by decision of the Canadian parliament. The Senate should be reformed, but to do that, the constitution would

3 The United Farmers government, of which Raney was a member, lost a provincial election to the Conservatives on 25 June 1923.
4 *The Globe*, 1 November 1922.

have to be revised. Canada's Supreme Court should be the court of last appeal, in my view, and Canadians should no longer have to take their cases to the Judicial Committee of the Privy Council in London for final judgment. Equal status with Britain was better than continued subservience or an outright declaration of independence. As the debate grew wilder, I raised my voice in make-believe anger to insist, "Canada first and England second!" but then I affirmed that although I believed this, it did not mean I was a follower of Bourassa. The *Toronto Telegram* reported that the *aqua pura* on the clerk's table was in danger of upsetting as I banged the desk with "a few Indian club stunts."

In light of his later career as a staunch anti-imperialist and leader of the Canadian peace movement, it was ironic that Jim Endicott opened for the negative by praising Canada's continuing connection with the British empire, arguing that ordinary citizens would not understand constitutional change unless it was introduced at their request. For the affirmative, W. E. Raney supported my arguments and urged the removal of the colonial "red tape" that was still binding the country. Summing up for the negative, Maurice Cody reflected on the merits of the gradualism of the British constitutional process and the importance of custom and convention. Although we narrowly lost the debate, Mr. Raney and I did quite well, considering that we were putting forward rather advanced ideas for the 1920s. Perhaps I can derive some satisfaction from realizing as I write that though we lost the day, many of our arguments were subsequently accepted. As a member of Mackenzie King's government in 1946, I proposed the Canadian Citizenship Act, which provided all eligible Canadians with a new status — that of citizens of their country. Later, in 1949, I was one of those who approved the abolition of appeals to the Judicial Committee of the Privy Council. In public life, I was ever imbued with the desire to further Canada's status as a sovereign state in the commonwealth, as opposed to the empire.

The intervarsity series enabled us to travel to other cities. During my final year, I went to Montreal to debate with a team from

McGill. Ernest Schmidt and I successfully defended the resolution that the League of Nations had justified its existence. Both my convictions and my arguments had gained strength from a meeting with W. A. Riddell, Canada's permanent representative at the League. Morley Callaghan, C. R. Philip of the Ontario College of Education, and I also represented the University of Toronto in the first-ever cross-border university debate at the University of Pittsburgh (it was my first time in the United States). Our team successfully defended the motion that citizens should have the right to advocate any political or economic doctrine.

Yet although I greatly enjoyed debating, it was not something I did just for fun. I had a goal: to prepare myself for public life.

By the time I received my bachelor's degree, I numbered many students and professors among my friends. The university's history club was popular with arts students, but its membership was largely restricted to those in honours history. Maurice Cody invited me to attend a meeting at the home of Professor G. M. Wrong, chairman of the university's department of history. His house on Jarvis Street, furnished with comfortable chintz in the English style, was the finest I had ever been in and made me realize again that my parents' standard of living was not that of the Wrongs and many other Torontonians. George Wrong impressed me, although at first I was irritated by what I thought was an affectation in his speech.

In retrospect, that particular meeting was a memorable one, not least because Hume Wrong, the professor's son, another history lecturer at the university, was there. Tall and good-looking, Hume had an impaired eye that nevertheless gave him an air of distinction. I got to know him better when he was one of Canada's ablest foreign service officers, but he certainly made his presence felt on this occasion. A brilliant man who never spared others his most critical thoughts, Hume at one stage in the evening tartly corrected his father on a particular point. The senior Wrong was very annoyed because some of those present found the incident amusing. One who did not laugh was Mike Pearson, another young history lecturer. In fact, he remonstrated with Hume about his remark. Later Hume said to me, "You know, Mike sometimes reflects the narrowness of Methodism and of Victoria College." This remark took me a little aback. Two friends of mine at Victoria, Ernie Livermore and Eric Beecroft, did not strike me as narrow-minded.

I was just getting into the circle, but I quickly observed that Mike Pearson did not inspire anything like the admiration accorded Hume Wrong. We met several times at the university — Mike was a football coach, while I managed the college rugby team — and I found him an amiable and outgoing fellow. At that time, he wore a fedora pulled down at the front and back and was never without the bow tie that became his trademark. At the Hart House ball in 1925, he escorted Maryon Moody, the woman he married that August. Maryon was extremely charming, and I complimented her on her coloured shawl. In later years she used to say, "I'll always think well of you because you remarked on that shawl."

I never worked on *The Varsity* student newspaper or belonged to a fraternity; I could not afford to and, in any case, was not particularly interested. The "rah rah" aspect of college life — football hoopla and pennants festooned on one's walls — was not my style. In my final year at St. Michael's, as president of the student council, I disagreed with the inordinate attention being paid by the college to the Ontario Hockey Association instead of to intervarsity sport. I decided to do something about it and got together a hockey team that almost won the Jennings Cup.

As graduation grew near, I hoped to get a Rhodes Scholarship; but it was not to be. I called on Vincent Massey, who lived near the university in a large house he hated, to see whether the Massey Foundation might provide help for me to continue my studies. Massey welcomed me very nicely over a cup of tea but explained that while he was sympathetic about my difficulty, my B average was just not high enough to justify help from the foundation. He seemed not to know much about St. Michael's but, perhaps as a way of showing his interest in the Catholic world, told me that in a recent stage production he had played the role of an archbishop. Because he wanted to do well in the part, he had gone to see Neil McNeil, the Catholic archbishop of Toronto, to discuss his deportment on stage. Massey, like his brother Raymond, was a born actor. Not only did the archbishop tell him how to comport himself on the boards; he lent him his episcopal ring. My reaction was not the one Massey had expected: I was amazed that the ring had been lent so cavalierly and told him so.

My days at St. Michael's were palmy ones; I loved the courses and appreciated the warm sense of community one finds at a university. Participation in all aspects of university life stimulated my interest and set the pattern for my future — one of ceaseless activity and study. Catholic colleges are perhaps more ingrown than secular schools. Yet I never felt that this lack of urbanity was a handicap; St. Mike's had scholarship and teamwork — in short, an esprit de corps. Although I was a committed college man, I was always conscious of the wider sphere of university life and made certain that I got the most out of it.

Nowadays universities are not the places of learning they once were; I often wonder whether the primary purpose of the university — not to give man knowledge but to train him to acquire knowledge — is being met. For instance, I feel quite critical of many political scientists. Their knowledge of history and literature often seems so inadequate, and their behaviourist approach, designed to provide comprehensive answers, is such a rarefied one. Very few compare with my professor of political theory and government at Toronto, R. M. MacIver, the author of *The Modern State* and a scholar of admitted greatness, who exerted such influence on students all over the continent.

The second stage of my Toronto years, my legal studies at Osgoode Hall, began in September 1926. I was now on the way to becoming a barrister and solicitor, pursuing a three-year course and working part-time in a law office, where I learned something about litigation, wills, title searches and suchlike.

At that time, Osgoode Hall, under the direction of the Law Society of Upper Canada, had two classes of aspiring lawyers: those who qualified for admission by virtue of a bachelor's degree from a university, and those who had spent two years studying under a lawyer in professional quarters. It was understandable that lawyers would talk to one another about the advantages of each system for entering law school. Inevitably a change in the qualifications for entry developed under the impetus of Dr. Cecil Wright, a brilliant legal scholar who thought the law school should be under the authority of a degree-granting university. A number of my first-year contemporaries — my friends Donald Fleming and Wishart Spence, for example — also thought this a better arrangement. I saw every reason for lawyers to enjoy the benefits of training beyond their profession. Some of the best judges in the common law and civil law systems are men who, before taking up the study of law, read other subjects at university, such as philosophy, history, literature, politics, and economic theory.

Osgoode Hall Law School provided morning lectures and library facilities. Housed in one of the finest buildings in Canada, it was named after William Osgoode, chief justice at the time of Governor Simcoe. In the building were the divisions of the Supreme Court of Ontario, the Master's Chambers, the Wellesley Courtroom, the offices of the justices and the inner sanctum of the benchers of the Law Society, as well as the classrooms of the law school and the professors' offices. The school's main library, chiefly for the use of professional lawyers, is the building's finest adornment. This was a room in which I loved to study on those days set aside for my law courses.

The dean of the school, J. D. Falconbridge, was a widely respected teacher. His lectures on the conflict of laws and the law of contracts were orderly yet challenging, and his quiet manner belied an active mind. Looking back at Falconbridge, one becomes aware of the bigness of the life of a good professor. He and other teachers at Osgoode Hall could speak with the pride of achievement when they recalled their law, life and times. This was surely true of Professor Donald MacRae, who taught me torts and the history of English law. His writing on torts served both the student and the practitioner, as I well recall from his digest.

Like MacRae, Sidney Smith, a professor of real property law, had come to Osgoode Hall from Dalhousie Law School in Halifax. He was a brilliant professor, who later, as president of the University of Toronto, revealed exceptional administrative talents. Smith came close to contesting the leadership of the federal Conservative Party in 1942, but the job went to John Bracken, the Manitoba premier. Prime Minister John Diefenbaker seemed to have reached a masterful decision in the appointment of Sidney as secretary of state for external affairs in September 1957; but, like others, I felt that this was not Smith's most successful role.

When Dr. Cecil Wright returned from Harvard to teach the law of wills at Osgoode Hall, the theories he propounded, while often ingenious, were frequently regarded with suspicion by less able observers. Perhaps it was this academic quality that helped poison the minds of some of my cabinet colleagues and certain judges and practitioners who stood in the way of Wright's appointment to the Supreme Court of Ontario in the early 1950s. Despite my argument that Wright's elevation would bring substance to the bench, Prime Minister St. Laurent's reaction suggested that the time for an academic judge had not yet arrived.

The friends of one's college days are precious, and I was fortunate in mine. Lionel Chevrier, who had come to Osgoode Hall from the University of Ottawa, was a true companion, as was Wishart Spence, a future justice of the Supreme Court of Canada. Another close friend was Donald Fleming, who, like Wishart, had attended the University of Toronto with me; but Lionel and Wishart were easier for me to understand because we had common political sympathies. Donald and I first debated at Osgoode's mock parliament; we continued our verbal jousting years later on the floor of the House of Commons, when I was minister of national health and welfare and, afterwards, when he became Diefenbaker's first minister of finance.

After mornings at the law school, I toiled away each afternoon in the law office of Henderson and McGuire, in a position arranged for me by Senator Andrew Haydon, the Liberals' national organizer. Mr. Henderson, a solicitor, taught me the importance of detail, and another partner, Henry Bowles, instructed me in legal procedure and how to search a title. My remuneration was five dollars a week.

I learned much about the practical side of the law at Henderson and McGuire, and experience is a great teacher. One day in the division court, I arrived with an armful of books, from which I intended to make a rousing plea for my client, the plaintiff. I did not realize that citing numerous reports and precedents was not the custom in small claims proceedings. The case was being heard by Judge Morrison, who had got into the habit of running his eyes over the racing form while he was listening to evidence. He let me work my way through a carefully documented argument that ended with the exhortation, "That, your Honour, is the law!" I felt I was back at Hart House and had just demolished my opponent. Languidly raising his eyes, Judge Morrison observed, "If that is the law, young man, I am going to change it. Judgment for the defendant."

I had an aptitude and liking for law but found Osgoode Hall a little dull. The professors were stimulating, but it was not a community with the university's intellectual animation. Because philosophy and history were still my main interests, I concurrently pursued a master's degree in philosophy at St. Michael's, under Dr. Gerald Phelan, the college's director of graduate studies. He supervised me, Joe Mahon, and another close friend, Frank Flaherty, in addition to presiding over a limited number of weekly courses.

With Dr. Phelan's encouragement, I wrote my thesis on Cardinal Newman's *An Essay in Aid of a Grammar of Assent.* Although Newman had been greatly disturbed by the growth of atheism, he held that one generation had no right and no capacity to pass judgment on the traditions of mankind, contending that the fashion of the moment is not likely to be right. Newman did not write on social problems, but he was concerned about the question of war; the Crimean War he regarded as unjust. When he was still an Anglican minister, Newman had been a leading light in the Oxford Movement, which raised so many religious questions and excited such great spiritual energies. In 1963 I was thrilled to hear Paul VI say at the Second Vatican Council that Newman's influence had been great, and during the debates on collegiality, Cardinal Garcias of Bombay proclaimed that Newman's *An Essay on the Development of Christian Doctrine* was the signpost by which Vatican II ought to proceed.

During this time, my outlook was broadened by the lectures of certain distinguished philosophers who visited St. Michael's. In 1926, Father Léon Noel, of the University of Louvain, came to Toronto to give two lectures on the philosophy of St. Thomas Aquinas. The college tried to get him to remain as head of the projected Institute of Medieval Studies, but he would not leave Louvain. Later that year, the eminent French philosopher Etienne Gilson of the Sorbonne visited St. Mike's. Eventually, in 1932, he settled in Toronto as the first head of the Institute of Medieval Studies. In his noted book, *The Philosopher and Theology*, Gilson recalls that it was his master, Lucien Lévy-Bruhl, who in 1905 introduced him to St. Thomas Aquinas by suggesting a study on Descartes and scholasticism.

It is not too much to say that Gilson revolutionized the portrayal and understanding of St. Thomas Aquinas, but he was careful not to confuse his religious beliefs with Thomism. He did not approve of the way scholastic philosophy was taught in the textbooks because they drew their inspiration from church dogma — a source foreign to other philosophies — and made little attempt to understand *the raison d'être* of these philosophies. Gilson thought it high-handed for theologians to concentrate on demonstrating that the philosophy of Kant was false; he maintained that, unlike the theologian, the philosopher does not base his condemnation on biblical or religious authorities. The contrast between the philosopher and the theologian, as Gilson saw it, is that the philosopher argues from premises drawn from natural experiences, while the theologian draws some of his premises from divine revelation. The philosopher and the theologian both employ rational methods, including syllogistic reasoning, but the theologian, through faith, has access to truths that can neither be supported nor refuted by strictly philosophical methods. At the same time, since philosophy is an enterprise of natural reason, the theologian must not impose on the philosopher, as philosopher, conclusions that cannot in principle be reached by natural reason. Gilson believed that the mind of the Thomist, who welcomes truth from all sources, is free.

Etienne Gilson's liberal approach had great significance for me. During his twenty-five years as pontiff at the end of the nineteenth century, Leo XIII had encouraged the revival of Thomistic teaching begun by Cardinal Mercier at the University of Louvain; this initiative helped to pave the way for his co-religionists to take more active roles in the development of the modern state. It was certainly unwise of Leo's successor, Pius X, to proscribe in 1907 the Modernist treatment of social questions and progressive institutions. Proposals for the betterment of society are political questions, and the Catholic church was taking an all-embracing stand when it included them in its condemnation. What would have happened to me as minister of national health and welfare if I had been in office during Pius's reign before World War I? I doubt very much whether my proposals to improve the lot of Canadians would have been possible; they would not have been tolerated in Québec or by Catholics elsewhere if the directions of Pius X had prevailed. Under that kind of restriction, what politican could exercise a role in the modern state? Leo XIII did not make this mistake, and neither did Gilson.

Because of the heavy load of my legal work and my master's course, extra-curricular activity was inevitably curtailed. But what

I could undertake provided me with interesting contacts. Some of them arose from my preparations for a debate on western civilization with a team of visiting British students in 1926. I was urged by Father McCorkell to talk to W. H. Moore, so I went along to his office on Victoria Street to see him. Moore had previously judged a debate at the university, but I had not then been aware of the range of his intellectual interests. He suggested that I come to his house that evening. There, I found myself seated in the library of a rather grand Rosedale home with my host and Archbishop McNeil, discussing the problems of western civilization. Moore was not a Catholic, but it was fascinating to see these two men, so different in their interests, their religion and their daily lives, pulled together by the lure of intellectual exchange.

I gained a good friend in Moore. He offered me summer employment for the next four years at Thorncliffe Racetrack in Toronto, where for twelve dollars a day I sold parimutuel tickets with other students. Eventually, I found work at the Woodbine racetrack and also at three tracks in and about Windsor; every summer I would spend at least six weeks down there. One year, when I had more time on my hands, I also worked from the evening until the middle of the night at the Ford plant, cleaning up and doing odd jobs.

It disturbed Sidney Smith that my time was divided between Osgoode Hall and St. Michael's, but Henderson and McGuire never seemed to notice the hours I spent working on my thesis. I spoke in my last debate early in March 1927, across the floor from the acting leader of the opposition, Hugh Guthrie.[5] We discussed the merits of implementing the recommendations of the Royal Commission on Maritime Claims, which supported increased federal subsidies to the Atlantic provinces.

At the end of my first year at Osgoode Hall, I was elected president of the Newman Club and took up residence in the club's fine old quarters at the corner of St. George and Hoskin, not far

5 Guthrie was chosen on 11 October 1926, after Arthur Meighen's resignation.

from Trinity College, Hart House and University College. One of the arguments against my candidacy was expressed in a letter published in the club newsletter by "Laura," who I suspected was my friend Frank Flaherty, mischievously trying to drum up interest in the contest. The letter suggested that I might not be good for the club because I never took out girls. This gave me a good laugh.

As president, I set about inviting prominent figures to speak to the club and managed to get the minister of justice, Ernest Lapointe, to one of our meetings. After my welcome in English, Lionel Chevrier greeted Mr. Lapointe in French. The minister then urged the audience to demonstrate tolerance and to unite for the common good of Canada. Fernand Rinfret, the secretary of state, who was accompanying Lapointe, commented on Lionel's cordiality and said it was always moving to hear French spoken in Toronto.

My Newman Club activities brought me into contact with an outspoken defender of Catholic rights, Senator Charles Murphy. Although I could not persuade him to address the Newman Club, he kept me informed about political matters that interested him.[6] Murphy was greatly disturbed after the 1926 election by the reunion of the pro-conscriptionist and anti-conscriptionist Liberals; that, he believed, would lead to a loss of influence by Catholics in the Liberal Party.[7] He was particularly upset about Mackenzie Kings's reliance on those, including Newton Rowell, who had deserted Laurier and joined Borden's Union government. As a representative of the Newman Club, I objected to King's appointment of Rowell as counsel in a probe of the federal customs department. To substantiate my objections, I cited Rowell's criticism

6 Martin to Murphy, 17 January 1926, 23 January 1926, Charles Murphy Papers (vol. 18, folder 85), Public Archives of Canada, Ottawa, Canada (hereafter PAC); Murphy to Martin, 23 January 1926, 4 October 1926, ibid.
7 Murphy to Martin, 2 November 1926, ibid., see also Margaret Prang, *N. W. Rowell: Ontario Nationalist* (Toronto: University of Toronto Press, 1975), p. 421 ff. For more on relations between the Catholic and Protestant wings of the Liberal Party, see idem, pp. 240-243, 263-64, 276-78, 322-24, 337-38.

of the French clergy during the 1917 conscription crisis, something I much regret having done.[8]

I saw Rowell perform in court in a number of important cases. His great ability and manner so impressed me that although merely *in statu pupillari*, I urged Father Carr to engage a good lawyer to act for St. Michael's in an expropriation proceeding over the city's takeover of college property. (That property is now a large block of the present Bay Street, in the St. Joseph-St. Mary Street neighbourhood.) I suggested Rowell. "How can you make such a recommendation, remembering his attitude towards Catholics and their school rights," Father Carr remarked, "let alone his abandonment of your great Laurier?" I was chastened, although I did not relent in my view that the college needed a good lawyer. As I was leaving, Father Carr said, "Thank you for your interest. I should tell you that we have engaged counsel." To my astonishment and pleasure, he then told me that Rowell's services had been secured.

Dr. Matthew McKay, a Pembroke dentist, combined his professional skill with a consuming interest in public affairs and a condemnatory eye for all that was conservative in life and politics. He was the mainstay of the Liberal Party in North Renfrew both federally and provincially. In June 1928, Dr. McKay led a deputation of Liberals from the provincial constituency to invite me to contest a byelection in North Renfrew brought about by the sudden death of the Conservative member, Alexander Stuart. This unexpected turn of events, just as I was finishing my law examinations, diverted my attention from my studies and led me to fail in one subject and to postpone my call to the bar until the end of September.

I suppose the deputation's blandishments goaded me to jump

8 Telegram, Martin to King, 1 October 1926, W. L. Mackenzie King
   Papers (J1 series, p. 115,153), PAC.

into the election fray even though I had many more immediate concerns. That all my scholastic and political obligations were faced and met must have been due to considerable self-assurance, a taste for adventure, and a love of learning. There was nothing calculated in it at all; I had decided to enter public life, to be sure, but I wanted first to complete my education and professional training.

During my time in Toronto, my emotional and intellectual attachment to liberalism had assumed a more formal connection. I had spoken to the Toronto District Women's Club, had participated in the student parliament, and had served on the executive of the Liberal Club at the university and at Osgoode Hall. Throughout my college years I had followed the national party's fortunes closely and had been greatly interested in Mackenzie King's career ever since he had won the national leadership convention in 1919 by thirty-eight votes. As one of the two candidates seeking to succeed Laurier who had remained loyal to the leader in 1919, Mackenzie King struck a sympathetic chord in me.[9] His convention victory and his subsequent election as prime minister in 1921 had, I believed, vindicated my hero Laurier and his conscription policy.

About this time I came to know a number of leading public figures. Around 1926, Senator Andrew Haydon, the Liberals' national organizer, came to Toronto to address a Queen's University dinner. Hearing him speak so knowledgeably on university scholarships and the relations between scholars and public life, I was encouraged to think that it was possible for a political organizer to have intellectual interests and to speak about them publicly. On my way to Pembroke, I frequently made a point of dropping in to see Haydon at his home on Ottawa's Driveway, and I got to know him quite well. We would talk about Canadian history and also about the broad aspects of political life. International affairs did not interest him at all, but he had a very good library and loved

9 D. D. McKenzie, MP for Cape Breton North, was the other. He served as Liberal House leader after Laurier's death.

literature and local history. When Haydon was implicated in the Beauharnois scandal in 1931, I was very disappointed at the way Mackenzie King treated him. As the Liberal's national organizer, Haydon was inevitably involved in the affair, but I still believe that the prime minister did not defend him as he should have done.

As well as managing his businesses, my summer employer, W. H. Moore, served as the unofficial treasurer, or "bagman," of the Ontario Liberal Party. He introduced me to some other prominent party members: W. E. N. Sinclair, the Ontario provincial leader; Peter Heenan, former minister of labour; future senators James Spence, Wishart's father, and Frank O'Connor, owner of the Laura Secord candy shops. Nelson Parliament, the Liberal's provincial organizer, had been an acquaintance since my first years at St. Michael's and had taught me a great deal about the practical side of politics.

My interest in public affairs grew even more intense when, in late June 1926, I witnessed part of one of the more compelling episodes of these years in the House of Commons. On my way to Pembroke for a brief visit with my parents before beginning work at the Thorncliffe racetrack, I met Mike Pearson at Ottawa's old Union Station, opposite the Chateau Laurier. Mike said he was in town to visit the Public Archives, but I had a hunch he was doing more than that — perhaps laying the foundation for his career in the department of external affairs.

At his suggestion, we walked up to Parliament Hill, where Mackenzie King's minority government had been fighting off a vote of censure over charges of corruption in the customs department. The two of us sat in what is now called the Diplomatic Gallery, over the clock and facing the Speaker. (In later years, as we sat side by side at our desks on the floor of the House, Mike and I often talked about the first time we came there together.) We heard King curtly announce his resignation as prime minister to a stunned House. Because the governor general, Lord Byng, had refused a dissolution of parliament, King had no other recourse.

Mike suggested that we search out a member of parliament who could give us an interpretation of this dramatic turn of events. I did not know any MPs, but he took me along to meet J. S. Woodsworth, the Labour member for Winnipeg North Centre who later helped found the Co-operative Commonwealth Federation. Mike knew Woodsworth, a former Methodist minister like Mike's father, through their affiliation with Victoria College. So Mike and I, the future prime minister and the future cabinet minister, went to Woodsworth's room and shared a meal of brown bread, cheese and tea. Woodsworth was dressed in a gray suit and impressed me as a kind and gentle man. King had resigned to avoid censure, Woodsworth explained, and the governor general had no choice but to call on Arthur Meighen, the Conservative leader, to form a government.

Although King did not get his dissolution, Meighen was given one after he lost a vote in the House five days later. This brought on a general election campaign. On 23 July, during another, more extended visit to Pembroke, I drove down to Ottawa with two local Liberals, Dr. J. C. Bradley, the president of the North Renfrew constituency association, and Dr. C. T. Fink, to hear Mackenzie King deliver the opening speech of the campaign. The weather was warm, but the steamy Days Arena was packed to the rafters. I had never heard Mackenzie King speak, but now I listened with rapt interest from the back row of the arena as he defended his constitutional stance for two solid hours; it was masterly, and I never again heard him speak as well. King did not call Lord Byng's personality into question, but cast doubt on the constitutionality of a course where the governor general could refuse a dissolution to one prime minister and yet grant it days later to another. Never in Canadian history had a governor general refused a request for dissolution from a responsible prime minister, King maintained. To follow this course, the Crown's representative would have had to be certain of finding a prime minister both willing and able to take responsibility for the governor general's decision. This, King asserted, Arthur Meighen had been unable to do: he had carried on the proceedings of the House for only three days before losing its confidence. King denied that he had asked for a dissolution to avoid a vote of censure and reiterated that it was the constitutional issue, not the customs scandal, that formed the all-important principle to be decided in the election. He then called "in the name of our King and of our Country" for his "fellow Canadians, because of all that the British Constitution serves to inspire in Canada of liberty, freedom and loyalty, to vindicate its rights and majesty at the polls."[10]

This issue of the 1926 election continues to excite constitutional experts. Eugene Forsey wrote a book upholding Byng's action.[11] My able friend, Basil Markesinis, a law lecturer at Trinity College, Cambridge, argued against Forsey and reinforced my own belief that the governor general had acted incorrectly in refusing King's request.[12]

In any event, stirred by the speech and the occasion, I returned with my friends to Pembroke to give full but unsuccessful battle in support of Dr. McKay, the Liberal candidate in Renfrew North.[13] I worked in his committee room and made a few speeches on his behalf — my first election addresses. But my most notable contribution was to arrange a visit by Vincent Massey, who came to speak in Pembroke in early September.

---

10 For a complete text of the speech, see Arthur Berriedale Keith (ed.), *Speeches and Documents on the British Dominions, 1918-1931: From Self-government to National Sovereignty* (London: Oxford University Press, 1961), pp. 150-60. Lord Byng, a distinguished British soldier in World War I, thought that after King's resignation Arthur Meighen, the Conservative leader, should be called upon to form a government; assurance had been given by Meighen that he had the promise of support from Robert Forke, the leader of the Progressive Party in the House of Commons. The Progressives, however, quickly deserted Meighen and voted with the Liberals on a resolution that questioned the legality of the Meighen government. (Meighen alone had accepted office, an act that required him to resign his seat in the House. His ministers had accepted only acting portfolios, and Meighen claimed that they therefore did not have to resign.)

11 Eugene A. Forsey, *The Royal Power of Dissolution of Parliament in the British Commonwealth* (Toronto: Oxford University Press, 1943).

12 B. S. Markesinis, *The Theory and Practice of Dissolution of Parliament: A Comparative Study with Special Reference to the United Kingdom and Greek Experience* (Cambridge: Cambridge University Press, 1972), pp. 89-91.

13 Dr. McKay had been elected MP for Renfrew North in 1921 but had lost his seat in October 1925. When I won Essex East in 1935, he regained Renfrew North, and I was pleased to sit in the House of Commons with him until his death in 1937.

Massey had lost in his effort to capture the Durham federal constituency in 1925 and had failed to get a nomination the next year.[14] Although he had important connections in political, social and academic circles in Ottawa and Toronto, his name meant little in Pembroke, apart from his association with the Massey-Harris farm implement company. In my introductory remarks, I tried to ascribe the country's prosperity and progress to the Liberal Party's program. Massey's speech went badly; he was not a stirring speaker or a true "political animal." Despite his shortcomings as a politician, I had a great respect for him and for the much-needed character he gave to public life at that time. In Canada, Massey was one of the few intellectuals with considerable political interests until Norman Rogers, a professor at Queen's University, became active in the Liberal Party in the mid-1930s.

During the 1926 election, I apparently developed a name as a campaigner, and that reputation prompted Dr. McKay and other local Liberals to urge me to stand in the provincial byelection two years later. When they asked me to consider running, I felt a little unsure, since my sights had been set on federal, not provincial, politics. I was in a quandary: by refusing to serve when I was needed, I might run the risk of finding my way blocked later when I would be more prepared.

The constituency and provincial Liberals were divided over whether the party should contest the byelection, and it was some time before I decided to seek the nomination. The Conservative candidate, E. A. Dunlop, was Pembroke's leading industrialist, a major employer in the town and a former member of the legislature. It was widely speculated that if he was elected and the Tories returned, Dunlop would become the provincial treasurer in Howard Ferguson's administration. Although few local Liberals wished to put up a candidate to oppose him, W. E. N. Sinclair and W. H. Moore pressed me to stand. The latter thought it would be valuable experience, if nothing else. Nelson Parliament also urged

14 Claude Bissell, *The Young Vincent Massey* (Toronto: University of Toronto Press, 1981), pp. 108-13.

me to run. In retrospect, it is easy to see why: they could not get another candidate because the local Liberals, who knew Dunlop would win, did not want an expensive fight.[15]

The nominating convention of 4 June was held, as had become the custom, in Pembroke's town hall. Considering that it was a Monday, the attendance was fair, but there was very little enthusiasm, at least at the beginning of the deliberations. The president of the Liberal Association, Tom Galligan, thought it expedient that the meeting first discuss the advisability of having a candidate at all. He himself spoke in favour of the Liberals' contesting the seat; George McNab and Lorne Humphries made the point that since it was just a byelection, the seat should be surrendered to the Conservatives, who would then win it by acclamation. However, the majority of those present wanted a fight, and the names of McNab and Galligan, as well as mine, were put forward. The others then peremptorily withdrew, and I became the official Liberal nominee.

Once nominated, I threw myself into the fray as though my candidacy had been generally welcomed. In my remarks to the convention, I sought to justify my nomination by referring to other people — Charles James Fox, William Pitt the Younger, my great Laurier — who had entered public life early, and I then outlined the issues upon which I would rest my plea for support. The Ferguson government, I argued, could be criticized for its failure to better the wages and working conditions of the unskilled labourer. I pointed out that in Pembroke there was no larger employer than the Conservative candidate, Edward Dunlop, and that in my view, a labourer was worthy of his hire. One of Dunlop's concerns, the Pembroke Electric Light Company, was effectively hindering the development of a publicly owned hydro

15 Interview with Paul Martin, Windsor, Ont., 22-23 June 1932, Escott Reid Papers (vol. 1, Interview transcripts, p. 128), PAC. In Escott Reid's papers is a typed manuscript of an interview I had with him in June 1932. It says that I was offered $10,000 by the Conservatives not to participate in the election. Escott was wrong. The story is ironic because when the election was over I was left with a personal debt of $3,500.

industry in eastern Ontario that could provide cheaper heat and light.

I find it hard now to describe my feelings during these first few hours as a candidate for the Ontario legislature. My parents were displeased with me for running against Mr. Dunlop, to whom they felt a sense of loyalty. My father reminded me of the months of privation suffered by our family when he had been out of work, before Mr. Dunlop gave him a job at his office-equipment factory. While I regarded Dunlop as an instrument of hindrance to social reform, my father looked upon him as a man who gave people jobs. He argued that Mr. Dunlop was good for the community, but I would have none of it: "Dad, you don't understand these things. Anyone who stands in the way of desirable social change must be challenged." My mother was even more outspoken. In her strongly expressed opinion, I was a young man just starting out in life, and should not encumber myself with a political obligation about which I knew little.

My parents' advice meant a great deal to me, but I had deeply held views too. Once the campaign got rolling, my mother and father supported me wholeheartedly and even worked for me. Still, things were not easy for them. One night I came home to find Mother crying. She told me that my father had heard that he was to be fired for taking part in the election. This naturally got my dander up, and I went along to Mr. Dunlop's house to protest. Fortunately he was not in. I made some soundings and found that there was no truth to the rumour; he was not going to be that foolish — such insensitivity would only prove my statements about industrial employers. That week I wrote a letter to the Pembroke *Standard* pointing out that "the treatment accorded my father in the particular plant in which he works should commend itself to the officials of other industries."

At the opening of the contest, Nelson Parliament helped me set up an organization. My headquarters were two small rooms below Dr. McKay's dental office in the town; from there I ran.my campaign and planned visits to party workers. An entry in my diary notes that "it requires patience and a maximum taxation of energy to enthuse those not already so disposed." Although I was not convinced that I could win, a women's organization was formed to assist me. I began to feel that there would be some votes for us, particularly after *The Globe* published an editorial favouring the entry into political life of one so young.

As I toured the riding with Nelson Parliament, speaking two or three times a day in the smaller communities, I stuck with the program I had outlined at the nominating convention. At the end of the first week, I spoke again in Pembroke, this time to a more enthusiastic crowd, who seemed pleased that I was recommending universal minimum wage legislation throughout the province and improved local facilities — especially roads, which were in poor shape. I was criticizing an economic condition, firmly believing that government intervention could help in a material way to change things for the better.

The next day Dunlop made it clear that he paid thirty-two cents an hour for work that would receive only twenty-five cents an hour in Toronto. He also noted that the rates charged by the private suppliers of Pembroke's power were lower than those of Ontario Hydro. My riposte was that the thirty-two cents an hour was the rate for skilled labour; those without skills received only fifteen cents an hour.

Such local issues increased the tempo of the campaign. Responding to my challenge, Dunlop agreed to debate with me at Cobden; public debates were an extremely rare occurrence at this time. Dunlop and I were to be supported respectively by Charles McCrea, the minister of mines, and W. E. N. Sinclair, who travelled up from Toronto and spent several days with me boosting my campaign. A big crowd assembled at the Cobden Fairgrounds to hear us. Quoting my opponent's own words, I contended that the wage scale in Pembroke was so low because there was a surplus of labour and that employers were really concerned not with fair wages, but with profit.

At Douglas, three days later and on my twenty-fifth birthday, Dr. M. J. Maloney, federal MP for Renfrew South, replaced McCrea at another public debate. My party leader was again on the platform; but his speech contained a rather flat statement about prohibition, and he was unable to respond to a Conservative heckler, who asked him if he would commit the Liberal Party to a universal minimum wage law. The liquor issue caused difficulties for me: Sinclair favoured prohibition, while I did not — if for no other reason than that a prohibitionist stance would have alienated the Irish and the French voters, the chief sources of Liberal support. Sinclair's evasions were so transparent that the Tories were able to ask thereafter whether I had convinced my own leader of the efficacy of the policies I was proposing. It was not hard to deduce that I would have little influence in a legislature dominated by the Conservative Party and by Liberals of the Sinclair stripe. Perhaps he impressed me somewhat at the time because he was the first political leader I had met, but Sinclair did not have the magnetism to touch the electorate.

In its final days, the campaign really heated up and began to arouse great interest. I wrote in my diary: "Brass bands are useful creations during an election. Noise and glamour help the spirit of things." The Tories knew this, and the wealthy Conservative establishment arranged for the band of the governor general's foot guards to visit Pembroke. It was a rousing display, but many locals thought it a pity that the town band had been passed over. On election eve, two meetings took place, mine at the Armouries and Dunlop's at the O'Brien Opera House. Considering the rival attraction, the attendance at ours was beyond my expectations; no doubt the appearance of the local citizen's band helped! My opponent, though, had learned his lesson and had hired the Renfrew Pipe Band for his gathering.

Outside Pembroke, interest in the contest had grown as a result of a number of stories written for the *Toronto Daily Star* by R. C. Reade. An acquaintance from my university days and the Hart House debates, Bob Reade had been writing for the *Star* since his return from Oxford, where he had studied on a Rhodes Scholarship. Holidaying at nearby Golden Lake, he had heard about the byelection and one day sidled into my committee rooms, puffing on a cigarette. He looked around and said laconically, "I think you can improve your organization." Bob soon helped me to do just this. While Nelson Parliament had talked to me about publicity and organization, I had not done what he had recommended. My instinct told me that the first thing I had to do was to get to know the people.

In his reports about my campaign, Bob Reade made the small meetings of a few people sound like enthusiastic gatherings of five hundred. He even managed to get me the editorial endorsement of his paper for my stand supporting the extension of the public power system to eastern Ontario.[16] We had "razzle-dazzle," he would say, giving the impression of an avalanche of support in my favour. Bob was a very clever fellow, bubbling with ideas, and he urged me to subtly get over the notion that Dunlop, out of touch with the principles of big business, ran his plants with little recognition of individual merit and talent.

By the end of the campaign, I thought I had a chance to win, but when the votes were counted on election night, I could say, as Laurier had before me, "They welcomed me warmly but they did not vote for me." Despite the turnout for the rallies and my father's assurance that the mill workers in Pembroke would support me, I lost by 2,201 votes, giving the victor the largest majority ever in Renfrew North.[17] I had certainly not expected such a drubbing, although the Tories had boasted at one point that they would win by 2,500 votes. Our machinery for getting out the vote was not up to the mark, and the poll captain system did not really work as it should have. The greatest surprise to me was the Pembroke vote, where roughly three-fifths of the ridings's electorate lived: Dunlop carried a 750-vote majority.

Some campaign workers thought I had chosen poor ground on which to fight the three-week campaign. I disagreed. I had fought for a program and a political philosophy in which I believed.

16 *Toronto Daily Star*, 23 June 1928.
17 Dunlop received 5,385 votes to my 3,184. In the previous election, the Conservative candidate, Alexander Stuart, had received 5,000 votes to 3,370 for R. M. Warren, a prohibitionist candidate who had formerly belonged to the United Farmers of Ontario.

Although my ideas were somewhat ahead of their time, I spoke throughout the campaign of social progress, which was to become a major theme for the rest of my public life. After the election, I wrote in my diary that the experience was worth the effort: "I feel particularly happy in the thought that my fight was sincere and that I was not playing politics in the cheap sense of the word. I would sooner be right and be a defeated candidate than be wrong and be the member for Renfrew North."

As soon as the initial returns indicated what the result would be, I crossed the street between the two headquarters to congratulate my adversary. Bob Reade later urged me to attend the Tory victory celebrations where I could do the same thing publicly. This to me seemed unnecessary because I had already complimented Dunlop on his win, but Bob was insistent. While Dunlop was in the middle of his victor's speech at the Armouries, I walked into the hall and up onto the platform. He was flabbergasted. As I shook his hand, he said quietly, "You little son of a bitch." The crowd applauded my magnanimity, oblivious of the earlier handshaking. Reade's advice was sound in every way; it is always wise in politics to be generous with one's opponents. The following day, the arthritically conservative *Ottawa Journal* did not praise Dunlop for his win but commented instead on sportsmanship in politics; shortly afterwards, the story appeared in newspapers all over the country.

Unhappily, I received more commendation for my part in the campaign than funds with which to pay electoral expenses. Two leading Conservatives, Mayor Ellis of Ottawa and Canon H. J. Cody, Ontario's minister of education, both referred to my unselfish public gesture and to the tough fight I had put up. My former professor, Father Basil Sullivan, applauded me for my defence of labour. Reade and I kept in touch for years and frequently reminisced about the relentless campaign manager who made the "reluctant candidate" mount the stage "in the full flush of defeat" and steal the show.

III

A Wider World

W H. MOORE HAD RAISED my spirits about the election defeat by suggesting that I take a trip to western Canada, kindly giving me $250 to finance it. It is unlikely that I was ever as enthusiastic about a venture as I was the night my parents and sisters saw me on board the train for the initial leg of my journey to the West. First I went to Ottawa to get the names and addresses of various Liberals whom I should see on my journey. R. J. Deachman, who represented the Consumers' League of Canada and the national Liberal organization, gave me a number of suggestions; Bob would later sit with me in the House of Commons during several parliaments. From Ottawa I went to Windsor and worked at the racetrack for a week.

By this time, I had come to consider Windsor as a possible home, and so I used this week in July to investigate the city and to determine what opportunities it might have for a young lawyer when I returned from further study. Among those I got to know was Leo McLaughlin, president of the Essex Liberal Association, who in turn invited me to meet several well-known local Liberals. After calling on Mrs. W. C. Kennedy, widow of a former minister of railways and canals, I was introduced to Norman McLarty, a widely respected lawyer, with whom I was later to be closely associated in parliament. Norman would play an important role in Mackenzie King's cabinet as minister of labour, postmaster general and secretary of state. When I first met him, he suggested that before starting a practice I should talk to him about the possibility of joining his firm.

To see Canada in all its parts is "a joy forever." From Windsor, I took *The Noronic*, the largest cruiseship on the Great Lakes;[1] as I recorded at the time, it was "the last word in luxury." With a good orchestra on board, a splendid dance floor and comfortable lounge rooms, I could not but enjoy the trip. Twice a day, the passengers joined the official one-mile walk around the promenade deck, kept in marching mood by a bagpiper attired in Highland costume. In the evenings, concerts and dancing took up the time of the sociable group on board. My congenial cabinmate, Mr. Dunlop, of Stettler, Alberta, shared the political persuasion of my erstwhile opponent but not his kinship. At Sarnia, I swam in Lake Huron, but even at that time of year, the water was very cold.

From Port Arthur, I took the train to Winnipeg, feeling quite unstrung at the thought that this was the city of Aileen MacDonnell, my first romantic attachment. I was ill at ease with young women and did not get used to taking them out on dates until I was well into my university years. Aileen had been a student at St. Joseph's College when I was at Osgoode Hall and was the cause of my spending more time at the university than I perhaps should have. I was heartbroken when she did not return my affection or allow me to be her suitor. She had been sent to Toronto by her family to escape a young man who was pursuing her, but he followed her from Winnipeg and they eventually became engaged. However, by the time I arrived in Winnipeg, I was more or less cured, if that is the proper word, of any desire to "make up."

Because Aileen's older brother, Beau, an active Liberal, had known I was coming to town, he called me at the hotel and offered

1 *The Noronic* was owned by Canada Steamship Lines, a company that has since vicariously formed an important part of my life.

to show me around Winnipeg. I was struck by the impressive width of its streets, compared to Toronto's. While I would have liked to be the MacDonnells' guest for other than dinner, I declined Beau's invitation to stay at their home. That evening, I had mixed feelings about seeing Aileen, who was as charming as ever. My rival appeared after dinner, and it was plainly evident that he disliked my being there. As I bid farewell to Aileen, she showed little enthusiasm for keeping in touch, and I resolved not to write or communicate with her again, although it hurt me to do so.

The highlight of the next day was an encounter with J. W. Dafoe, editor of the *Winnipeg Free Press* and the *rex regis* of Canadian editorial writers. I had no difficulty in getting to see the distinguished editor; as I walked in, he was seated at his office desk, his sandy hair very much tossed up and his bright eyes revealing great mental agility. When I told him I was Paul Martin of North Renfrew, Dafoe astonished me by saying that he had heard my name. The Dafoes came from Combermere, not far from Pembroke, and apparently he had followed my byelection campaign.

We began to discuss Canada's international status, and I made it plain that I shared Arthur Berriedale Keith's view that Canada was not equal in status to Britain. Dafoe, like Mackenzie King, was of the opposite opinion and had written a recent editorial to that effect. That Canada did not have a foreign policy of its own, that its citizens could not, of their own will, amend the constitution, and that they were still subject to the Colonial Laws Validity Act were, I suggested, palpable demonstrations of our inequality and inferior status vis-à-vis Britain. Dafoe brushed aside my arguments as academic dogmatism reminiscent of the views of W. P. M. Kennedy, a lecturer in constitutional law at the University of Toronto. In Dafoe's view, the most important point to remember was that Canada could remove these marks of inferiority at any time. Although I thought there was something in what Dafoe said, I was not entirely convinced; for instance, Canada's sovereignty would be compromised by a British declaration of war, which would similarly commit the rest of the empire, at least in international affairs.

The landscape I saw from the train after we left Winnipeg behind was a little disappointing; yet the vastness of the prairies was startling. Brandon reminded me very much of Pembroke, while Regina put me in mind of an overgrown county town. Calgary I liked from the first. Out walking through the city, I heard some church chimes and found out that the locals said about them, "There is Bennett speaking again." Apparently the Conservative chieftain had donated them to the church, but it amused me to hear that Calgarians would make a joke at the expense of the loquacious R. B.

In all my ports of call, I visited Liberal luminaries and workers to exchange information and ideas. While in Regina, I was taken around by the president of the city's Young Liberals, who made sure I met Charles Dunning, former premier of Saskatchewan and then the minister of railways and canals in the King government. I knew that Saskatchewan was a "den of Liberals" but recorded in my journal that they were slightly "too practical, perhaps at the expense of giving the best sort of government." During visits with provincial ministers, including Dr. J. M. Uhrich, Saskatchewan's minister of public health, the distressful anti-Catholic and anti-Liberal feeling being whipped up by the Ku Klux Klan in the province was discussed; it was lamentable that such an odious set of prejudices had engaged the public mind.

After the prairies, I found the Rockies breathtaking. Banff was the most beautiful spot I had ever seen. As lofty as the mountains, though, were the prices at the Banff Springs Hotel, and I quickly had to move on to the coast.

In Vancouver, a pretty young girl staying at the same hotel asked me whether I golfed; I had bought a pair of white linen plus fours, and she no doubt thought I spent time on the golf links. After admitting that I didn't, I found out that she was going riding in Stanley Park and asked to accompany her, even though I had never been on a horse in my life. The stable hands had to help me up onto my hired steed. I followed the young lady onto the bridle path, where she spurred her horse faster and faster, despite my pleas to her to slow down. When she did eventually slow her horse to a trot, I reached over to hold her hand — I was gauche with both women and horses — but just at that point my nag took it into its head to gallop, and I found myself on top of a pile of leaves. My riding companion helped me up, laughing, and then cantered off, thus ending my equestrian courting.

During my five- or six-week western excursion, I tried to put the future out of my mind, but I could not long postpone a decision once I returned to Toronto in late August. Right away, I had to work at the Thorncliffe racetrack to earn $161 for fees to enable me to be called to the bar.

By this time, I had determined to go to Harvard. Dean Falconbridge and Dr. D. A. MacRae of Osgoode Hall both had urged me to work towards an LL.M. and had written to Roscoe Pound of the Harvard Law School on my behalf. Some of my friends thought it was foolish of me to consider further education, and since the Ontario Liberal Party had refused to assume further responsibility for my election debts, I myself would have to repay them. For a while, I considered taking up a quasi offer to join the Windsor law firm of Roach, Riddell and Baillargeon as a means of immediately meeting those debts, but Harvard beckoned; a degree from its famous law school not only would mean greater remuneration when I finally began practising but also would give me the kind of training that is obtainable only in great centres of learning. On 14 September, I received a telegram admitting me to the Law School. My joy was tempered by the very sad news the same day that my Uncle Edward, my father's brother, had died. Three days later, I went to see Senator Haydon, who presented me with $600 for my studies, insisting that it was a gift. Still not sure whether I ought to go to Harvard, I looked into another possibility — and met a future cabinet colleague — when I called upon Ralph Campney to see about the prospects of securing a job similar to his; he worked as private secretary to a cabinet minister in Ottawa.[2] Such a position, I thought, would tide me over my

2 The minister of trade and commerce, James Malcolm.

financial impediments and enable me to save enough to begin a law practice. But Ralph discouraged me from pursuing the idea.

That visit to Ottawa gave me much to think about. First of all, there was the pleasure of seeing my parents again, albeit at a sad family occasion. As my uncle's funeral procession entered the gates of Notre Dame Cemetery, I saw for the first time the memorial to Laurier. Later, at dinner, Aunt Aglae, my father's sister, gave me a little picture of Thomas D'Arcy McGee that, according to family lore, had been handed to my grandfather, James Martin, by McGee himself a week before his assassination in 1868.

A hectic week followed my return to Toronto. I was called to the bar on 20 September in a solemn ceremony, full of admonitions by the treasurer of the benchers of the Law Society and by Chief Justice Anglin, whose son Eddie was called along with me. After taking the oath, I returned my borrowed gown and celebrated with some of my classmates, relaxing afterwards at a movie with a young lady friend. My Harvard plans fell into place the following day, when I went to see Frank O'Connor, the confectionery magnate. I was a little taken aback when he would not provide financial aid, for as president of the Newman Club I had helped him dispense assistance to students. But in order to help me work my way through law school, Frank kindly gave me a letter of introduction to the manager of Fanny Farmer, the American candy company, which he owned. Although I felt embarrassed at having to ask for funds so pointedly, it had become imperative. In between packing, I worked my last day at the track and, on 22 September, left Toronto by train for Montreal and Boston.

Even though my bags passed customs just before the Canada-US border in Vermont, I did not. A customs official who boarded the train there told me that I needed a visa for my year in Boston and insisted that I procure one from the American consul in Montreal. My pleas were to no avail. When I reached Farnham, a small town to the southeast of Montreal, I had to get off the train and hang about the waiting room until another one could take me back the next morning. Despite my disappointment and the hostility I felt for the regulations and the law-abiding inspector, I slept soundly on a long wooden bench until dawn and the train's arrival. In Montreal I was able to collect papers proving my bona fides; later that day, I presented them to the same inspector, but with no generous greeting.

My first view of Boston and Harvard did not meet my expectations. I found the city uninteresting and smaller than I had imagined and was also a little let down to see that Harvard, although across the Charles River in Cambridge, rested so close to a noisy and bustling city. My first stop on arrival was the office of the eminent Dean Roscoe Pound, who, to my amazement, was wearing a newspaperman's green eyeshade. He buoyed up my spirits and spoke of all that Harvard offered. Aware of my aspirations to serve in public life, Pound suggested a particular course of study: Roman law with James Thayer, international law with Manley O. Hudson, administrative law with Felix Frankfurter, and jurisprudence with himself. Dean Pound looked quite unlike a great professor; in fact his appearance reminded me of my former mill boss in Pembroke. But the more I saw of him, the more I came to admire that rare combination of scholar, professor and able administrator.[3]

I quickly found a room in Cambridge at 23 Ware Street, a "digs" owned and operated by a giant of a woman, fittingly called Mrs. Stone. Close by was the drugstore where I breakfasted for the next ten months on doughnuts and milk, a ten-cent repast. After settling in, I went out for a stroll and unexpectedly bumped into Médard Carrière, an old schoolmate from St. Alexandre then in the second year of his studies for a doctorate in French literature at Harvard. We went back to my room to reminisce about Ironside; later that night, I recorded my joy at coming to Boston: "Every man resorts to tradition and, although I am primarily impressed

3 At nineteen, Pound had an M.A. from Nebraska but never took a law degree. In 1889 students came to Harvard for a particular period of study and left at will. Pound got a doctoral degree in botany, but in 1898 he began to teach law in Nebraska and carried out a botanical survey in the state. He taught law at both Northwestern and Chicago before moving to Harvard in 1910. He served as dean at the Harvard Law School from 1916 to 1936.

with the intellectual and scholastic halo encircling the university, I cannot help but hope and think that my coming to Harvard, just as Mr. King came in 1907, has a tinge of significance. . . . It will be interesting many years hence to know whether my association with Harvard will have as enriching an influence."

Since Roman law had not been taught at Osgoode Hall, I was given it as a compulsory subject at Harvard. The course was a muddle and was not made any clearer by Professor Thayer's stuttering manner. For a while, it was difficult to decide whether I was a poor listener or he a poor lecturer. After working our way haltingly through the *lex aquilia* and such subjects as "mistake," I grew disgusted with the class and made up for it by reading on my own.

I was stimulated from the first by the freedom and intellectual activity of Roscoe Pound's course. He singled me out right away as a student of philosophy, and at our first seminar I found myself outlining Aristotle's definition of nature. Pound and I often engaged in friendly disputation over the attributes of sociological jurisprudence, in which he firmly believed. I held that it could not be said that this approach provided a scientific basis for law or for its interpretation; Pound maintained that there was little to be gained simply by a discussion of method, and he questioned whether there was any such thing as "science," in the sense of the absolute attainment of certainty. I was startled but refreshed to hear jurisprudence being related to philosophy and science. In Pound's view, the isolation of jurisprudence from the social sciences had been responsible for the failure of law to meet social objectives. The notion that law exists to serve the interests of the community is widely accepted today. But it was a novel idea when Pound began to teach at Harvard just before the Great War, and it had come to be the dominant theme of his course in jurisprudence.

Looking out from under his emerald eyeshade, Pound spoke with great erudition about four aspects of the philosophy of law: the analytical, the historical, the philosophical and the sociological. He lead us through the Greek theories of justice, from Aristotle and Plato, to his own articles on "the maxims of equity," set out in various issues of the *Harvard Law Review*, to help us study the genesis of legal analysis. For the *jus gentium* we followed W. W. Buckland, while our commentators for the *jus naturale* were Cicero, Maine and Bryce. Pound then swung to the twelfth century and moved into what he believed marked the beginnings of modern legal science. How astonished I was to hear the dean of the Harvard Law School speak of Thomas Aquinas; he reminded me of how much I had learned from Maurice de Wulf's *Histoire de la philosophie medièvale*. Like Etienne Gilson, Pound looked on Thomism as philosophy, not theology — using reason to understand the nature of the world. Thomism has been described as Christian philosophy, but this is a wrong connotation. He also spoke of the Protestant jurist-theologians and the emancipation of jurisprudence from theology.

Pound's lectures were frequently applauded. Here was no ordinary teacher but a great man at work — a lawyer, philosopher and historian telling his students about the end of law, illustrating the theories of justice of Kant, Pufendorf and Oliver Wendell Holmes, among others. To watch and to hear him was an unforgettable experience. But not all my fellow students thought so. Angus Macdonald, a future premier of Nova Scotia and Canada's wartime minister of national defence for naval services, took Pound's course with me as part of his sabbatical from Dalhousie University. Angus's less admiring reaction surprised me because his background in philosophy was not so different from mine, and he was a friend of my M.A. supervisor, Dr. Phelan.[4]

One blustery November Sunday, Roscoe Pound invited me out to his suburban home. Never had I seen as many books in a private residence — he even had bookshelves in his garage! As we sat chatting, Pound ridiculed the prevailing view that there was too much law. In our complex civilization, he said, the absence of law would produce discomfort and injustice. He wholeheartedly agreed with my belief that governments must legislate social

4 Listening to Angus, I soon realized that the philosophy curriculum at St. Michael's was more scholarly, liberal and rational than that of so many Catholic colleges.

reforms, such as universal minimum wage legislation. Although I did not subscribe to his view that society is more than the sum of its particular parts, I could see that society was distinct from the individual. Discovering that Pound's early circumstances paralleled my own, I surmised that his relatively unprivileged background had stimulated his instinctive sympathy for the oppressed and the poor and his adherence to the sociological side of jurisprudence. He said that there were other, more essential qualities for the public man than a knowledge of economics: the courage to speak one's mind despite the call of expediency, for example. Pound told me that when he had sat as a judge on the Nebraska bench, he had earned the nickname of Pontius Pilate. His approach to the interaction between law and society reinforced my own views, as did his encouraging letters during my years as minister of national health and welfare, when I tried to follow our shared precepts in my legislative program.

The first seminar with my professor of administrative law, Felix Frankfurter, a short and pudgy man who wore spectacles, left me with some reservations. Despite Burgon Bickersteth's enthusiastic recommendation, Frankfurter's criticisms of other legal scholars seemed too dogmatic. But after two months in his class, I came to regard him as an imaginative teacher, listening tolerantly but never willing to become embroiled in idle argument. He did not lecture our small group but preferred to base the discussion on case law.

In 1928, administrative law had barely achieved *de jure* recognition by English and American lawyers, and Frankfurter's course pioneered a study that has since become so all-embracing. He reminded us that industrial change made inevitable the emergence of legal controls over economic and social interests and that such a development must be countered by devising effective legal standards. We began with the implicit understanding that at the beginning of the present century, the growing powers of the state were not beyond the grasp of administrative law, but as the power of the executive grew, the law had not always exacted standards of justice under statutory authority. Judicial surveillance seemed to lack the necessary vigilance, and criticism of the bureaucracy had become rampant. The lord chief justice of England, Lord Hewart, had just defined the problem in his book, *The New Despotism*,[5] which was part of our reading for Frankfurter's course. Our statutory rules and orders-in-council had also begun to raise questions in Canada. Judicial review and administrative discretion could not exist in isolation, and administrative law needed students trained in the common law.

There is a relation between administrative law and the control by law of administrative abuse through the device known as the declaratory judgment, the subject of my LL.M. thesis prescribed and directed by Felix Frankfurter. The declaratory judgment resolves conflicts before the infringement of a right takes place; it derives from Scottish law, which gives one the right to go into court and ask for a declaration of rights regarding a potential violation or conflict. In short, it states the rights of the parties without specifying the action to be taken. The English judicial system first provided for it in the rules of court in 1883. This statutory remedy, so essential in any current system of law, took a long time to be adopted. In administrative law, the advantages of the declaratory judgment arise where it is difficult to select the appropriate remedy or where the ordinary correction is unsatisfactory. Since the time of my thesis in 1929, the declaratory judgment has been increasingly used in both the United Kingdom and Canada.

My growing admiration for Frankfurter was not universally shared. In many quarters, he was looked upon as a radical, and his book declaring the innocence of Sacco and Vanzetti, the Boston anarchists executed in August 1927, only increased the hostility towards him of the Harvard establishment. I decided to take the man as he was, and my impression bore out his brilliance. I was not concerned about what others thought, since most of his critics had probably never met him or read his writings.

My one reservation about Frankfurter grew out of a feeling that he played favourites by choosing certain students, usually because of their intellectual merits, and then pushed them to "perform" in

5 Gordon Hewart, *The New Despotism* (London: E. Benn, 1929).

class. In my group of about fifteen, the most noteworthy of these was an undergraduate who because of his academic achievements had been given special permission to join us. He was a tall, well-dressed, good-looking and able youth called Alger Hiss. No one could deny that Hiss had talent. From his bearing, I always assumed that he was the son of wealthy American parents — Ivy League types — since these were the kind of people Frankfurter appeared to lean towards, but I later learned that Hiss was the son of a milkman. I met him again in 1946 when, as secretary of state, I served as a delegate to the first General Assembly of the United Nations in London; he was working at the time as the secretary of the United States delegation.

Our paths crossed once more after he stood accused of perjury. It was at a cocktail party at the end of 1948, when I was in New York as a delegate to the United Nations. Whittaker Chambers had accused Hiss of being a communist, and the press were sniffing at his trail wherever he went. Dodging Hiss throughout the party, I deliberately left early. I felt great admiration for the courageous position taken by Dean Acheson, a prominent lawyer and later the US secretary of state. While he did not comment on the legal issues, Acheson never denied his friendship even after Hiss had been convicted and before the appeal was heard. Thinking about this incident and comparing Acheson's courage with my lack of it, I felt ashamed.[6]

Despite my thesis, administrative law was really a sideline for me; my main academic interest remained international law. I had gone to Harvard to work with Manley O. Hudson, an outstanding scholar in international law, and was very disappointed when, as was the current custom, the law professors assigned me a thesis

6 Whittaker Chambers had told the House of Representatives' Un-American Activities Committee in the summer of 1948 that he had worked with Hiss in the 1930s and that the latter was a member of the Communist Party at the time. Chambers asserted that Hiss, then in the state department, had passed on confidential documents for transmittal to a Soviet secret agent. Hiss denied Chambers's allegations but was later indicted for perjury. As a matter of record, it is interesting to note that John Foster Dulles had written in 1946 that "there is no reason to doubt Hiss's complete loyalty to our American institutions."

topic in another field. As professor of the seminar on international law, Manley Hudson exerted a powerful influence on me. This association extended into studies on the International Court of Justice at the end of World War II and my efforts in 1946 to have him selected by the United States as its nominee to the postwar successor of this judicial body that he had served so well. While most of his life was spent teaching and writing on international law, he worked tirelessly for international organization in relation to the law of nations.

Manley Hudson was a superb teacher, articulate and theatrical. On one occasion, he censured me for quoting from a columnist in *The New York Times* to help buttress a legal argument. My seminar colleagues, graduate students from all over the world, were shaken in their seats as Hudson, in strong language, deplored the fact that any student of law would rest a case on such a flabby authority. His impatient manner used to make me nervous — it was well-nigh impossible to argue with him — but some students lost their tempers, and a classmate known as "Alabama Pete" Cox once had a spat with him in class. Hudson displayed great reverence for rare books of legal scholarship. One day, with profound respect, he passed a precious book around the table, allowing each student to touch it. Perhaps my regard for scholarly works is partly attributable to this incident.

Although it is now used in law schools throughout the world, the case system in legal studies will always be identified with Harvard. Students arrived in class thinking that a case was clear-cut and believing categorically that the decision rendered was a proper or an improper one. Hudson would turn this apparent simplicity into a factual and legal complexity, which he would then explain. Later he would unravel the legal arguments in a summing-up of pristine elegance. Apart from teaching, between 1925 and 1935 Hudson directed "The Harvard Research" studies by American scholars — draft conventions on various questions of international law.[7] The year after I left Harvard, Hudson's group published a

7 Manley O. Hudson, general editor, *Harvard Studies in International Law* (Cambridge, Mass.: Harvard University, Bureau of International Research, various dates).

valuable collection of laws on nationality. I cherished these and later found them of great help when I came to draft the Canadian Citizenship Act in the immediate postwar years.

The recognition of states was a matter of great interest to me and one that I pursued after my year at Harvard. Our seminar examined the status of the British dominions in international law. Discussions then under way in London led in December 1931 to the enactment of the Statute of Westminster and the abolition of the right of the United Kingdom parliament to withhold consent from dominion legislation. As I busied myself preparing my first paper for the seminar, my research reinforced the position I had taken with J. W. Dafoe the previous summer. I came to the conclusion that although Canada was not a sovereign power, the country *was* an international personality and, in consequence, could legally remain neutral if Britain declared war. Furthermore, I argued that the British empire would inevitably disappear as countries gained their independence. I did not foresee the growth of the commonwealth but assumed fatalistically that any change would ultimately lead to disintegration. Happily, I was wrong.

My second seminar report presented views on the status of the Vatican. Strangely, by a majority of one, the class decided that this city-state should be admitted to the family of nations. Asked for my personal view, I said I thought it would be a mistake. A number of things led me to this conclusion, despite all legal arguments to the contrary: the history of the papacy as a temporal power, the universality of the church, and the fact that the Vatican's main concern was religious. For its own sake, I believed the Vatican should uphold the principle of rendering unto Caesar that which is Caesar's. In February 1929, Mussolini signed the Lateran Treaty, which recognized the Vatican as a separate state under the direct sovereignty of the pope. My opinions prompted Wishart Spence to tell me after the class that in argument I freed myself from religious prejudice more than anyone he had ever known.

While the undergraduate course was pragmatic, the postgraduate courses at Harvard for students who were already lawyers constituted an intellectual study of the law. In many ways, I found Harvard to be an academic "factory": students given study cubicles

in the library stacks would peek into their colleagues' carrels to
see if they were hard at it. We worked diligently, knowing full well
that the school would fail a certain percentage of its students. I was
very anxious to get my LL.M., particularly since most of the other
students, Wishart Spence for instance, were top graduates. Harvard was without doubt the most rigorous legal training I received.

Manley Hudson urged us to supplement our interest in international law by attending the meetings of the Foreign Policy Association in Boston's Copley Plaza Hotel. There we listened to
J. L. Brierly of Oxford outline the arguments in his book, *The Law
of Nations,*[8] and spent an evening with Norman Angell, who was to
win the Nobel Peace Prize in 1933. I attended other lectures, too,
including those by Professor F. W. Taussig on economic theory.
Taussig's name was as respected then as Maynard Keynes's would
be later. He had taught Mackenzie King and, during my time at
Harvard, lectured to Norman Robertson, who later became one of
Canada's most remarkable public servants. When the great advocate Clarence Darrow visited Boston, I found his topic — Tolstoy's
philosophy — a surprising one. Darrow spoke clearly, almost
coldly, both then and later at the law school, where he expounded
his philosophy of man as a machine and his refusal to consider most
criminals as completely responsible for their actions.

During the autumn, my chief extracurricular activity was the
American presidential elections. In early October at a Democratic
rally in Boston, the playboy mayor of New York, Jimmy Walker,
defended Tammany Hall and attacked religious intolerance. The
following week, Franklin Delano Roosevelt, governor of the State
of New York, visited Boston. Jim, his son and my classmate,
accompanied his father to the podium in Orchestra Hall.

When the Republican presidential candidate, Herbert Hoover,
came to town, I arranged to get a seat in the press cavalcade that
wound its way around the city with him. The public did not greet
Hoover very keenly, and he appeared tired and unenthusiastic.

8 J. L. Brierly, *The Law of Nations: An Introduction to the International Law of Peace*
(Oxford: Clarendon Press, 1928).

His speech fascinated me; he did not play on the crowd's emotion but spoke in a simple conversational tone that evoked a practical and businesslike disposition. He argued that the economic policies and efficient administration that he was advocating were not ends in themselves but were means of effecting happiness for the people. While my sympathies were with the Democratic Party, I must confess that I found Hoover more prepossessing than I had expected.

The Democratic hopeful, Al Smith, arrived later in October. I do not know how much he saw, but he certainly conquered. In the *Toronto Daily Star* press car once again, I passed a crowd unprecedented in Boston — even Charles Lindbergh was not as lionized. Adeptly playing on human nature, the former New York governor waved his brown derby aloft to the accompaniment of choruses from his theme song, "The Sidewalks of New York." Although I had secured a press ticket, it was only by slipping past the police that I got into the arena, so congested was the mob. Smith was unable to stop the delirious cheering. Standing on a chair and joining in, I initially dismayed my more sedate companion, Angus Macdonald. Then, when Smith tried to make himself heard above the uproar, I looked over and there was Angus on his chair, lustily shouting his approval. Smith ridiculed those who charged him with socialism, pointing out that the so-called prosperity of the United States was not shared by all its citizens. While the Happy Warrior's speech did not impress me with its intellectual content, I could not help but admire his humanity and bluntness. The traditions of the Democratic Party were personified by the introduction on the platform of Mrs. Francis Sayre, daughter of the great Woodrow Wilson and wife of a Harvard Law School professor.

Hoover, I felt, would prove abler in understanding the international situation, but if I had had a vote, it would have gone to Smith. As to the question of a Catholic president — Smith would have been the first — his election, in my view, would settle that issue once and for all.

On election night, I listened to the early results on the radio in the Harvard Club. As I walked home to bed without knowing who the victor was, an airplane passed overhead with a red light glowing from its tail. That was supposed to signify a Republican president, and the following morning I found out that it was disappointingly true.

The pressure of studies and finances kept my other extra-curricular activities in tight rein. The election debt still nagged at me, and I kept receiving dunning letters from the Pembroke *Standard-Observer*, to whom I owed money for advertising in the election campaign. One evening, while I was out, an unnamed visitor called; he told my landlady that he would be back the following day. With some consternation, I awaited the bill collector and felt considerable relief when he turned out to be just a book salesman. I had written to W. H. Moore, expressing my anxiety about the large debt, but he did not answer my letters.

Despite the financial pressures, I managed to enjoy myself with my close friends Wishart Spence and Don Carrick, a Toronto student taking the three-year undergraduate course in law. Don was an outstanding athlete, and we often went to university football matches; when Wishart got a car in October, he took us on drives in the countryside around Boston. In mid-November, we drove to Montreal for the Varsity-McGill football game. McGill won, and that evening we went with some local students to see Lon Chaney's "While the City Sleeps"; their rambunctious celebrations provided more diversion than the film. Back in Boston, on a visit with Wishart to some friends of his, I was intrigued when a lady produced letters to her from Mackenzie King. Their contents shocked me; they were mushy and replete with Victorian sensibilities — not the type of correspondence to be carried on with a married woman. I went on my own to the theatre, movies and concerts as my funds allowed. Attractions available ranged from Al Jolson in "The Singing Fool" to the coloratura soprano Amelita Galli-Curci, whom I had heard before only on the gramophone. I went on a few dates arranged by various friends, but wrote in my diary that most girls were "more interested in the 'flask' and in dancing," and this made me uneasy in their company. Quiet evenings, sitting around chatting at Dorothy Agnew's parents' house — she had been an acquaintance in Toronto — were more to my taste.

I passed a rather lonely Christmas after deciding to spend my first holiday away from my family. Harvard provided for students who remained in the city, and the university president, Lawrence Lowell, and his wife inaugurated the holiday season by inviting us to tea a few weeks before Christmas. (When I was confined to the Stillman infirmary with the flu later that year, Mrs. Lowell kindly stopped by my bed on one of her regular visits, and she later asked me to dinner.) Taking advantage of free time from classes, I put in a few hours each day working at the Fanny Farmer Candy Studio; the change was enjoyable. On Christmas Eve, the Lowells again entertained us, and we listened to readings, religious and secular, including "My Financial Career," by Stephen Leacock. At midnight mass, I heard Father Cushing, who later became cardinal. Mr. Gregory, the manager of the candy studio, saved my spending a melancholy day by inviting me to his home for Christmas dinner. His little daughter and the family cat presented me with a tie and a pair of socks, my only presents that year.

On Boxing Day, with twenty-one dollars in my pocket, I took the bus to New York and put up for twenty-five cents a night at the Hermitage Hotel, the cheapest flophouse I could find. In my innocence, I had not known that this neighbourhood, near 7th Avenue and 42nd Street, harboured a good number of the ladies of the night. After watching the film "Interference," starring Eddie Cantor, I walked around Broadway, a little lost, and decided that the nightlife and bright lights were not for me. The following day, Wall Street "played host to a poor man," as did the Woolworth Building — a Cathedral of Commerce — with its soaring Art Deco lobby. At a vaudeville act the next afternoon, a blindfolded pianist amazed the audience by her ability, apparently unprompted, to play selections whispered by people in the audience to her male assistant but not to her. I was convinced it was all bunk, but when I asked him for the Canadian national anthem, she astounded me by striking up "O Canada."

Off the tourist track, I visited New York's ghetto and found it another world; pushcarts lined the streets, selling everything from toothpicks to potatoes. On the bus to Chinatown, I met a fellow from a mission, a rehabilitated derelict who counselled the down-and-outs sleeping rough in the Bowery. We went to the mission, facing several gambling dens on a rundown street. Each night after a service of hymns and testimonials, the unfortunate inmates received food and a bed; among them, I was told, were doctors, lawyers and even clergymen. Moved by this scene, I pondered my own relative good fortune and wondered about the future.

That future took another twist towards the end of my year at Harvard. For a while, I had considered continuing my studies and had entertained hopes of pursuing a doctorate in jurisprudence, as Angus Macdonald had done. Reluctantly, I had more or less abandoned my dream of studying in England on a Rhodes Scholarship or a Massey Fellowship, but Burgon Bickersteth and probably Father McCorkell had made up their minds that I might benefit from a year in Europe.[9] Because of their efforts, I received the first William E. Wilder Fellowship, established by J. H. Gundy to assist young Canadians who wished to be politically active. Vincent Massey, Burgon Bickersteth and Manley Hudson agreed that it would be useful for me to apply to Trinity College, Cambridge, where the law tradition was second to none. My Harvard professor provided further inducement by informing me that he, too, intended to spend part of the next year at Trinity, working on a new book. In the end, he did not come.

That summer, while working at the racetracks in Toronto and Windsor, I heard that I had been accepted at Trinity College. By this time, I had definitely decided that I would establish my law practice in Windsor. C. P. McTague, the head of the firm I hoped

9 Bickersteth to King, 7 May 1929, W. L. Mackenzie King Papers (J1 series, p. 135735 ff.), PAC.

to join, had promised to hold a position open until I returned from England. My father and mother, who until then had never discouraged me in anything I wished to do, did begin to wonder whether I was developing a propensity to be a perpetual student. It was worrying me too, but I loved university life and felt that my broader horizons would prove beneficial in the long run.

On 4 October, I journeyed to Montreal and embarked for Liverpool. My father came to the dockside to see me off, and although I missed my mother and sisters, I was very happy to spend my last day in Canada with him. The following morning, I sailed on *The Doric* — not the largest ship of the White Star Line but a mighty 20,000 tons nonetheless. Since no Catholic priest was on board, the following morning, as we sailed in fine weather down the St. Lawrence, I attended the Protestant service. After we passed Belle Isle and moved into the open ocean, time became unimportant, and my travelling companions and the books I had brought with me on the voyage marked the days. Of the passenger complement of two hundred, fewer than forty were in my section — tourist third. My cabinmate was a very pleasant Methodist clergyman, Mr. Balch. Promenading, reading, attending the morning and afternoon musical recitals, deck quoits and golf kept us amused as we crossed the Atlantic.

The first sight of England as we docked at Liverpool is still fresh in my memory. Before getting on the train for London, I had just enough time to see the city's fine Anglican cathedral, in a state of construction since the year after my birth, and the house where the great Liberal leader William Ewart Gladstone was born in 1809. The old compartments of the British trains, smaller and more private than our Canadian coaches, intrigued me as we headed for London, from where, after a few hours, I would proceed to Cambridge. I remember standing in Whitehall, looking across at Canada House in Trafalgar Square. Seeing the Houses of Parliament, so familiar in photos and yet so much more majestic in reality, was a great thrill and stimulated future dreams; the parliamentary and common law tradition that I had studied and revered was embodied in that pile of stone. Determined not to look like a tourist, I went into a tobacconist's and bought a pipe, a cheap one, and some tobacco. By the time I got to Cambridge, my mouth was so sore and burnt that I just threw the pipe away.

Darkness had descended when I reached my destination. Gowned students were walking and bicycling in all directions through streets unfamiliar to me. Yet I did recognize King's College Chapel from paintings and photographs — "this immense and glorious work of fine intelligence," as Wordsworth called it. Most of the other buildings I could not identify, but there was no mistaking Trinity College when I found myself in front of its Great Gate, adorned with the effigy of its founder, Henry VIII. I made myself known to the assistant bursar, whose office was in Great Court, the largest college court in England. Near the middle is a fine Renaissance fountain. I did not know on my first night how much history is attached to this court, its college and the wider university. On a ground floor were Thackeray's rooms, opposite those of Macaulay. Isaac Newton once had rooms on the first floor, next to the Great Gate. Nearby lie "sets" occupied in their several times by Francis Bacon, Dryden and Tennyson, by royal princes and future kings, together with great scientists such as J. J. Thomson and Baron Adrian, the architects of our changing world.

That first night there was no time to get more than a quick impression before I left the college to take up my digs at 1 Malcolm Street, close by Jesus College, the home of Bishop Cranmer, who served his king diligently. I did not stay long in these lodgings, but moved up the street to number 20, where I had more space for sleep, study and hospitality. I was now able to detect the difference between Cambridge and Toronto, or even Harvard for that matter. The leisurely but purposeful life in an ancient English university had already begun to add a new dimension to my experience. The next day, I was introduced to my senior tutor, J. R. M. Butler, a history don who became a lifelong friend and my continuing contact with Trinity. His rooms, next to the Master's Lodge, were reached by a long staircase winding to the corner turret on the third floor. Jim, the son of Henry Montague Butler, a distinguished headmaster of Harrow and later master of Trinity

College, was tall, thin and bald, very much the Mr. Chips type. An enthusiastic climber, Jim had his rooms festooned with photographs of mountains he had conquered. Because of my age and experience, he was less a tutor than a directing friend. He explained that in British universities a student attended lectures on any subject that absorbed him or her. Since my special interest was international law, I sought out appropriate lectures in that and related disciplines.

Butler had assigned Professor Pearce Higgins, Whewell Professor of International Law, to be my supervisor. Higgins's lectures were far less stimulating than Manley Hudson's had been, and he read his way drily through texts he had presented dozens of times before. His emphasis on the historical evolution of naval law and history did not seem too relevant in a day when international law was evolving rapidly. I met privately with Higgins, usually over lunch or a cup of tea, and our discussions generally centred on the recognition of states. Continuing the interest that I had developed at Harvard, I explored with him the close relationship between law and politics in gaining recognition for a state. Despite the kinship between the two, Higgins believed that the recognition of states should remain essentially a question of international law and not of the politics of the day.

More satisfying as a teacher was Dr. Arnold McNair, who lectured on war and neutrality during the Lent term. Besides, his subject appealed more directly to my own interests. Later on, McNair became a justice of the International Court; he also coedited the *Cambridge Legal Essays*,[10] one of the first books I read in the Squires Law Library. It pointed out the difference between the study of law in Britain and the United States. True to the concepts of education derived from Germany, the American university emphasized research and precision in arranging evidence for argument, while the English system stressed legal principles in a manner more closely allied to philosophy.

10 A. D. McNair and P. H. Winfield, *Cambridge Legal Essays, . . . Presented to Doctor Bond, Professor Buckland and Professor Kenny, etc.* (Cambridge: W. Heffer & Sons, 1926).

The Squires Library was a fulcrum for law students from all the Cambridge colleges, and I spent a lot of time there. But unlike Harvard, where studying took up all one's time, a great deal of the day at Cambridge was spent talking and socializing around the meal table. I would eat breakfast and lunch in the town but more often than not would take dinner in hall, a practice I liked. To lunch with the master of the college was a special privilege. In my years at Trinity, I was twice asked to lunch by J. J. Thomson, one of Cambridge's most renowned scientists and the Nobel Prize winner whose research led to the discovery of isotopes.

I quickly felt at home with both the British people and their institutions. They never made me feel like a colonial, and I grew very proud of my nationality and of my French origin — I think I must have been the only French Canadian in Cambridge at that time. I had not lost my nationalism, however, and the only thing that I objected to was an exaggerated emphasis on the "empire," since that implies some type of supremacy of one nation over others.

The Cambridge atmosphere encouraged students to diversify their interests, and the personal libraries of many dons and students reflected this catholicity of taste. As an undergraduate, I had had money only for essential texts, and during my year at Harvard I had managed to buy more books, including some outside my discipline. But at Cambridge, rooting through secondhand bookshops for the unexpected "find" turned into a passion. One of my enduring impressions of Britain has to do with the manner in which people know and value their books.

In one memorable lecture, I heard W. W. Buckland, an emeritus professor of Roman law, maintain that jurisprudence was not a philosophy and that John Austin and Kant were not in disagreement but were interested in different matters — Austin in existing bodies of law, Kant in law in the abstract.[11] Since Ernest Barker, the noted political philosopher and a staunch Yorkshireman, often

11 Austin (1790–1859) had a strong influence on legal theory and particularly on John Stuart Mill.

touched on matters close to the law, I used to drop into his lectures whenever I could. Barker was the only Cambridge academic I heard refer to St. Thomas Aquinas. Another lecturer, Sir Arthur Quiller-Couch, the noted Shakespearean scholar, always refused to acknowledge the presence of women in his classes, beginning them with the simple "Gentlemen." This was a source of great amusement, and students would pack his lectures merely to hear the salutation.

My friend Wynne Plumptre, a brilliant student of John Maynard Keynes, took me several times to the weekly evening gatherings in his professor's rooms. There, thirty or forty students sitting wherever there was space would wait until Keynes opened the discussion on a particular topic for that evening. My attendance was frequent enough that although I did not participate actively, Keynes knew who I was. Later, during World War II, I saw him in the lobby of the Chateau Laurier; he was in Canada to discuss war finance. When I introduced myself as the member of parliament for Essex East, he appeared quite unimpressed. Keynes's economic philosophy had a profound influence on me, particularly during the 1930s. His theories proposing active government stimulation of the economy to eradicate unemployment struck me as an important departure from economic orthodoxy, and I became a Keynesian.

The only thing I found a little difficult at Trinity College was its Anglican affiliation. One of the rules of the college concerned going to evensong a certain number of times each week. When I brought up the religious requirements with Jim Butler, he sent me to see the chaplain and deputy master, Dr. Parry. Explaining that I was a Catholic, Dr. Parry replied, "Oh, yes, Mr. Martin. You belong to the Minority. But these religious obligations will not hurt you." And that was the end of it. Still, I grew to like the Anglican service, especially its hymns, and soon found out that I was more diligent in my attendance than many with a formal adherence to that faith.

The leisurely pace of life at Cambridge allowed me to resume my debating interests. My first debate, at the Cambridge Union in mid-November, pitted me against Wynne Plumptre, who argued that "this House does not approve of the early liberation of the Indian people." Many distinguished figures from the subcontinent, including the Maharajkumar of Kharagpur, were in the audience that night. Wynne lost the debate and the negative to me — perhaps fortunately, given the sensitivity of the subject and the listeners. The Cambridge Union debates also gave me an opportunity to spend some time with my greatest friend in Cambridge, C. Wilfred Jenks, an undergraduate in law and a protégé of Dr. Arnold McNair. Later, McNair helped shape Jenks's brilliant career in law, international affairs and international organization. The president of the Union and another friend of Jenks was John Sinclair, Lord Pentland, a grandson of Lord Aberdeen, Canada's seventh governor general.

In November, Pentland came to see me in my digs. He told me that Lord Beaverbrook had agreed to debate the issue of empire free trade at the Cambridge Union in early December but had then declined because he did not like the wording of the motion. Pentland enlisted my help to convince R. B. Bennett, who happened to be in London, to step in for Beaverbrook (it was not uncommon for well-known personalities to "speak on the paper" as an invited guest of the Union). Pentland wanted me to go to London with him to support his invitation to Bennett to speak in Beaverbrook's place. I did not know the opposition leader, but, goaded by Pentland and keen to meet a possible prime minister, I went down to London with him. John and I spent many hours tracking down Bennett, who received us graciously and requested time to consider the invitation. Pentland had to return to Cambridge, but I stayed on to receive Bennett's answer; I suspect the Tory leader wanted to talk to Beaverbrook before making up his mind. What we did not know was that, to Beaverbrook's annoyance, Bennett had already expressed reservations about empire free trade. In the end, he agreed to come to Cambridge as a guest of the Union but would not to speak in the debate. This way he could meet the thirty or so Canadians at Cambridge but not compromise his position.

My satisfaction knew no bounds when the leader of the opposition asked me to dine with him the next day at the Mayfair Hotel, near Berkeley Square. The following morning, as I was waiting to go into the House of Commons, in a long line near Westminster Hall, I was startled to see Ernest Lapointe, Canada's minister of justice. I had met him when he spoke at Newman Hall, and we now exchanged a few words. Later, in the Mayfair's dining room, Mr. Lapointe and the undersecretary of state for external affairs, Dr. O. D. Skelton, saw me with R. B. Bennett; Lapointe jokingly wagged his finger at me. I took the earliest opportunity to explain the circumstances to him and Skelton. Mr. Lapointe, a witty man, warned me that hobnobbing with such a true-blue Tory might be corrupting, particularly because we had also tried to convince *him* to visit Cambridge.[12]

My dinner with Bennett introduced me to a well-endowed, informative mind — one that I came to appreciate later during our years together in the House of Commons. He proposed to drive to Cambridge the next day and invited me to join him. I was not asked where I would spend the night in London. Young students, however, are resourceful, particularly when they have to take their pocketbooks into account. The Imperial Hotel on Russell Square had a famous Turkish bath where one could spend the night for three shillings, and this is where I made for.

My final debate at Cambridge took place at the beginning of May, when I proposed a resolution to increase funding for Roman Catholic schools. No holds were barred as my chief opponent, G. G. Coulton, the celebrated medieval historian, argued the contrary. His criticism of the Church of Rome and its emanations were thought by many Catholics to be prejudicial and unfair. This time, I argued strictly from a forthright legal basis; the *Cambridge*

12 Mr. Lapointe and Dr. Skelton were in London to discuss dominion legislation and merchant shipping at an imperial conference. At my suggestion, C. A. E. Shuckburgh of the Seeley Club had invited Mr. Lapointe to speak (Shuckburgh to Lapointe, Ernest Lapointe Papers (pp. 2050-51)). John Pentland also tried (Pentland to Lapointe, 14 November 1929, ibid. (p. 2045)) after I told him of the encounter.

Review, not known for its magnanimity, could not find "an ill-turned epigram," and I succeeded in carrying the day.

I met Oswald McConkey at about the time of Bennett's visit. Mac, as we knew him, was a professor of field husbandry at the Ontario Agricultural College in Guelph and had come over to Cambridge to do research towards a doctorate on grass. He was a happy-go-lucky fellow and we became quite chummy. His rooms at Christ's College, over the entrance, put my digs to shame. Our friendship was strengthened by our common ownership of a secondhand Harley Davidson one-cylinder motorbike. Mac had bought the vehicle for £5, to get him to the flat open fen country outside Cambridge, but he proposed that we share the cost of the bike so that I could use it at night and on weekends.

At the end of term, in the spring of 1930, I took a week's trip on the bike down towards the south coast. On the way to Bournemouth and Weymouth, past the famous White Horse, I was riding along cheerily when something happened, and the next thing I remember was waking up in a nursing home on Weymouth's seafront. Apparently I had been unconscious for several hours. When I came to, I was looking into a nurse's lovely face. "Kiss me," I said, and she did. After I had convalesced for a few days, I courted her briefly. She was a delightful Welsh girl, Violet Davies; but I was on the point of going to Geneva, and our little romance had to end. While I was high commissioner to Britain and paying a visit to Weymouth, I mentioned this story to a local journalist. His report in the paper brought a response from Violet, who visited me to reminisce about old times.

Britain's universities provided long Christmas and Easter holidays. These breaks were considered part of the program of study and university experience. To see places one has read about is very much part of the joy of learning. During the Christmas vacation, I went to Paris for the first time. Frank Mallon, whom I had known at St. Michael's, and my old friend Médard Carrière arranged for me to stay at La Maison Canadienne. It met the grasp of my purse and gave me a feel of *la cité universitaire*, with its meals *à bon marché* — the diet was mostly potato pie. A bar we went to, lined with mirrors, employed nude waitresses to serve drinks. This was the first time I had seen a naked woman and it shocked me, but not so my more worldly friend Médard. Of course, I visited all the tourist places, including Notre Dame, La Madeleine, and Le Dôme des Invalides, where Napoleon's remains are buried in the crypt. The red granite sarcophagus is lighted by a circular opening in the dome, and the tomb is surrounded by tattered flags — symbols of the great regiments that served France's imperial dreams.

After Paris, Frank and I took a train into Belgium, arriving in Brussels at New Year's. The snow had fallen on this city of Albert I, the king whose heroism in the Great War I had greatly admired. The *mannequin qui pisse* in the Grande Place somewhat offended our Canadian sense of decency: Frank, more of a puritan than I, refused to cast more than a furtive glance at it. We went out to Waterloo and tried unsuccessfully to get into the room in the tavern where Wellington had spent the night before the battle. They told us it was closed, but we suspected it was occupied by a living "Wellington," possibly a New Year's guest. In Mercier's cathedral at Malines, we saw the famous wooden carvings, and at Louvain we called on Maurice de Wulf, our teacher of medieval philosophy at Toronto. Then, a few days later, Frank and I walked through the battlefields at Ypres and Passchendaele, eloquent reminders of the folly of man.

During the Easter vacation, Wynne Plumptre, my bosom Toronto friend Jack Beer, and I again stopped in Paris on our way to Italy. We reached Rome via Milan and Bologna. Once there, one could understand why Shelley and Keats had resolved to stay in this most exciting of cities. We took a *pensione* close by the Piazza di Espagna. How happy a trio we were seeing the sights: San Pietro in Vincoli, Santa Croce, and the basilicas St. John Lateran and St. Paul's Outside the Walls. Meanwhile we awaited the results of our appeal for tickets for an audience with Pope Pius XI. Although we did manage to get three through the superior of the Canadian College, Wynne decided at the last moment that he ought not to go, anticipating the disapproval of his father, Canon Plumptre of Toronto. Pius XI looked a powerful man and made a great impact on the hushed crowd in the hall. The mystique of authority is impressive, and I sensed it on this occasion, as I did much later when I had audiences with Pius XII and Paul VI.

At the Camera di Deputati, we saw Mussolini sitting below the podium. Like many another parliamentarian in legislatures throughout the world, he was reading a newspaper — probably one he owned. A day or two later, near the spreading monument dedicated to Victor Emmanuel II in the Piazza Venezia, we heard Il Duce giving an oration from an open window. He did not speak for long, but it was a sight to see; all his gestures were in high gear.

At mass on the day we were to return to Cambridge, I felt a tap on my shoulder. It was none other than Frank O'Connor, the Laura Secord and Fanny Farmer proprietor, who always seemed to be popping up in my life. After the service, he told me that he was holidaying with three friends, including the maître d'hotel of the King Edward in Toronto, who had been brought along to advise the party on food. O'Connor was planning to visit Florence and insisted that I accompany him and his troupe. So Wynne and Jack went off while I travelled to Florence, before returning to England.

During the new term, a South African graduate student, I. J. Rousseau, suggested I join him as a representative of Cambridge's Seeley Club at a Ralegh Club dinner at Rhodes House in Oxford. Rousseau spoke of Britain's prime minister, Ramsay MacDonald, as though he knew him, and, sure enough, just before dinner, he ushered me into a room and ceremoniously presented me to MacDonald. After a minute's conversation, by which time Rousseau had vanished, a puzzled MacDonald asked, "Who was that man?"

Cambridge begins to close its year with the May Back, a ball and celebration on the first day of May. Until early in the morning in the quads, on Trinity Lane and on the banks of the Cam, young ladies in fine long dresses and young men in tails party and dance. What a happy bunch we were: Jack Beer, Wynne Plumptre and I, and our lady friends.

I had agreed to begin working that fall as a junior solicitor in C. P. McTague's law firm in Windsor, but my last experience in Europe was to spend the summer at the Geneva School of International Studies run by Professor and Mrs. Alfred Zimmern. Wilfred Jenks had arranged for me to go to this world-famous gathering, held in La Grande Boissière near Lac Léman. Without doubt, I was under Jenks's spell; no man in my life has so captivated me by his knowledge and zeal for a new international order based on law and justice. He did not compromise his principles, believing steadfastly in the ultimate destiny of the League of Nations and (eventually) the United Nations. My own deep attachment to these institutions was encouraged by his dedicated example; Jenks worked energetically for the International Labour Office, which he directed for many years. He died in Rome in 1973, while addressing a conference on the growth of international law.

The Zimmerns ran their school principally for postgraduate students in international affairs — but occasionally they admitted exceptional undergraduates such as Wilfred Jenks. They also found money for grants to worthy students who had no means, and that is how I came to attend the seventh session. Although Alfred Zimmern had written a monumental book, *The Greek Commonwealth*, he published little more, deciding instead to lecture. The course, from mid-July to the end of the first week in September, was given in the evenings at the Conservatoire de Musique, where we also listened to chamber music concerts, and at La Grande Boissière.

That summer we heard the Indian philosopher and poet Rabindranath Tagore, read from his work; later, Jan Paderewski, the virtuoso Polish pianist and statesman who had briefly headed the government in 1919, spoke to us and gave a recital.

Zimmern introduced each week with a lecture on the subject we would study for the next seven days; then he would turn the sessions over to his invited lecturers. In 1930 we examined geography, the United States, Asia, l'Enseignement, history, sociology, economics and law. The brilliant corps of teachers included

Manley Hudson; Arnold McNair; J. L. Brierly; André Siegfried; Anthony Eden; Raymond Moley, soon to advise President Roosevelt; Edward Hambro of the League of Nations secretariat; Henri Rolin, the Belgian senator; and René Cassin, the French jurist who later won the Nobel Peace Prize. Aristide Briand, France's socialist foreign minister and the champion of Franco-German cooperation, addressed the school in a special lecture.

At the summer school, many men and women of my generation were encouraged to look upon the beginning of international organization as an essential element in the realization of world peace. Jenks and I had great hopes in 1930, but we were not impractically idealistic. It had taken a long time to bring about and maintain peace in the simplest community, and Zimmern was no stargazer. I did not go along with all his views, particularly his rigid adherence to the Treaty of Versailles and the imposition of war reparations on Germany. Most of us agreed with Keynes, who claimed that a Carthaginian peace was too severe and therefore counterproductive. Zimmern's students believed in the League of Nations but realized that unless the commitment of its members was stronger, it could not prevent future wars. My own view was that even lack of such a commitment was not a reason to abandon the organization but an indication that an international legal system was needed more than ever. Jenks later called the new international order the "common law of mankind," which imposed a shared responsibility for a common peace. We were not sure that it would come immediately, but as Wilfred concluded in his *Law in the World Community*: "The task is not for today, nor for tomorrow, but for all time."[13]

Canadians in Geneva inevitably compare our Rockies with the Swiss Alps. None of us at the Zimmern school were mountain climbers, although the great peaks enthralled us — Mont Blanc most of all, because on a clear day it was possible to see it from Geneva. On weekends we would go hiking in the mountains. A particularly good day was the one we spent climbing the Great

13 C. Wilfred Jenks, *Law in the World Community* (New York: D. McKay, 1967).

Saint Bernard, the pass that Napoleon and his army crossed in 1800. By the time we reached the top, I had no energy to go back down again. No wonder: young, adventurous and unknowing, I had worn running shoes, not climbing boots. We made the return journey to Geneva by bus.

After the summer school closed, many of us remained for the first week of the Assembly of the League of Nations, held in Le Bâtiment Electoral. We sat in the gallery next to Zimmern, who identified the speakers and gave us a running commentary on the proceedings. Lord Robert Cecil, Britain's League champion, was there, as was Arthur Henderson, who had presided for such a long time over the abortive disarmament discussions. Aristide Briand and Italy's Dino Grandi were also at the Assembly, but what amazed me was that at this time, few of the world's leaders of the 1920s were present. Sir Robert Borden, the head of Canada's delegation, was one of the few survivors of the generation that had dominated Versailles twelve years before. He was warmly received when he rose to speak.

I called on Sir Robert at the Hôtel de la Paix. Invitations to official functions and receptions were spread across his desk. Gathering these into a pile, he rumbled, "If I were Mackenzie King, I would tie these cards with a red ribbon and put them in my archives. But I am not Mackenzie King." And, with that, he swept the invitations into a basket on the floor.

In 1930, my friends and I hoped that the League would develop supranationally, believing that if it had commanded a stronger consensus, it would have sown the cause of peace more fruitfully. We were moved by idealism; where else could this idealism be better focussed? Zimmern urged us to think of the League as a means for states to pursue relations with one another. The statesmen who devised the League hoped to provide a mechanism to prevent a repetition of the catastrophe of the Great War and other careless and criminal acts in international affairs. Only a few states did not assume the obligations of full membership, and the new organization was intended to be a universal one. Zimmern preferred the French term, "Société des Nations," since, for him, the word "League" denoted a conspiracy against another party. He emphasized that there is implicit in the League's code the acceptance of states as they exist.

My first encounter with the League of Nations coincided with the advent of the great Depression. Unemployment and poverty were widespread throughout the western world. Aristide Briand had advocated his plan for a United States of Europe, but the Depression destroyed the prevailing spirit of economic cooperation. The United States raised its tariff barriers, and self-interest took over as each state looked to its own defence.

The full significance of what was happening had perhaps escaped my notice, as I gathered my belongings in Cambridge in preparation for my return home. My studies had not been for fun. What I had learned must be put to use.

That summer, I met W. L. Grant, the headmaster of Upper Canada College. As we walked across the Quai Wilson in Geneva, he asked me what I proposed to do on my return to Canada. I had really only one objective in mind — to practise law. Grant looked at me in surprise: "But surely you don't want to be *just* a lawyer." His words never left me. I knew what I eventually wanted to do, but before I embarked on a public career, I wished to practise law and to establish myself.

IV

Life, Law and Liberalism

WHEN I WAS YOUNG, the cities on both the Canadian and the American banks of the Detroit River were meccas for the working man. Hundreds of people from the Ottawa Valley moved there — to Windsor and Detroit — hoping to make money in the automobile factories. Early in the second decade of the century, Henry Ford had introduced an eight-hour day in his plants on the Canadian side of the border. The five dollars a day that he then paid his workers seemed like a small fortune to those of us from households whose providers earned a great deal less. When the young men came home on visits to Pembroke and the Ottawa Valley, they seemed like beings from another planet. What kind of cities were Windsor and Detroit? we all wondered.

While I was at Osgoode Hall, I had an opportunity to find out during those summers when I worked at Windsor's racetracks and, for a short time, at the Ford plant. Quite early on, I realized that Windsor was the city for me. In the late 1920s, it was a progressive industrial centre of nearly 100,000 people, with rapidly expanding suburbs and rich adjacent farmlands. One of the reasons I felt so much at home was that the city and surrounding area had a large

French community; many of the forebears of these families had
been there for a few hundred years. But most important of all, I
had made plenty of friends in Windsor and Essex County and
realized that I had grown to love urban life, enjoying contacts with
the wide variety of people one meets in a city. And those who
thought Windsor was not large enough could take the ten-cent
ferry ride over to Detroit, one of the biggest cities in North America, with impressive libraries, theatres and universities.

After finishing my legal studies, I had inquired about employment with several Windsor law firms and generally received warm
encouragement. For a while, I had considered setting up a practice
with J. Ramsay Morris, a fellow lawyer from Pembroke who had
come to live in Leamington, about thirty miles from Windsor.
Then Norman McLarty, a successful and well-liked lawyer, whose
partner, Gordon Fraser, was one of Windsor's leading counsels
and a great character, invited me to join his firm. But while I was
in Europe, I made arrangements with C. P. McTague to start in
his partnership. Even though McTague offered me five dollars a
week less than McLarty, I knew him better because of his connection with St. Michael's College; he had set up a busy and well-
respected legal practice in Windsor, with clients throughout
southwestern Ontario and Detroit. All in all, McTague's firm
offered a wider variety of opportunities and experiences for the
lawyer about to begin in his profession than did the other
possibilities.

Although Charlie McTague was a strong Conservative, I supposed that given the population of Windsor and Essex County,
the political situation ultimately would be good for a young and
earnest Liberal. Dr. Matthew McKay's repeated rebuffs at the
polls and my own shellacking in the byelection offered me little
encouragement to enter political life in Pembroke; but the sizeable
French Canadian and immigrant population in Essex County
could be helpful to me if and when I ventured into politics. Several
Windsorites of French descent had served in provincial cabinets,
and the Conservative member for Essex East, Dr. Raymond
Morand — a Franco-Ontarian — had been sworn in as a member

of the short-lived Meighen government in 1926. It was my belief that, deep down, the electors in this industrial centre were very sympathetic towards the Liberalism of Laurier and Mackenzie King, even though Essex County had returned three Tories to Ottawa in the 1930 general election. But this clean sweep did not concern me unduly because I had no immediate wish to run for parliament. My financial obligations would first have to be met — the debt from the Renfrew byelection must be paid off, and I was anxious to send money to my family whenever I could afford it. So, by the fall of 1930, all things considered, I was pleased with my decision to practise law and believed that I had done the right thing to settle by the shores of the Detroit River and Lake St. Clair.

In late September 1930, as I returned from my year in Europe aboard *The Empress of Scotland,* I was full of hope and confidence about what lay ahead, exhilarated by the thought that a whole life was before me, even though I had come back with hardly a cent. We passed along the banks of the great St. Lawrence very soon after summer's green had changed to autumn splendour; Canada seemed more picturesque than I had ever known it. Passing Ste. Anne de Beaupré, where my mother had taken me so long ago, I looked forward eagerly to my homecoming and her fond welcome.

My visit to Pembroke was a short but happy one. I went out walking with my sisters, who scolded me for striding along too quickly; it was, I said, a way of working off my high spirits and the joie de vivre that had been kindled by my adventurous year abroad. In my grey Oxford "bags," the floppy trousers then in vogue in England, I must have looked very odd to the townspeople of Pembroke.

Expectantly awaiting professional life and further experiences, I left for Windsor at the end of October. But first I had to ask a friend who also had worked at the track to wire me a loan of sixty-five dollars for my train fare and to enable me to pay for a few things I needed to set myself up in a rented room. For the first couple of months, I boarded in the home of a Mr. and Mrs. Hurtubise on Oak Avenue. My living quarters certainly were not comparable to those of the prosperous lawyers of Windsor, many of whom lived in the grand houses and well-appointed apartments on Victoria and Ouellette Avenues. But I knew that that would come; one must creep before one can walk.

From the seventh floor of the Security Building, Charles McTague, K.C., directed Windsor's most promising law firm. His offices overlooked the waterfront, and I would often gaze out at Detroit's imposing skyline, at the ferryboats plying back and forth, and the huge cargo ships moving majestically up and down the river. With five partners and an equal number of lawyers,[1] the firm impressed me from the start. Charlie McTague was a brilliant lawyer, although he was not a great trial counsel. He did not really have an instinctive grasp of the forensic art, but he had a fine legal brain and had built up a successful business based on corporation law and general practice.

McTague had gained quite a reputation in Windsor.[2] Shortly after I began working for him, he received a threatening phone call from some bootleggers, telling him to stop representing clients the gang did not like, or they would "get him." This group, known as the Purple Gang, were the quintessential liquor smugglers in our neck of the woods. Mostly east-side Detroit hoodlums, with a few Canadian "associates," they supplied many of the blind pigs — the

---

1 C. P. McTague, J. H. Clark, A. Racine, S. L. Springsteen, H. M. McTague, N. L. Spencer, L. R. McDonald, A. H. Stevenson, Léon Lalande and me.

2 R. B. Bennett appointed McTague an Ontario Supreme Court judge. Had he stayed on the bench, I have no doubt he would have ranked with our greatest judges. Although he found judicial work interesting, it did not satisfy him, and he eventually returned to practise in Toronto.

   Later, during the war, I was pleased when Mackenzie King appointed McTague chairman of the National Labour Relations Board, a position from which he resigned to manage the national Conservatives' 1945 election campaign. Charlie himself became a candidate in his native city of Guelph, despite King's great annoyance that he had left the Board in wartime to pursue a political career. Of course, McTague had every right to follow the path he had chosen, although he was offended when I told him that in my opinion he was not a potential parliamentarian.

illegal liquor outlets across the river — and even had dealings with
Al Capone in Chicago. Since several of these gangsters had already
committed murder, Charlie knew they meant business but nonetheless told me that after the phone call, he happened to drive
out to a cottage on Lake Erie to visit friends and noticed several
American cars parked in the next-door lot. By the time he was set
to leave, the cars had vanished. "I don't know who they were," he
chuckled, "Democratic politicians or the Purple Gang?" A few
years later, a client for whom I was drawing up a will asked if I
remembered McTague as a brave individual. "I was a rum-
runner," he said, "a member of the Purple Gang — and one day I
called and threatened McTague, just to scare him. And do you
know, that afternoon he came right next door to our headquarters.
We thought he knew who had called and was going to bring in the
police, so we moved out fast." Of such incidents are reputations
made!

In the McTague firm, I shared a spot at the very bottom of the
roster with Léon Lalande. Our offices adjoined, and we spent a lot
of time together discussing the law. McTague, as the *magister*,
encouraged his staff to exchange views in this way, and on Monday evenings, all the firm's lawyers met around the big table in the
library to discuss cases reported in the law journals. These meetings stimulated my critical faculties just as much as a university
seminar. It often seemed to me that a lawyer's position in the firm
did not always reflect his knowledge of the law, but McTague
proved himself a profound exponent of it at these weekly sessions.

Unlike his British counterpart, the Canadian lawyer is both
barrister and solicitor; the Canadian profession therefore does not
deny the novice an opportunity to make a go of practising both
divisions of the law. I certainly did not find my duties an oppressive
comedown from Roscoe Pound's interpretations of legal history,
and it was particularly satisfying to work as a counsel and argue a
case in court. Stanley L. Springsteen, the firm's chief counsel,
allowed me to serve as his understudy on important commercial
cases and asked me to lend him a hand with all sorts of litigation.
One of the most important cases went from trial to the Appellate

Division of the Supreme Court of Ontario and then to the Supreme Court of Canada. A man named Kovinsky had borrowed a substantial sum from the Bank of Montreal and had then run into financial difficulties; so the bank put one of its employees in charge of his business. Despite the trial judgment and the appeal ruling — that the bank's employee was really the agent of the bank — McTague disagreed and argued that he was the debtor's agent. He was like a dog with a bone and urged me to turn over the library to find a case to prove his point. After a lot of digging, I turned up an old British case that did so. It was a great thrill when the Supreme Court agreed with our submission.

After I had been with the firm for well over a year, I asked McTague to consider the possibility of me becoming a partner. But although he was sympathetic to the straits of the junior lawyer, McTague said that he could not elevate me, pointing out that he was unable to give even his sister, a lawyer hired by the firm, this promotion. Feeling that I might do better on my own, I moved down a few flights in the Security Building and hung out my shingle.

Sometime in 1931, I met an able young lawyer called Keith Laird, and we quickly became friends; Keith spoke French and shared a number of my intellectual interests. A native of Blenheim, a town between Windsor and London, he had graduated from Windsor Collegiate and the University of Western Ontario, where he received the gold medal in economics. After Osgoode Hall, Keith was called to the bar and joined the firm of Kenning, Cleary and Grant. Léon Lalande, Keith and I would often meet in Windsor's Wyandotte Hotel, owned by Léon's father, to review the law reports, discuss articles in *Revue des deux mondes* and generally comport ourselves as educated young men.

In 1932, when the Depression was at its worst and Keith had little legal work, his parents gave him the chance to study in Europe. I persuaded him not to go to the Sorbonne, as he had planned, but to apply to the Zimmern school in Geneva. He did so and, when he returned, opened his own law office next to mine. About the end of 1933, we decided it was foolish to keep on running back and forth to answer each other's phone and so set ourselves up as partners. Although we retained separate clients, we shared a small office staff and frequently consulted each other about cases.

The early 1930s in Windsor were difficult years for any young person trying to get established. When I first moved there at the height of the Depression, I probably did not appreciate the seriousness of the economic situation for Canada and the world; but I was in no way daunted. I soon realized, however, that any growth in Windsor's economy or population had long since stopped. A few years before, in 1927, more than 15,000 Windsor residents were employed in Detroit, but then, to protect the jobs of their own citizens, the Americans cut down their Canadian workforce. There were no jobs in Windsor either, and between 1930 and 1933 more than 13,000 people left the city for want of work.

Taking advantage of the situation, some employers often hired workers at less than a decent living wage. Twelve percent of the city's houses were left vacant, and thousands of people went on relief — an inhumane system that compelled recipients to line up each week for food vouchers and other necessities. These unfortunates were not given cash and were told exactly how much of each item they were allowed to have. I remember Windsor citizens on relief being obliged to cut wood in Ford City on the banks of the Detroit River as part of an abortive works program to make citizens "earn" their keep. Much of the work was foolish and degrading, and merely served to deprive respectable victims of the economic times of all human dignity. Many of the better off objected to relieving those on welfare of the obligation to perform a service; relief, they argued, was creating a group of people who had made up their minds never to work. As I viewed the situation — the municipalities, the provincial governments and Ottawa all squabbling about who should take responsibility for alleviating the misery of the jobless — I grew even more strongly convinced of the necessity of legislative measures that would provide security for those who were temporarily unemployed.

Despite the hard times, I had no shortage of clients. Keith and I had very little real estate work because no one was buying property; lawyers who relied upon real estate suffered terribly during the Depression. In the beginning, I spent most of my time collecting small debts for clients, drawing up wills, and appearing in the police court to defend speeders, drunks and petty thieves. I had considerable scruples about working on divorce cases. When Mr. Justice E. R. E. Chevrier of the Ontario Supreme Court came to Windsor, he was due to hear a divorce case that I was being pressed to assume for the plaintiff. I went to the judge's hotel to talk — not about the case, but about the propriety of my taking on the brief. He told me, "Well, it's just as proper for you to argue it as it is for me to sit on it as the judge. We do not perhaps agree with the law, but your duty as a lawyer and mine as a judge is to make the law work." Convinced by his argument, I took on the case, successfully as it turned out.

My activities as counsel came to the public's attention when I defended Abby Viggers, a man in his late twenties who had been a contemporary of mine in Pembroke; he was facing extradition for murder. Both the Detroit and Windsor papers played up the case with sensational headlines and photographs of the victim's widow pleading for revenge. Abby had been in and out of trouble since moving to Windsor, and I had already defended him and his brothers on a previous charge of selling liquor illegally. The charges against him were that within a few hours, he had fired a gun at a bartender, robbed a grocery store and kidnapped and shot a stranger in a Detroit beer garden. He phoned me after the Windsor police had picked him up almost immediately on a vagrancy charge. In my view, Abby was mentally unbalanced, but I agreed to fight extradition proceedings on his behalf.

Contending that no man could be deported for a crime unless that crime was contrary to the laws of Canada, I argued before the court that Viggers was insane at the time of the alleged acts and therefore could not be guilty of an extraditable crime. Judge Mahon ruled against me, although he complimented me on the defence I had made. When the murder trial began in Detroit, the

American judge refused to allow me the status of *amicus curiae* and would not let me sit at the counsel table to assist Viggers's lawyer. There was nothing I could do but testify that Viggers was indeed insane. Even this, however, proved fruitless, for the judge refused my evidence on the grounds that I was not a qualified psychiatrist. Viggers was convicted of first-degree murder and was sent to Jackson State Prison in Michigan, where I visited him later.

One of my cases that came to trial involved a Detroit taxi driver charged, after a raid, with the illegal consumption of liquor. I appealed for bail by trying to arouse the judge's sympathy for the plight of the accused's wife and children, arguing that if he was found guilty, his job could be jeopardized. The magistrate, not noticeably moved, remarked that American courts showed little leniency towards Canadians. "Nobody invites these people over here," concurred the crown attorney, J. S. Allan, who went on to jibe, "Of course we can easily understand Mr. Martin's interest in this man, knowing as we do his activities for international peace and amity."

Apart from the odd assignments that compose the work of a neophyte practitioner, for most of 1933 I was engaged by the city of Brantford as counsel in a probe of several municipal departments. A classmate of mine at Osgoode Hall, John Reycraft, was an alderman in Brantford and had convinced the city to retain me. Controversy surrounded the investigation since the new mayor, M. M. MacBride, had a reputation as a rebel and wanted, I suspected later, to expose the Brantford "establishment."

My own detective work and the audit of the books of various civic operations led the Brantford council to request a judicial inquiry. The auditor had discovered almost $43,000 missing from the accounts of the Brantford Municipal Railway, and the commissioner, Judge Boles, of neighbouring Norfolk County, opened his enquiry towards the end of July by investigating the alleged misappropriation. Other counsel — most notably J. A. D. Slemin;

W. Ross Macdonald, a future colleague in the House of Commons; and J. C. McRuer, later the chief justice of Ontario — represented some of those who had been implicated. When the evidence began to show that the secretary of the municipal railway was implicated in the affair, I questioned her about an uncommonly large personal bank account, her frequent trips to New York and Europe, and her expensive clothes and carefully marcelled hair. The Brantford press found my line of questioning "approaching the dramatic." The public hearings produced almost 700 pages of testimony before Judge Boles heard the concluding arguments.[3] After I had made my final submission, J. C. McRuer commented on the fairness and zeal with which I had prosecuted the case, and when the judge handed down his findings, I was pleased to hear him support my contentions. He found that some of the employees of the street railway had misappropriated money, and he went on to criticize former municipal officials for not running their operations wisely. It always seemed odd to me that in view of the judge's findings, no remedial action was taken by the authorities.

The money I earned from the city of Brantford went a long way towards liquidating my long-standing debts. Yet even though I charged about one-fifth the fee of more experienced counsel, my bill was not paid promptly. When the invoice was taxed by the registrar of the court, I was awarded $500 more than I had asked for. John Aylesworth, later a member of the court of appeal in Ontario, represented me at the taxation hearing. The city of Brantford appealed the registrar's decision but eventually withdrew its objection.

Although the Brantford investigation and my court work in Windsor enhanced my reputation, my involvement with a famous family of the 1930s provided me with much more notoriety. In a

---

3 Among the fields of investigation was the cemetery commission. In that inquiry, a mausoleum salesman, a Mr. Smythe, told the commissioner that he had given $620 to the former mayor to facilitate the purchase by the city of sixty-eight crypts!

despatch dated 22 February 1935, the Associated Press informed the continent that I had played host to Elzire and Oliva Dionne, from Corbeil in northern Ontario, the parents of the famous girl quintuplets, who at that time were five months old. Leo Kirwin, a friend of the Dionnes, had phoned to ask me to look after the interests of the quintuplets' parents, who were simple people and did not understand the ways of business and government. When the Dionnes walked out of my office, photographers and reporters were milling around, trying to find out what was going on. I decided that Oliva Dionne should stay in my apartment, and this enabled us to carry on our conversation in private for two days. I found him a friendly, decent man, bewildered by all that had taken place.

In order to guard the infants' health and to prevent their being exploited commercially, the Ontario government had established a two-year guardianship for them shortly after their birth. Their guardians controlled a great deal of money that belonged to the infants as a result of royalties for the story rights from magazines, newspapers and newsreels; the parents received only seventy-five dollars a month for themselves and their five other children. In effect, the province had created two separate families, and I believed this to be wrong. Although the interference in the family's arrangements disturbed me, it agitated the bishop of Pembroke, C. L. Nelligan, even more; he had suggested that I represent the parents in their dealings with the government and try to reunite the family. The Catholic church viewed the separation as a contradiction of the idea that the father and mother are the heads of a family. Taking the children and making them wards of the state was — understandably — questioned in the Ontario of the 1930s. Because I knew the Liberal premier of the province, Mitch Hepburn, and David Croll, the minister of public welfare, who had direct responsibility for the children, the bishop had sent the Dionnes to me to try to head off imminent legislation that would provide for permanent guardianship over the quintuplets, thus denying the sanctity of the family.

When Hepburn heard of my meeting with the Dionnes, he told the press that he was too busy to see me and expressed intense irritation that promoters were trying to use the parents to put the girls on display. The following day, the legislature considered a motion to provide for permanent guardianship of the children. Despite Hepburn's bluster, he met me and stated afterwards that the two of us and the parents had agreed in principle that the quintuplets needed protection. He had meant to say earlier, he told the press, that he would not discuss any proposal that might endanger the children's health. I reiterated that there should be no exploitation and that I was anxious that nothing should create a division in the family. The Ontario government took the view that the only way to avoid exploitation was through legislation that would allow the guardians — including the father and Allan Dafoe, their physician — control over the children's finances, education and health. During the debate on the bill in the Ontario legislature in March, the members banged their desks with approval when Croll mentioned that Oliva was in the chamber. Leo Macaulay, a Conservative member, expressed concern about "political lawyers hovering around from Detroit and Windsor," but the minister's reply was suitably droll: "Because the father had the wisdom to hire a Liberal lawyer, you can't say his children are in politics."

Essentially, I had failed in my task to get the government to modify the bill, and Oliva Dionne soon issued a statement expressing his dissatisfaction with the Hepburn administration. As usual, whenever the quintuplets were involved, the press wallowed in the controversy. Croll, said Dionne, "told us that God never intended us to have money . . . and to forget about the babies until they were eighteen and then we would have $1,000,000. . . . All we want is a chance to show that we are able to raise our babies."

But I had done all that I could in a hopeless situation and had to leave the case, disappointed that I had not been able to effect a solution.

Although I enjoyed the practice of law and worked hard to do it well, I never forgot W. L. Grant's admonition: "Surely you don't want to be *just* a lawyer." I must have had this advice in mind when the president of Assumption College invited me to take up residence there several months after I arrived in Windsor. Like St. Michael's, Assumption was under the direction of the Basilian fathers. Would I be agreeable to giving a course in political theory for two or three hours a week? the president asked. As part of the honorarium, I would be given room and board in the college. Since I knew most of the professors, some of whom had been fellow students at the University of Toronto, the president's suggestion dovetailed perfectly with my desires and interests. My teaching duties were not heavy, and I have always enjoyed university life and the company of intellectually inclined men and women; this arrangement with Assumption brought me into close contact with academic life yet enabled me to carry on my professional responsibilities. Even better, it brought me some clients!

In my course on political theory, I paid particular attention to the nature of the state. I urged the students to supplement my lectures by reading William Archibald Dunning's magisterial work on political theory.[4] Looking now at my copy of Dunning, I can see from the underlinings that I paid a lot of attention to Plato and Aristotle. Plato's argument that the true statesman would seek to establish standards of virtue for the citizens to observe was of particular interest to me. Although the all-wise philosopher did not exist, to my mind the law as the reflection of experience and practical sagacity was of bedrock importance. In one of my later political campaigns, a former student asked me if Plato's ideals were put into practice in the House of Commons. Taking the question as the joke it was intended to be, I replied, "It all depends whether the members of the Commons had the good fortune to follow my course of lectures."

4 W. A. Dunning, *A History of Political Theories*, 4 vols. (New York: Macmillan, 1919).

The Windsor area has an advantage over many Canadian cities since it shares a community of interest with one of the biggest metropolitan centres in the United States. As a result, some call the people of Windsor more American than Canadian. This is a mistake; in no way are its denizens American except by propinquity. In fact, historically, this part of Ontario has always displayed an anti-republican disposition. The coexistence of these two traditions lay in the back of my mind when I prepared a paper, "The Philosophy of Internationalism," for the American Catholic Philosophical Association at Duquesne University, Pittsburgh in December 1933. In my view, internationalism would not reduce the world to a colourless cosmopolitan homogeneity. "The philosophy of internationalism," I told my audience,

> is not for a world to come, but arises out of the fact of contemporary world interdependence. The need is not for reconciliation between national interests and the interest of humanity as much as an attempt to guarantee that the policy of nationalism shall not be likely to affect the well-being of humanity. This presupposes a change, if necessary, in the unit of allegiance. It involves a limitation of national authority — in the interests of social peace.

These are ideas that I have found little need to modify over the years, and since 1933 I have propounded them the world over. In putting my case at Pittsburgh, I had very much in mind the contention, advanced by some Catholics, that the League of Nations was a godless institution, an assertion that I have always steadfastly resisted.

Right on my doorstep, reactionary Catholic sentiment was being stirred up. A former Basilian priest, Charles E. Coughlin, had taken to broadcasting to the continent from Detroit each Sunday afternoon. In no time at all, he was almost as well-known as the president of the United States. His fulminations, more political and economic than theological, even touched on foreign policy and reflected a bigoted interpretation of the developing international order. When Coughlin attacked the International Court of Justice, I wrote a letter to him, challenging his thesis, but my letter was never acknowledged.

Despite Couglin's influence over some Catholics, I was not the only resident of Assumption who drew a line between demagoguery and responsibility, and many of the priests there supported my efforts to form a Border Cities branch of the League of Nations Society in the fall of 1931.[5] This proved a great success, and from the start our meetings were attended by hundreds of people. Our branch was affiliated with the League of Nations Society of Canada, of which I became a national officer in 1933; the society served as a public information organization for promoting the efforts of the League as an instrument of world peace. The Windsor branch filled a special place since there was no other body, a local Canadian Club for instance, to represent the city. As Mr. Brown, the *maître d'hôtel* at the Prince Edward, where we held our meetings, used to say: "Well Mr. Martin. Another smash hit."

Quite often, I felt that the national organization in Ottawa did not share our drive or appreciate how much we were doing in Windsor; the executive appeared to be really out of touch with the branches, and particularly ours. I got impatient that the League of Nations Society as a whole seemed unable to take such initiatives as ours when we arranged radio broadcasts of addresses by important speakers. My exasperation probably stemmed from the fact that I firmly believed in the principles of international order and had always been very active in organizations to which I belonged. Other people were interested and committed but did nothing about it. I am not built that way.

At our first gathering, D. A. Stevenson spoke about the operations of the International Labour Organization; then we managed to persuade Newton Rowell to come and speak on the relationship

5 I served as president of the branch in 1931 and 1932. The other officers were
   vice-president, Miss Catherine Straith, a public school teacher; secretary, Miss
   L. J. Campeau; treasurer, Léon Lalande; cooperation committee, Mrs. W. E. Mat-
   thews; study circles committee, Charles Quenneville; education committee, Miss
   N. L. Spencer, Mrs. H. R. Casgrain, Mrs. J. C. Pennington, Mrs. W. D. Kennedy,
   mittee, Mrs. H. W. Bull and Harold Hough. Others associated with the branch
   included Senator LaCasse, Dr. R. D. Morand, Dr. P. Poisson, Judge J. J. Coughlin, Rabbi Israel Lebendiger, E. M. Eagle, W. F. Herman, W. D. Lowe,
   N. L. Spencer, Mrs. H. R. Casgrain, Mrs. J. C.Pennington, Mrs. W. D. Kennedy,
   Rev. Father D. L. Dillon, Angus Mowat, E. A. Stone, and Rev. A. H. Foster.

of disarmament to economic problems. It was a huge success. Since the hall could not accommodate the audience — more than a thousand strong — a group of teachers collected money and paid for a broadcast of the speech on Windsor's new radio station. For our 1932 program, we secured Hugh Guthrie, the minister of justice and the head of Canada's delegation to the recent Assembly of the League of Nations. Guthrie warned that the Chinese situation was endangering world peace. Pursuing this topic, Mrs. Adelaide Plumptre, my friend Wynne's mother and another Canadian delegate to the League, spoke of her hope that the League's investigation of the Manchurian dispute would help end the crisis. Japan, however, took little notice of the League and in February 1932 set up its puppet government of an "independent" Manchukuo. The League had no means of enforcing its resolutions.

In 1933 my teacher from Geneva, Alfred Zimmern, came to Canada and addressed our branch. By this time, the Japanese had left the disarmament conference and the League of Nations; in October, Adolf Hitler, who had become head of the German government ten months before, had ordered his delegates home. My fellow Windsorites, having heard me speak of Zimmern's eminence, keenly awaited his comments on the worsening political climate in Europe. He and his energetic wife shared the podium. In his address, Zimmern called for control of armaments by eliminating the profits of the arms dealers — whom he referred to as the "merchants of death." He still insisted that the Treaty of Versailles had not caused the present crisis by being too hard on Germany — a view I could not uphold. Because Germany had left the League, Zimmern did not feel that the other members should coax Hitler into changing his mind. I had argued that the position we had taken had played into Hitler's hands, although, no less than Zimmern, I was in favour of arms control. Other countries, he noted, had also failed to keep their promises to disarm, and he pointed out that Canada, the source of eighty-five percent of the world's nickel production, had a special responsibility to restrain the growth of arms manufacture.

Throughout this increasingly tense international situation, I strongly defended the League of Nations from attacks by isolationists, who claimed both that it had failed and that Canada would find itself involved in wars because of its membership of the League. In a letter written to me in the spring of 1934, Senator Charles Murphy called the League a "glorified debating society at Geneva." Like many others, including some prominent public figures, Murphy failed to distinguish between Canada's membership in the League and the justifiability of our nonparticipation in European conflicts. In my reply, I told him that I agreed that Canada ought to keep out of foreign wars, but "with a world as interdependent as ours now is, it is impossible . . . not to have something to do with the existing machinery for minimizing the occasions of war." Of course, the League was not a faultless body, but I held that "its imperfection is due not to its structure or to the principles upon which it is built but rather to the lack of good faith of certain of its members." Deliberately misunderstanding my comments, Murphy accused me of wanting to have "a finger in the European pie" and of joining "our worthy citizens [who] think that we are a very important country and that we really have something to say about military and other happenings in Europe." Isolationists such as Murphy and Senator A. D. McRae felt that the "future of the Dominion of Canada, like that of the United States, lies on this continent — and not in Europe. . . . Not one of the Big Powers is honest, and it is because of their dishonesty that the League has failed." Murphy further claimed that the League was the "the creation of theorists and utterly lacking in the machinery to deal with the practical problems that lead to war or peace."

It was a bit like banging one's head against a brick wall, but I put a final argument to Murphy, noting that because of the economic interdependence of the world,

> whether we wish to or not, the concerns of Europe and, for that matter, the concern of the East is likewise ours. To deny this would mean an acknowledgment that we were to retrace our steps, accept a lower standard of living which would involve ceasing to trade with other nations, ceasing to travel, ceasing, in fact, to have any

connection with them except in an indirect way. Just as individual
man living in society has to accept the disadvantages of the collective life, so, too, nations cannot enjoy the benefits of membership in
the family of nations without submitting to restraint, which presup-
poses submission to law and a regard for the interests of other
nations.

I did not deny the hypocrisy of the United States in its attitude of
pretended aloofness from Europe, but I asserted that "the situation
is such that, whether or not we want international order, we must
and we are going to have it. After all, the boast of nations that they
are self-sufficient is neither consistent with the fact nor is it beautiful." In my view, it was not the theorists who were responsible for
the League's problems; I told Murphy, "Propaganda in this sort of
thing is as essential as in anything else, and it is not the propagan-
dists who have been at fault but the minister of foreign affairs, and
in some cases the prime minister, together with a group of dishon-
est men in all countries who have nothing at heart but their own
pecuniary welfare."[6]

My drive to bring into being a forum where citizens could
inform themselves about international affairs did not stop with the
League of Nations Society; I also helped organize two rather
private study groups. Given the size and proximity of Detroit, it
was only natural that I should seek an outlet there for my interest
in foreign affairs. Judge Homer Ferguson, later a Michigan senator and governor of the Philippines, and Mrs. Aloquoia Miller, an
imposing figure and ardent student of international affairs, joined
me in founding the Canadian Affiliates of the Foreign Policy
Association, a group of a dozen or so people who met on alternate
Saturdays on either side of the river to discuss world politics. We
were able to attract eminent speakers from all over the United
States, and Jesse S. Reeves, professor of international law and
diplomacy at the University of Michigan, and Carl F. Remer,[7]

6 Murphy to Martin, 24 April 1934, Charles Murphy Papers (vol. 18, folder 85),
   PAC; Martin to Murphy, 1 May 1934, ibid.; Murphy to Martin, 14 May 1934,
   ibid.; Martin to Murphy, 25 May 1934, ibid.
7 He taught in China and edited an important book, C. F. Remer, (ed.), *Readings in
   Economics for China* (Shanghai: Commercial Press, 1933).

one of the world's most distinguished experts on the Asian economy, joined us in our animated exchanges.

We also organized a strictly Canadian group. Keith Laird and
Judge Joseph Coughlin, a county court judge, helped me organize
the Windsor branch of the Canadian Institute of International
Affairs in 1934. Escott Reid, the secretary of the national body
since 1932, came down to Windsor to lend a hand in setting up the
branch. The CIIA was composed of groups of people from across
the country who had a special interest in foreign affairs; they would
get together to talk about the great issues facing the world. We had
about fifteen members in Windsor out of a national total of some
seven hundred. Academics, professionals, journalists and members
of the business community all joined the CIIA, and their political
opinions covered the spectrum. Meetings were private, unless it
had been specifically decided otherwise, and speakers were encouraged to be candid.

Publicity is of the greatest importance for a young lawyer and an
aspiring politician. Keith Laird always maintained that the
Dionne case did more to bring my name before the public eye than
anything else. While I partly agreed with him, I thought that my
community activities for the League of Nations in Windsor played
a large part in establishing my reputation. I wanted to keep my
foot in the door as an eventual contender for public office and was
keen for the public to be aware of the breadth of my interests.

After North Renfrew, I continued to be active in Liberal politics. While at Cambridge, I was delighted to receive an encouraging reply to a youthfully effusive note I had sent Mackenzie King;
we shared friends, the Pentlands and Burgon Bickersteth, who had
spoken to King about me.[8] In his note, King wrote: "I am quite

8 Bickersteth to King, 8 December 1929, W. L. Mackenzie King Papers (J1 series,
   p. 135746), PAC, I did not know that Bickersteth had brought my name so forcefully to King. "I believe that boy will find himself in politics before long and I think
   he will go a long way. [Hart House] did something for him and that, whereas he

confident that it will not be long before we will see you in Parliament and I am glad to know that you are keeping that objective in view."[9] Of course, although I thought that I should not be in too much of a rush to get a seat in the House, the prime minister's support of my ultimate objective gave me great hope.

While at the Zimmern school, I had heard about the defeat of King's government on 28 July 1930 and wrote to the new leader of the opposition to send him my sympathy. Yet again his response pleased me — an invitation to call and see him in Ottawa to discuss our mutual friends and — portentously — "your future."[10]

On my way from Pembroke to Windsor in the fall of 1930, I stopped off in Ottawa to see Mackenzie King and Bob Deachman, of the national Liberal office, determined to scotch rumours that I was interested in the Liberal leadership in Ontario. Stories had appeared in the newspapers suggesting me as a possible successor to W. E. N. Sinclair, who many in the party thought was a weak leader. While fully aware of Sinclair's shortcomings, it was out of the question for me even to consider provincial politics; I was just not interested. My academic studies in international affairs propelled me in another direction, and I wished to make a success of practising law before attempting a political career. Some young Liberals, encouraged by the recent selection of my Harvard classmate Angus Macdonald as leader of the Liberal Party in Nova Scotia, apparently hoped that I would run and win in Ontario. But Bob Deachman mentioned when I saw him that most young party members hoped that Mitchell Hepburn, the federal MP for Elgin, would take over the leadership. Deachman told me he liked

---

came here as an undergraduate with strongly developed racial and religious prejudices, he has now got rid of those and finds he receives the warmest welcome in England."

The Pentlands were friends of King. Marjorie, Lady Pentland, was the daughter of the Earl of Aberdeen and knew King from the time when her father was governor general.

9 Martin to King, 9 November 1929 King Papers (J1 series, p. 140268 ff.), PAC; King to Martin, 20 January 1930, ibid. (p. 140272 ff.).

10 Martin to King, August 1930, ibid. (p. 151630 ff.); King to Martin, 28 August 1930, ibid.

Hepburn: he had charisma and was capable of reviving a moribund provincial party, which had not been in office since 1905 and since then had changed leaders half-a-dozen times. In the 1929 election, the party had won only fourteen of the one hundred and twelve seats in the legislature.

Later, after seeing Deachman, I was taken out to Kingsmere to meet Mackenzie King. He asked me about my studies at Harvard and Cambridge, and we discussed his efforts to establish the federal department of labour. Encouraging me in my hope eventually to enter public life, King also mentioned the adjustments that both he and the party were making as a consequence of their electoral loss three months before, after nine years in power. Unlike Deachman, King gave no indication that he believed Hepburn would be a good choice as Ontario leader; indeed, it was clear that he thought otherwise because he had had difficulties in the caucus over Hepburn's attacks on the Sun Life Assurance Company. King's apprehension about Hepburn led me to believe that Deachman's view had merit. Canada was suffering from an economic malaise, and I felt that a young, energetic leader might restore confidence. That Mitch Hepburn would be an effective leader was not enough for King; his concern was whether the new leader would be cooperative and help the interest of the federal Liberals.

As a newcomer to Windsor, but one known to local party members, I was pleased to be nominated as a delegate to the provincial leadership convention in December 1930. By the time the convention was held, I had made up my mind that if Hepburn stood, I would support him. Percy Parker, King's apparent choice, had decided not to run. I spoke to Hepburn on the telephone and pledged my backing. He appreciated my interest and wanted to meet me. Frank O'Connor, who had helped me get a job while I was at Harvard, told me that Hepburn had greatly impressed the Toronto Liberals. At the convention, I worked actively to convince him to run and then, given his readiness, to elect him. W. E. N. Sinclair had become embittered about the attempt to dump him and decided he would not leave office until he had to.

When the convention gave Hepburn an enthusiastic reception, Sinclair knew that he could not win and stepped down. Hepburn won handily over Elmore Philpott, never really a serious contender.

Mitch Hepburn was a remarkable man. His friendly smile and sunny nature made it hard not to warm to him. He had boundless energy, could rouse an audience and, although no intellectual, had all the necessary leadership capacities. As a farmer and a believer in low tariffs, he was capable of winning strong rural support. Hepburn appealed to me in the early 1930s because he shared my independence and was working for political and social change. A former member of the United Farmers of Ontario, a rural protest group that had formed the provincial government from 1919 to 1923, Hepburn was elected to the House of Commons in 1925 as a progressive Liberal. In parliament, he attacked what he called the "big interests," particularly Sun Life, which he claimed was assisting its few large shareholders by hurting numerous small policyholders.[11]

By openly voicing reservations about Hepburn as Ontario leader both before and after the convention, Mackenzie King acted unwisely. In essence, the federal leader invited Hepburn's hostility by speaking about his inadequacies to many party members. What King forgot was that most men would resent the criticisms he made of Hepburn. This is in no sense a justification for Hepburn's later intransigence and pettiness, but King would have been prudent to accept the inevitable and welcome Hepburn's leadership by offering his support.

When Hepburn grew miffed at King's slight, I was one of those who tried to smooth his ruffled feathers. Bending the truth, I told Hepburn that King would support him and was more enthusiastic about his leadership of the Ontario party than might appear. There is a streak in me that welcomes independent action, and for

11 See Neil McKenty, *Mitch Hepburn* (Toronto: McClelland and Stewart, 1967), pp. 23-24.

that reason I was anxious that Hepburn should have an opportunity to make a go of things. In his championship of the little man, we were of one mind, and from 1930 to 1935 I had my baptism of fire outside North Renfrew when, as a representative of the young Liberals, I sometimes shared a platform with him.

In my home town of Pembroke, Hepburn called for a reform of the tax system to prevent the rich from getting richer and the poor from getting poorer.[12] At Dutton, in his home area, I supported Hepburn and told an audience that "Liberalism holds for a modification of the present capitalistic system. It is inevitable. The man who thinks that, if the recovery comes, conditions are going to be the same as they were before 1929, is a fool."

My ideas about the necessity and direction of reform had been greatly influenced by Franklin Delano Roosevelt. No political leader, with the single exception of Laurier, has ever impressed me as much as Roosevelt did. During the 1932 election campaign, when Roosevelt was running against Herbert Hoover, I had read in the paper that FDR was to speak at the Naval Armory in Detroit one Sunday. I sent a wire to Jim Roosevelt, my Harvard classmate, who was travelling with his father, telling him I was practising law in Windsor, was following the US elections keenly, and hoped very much to see him, and perhaps his father, when they came to Detroit. Jim replied speedily with a telegram inviting me to the Book Cadillac Hotel to meet his father and to breakfast before the big rally at the Armory. I had almost ten minutes with Roosevelt, to the considerable concern of Governor Comstock of Michigan. Roosevelt asked me to sit at his table for breakfast. In the next morning's *Detroit Free Press*, I was surprised to see a picture of the future president shaking hands with me; I have cherished this photograph ever since. In the 1970s, in London, on my daily walk through Grosvenor Square to the High Commission, I gave FDR a greeting as I passed the fine monument to a great leader.

At the afternoon rally, even Father Coughlin sat in the front row on the platform — at this time he was still supporting the

12 *Ottawa Journal*, 24 August 1933.

Democratic candidate. When Roosevelt opened his speech, he noted that it was a Sunday afternoon and that a normal political address should not therefore be expected. Despite this disclaimer, I cannot recall hearing many abler political utterances. We were reminded of how the nation faced heavy unemployment and economic distress. FDR pledged himself to a New Deal for the American people that would bring social justice to all. This program would involve not just alleviating the burden of the Depression but also reforming the economic system to protect the elderly, the unemployed, the factory worker, the farmer and the homeowner. To achieve relief, he promised great public works to create jobs and stimulate investment.

After his election victory, Roosevelt soon demonstrated that he was a liberal among liberals. He personified my own ideas and ideals of government. The collapse of the banking system in the United States just as Roosevelt assumed the presidency posed an awesome challenge. By closing the banks, he showed a decisiveness that rallied the nation to his side.

Roosevelt was masterly on the radio. In his fireside chats, he used the medium perfectly as an instrument to mould public opinion. On the night of one of these chats, I was in Buffalo on business. It was snowing — wet snow that makes the night look darker — when I passed a small bar and heard Roosevelt's clear and resonant voice. I went in and found everyone, even the bartender, listening raptly. The crowd in the bar laughed and applauded. Roosevelt had a tremendous capacity to communicate, a prerequisite in a national leader. In the darkest of times, by words and actions, he always gave his people the feeling that things would improve.

There is no doubt that Mackenzie King was clever and perhaps even a more sagacious political leader than Roosevelt; but he did not give the appearance of being in command of political events. During the early 1930s, I was influenced by what I thought was King's intellectualism. I saw this in both his academic career and his book, *Industry and Humanity*, which appealed greatly to me despite the generality of its scope and the opacity of its prose. Until

I went to the House of Commons, I tended to regard King as more of a scholar than he turned out to be.

I had a hint of the real Mackenzie King when I went to Ottawa shortly after Roosevelt's first election. By then, I knew some of the New Dealers; I had met Rex Tugwell in Detroit and had been in touch with Raymond Moley, whom I had first run across during my stay in Geneva. Fired up by the New Deal, I wanted King to espouse policies similar to Roosevelt's to tackle the problems posed by the Depression and to put forward a new deal for Canada. But King refused to see me right away, and I was left to cool my heels for several days before he granted me an interview. I could tell that he was displeased when I expressed surprise that the author of *Industry and Humanity* was not more fired up about the Rooseveltian New Deal.

However, the federal Liberal Party was not totally arid ground for reformers, and those who advocated a program of social change found an ally in the new president of the National Liberal Federation, Vincent Massey. Massey had resigned as minister to Washington when R. B. Bennett's Conservatives won the 1930 election and not long afterwards had been asked by Mackenzie King to take over the administration of the Liberal national organization. Massey and I had renewed our acquaintance on his return from Washington, and during a weekend visit to "Batterwood," his home in Port Hope, in the late summer of 1931, he spoke to me of King's offer.

This was the first of many weekends and Christmas holidays I spent with the Masseys; I had never met as many luminaries from Canada and abroad as I did at "Batterwood." Massey loved the intellectual and academic community; he was not afraid to seize upon new ideas and would accept a progressive point of view largely for intellectual reasons. Although many thought he was a snob, I always found him approachable; he did not invite guests to his home just because they were prominent people. I remember mentioning a young Lithuanian girl, a promising violinist, to him. Massey made a point of seeking her out, and she ended up spending Christmas at "Batterwood." She certainly was not the type who would be mentioned in the social columns; but she was stimulating company, and that was enough for Massey. I often saw the young Dominican, Father Georges Henri Lévesque, there, in the early 1950s. He was a colleague of Massey on the Royal Commission on National Development in the Arts, Letters and Sciences, and he became one of Québec's strongest intellectual and liberal forces. Sometimes the main house and the neighbouring Durham House were full of guests, and the evenings were enlivened by music, good conversation and Vincent's favourite charades. The Masseys had a marvellous library, and their home served as a refuge for me when I needed the company of people of ideas.

On that first weekend at "Batterwood," the prospective head of the Liberal Federation wanted to discuss the party's future, and it was clear that Massey was eager for me to work closely with him during the next few years to build up the party nationally. But before he finally accepted King's offer, Massey decided to test the waters. He and his wife, Alice, were to make a trip to the Far East during the last few months of the year; they had arranged a speaking tour of western Canada afterwards, under the auspices of the Canadian Club, ostensibly to talk about his experiences in the Orient. But the speeches were only part of the reason for the tour; Massey had decided he wanted to confer with western Liberals before giving King his answer. He invited me to accompany him and his wife, and after I had arranged to free myself from my commitments for a few weeks, we left for Winnipeg at the beginning of February 1932. Vincent was keen to meet leading members of the party wherever we went, and it was my job to help arrange these meetings.

Our first stop in Winnipeg proved important: Massey had been in touch with J. W. Dafoe before we left, and the great editor gave a dinner for him at the Manitoba Club. Dafoe seated me next to Norman Lambert, who he believed was the man Massey should select to organize the proposed Liberal Federation. Lambert had come to Winnipeg as the western correspondent of the Toronto *Globe* and subsequently worked for the United Grain Growers of

Manitoba; both Massey and I echoed Dafoe's good opinion of him. During the dinner, the talk turned to the need for the Liberal Party to gather together progressive sentiment by enunciating reform policies. It may be presumptuous to say so, but I think my touting Norman Lambert's name may have done the trick. He later came to Ottawa as secretary of the National Liberal Federation and played a notable role in the party's electoral success in 1935.

While I agreed with the opinion constantly expressed throughout the West that the party should be advocating reform, I did not completely approve of the policies the westerners were proposing. I suppose I was affected by my experiences in the industrial heartland of Windsor, just as the westerners were influenced by their prairie environment. Many of them maintained that the solution to the Depression lay in low tariffs and an aggressive export policy for Canadian wheat. To my dissatisfaction, a belief in social welfare and unemployment insurance — the hallmarks of my Liberalism — played a very small part in their considerations. Many of their political beliefs seemed akin to nineteenth-century liberalism; the New Deal did not mean a great deal to them, and in some ways they were tenaciously opposed to it. Nonetheless, after the western excursion, I returned to my law practice exhilarated by the prospect of change in the Liberal fold. Massey accepted the job of president of the Liberal Federation and set to work infusing the party with new life.

The fall and winter of 1931-32 produced another challenge for the Liberal Party and yet another stimulus for reform. Organizations, mainly of young intellectuals, many of whom had been Liberals, began to agitate for socialism. The first of these, the League for Social Reconstruction, came to life in 1932 as the brainchild of Frank Underhill, a professor of history at the University of Toronto, and Frank Scott, a law professor at McGill. A few months later, a new radical political party, the Co-operative

Commonwealth Federation, came into being. Although I knew that the League had stated its purposes in non-political terms, I was aware that a large part of its impetus came from those who held socialist views. Some of my friends joined it — a few were socialists, others were not. In its manifesto, the League vowed to establish a social order that was based on the common good, not private profit. To educate the public to accept its ideas, it held lectures and disseminated pamphlets. Like Norman Rogers, a professor at Queen's University, I declined to participate in the League's activities, preferring to work for reform from within the Liberal Party. In my speeches, I tried not to hit the CCF or the League too hard since I knew many of their members and shared their desire for radical change. I would point out, for example, that I appreciated the sincerity of J. S. Woodsworth, the CCF's leader, but could not subscribe to his political program. "To say that we must overthrow all we have built up does not sound rational," I said when I spoke in Dutton; "that . . . is one of the weaknesses of the CCF policy. . . . I feel that more good can be accomplished by taking the middle course than by taking the extreme."[13] Furthermore, I declared that "when recovery comes, there will be a new order. . . . It may be a move towards state control. The CCF would throw capitalism overboard. The Liberals would prune out what is bad and keep what is good."[14]

Vincent Massey spoke and thought along much the same lines. Little did we know that his speech at Windsor towards the end of March would enrage Mackenzie King so much.[15] I had convinced Massey to address the Essex County Liberal Association, and he had resolved to try to enunciate some of the ideas of reform liberalism at the meeting. While he continued to repudiate doctrinaire state socialism, Massey welcomed cooperation with all those who wished to check the abuses of capitalism and to work for a

13 Speech at Dutton, 3 April 1933.
14 Speech at Hamilton, 11 April 1933, reported in the *Hamilton Spectator*.
15 These remarks," wrote Massey, "have caused a certain amount of discussion in the Liberal caucus at Ottawa. Some of the laissez-faire die-hards felt I went too far. . . . I don't think the controversy did any harm" (Massey to J. W. Dafoe, 3 April 1933, J. W. Dafoe Papers (reel M76), PAC).

more equitable distribution of wealth. In this regard, he saw little difference between the Liberals and the CCF and urged them to work as a team. We expected this kind of talk to be resisted by some old-guard Liberals, and so were surprised to find how many of them liked the tone of Roosevelt's inaugural address, to which Massey referred in glowing terms.

Massey and I had talked about setting up a summer school to bring together those who shared our reformist views. In May 1933, I joined him and a small group that met at Port Hope to plan the next step. His brother-in-law, Raleigh Parkin of Montreal, agreed to invite some people from there, including Percy Corbett of the McGill Law School. Others with whom Massey discussed his proposal were his secretary, Steven Cartwright, and two Ottawa lawyers — Oliver Mowat Biggar and Ainslie Greene. As Massey observed, of all of them, I was the only person clearly identified with the Liberal Party day in and day out. In addition to the Canadians, Massey intended to invite some prominent reformers from the United States and Britain.

The summer school took place at Trinity College School, Port Hope, from 4 to 9 September 1933, under aegis of a committee of twenty-seven, including J. E. Atkinson, the publisher of the *Toronto Daily Star*, and J. W. Dafoe. It was a great success. There was an undercurrent of disagreement, however, between the vast majority of the younger people, who strongly supported the philosophy of the New Deal, and the older party members, who took the more mainstream stance of official Liberalism.

The conference's program provided an opportunity to discuss the gamut of economic and political issues. Sir Herbert Samuel spoke about Liberalism and state action in the United Kingdom; Floyd Chalmers of the *Financial Post* dealt with the world economic conference; and Percy Corbett, in his address on a foreign policy for Canada, acknowledged his unhappiness as a Canadian that our country was the first to undermine the Covenant of the League of Nations.[16] I remember the look of displeasure on Mackenzie

16 P. E. Corbett, "A Foreign Policy for Canada," First Liberal Summer Conference, Port Hope, September 1933, *The Liberal Way* (Toronto: J. M. Dent, 1933).

King's face as Corbett spoke, but I thought Percy's presentation was one of the best at the conference and told him so.

The greatest interest at Port Hope, however, centred on an analysis of Roosevelt's New Deal. Averell Harriman, of the National Industrial Recovery Administration, and Raymond Moley, recently resigned as a troubleshooter for Roosevelt, set out the basis of the American president's reforms to combat the Depression. Many of us at the conference wondered what was going through Mackenzie King's mind as these men spoke of Roosevelt's leadership. Francis Hankin and Terry MacDermot discussed the New Deal from a Canadian perspective. The problems of the 1930s, they pointed out, could best be resolved by using the institutions of a free society and building on them in the changed circumstances. In this way, freedom and individualism would be preserved. MacDermot's defence of the New Deal was, for me, more effective than Harriman's or Moley's, and I fully agreed with his contention that the New Deal was applicable to Canada; King must again have squirmed when MacDermot said, "We need a man who can lead and with the courage and wit to act."[17]

My former professor of political theory, Robert MacIver, then teaching at Columbia University, asserted that Liberalism was capable of meeting the challenge of the day better than any other political creed. "The old individualism," he told us, "is meaningless in a world of giant corporations . . . and of national economic systems. . . ."[18] Liberalism sought not abolition but control.

Throughout the meetings, Mackenzie King sat uncomfortably at a small desk, taking notes. It was a strange image: the political master, placed in the position of schoolboy, while the younger men stood at the podium and lectured. There were many at the conference who shared the beliefs of the CCF. That new party's Regina Manifesto had declared the party's position only a few weeks

17 T. W. L. MacDermot, "The Significance for Canada of the American 'New Deal,' " *The Liberal Way*, p. 196.
18 R. M. MacIver, "Liberalism and the Economic Challenge," ibid., p. 214.

before, and we were worried about King's reaction to the doctrines being put forward at Port Hope. The party leader and Frank Scott had a heated discussion about general trends in the Liberal Party.

King had his undisputed say, however, when he closed our deliberations. He publicly stated that he thought the conference demonstrated the need for wider knowledge and a new perspective (we now know that privately he viewed the conference as a threat) and went on to question the use of the word "planning" and the reliance on experts which had been referred to so frequently in the presentations. King cautioned against its overuse in present-day Liberal rhetoric and did not agree with those who criticized "the Liberalism that means *laissez-faire.*"[19] Here, I thought, the Liberal leader missed the point and revealed how much he lacked Roosevelt's drive and modernity. Those of us who spoke against laissez faire were urging action to correct the abuses of the Depression.

The value of the Port Hope conference lay in the wider intellectual base and the stimulus towards more progressive ideas that it afforded the Liberal Party. While it may have driven some waiverers into the CCF fold, it provided others of us with a greater sense of purpose. Much later, my active participation and criticism of the party establishment at Port Hope was remembered and undoubtedly affected the perceptions of some of my older colleagues in the King and St. Laurent governments about my position in the party.

Massey was the right man at the right time to head the National Liberal Federation. He brought it prestige and, more than anyone else could, dispelled the notion that the Federation was a mere party machine. The organization headed by Massey *was* political; but to the extent that he could influence it, there was some consideration of matters beyond day-to-day politics. For Massey, the Federation served as a "clearinghouse" of Liberal opinion — one of the few means by which party workers could make known in Ottawa their opinions on matters of policy. The president had not previously been able to direct discussion within the party in order

19 W. L. M. King, "The Practice of Liberalism," *The Liberal Way*, p. 278.

to present its parliamentarians with a consensus. Massey hoped to correct this state of affairs. At Port Hope, the party held its first open discussion on international affairs. We baulked at what we regarded as King's isolationism, and he was against us airing our views on party policy, because he erroneously believed that it fomented public disagreement among fellow Liberals.

While the federal party was trying to reach an accommodation on the issue of a revival of Liberalism, Mitch Hepburn was busily concocting a strategy that would unseat the Conservative government of George Henry and get himself elected premier of Ontario. Hepburn assiduously created issues by which to measure public opinion. One matter that divided the party was prohibition: Liberals had long espoused a policy of prohibition, but many argued against it. Although I did not drink, I felt prohibition had been a great mistake. The president of the Ontario Temperance Union, Roscoe Rodd, was a fellow Windsor lawyer and Liberal, and the Windsor Chamber of Commerce asked the two of us to debate the merits of selling beer and wine by the glass in licensed establishments. I argued that the Ontario treasury lost money each year, that the current government policy of allowing only bulk sales of liquor to the public discriminated against the poor, and that the sale of beer and wine by the glass would allow taverns to reopen, hence making law enforcement easier. The vote on the debate confirmed that my point of view was shared by most of those present.

His soundings led Hepburn to declare that the Liberal Party no longer supported prohibition. But when, just before the 1934 Ontario election, the Conservative government introduced legislation permitting the sale of beer and wine by the glass, the Liberal Party split once more over the issue. Those of us in the Border Cities firmly believed that fear of Liberal restrictions might lose the Essex County seats to the Conservatives yet again.

It was not easy to keep out of provincial discussions. Hepburn lived in southwestern Ontario, and I generally saw him when he came my way. More than this, I went on speaking tours with him, as a representative of the young Liberals, in the years before the 1934 provincial election. While the average voter does not necessarily vote for the same party federally and provincially, it is difficult for the party worker not to be involved in both jurisdictions. The organization in the federal and provincial constituency is essentially made up of the same people. At this time, I was a party worker and felt it was my duty to assist at both levels, particularly if I wished to be a candidate myself at some time in the future.

While working on Hepburn's behalf, I almost got myself in serious trouble. Late in 1932, the provincial government had taken over the almost bankrupt Abitibi Power Company. Under pressure from the Liberals, the premier admitted that he had held bonds in the company, awaiting takeover. I was due to speak five days later in Hamilton and beforehand had discussed the Abitibi bonds issue with Harry Johnson, the secretary of the Ontario Liberal Association. I made it clear that the party was about to implicate other Conservative ministers. My speech in Hamilton caused more of a stir than I had intended because I declared that further disclosures would occur during the current session. Premier Henry, I said, was "honest but stupid." My statements caused Henry to inform the legislature that he had asked the attorney general, W. H. Price, to send me a telegram urging me to provide the House with any information I might have that would support my charges. Realizing that my rashness had placed me in a very precarious position, I phoned Hepburn. Even though I had exposed the party as well as myself, Hepburn told me not to worry. The legislature was about to adjourn, and so I did not acknowledge the telegram, but kept my head beneath the parapet.

George Henry called the long-awaited provincial election for 19 June 1934. Keith Laird undertook to organize James H. Clark's campaign in Windsor-Sandwich; Clark was an outstanding lawyer and a partner in the McTague firm. I made a number of speeches on his behalf and also campaigned for other Liberals throughout the province.[20] Generally, I urged unemployment insurance and minimum wages for labour when I was in the cities; at the rural meetings, I pointed out that George Henry had done

---

20 *Border Cities Star*, 28 May 1934. I spoke in Lucan, Stratford, London and Sault Ste. Marie.

little for the farmers. Of the local candidates in the Essex ridings, Dr. A. H. C. Trottier in Essex North and David Croll in Windsor-Walkerville put forward the same policies I had advocated. We argued that the Liberals would seek to create jobs; money lying idle in the banks and the treasury would be put to constructive use to stimulate the economy. The socialists did not have a monopoly on the philosophy of the New Deal.

On election day, I served as a poll captain, helping to get out the vote. That night Essex County returned four Liberals, who were all pledged to support Mitch Hepburn's new administration. As it became clear in Clark's committee rooms that Hepburn had a substantial lead, my friend Bill Tubman turned to me and said: "Your turn is next. These are Liberal times. You must not lose the chance." I thought a lot about his advice that one must not lose the right opportunity. Although I had suspected that such a situation might arise, I was not prepared for it; my preference was to carry on with my increasingly prosperous law practice. Clearly, I was on the horns of a dilemma.

Shortly, other voices joined Bill Tubman's. In an editorial in the *Border Cities Star*, Lum Clark commented: "If we were running the Liberal campaign in Essex County, we would get busy right away to prepare for the federal election. There are half a dozen men who will make good candidates."[21] I knew Lum had me in mind. When I worked in Windsor as a student, I had met Ellison Young, chief of the *Star*'s editorial department; later, having established myself in the city, we became fast friends. Through him, I got to know his publisher, W. F. Herman; the editor, Harold Vaughan; and W. L. (Lum) Clark, who boarded with Mr. and Mrs. Herman. As an aspirant to public office, I have always recognized the importance of a friendly connection with the proprietor and his newspaper — the only one in town; rarely did I let a week go by without calling the newspaper's office. Mr. Herman and I took a liking to each other. A shy, retiring man, very proud of his paper, especially of its rotogravure department, he was pleased by my interest. Although

21 *Border Cities Star*, 27 June 1934.

he professed to be politically neutral, I knew that at heart Herman was a Liberal. All my activities — law cases, the meetings of the League of Nations Society, political speeches — were reported at great length in the *Star*.

These representations made me look again at the possibilities for election. If I was to run for parliament, it was obvious that I should do so in a constituency that conformed to my background as much as possible. The riding I looked at most closely was Essex East; it was urban but had a strong rural hinterland. It contained part of Windsor, the towns of Walkerville, Ford City, Riverside and Tecumseh, all inhabited, for the most part, by workers in the automobile plants and its allied industries. The rural areas of the constituency along Lake St. Clair took in La Puce, St. Clair Beach, Belle River, Pointe Aux Roches, St. Joachim, Tilbury North, and the townships of Rochester, Maidstone, Sandwich South and Sandwich East. The industrialization of the area was a major influence on its political complexion.

It was my belief that the weakness of the Liberal Party in the past could be attributed largely to the poor calibre of its candidates in federal elections. Since the death of W. C. Kennedy, who had served as minister of railways and canals in Mackenzie King's first government from December 1921 until his death in January 1923, the tide had turned against the Liberals. It was fertile ground for the CCF, and one communist had run in Essex East in 1930.

There was quite a strong French vote that it was important to win.[22] During the 1934 provincial election, Dr. Percy Gardner, the original Liberal candidate, had been superceded by Dr. Albert Trottier as a result of the French community's opposition. Moreover, in the federal constituency, the immigrant vote in East Windsor around Drouillard Road carried considerable weight. The town of Walkerville, where the executives of the automobile factories and the liquor distillery lived, was largely Tory territory.

---

22 The Conservative member, R. D. Morand, came from a French-Canadian family that had long been settled in the southwestern Ontario peninsula.

Once I had considered the matter, I realized that a federal election would be called no later than the autumn of 1935. By July of the previous year, the Conservatives had started to jockey for constituency nominations in the Windsor area, and I knew the Liberals would not be far behind. I went to "Batterwood" to spend a few days with Vincent Massey, and while I was gone, the *Border Cities Star* specifically mentioned my name as a possible candidate in Essex East. Worried that I would be seen as a Johnny-come-lately who was forcing his way into local politics, I kept my counsel. To say peremptorily that under no circumstances was I interested might have shut the door for a long time. My innate reluctance was competing with a recognition that I should seize the moment. Tubman and the Reverend Hugh Paulin, the Presbyterian minister of St. Andrew's Church, urged me to take the chance; and Norman McLarty, the mainstay of the local party, entreated me to join him as a candidate (he was planning to seek the nomination in Essex West). This convinced me that established Windsor Liberals did not see me as a carpetbagger, and when I did not stop the rumours that I was to be a candidate for the nomination, I myself came to accept it as a fact.

V

The Member For Essex East

I N EARLY NOVEMBER 1935, I paid my first visit to Ottawa as the member for Essex East.[1] It was an auspicious occasion both for me and for my companion, Murray Clark, the new MP for Essex South. Ottawa was my birthplace; it was here and at St. Alexandre that I had spun my first dreams of public life. Now an ambition had been fulfilled, and the opportunity to give it meaning, credibility and substance was at hand. With a feeling of solemn exultation, Murray and I walked up Parliament Hill through the East Block gates and past the monument to Laurier, who had served as my model from boyhood; now, as a man of thirty-two, I was following in his footsteps. We moved on to look around the House of Commons chamber, which, thanks to the voters of Essex East, remained the centre of my political life for the next thirty-three years. As we made our tour of the Parliament

---

1 In this book, it is inevitable that the official name of the riding I represented should be frequently mentioned. It became a household word in our family. On one occasion in the late 1940s, when my children, Paul and Mary Anne, drove with me to a church picnic, Mary Anne asked, "Daddy, what is Essex East?" My son, his sister's senior by six years, intervened: "Don't you know? Essex East is the Holy Land."

133

Buildings, I thought not only of what lay ahead but of the twelve months of strenuous effort that had preceded my trip to Ottawa — of the struggle to achieve nomination and then election.

Before I announced my decision to seek the Liberal nomination on 13 October 1934, I had been obliged to make some changes in my living arrangements. Reluctantly, I had decided to leave Assumption College, which was part of the Essex West constituency. It seemed prudent to move into Essex East, so I rented a flat on Argyle Road in a building appropriately called the Renfrew Apartments. This was my home for the next four eventful years; from there I planned my nomination and found refuge when I needed rest and quiet.

Up until this time, I had never owned an automobile. Now, as an aspiring candidate, it had become necessary to acquire one to get around the riding; I could make the necessary visits to potential supporters in the rural parts of Essex East only by car. So I walked into a Ford dealer's showroom, supremely confident of my capacity to operate any vehicle he had on display. With few instructions and no lessons, I proudly drove my new Ford down Ouellette Avenue. My adventures were newsworthy. The *Border Cities Star* noted with amusement that within a short time of each other, both Mitch Hepburn and Paul Martin had had similar accidents: Hepburn had hit a cow, but Martin had had the distinction of being hit by a cow! Alfred Quenneville, one of those who helped me over the years, was with me in the car and often chided me later about my driving. I must have had a charmed life. In one accident, the car skidded across the highway, flinging out my fellow passengers and me. Luckily, no one was hurt. Despite these incidents, the car gave yeomen service as it carried me over the winding dirt roads of Essex County, deeply rutted by farm machinery.

I knew from the outset that any effort to secure the Liberal nomination in Essex East would not be easy. Several other individuals had expressed an interest or had been mentioned in the press as potential contenders. The *Border Cities Star* had put forward the names of two other arrivals from Renfrew County: Dr. James Young, a respected physician, and Miss A. D. L. Robinson. The formidable Miss Dorothea Robinson had a considerable local following. As a boy, I had met her when she canvassed my mother for the United Farmers of Ontario in North Renfrew during the 1919 provincial election; I had never before seen a woman soliciting votes. Like most members of the United Farmers, she had long returned to the Liberal ranks by 1934. Apart from those with less recent roots in Essex County, three men were referred to as possible contenders — Ulysse Reaume, Leo Sylvestre and Gabriel McPharlin.

It quickly turned out, however, that my chief opponnent would be Dr. Percy N. Gardner, a seventeen-year veteran of the council in Ford City (a municipality that became part of the enlarged city of Windsor in 1935). Gardner, a popular alderman, represented the heart of the working-class section of Ford City. In essence, though, he was a local ward politician whose vision stopped at the city limits.

The campaign for the nomination brought on a storm that had been brewing since 1933. In that year, Gardner had originally been selected as the Liberal candidate for the provincial riding of Essex North (the federal consitutuency of Essex East included this provincial riding, as well as a large portion of the city of Windsor). But he subsequently lost the nomination, largely because of some tasteless remarks he had made about French Canadian Liberals in the constituency. A new nominating convention questioned his suitability to be the official candidate because he was not French, and the name of Tony Marentette, a popular Essex County Liberal of French descent, was put forward. Mitch Hepburn resolved the dispute, which could have split the vote and cost the Liberals the seat. In the behind-the-scenes negotiations, Gardner was induced to step down in favour of the greatly respected Dr. A. H. C. Trottier, a compromise candidate who lived in Windsor but who had practised medicine years before in Belle River. At the end of May, Marentette and Gardner withdrew in favour of Trottier, who was elected to the Ontario legislature in June 1934.

The question of Dr. Gardner's withdrawal came to the fore during the preliminaries to the federal nomination. It was spread about that he had been given a considerable sum of money not to seek the nomination. At the rally in the Scottish Rite Hall where the erstwhile doctor declared his candidacy, two hundred workers announced their determination to further his claim to a seat in the House of Commons and thereby correct what they felt was an injustice. Then another, more consequential, rumour emerged: that Gardner had been promised the nomination in Essex East. While some Liberals might have told him that there was a possibility of him securing the nomination for the seat, no promise could have been given; the choice would have to be decided by delegates at an official convention.

When I heard about the so-called commitment to Gardner regarding my — by then — coveted constituency, I took steps to dispel the story, letting it be known that any peddling of nominations was not in the tradition of Essex East and would not be sanctioned by the constituency executive. Gardner's supporters argued that he was entitled to the federal nomination by virtue of his long service in civic affairs. But my view was that if it was wise to give to a French-speaking nominee one of the four provincial seats in a region with a substantial francophone population, the same reasoning should apply to the federal seats.

To begin with, I set about assembling a strong body of workers to help my cause. Bill Tubman, who had first urged me to run for parliament, directed my campaign. He had proven his skills as an organizer by helping Keith Laird elect James H. Clark to the provincial house, but I did not get to know Bill very well until that particular campaign was over. Bill was an accountant and bookkeeper, but he had been on relief for some time. He was a forceful character, full of ideas, and I sometimes wondered whether he had lost his job for knowing more than his boss.

At the outset, I faced a mighty task: to get to know all my workers and the other Liberals in the constituency. I got in touch with the leaders of various communities in the riding and then drove around to see them all. It was important for me to find out their views on the issues of the day and on the other candidates. For instance, I soon learned from my supporters that Richard Benoit, a strong, able and independent personality with a prosperous farm in Tilbury West, did not necessarily favour me. So I went out and had a talk with him. When I left, I felt that this man would be on my side; he was a respected Liberal reformer, and we shared common views on many matters. In Belle River, I visited John D. Renaud, a merchant I hoped to win to my cause; I knew that if I could convince him (he also was the village policeman and undertaker!), others would follow his lead. Alice Renaud — no relation to John — was an important link, too, and had great influence among the Liberal women in the county. F. X. Chauvin, a suave and goateed individual who regarded himself as a litterateur, was one of my most fervent champions and an excellent public speaker.

In order to get my name abroad, I grasped every opportunity to address gatherings in the constituency. The local Liberals organized teas, addresses to women's associations and general meetings so that the party members would be better able to appraise the candidates. But I was not content with just meeting the party faithful and made a point of speaking to the North Essex Teachers, the Border Cities Life Underwriters Association, the Moderation League, the Shriners, the Canadian Legion, the Ukrainian Citizens and other multinational groups, and indeed anyone else who would hear me. Invitations from outside Essex County poured in. Bill Tubman and others thought it was a wise thing to be in demand, particularly since my opponents were somewhat confined to home territory; among the groups I spoke to were Brantford Young Liberals and the Chatham Home and School Club.

My law work suffered as a result, because I was on the road from the autumn of 1934 until the nominating convention the following June. But certain cases, such as my work for the Dionnes, helped keep my name before the public. It was hard slogging but a great opportunity to expound my views on all kinds of issues. Naturally, I did not restrict myself to local or even domestic themes. My speeches dealt with international questions that I considered important: the failure of the disarmament talks organized by the League of Nations and the need to reform the economic system. In effect, I was laying the foundation of my political platform, a platform that is better discussed later, in the context of the general election campaign.[2]

At some gatherings, I sensed that a number of Dr. Gardner's supporters were growing jealous of my appearances before audiences where the doctor was not likely to be invited to the podium. Of course, this was politically perilous for me. Dr. Gardner did not discuss the great issues of the day with any relish; at one point, he made the naive suggestion that two members should represent the whole of Essex County both at Queen's Park and on Parliament Hill. I remember that he once went after me for introducing St. Thomas Aquinas into a discussion about labour. Nobody was interested in that "academic stuff," he said tellingly, scoring points against me, as the applause his remark provoked made clear. Gardner proved that popularity among those who attended League of Nations Society meetings could spell the opposite in the working-class streets around Drouillard Road. In that neighbourhood, hit exceptionally hard by the Depression, voters wanted a candidate who showed an interest in their personal problems. So I learned to balance my activities and not to forget that most people have little interest in political philosophy.

In my public speeches, I suppose, I often tended to talk above the heads of many in the audience. But I believe that my developing reputation as someone who addressed more complex issues and was in tune with the universal desire for change helped me clinch the nomination. That does not mean that I was an academic dabbling in politics. My understanding of the political process was innate — I knew how to make a good speech and how to handle a crowd as well as anyone; but I had another side as well.

A speech by either Gardner or me was almost daily fare in the *Border Cities Star;*[3] but a meeting where both of us spoke was

2 See pp. 148-65.
3 The *Border Cities Star* became the *Windsor Daily Star* on 29 June 1935; that same day, many of the smaller municipalities in Essex County amalgamated with the city of Windsor.
   Readers will notice that throughout these memoirs, I quote extensively from the *Windsor Daily Star* (henceforth abbreviated to *WDS*). During most of my public life, this was one of the best newspapers in Canada, as cosmopolitan as a local paper could be.

covered *in extenso*, with pictures galore. I was always conscious of
having my political views and activities known in Essex County
and, in the language of the press, made the transition from "Liberal lawyer" to "Liberal stalwart" with ease. Soon after the campaign began, one of my clients asked me if I was running in the
next election. He greeted my non-committal answer with disbelief:
"You sure as hell ain't runnin' to keep warm."

The publisher of the *Border Cities Star*, W. F. Herman, knew how
to make an event newsworthy. His sympathies were with Dr.
Gardner, whom he had known for a long time; Gardner had
supported many of the *Star*'s proposals for municipal reform.
Although Mr. Herman and I were friendly, he felt that all things
considered, he should support my opponent. I was consoled by the
newspaper's staff: Lum Clark, Ellison Young, and Harold
Vaughan, all strong proponents of my candidacy.

The newspaper coverage helped to make the campaign for the
Liberal nomination a subject of great interest both locally and
farther afield. At the annual meeting of the Essex East Constituency Association in March 1935, over five hundred people — the
largest attendance at this type of meeting for many years —
jammed the pavilion in Belle River. Among those elected were
Richard Benoit, who served as president for the following year,
and several officers who did not represent the slate of the "old-time
Liberals" backing Dr. Gardner. Benoit pleaded for harmony since
Gardner and I disagreed on what type of nominating convention
should be held. My adversary favoured a "closed" convention, in
which the candidate would be selected by delegates who themselves were chosen by the local Liberal groups. A closed convention, he felt sure, would afford him the greatest advantage. I
wanted an open convention, where the candidate would be chosen
by all members of the party living in Essex East. In my view, an
open convention would prevent the nomination from being controlled by a small group who might have old scores to settle and
would stimulate even greater interest in and support for the nominee who eventually would contest the election. The meeting supported the open convention by 446 votes to 298.

This verdict increased Dr. Gardner's resentment and led to an

unedifying episode: a set-to between us at a tea for a group of
Liberal women. Gardner charged that I was spreading abroad a
rumour that he had received money for withdrawing from the
provincial election the year before. I countered by telling him that
he ought to declare that he had not received a cent. It was true that
some of my workers, still smarting from Gardner's anti-French
pronouncements, had not been entirely free of rumour-
mongering. Gardner had it put about that I had been kicked out of
Ottawa, and he further accused me of packing the Belle River
meeting. Understandably, some of the women were pretty upset,
even more so because the details of the tiff were well and dutifully
reported in the *Border Cities Star*.

The growing bitterness between Dr. Gardner and me encouraged other potential nominees, each of whom hoped to come up
with adequate support to win as a compromise candidate. "Gabe"
McPharlin, a graduate of the Ontario Agricultural College who
farmed at Woodslee, declared that if Gardner or I were picked, the
local party would split. While the doctor thought McPharlin's
candidacy an honest one, he complained that the others — Ulysse
Reaume, a Windsor businessman; Theodore Ouellette, an artisan
from Sandwich East; and Leo Sylvestre, a lawyer from Belle River
— were fronts for me. (Ouellette, Sylvestre and Reaume proved
his allegations false by remaining in the contest until they were
eliminated at the convention.)

One of the lighter moments in the campaign occurred during a
visit my father made to Windsor. I was showing off and said,
"Everybody knows me in this town, Dad." It was the typical
statement of a son trying to impress. "Oh, I can see that," my
father diffidently replied. To corroborate my boast, I then asked a
taxi driver who was taking us about, "What do you think of this
fellow Martin who is seeking the Liberal nomination?" "Never
heard of him," the driver replied laconically. My father got a great
kick out of that.

During this pre-nomination period, longer in Essex East than in
most other ridings, my schedule was an onerous one. I could not
give up working in my law office during the mornings: I needed

the income and to cover my flank in case I lost. Many of my callers, however, came on political as well as legal business. In the middle of the afternoon, I used to go out to petition the party faithful. Most evenings were taken up with meetings, at which I generally gave a speech. Since my contact with books and study was so restricted, I used to pull my car over to the side of the road from time to time during the hot summer afternoons, get out and read for an hour. Late at night, after a long day, I would return to the Renfrew Apartments and take stock of things, looking longingly at the books on my shelves before falling asleep exhausted.

In the week before the nomination convention, Dr. Gardner contrived to have it postponed by charging me with planning to bring in outside people to vote. Finally, on the eve of the convention, the *Border Cities Star* reported Dr. Gardner's most stinging attack. He claimed that I had been "thrown out of Renfrew," that I had moved to Essex East only recently, and was now trying to exploit the situation to prove that I was "God's gift" so that I could leave the area and join the group of big shots in Ottawa. Gardner further asserted that Ottawa and Toronto Liberals were promoting my candidacy over more deserving contenders. By this time, though, I was encouraged to think that Gardner was a desperate man and that his charges were just attempts to gain votes by stirring up further gossip. These accusations were mainly an attempt to play on the conscience of the owner of the *Border Cities Star*, because Mr. Herman, we all knew, would loudly and publicly denounce any candidate suspected of bringing in people to vote at the convention who were not qualified Liberals from the riding.

Despite Gardner's machinations, Essex East Liberals made their way on 8 June to the Lakeshore Pavilion in Belle River, right in the centre of the constituency. Not many, if any, political conventions had been held in this summer dance hall on the shores of Lake St. Clair. It was the biggest available meeting place in the riding, and there was heady talk that up to six thousand people might attend.

Since Belle River is eighteen miles from the Windsor portion of Essex East (the district with the greatest population density in the constituency), the prospective Liberal candidate in Essex West, Norman McLarty, in collaboration with Keith Laird, Bill Tubman and Alf Morrell, the indefatigable head of the Walkerville Liberals, ingeniously proposed that special provision be laid on to help those who had no means of transporting themselves to the convention. Why not a Martin special train? Thanks to Norman's pocketbook, it came about: a CNR special would take my supporters from the Walkerville station to the Lakeshore Pavilion. Such a gala event would spur them to attend the convention and would further ensure that they remained at the scene of battle until the expected rounds of voting had taken place. We hoped that participants supporting other candidates would tire of the rounds of balloting and would leave before the end. Only those authorized to travel on the Martin special could remain in comfort until the die had been cast.

The cleverness of the idea hit the mark, and the *Border Cities Star* saw in it the romance and colour of a great political outing. Naturally the train idea did not sit well with Dr. Gardner, who alleged that it would be used to pack the convention. People in Essex County still speak of the "Martin Booster Special," which has turned into a symbol identifying a whole generation of voters in the Windsor area.

Although the anxious night before the convention was a sleepless one, I boarded the train with hundreds of my supporters in a happy and confident mood, greeting them all as I moved from coach to coach. Their enthusiasm buoyed me for the coming ordeal. When we arrived in Belle River, my entourage was met by bands and cheers. But there were jeers, too, and it was obvious that certain delegates were decidedly not on my side. While my friends carried me on their shoulders to the pavilion, some supporters of Dr. Gardner set off stink bombs in the hall in an effort to stop the proceedings. Faced with a crowd of nearly three thousand, the riding executive issued cards to all eligible voters, thus averting the likelihood of any skulduggery.

Richard Benoit called the meeting to order in the early afternoon. Dr. Gardner's supporters showed their hand straightaway by placing in nomination three of my major supporters, George Scott, Alice Renaud and Miss A. D. L. Robinson. Our opponents hoped that the resulting withdrawals would prove to the delegates that I had somehow hindered the establishment of a fair contest.

Since there were chairs for only about a hundred of the delegates, the huge crowd milled about the pavilion during the speeches of the nominees, which for the most part merely reiterated pleas for support that the audience had been hearing for months. Although Miss Robinson withdrew in my favour, she said trenchantly that "no woman would have stood a chance." Gabe McPharlin made a pitch for a compromise candidate — namely himself; Dr. Gardner complained that the deck was stacked against him; Leo Sylvestre appealed for support as a native son. It was not the occasion for a great philippic, so I called for good judgment in selecting a candidate and asked whoever was nominated to follow true Liberal principles. In conclusion, I promised to support any other nominee who might be selected and pledged to fight for and serve the people whether I was chosen or not.

The simmering hostility between the various camps erupted during the balloting. At one point, Dr. Gardner actually fought for the microphone with the chairman, Richard Benoit. Gardner yelled that one man had thirteen ballots; someone else informed Benoit that there were not enough boxes and that ballot papers were being collected in hats. The chairman, in turn, claimed that the executive had no control over those ballots that already had been distributed and pointed out that if the situation got further out of control, the convention might have to be postponed. At this point, I lost my nerve and pleaded with Benoit to have the whole thing called off. But he would not give in and turned out to be an artful chairman, even getting the crowd to sing between the various rounds of voting.

The first ballot gave me a plurality, but not enough to win; Ulysse Reaume was eliminated. The second ballot left the situation much the same, although some voters moved over to Gabe McPharlin as the compromise candidate. This shift did not really come off, and the supporters of other candidates began to drift home. At ten past seven in the evening, I was declared the winner on the third ballot.[4] Dr. Gardner failed to move the customary motion that the nomination be made unanimous.

I was greatly relieved that it was all over. In my brief speech, I said that I would represent *all* the Liberals, although Dr. Gardner's claqueurs yelled back that I would not represent them. Although I knew that in time the divisions would be healed, I was under no illusions; at that moment, I was not everyone's choice. My supporters were ecstatic as the "Martin Special" chugged back to Windsor. I thanked them all as I moved inch by inch along the coaches — full of happy well-wishers shouting "On to Ottawa."

When I returned that night, bone weary, to my apartment on Argyle Road, I felt contented, but not a little confused. For the previous twelve months the strain had been severe. What lay ahead? I wondered. The past year had disturbed and would continue to disturb my plans for practising law. I knew that I could not stop making a living — and the nomination meant that I would be doing two things instead of concentrating on just one. Although I was strong and full of beans, this coming period would severely test my strength and endurance. Too tired to sleep and long after midnight, I walked reflectively about the silent streets of Walkerville, past St. Mary's Anglican Church and my own parish church of St. Anne's. It became clear to me on that nocturnal circuit how the quiet events of the past five years had merged. Perhaps my time had come; at least I hoped so, as early in the

4 The results of the various rounds were as follows:

	First Ballot	Second Ballot	Third Ballot
Martin	776	712	739
Gardner	562	557	517
McPharlin	188	223	177
Ouellette	17	7	—
Sylvestre	210	139	—
Reaume	10	—	—
Total	1,763	1,638	1,433

morning I knelt by my bedside to thank God for the day and for my life.

I have often reflected on the effort it required to achieve my initial place in public life; the process of gaining the nomination was a very tedious one. At first, all I wanted to do was to keep my foot in the door and make a good showing. Certainly I had no desire to spend all my time greeting people and speechifying, but I got so involved that I could not pull away. Contradictory as it may appear, I felt my priorities should lie elsewhere. This was not the only time I was faced with such a dilemma. It confronted me again after Mackenzie King's retirement in 1948, and once more when I ran against Mike Pearson for the Liberal leadership a decade later.

Contrary to what many people think, political campaigns have never really been enjoyable for me. But campaigning was the only way I could see of serving in the government of the nation. Appearances and my apparent success in winning ten successive elections in thirty-three years notwithstanding, campaigns were so enervating. It is said that I knew everyone, that I was a good door-to-door, store-to-store, supermarket-to-supermarket canvasser, and that I never forgot a face; in short, that I was a politician's politician. There were other designations that pleased me more. In my first nomination and election campaign, I found that I indeed had a good memory for names, faces and personal peculiarities. My interest in people was genuine; yet their difficulties often threatened to overwhelm me. Generally, I was on the go from early in the day until late at night; and on weekends, too, I climbed into my car and made my rounds.

Throughout my life, it has intrigued me to compare my introduction to public life with that of others with whom I shared the task of government. In 1941, before Louis St. Laurent had become a member of the House of Commons — at fifty-nine — Mackenzie King invited him to join his government as minister of justice. The fifty-one-year-old Mike Pearson entered the cabinet the same way, at the behest of St. Laurent and King in 1948. Pierre Trudeau came into the House of Commons in 1965 when he was forty-six and entered the cabinet eighteen months later, at Pearson's request. The candidate who enters politics in this way is generally presented with an uncontested nomination and often with a fairly safe seat. Those who enter the cabinet from outside politics in some respects take advantage of the hard work of others and cash in on that work to obtain the victory that generally ensues. Those who seek political office after they have made a reputation either in public service or in business are as politically ambitious as any others.

My circumstance was by far the more common one: the constituency ran the nomination and chose the candidate without outside interference. When I was thirty-two, I had to fight for and earn the nomination. The means that I and most others used to enter politics helped to build a strong political party. Most members of parliament set out about their career the way I did and are a little resentful of those who do not. After all, we are the ones who worked for years to build the party and who have painstakingly learned about government the hard way. John Diefenbaker, who also followed my course, made efforts to have the Conservative Party choose its leaders from among the members in the House of Commons. While I could not support this idea, I understand his point of view.

It would have been difficult to slacken my efforts after the euphoric Belle River verdict, and I worked hard to unify the party for the election. Dr. Gardner's supporters complained to the national Liberal office that the results had been achieved by chicanery, but nothing came of this rather pathetic charge. Some stories appeared in the press that Dr. Gardner would run as an independent in the forthcoming general election, but shortly after the nomination he shared the platform with me and pledged his support to the Liberal cause. The one truly disaffected candidate was Gabe

McPharlin, who left the party and, after running once for the Reconstruction Party, joined the Tories. A hard core of Liberals in East Windsor, where Gardner lived, was not at first easily amenable to my blandishments. One of his more formidable workers, Alice Shanahan in Maidstone, was an important person that I knew I must win over; not only were she and her husband the matriarch and patriarch of a large family, their influence and organizing skills had been demonstrated in municipal, provincial and federal elections. Soon after nomination day, I called on them and was thrilled to leave with their friendship and backing. In the working-class areas, David R. Croll, the provincial minister of public welfare and of municipal affairs, was very helpful during the campaign in consolidating my support and in winning votes. We had been political allies since he first ran for mayor of Windsor in 1930. At that time, few leading Liberals endorsed his candidacy, but, almost alone among the city's lawyers, I supported him, as did enough of the ordinary Joes that he won. A young, vigorous man, Dave Croll shared much of my political philosophy and zeal for reform. I worked on his behalf in the 1934 provincial election, after which he joined Mitch Hepburn's cabinet. With the help of Croll and others, by election time the Liberals in Essex East were foursquare behind their young candidate. It was to be that way for my ten elections to the House of Commons.

To make sure of the support of my friends at the *Star*, I went over to see them immediately after the nominating convention. W. F. Herman told me that Lum Clark, after following the proceedings in person, had assured him that Dr. Gardner's charges were untrue. It was clear that to the extent that any publisher in a one-paper community could be, Mr. Herman was now on my side. Part of his support may have been the result of his disgruntlement with the Bennett government, which had refused his newspaper a licence to operate a radio station. Because he did not get a licence, Mr. Herman resented the competition that radio gave him. When he heard me speak on the air during the 1935 campaign, he called me into his office and said: "Are you satisfied with the coverage we give you? Do you think this newspaper reports your position fairly? We do not like the other medium." This presented a challenge to me. Was I prepared to lose his support by using another medium, even though it was an effective one? Putting my cards on the table, I told Mr. Herman that radio was an important means of publicizing my beliefs and that I would continue to use it. Although he was peeved for a while, I think he respected me — in the end — for sticking to my guns.

The Liberal Party in Essex County soon completed its roster of candidates, and the excitement engendered in Belle River spilled over into Essex West. On 21 June, Norman McLarty defeated two other contenders in a packed Windsor Arena; he had been one of my first friends in Windsor, and I greeted his success enthusiastically. Murray Clark, a well-known farmer from Harrow, had been selected in March as the party's standard-bearer in Essex South. McLarty, most businessmen believed, was ministerial timber, and in the House Clark proved to be an energetic spokesman for the farmers.

Clearly the federal election campaign was on, and we all had great expectations. Provincial elections in Nova Scotia and British Columbia had been won by the Liberals in 1933, preceding Hepburn's win in Ontario and Jimmy Gardiner's triumph in Saskatchewan. In mid-August 1935, R. B. Bennett announced that polling day would be on 14 October, but in effect my campaign had been in high gear for almost a year.

As soon as the election was called, Bill Tubman installed himself in my campaign headquarters on Ellrose Avenue in East Windsor. Walkerville, Riverside and Tecumseh had separate campaign centres under Alf Morrell, Leo Renaud and Alice Renaud, all of whom worked like beavers on my behalf. Under Tubman's supervision, they organized the polls and recruited poll captains, canvassers and scrutineers, arranged cars to drive voters to the polling booths, made plans for babysitters, and set up meetings all over the riding — sometimes three in an evening.

There was no such thing as a "machine," but there did exist a zealous group of ordinary men and women — some teachers, the occasional clergyman, but essentially working men and women, who believed in the same things I did. People such as Connie Farquhar of Remington Park, one of the poorer districts in Windsor; Germaine Schiller, who lived with her mother in Riverside; Buster Riberdy, a maintenance man at Ford's, who served as my driver; and Tommy Couvillion, another Ford worker, who lived on Albert Road in East Windsor. It was much less of a machine than the "goon squads" that helped organize elections for the CCF. We did well because we worked hard. Never did a man have such loyal helpers; they are all part of my public life, and I know that the reason for the constancy of my electoral position in Essex East was that I did not forget them. As W. B. Yeats has said so truly:

> *Think where man's glory most begins and ends,*
> *And say my glory was I had such friends.*

I consulted everyone frequently and tried to assure each worker of his or her importance; this was essential. When there were disagreements, I would have to smooth ruffled feathers and try to keep everyone together. But I spent very little time in the committee rooms and relied on my campaign manager, Bill Tubman, who, like those who worked full-time, was reimbursed for his efforts. Strolling around town, I talked to voters in the stores on Ottawa Street or in the market, on church steps (I attended mass at a different church each Sunday), and sometimes at the factory gates early in the morning. Campaigning in the warm summer months was a particular delight.

The three Liberal candidates in Essex County ran well-coordinated campaigns, and we often shared a public platform. My law partner, Keith Laird, managed Norman McLarty's campaign, and Bill Tubman was ready to cooperate with anyone. Murray Clark had a different set of problems since his constituency was largely agricultural. He was a good organizer and normally would do most of the work himself, no matter who nominally managed the campaign. Murray would frequently call on me to speak at his meetings, especially in the small town of Essex.

During the campaign we basically ran our own show, receiving little financial help from the Liberal national office. The federal party paid for the newspaper display advertisements and sent us some pamphlets, but beyond that their contribution was minimal.[5] Our campaign funds were raised locally, mainly by Stan Springsteen and Keith Laird, who went out and solicited friends and local businesses for contributions. The corporations in the area diplomatically gave to both sides. All that Keith ever did was to point out that in a parliamentary democracy there had to be at least two political parties and that the Liberal Party was one of them. He promised nothing. Much of the money came from individuals who donated small amounts. Even Conservatives and CCFers quietly contributed to my campaign, although publicly they were working to defeat me. Finances were always a difficult problem, and my debts from 1935 were not paid off until two years later. The enormous cost of election campaigns always staggered me.

It was something of a sore point that the heads of the automobile plants — all Tories — gave the Liberal Party no financial assistance. Norman McLarty happened to be a great friend of Wallace Campbell, the president of the Ford Motor Company, and arranged for us to see him during the campaign to ask him to make contributions to all the political parties that were putting up candidates in Windsor. We left empty-handed. At the meeting, I told Campbell rather pointedly that donations helped our political system survive and reduced the likelihood of MPs receiving money from improper sources. The members in the Windsor area, Liberal or Conservative, spent more time working for the automobile companies than they did for any other interest group. The first donation we received from an automobile company was given by John Mansfield, the president of the Chrysler Corporation who,

5 Norman Lambert complained to his friend Grant Dexter that he feared a Liberal loss because of the shortage of funds (Dexter to Dafoe, 3 September 1935, J. W. Dafoe Papers, PAC).

during the war, handed Keith Laird a cheque on his own behalf, emphasizing that it had nothing to do with his company.

In politics one must be ever vigilant. Neglect or overconfidence is a common but dangerous attitude. I did not underestimate the risk of defeat and tried to leave nothing to chance. Lum Clark noted in the *Star* that "these are the days when the people show their resentment against conditions by voting out whichever group is in power, no matter what may be the politics of the governing party." In effect, the times were Liberal times; but I still felt like the underdog.

My Conservative opponent, Dr. Raymond Morand, had a very loyal following in the riding. If I had an advantage during the nomination tussle because of my French background, it was nullified during the election campaign. Morand's forebears had lived in Essex County for generations. He was a good doctor, as well as my personal physician and friend; all in all, far too strong a candidate for my liking and easily the most awesome of my opponents. Dr. Morand had faced no challenge for his nomination and arrived in Windsor after the parliamentary session, fresh for the struggle. When I developed a sore throat during the campaign, I sent for him. We were amused both by the situation and by his observation that he could render a public service by putting me out of commission.

The CCF candidate, Ben Levert, who ran a greenhouse business in Tecumseh, was also of French descent. Like me, he was an import — he came from Sturgeon Falls in northern Ontario. A powerful and witty speaker, Levert came close to demagoguery as he tried to mobilize the support of organized labour in the riding. I could not afford to overlook the potential appeal of the CCF in this industrial constituency. During this first national campaign for the CCF, Levert received the support of the local communists — most of whom lived in Essex East — and worked with their leaders,

Tom Raycraft and Reg Morris.[6] The Communist Party in Windsor drew its support from among the Ukrainian and Serbian communities, but some British immigrants and a few native-born Canadian workers were also party activists. In Essex East, the Ukrainian Labour Temple on Drouillard Road was their main gathering spot. Yet the communists were small in number — we arbitrarily said 3,000 votes in the Windsor area — and the great majority of the ethnic groups in the neighbourhood did not share their leanings or beliefs.

I knew Ben Levert quite well and at one point had to restrain my supporters from branding him a communist, telling them it was a mistake to start name-calling. One of my chief workers took me to task for this, insisting, "Paul, you cannot win elections this way." But I had meant what I said. Ben loved to explain the difference between socialism and communism; Saint Augustine, he said, was a communist in the social sense. When the communists gave Levert the kiss of death, Dr. Morand made capital out of the alliance. I called on Ben to deny the association, but he berated me for an "obnoxious" attempt to connect him with the Communist Party.[7]

Shortly after my nomination, H. H. Stevens, the former minister of trade and commerce in Bennett's government, announced that he was setting up a new political group, the Reconstruction Party, which would contest the election against his erstwhile leader and colleagues.[8] This created problems for Dr. Morand, who was a close friend of Stevens (before setting up the Reconstruction Party, Stevens had spoken at Morand's nomination). For a while, stories were bruited around Essex County that Dr. Morand would join Stevens, but in the end he did not, although he insisted on his right to take a stance independent of his party. Instead, the "Stevists" chose Gabe McPharlin, my opponent from the Liberal

6 I often wondered how much of Marx these two understood.
7 *WDS*, 8 October 1935.
8 Stevens resigned from Bennett's cabinet on 26 October 1934, exasperated that the prime minister was doing nothing to stop some retailers from price fixing.

nomination race, as their ensign-bearer in Essex East. He was not an effective candidate, but his entry into the race tended to draw support away from the official Conservative nominee and enhanced our chances of victory. The Stevists based their campaign on their leader's befriending the masses, and they claimed that people had to put up with high prices because of collusion among certain retailers. Stevens spoke to a crowd of three thousand at the Windsor Arena on 3 October; I quietly went to the meeting and came away deeply impressed by his stirring delivery and populist touch. The public at first seemed to look on the former minister as their champion, but his campaign eventually petered out.

The appearance of the new parties convinced me that many Canadians, agitated about the Depression, were willing to try radical measures. Even before I became the official candidate, I had formulated a position that, I hoped, would take into account the need for reform but at the same time would leave me space to manoeuvre within the Liberal Party. I was worried about the reluctance of Mackenzie King to espouse a reform platform. Every time I went to my law office, I saw evidence of the problem: there was always a line of people waiting to see me, pleading to help them find work and relief. If I had sat back and not talked about hopeful things, I would not have been elected. Dr. Morand understood the public mood and, long before Bennett had made his proposals for reform, had been pressing him to take measures to relieve the lot of the poor and the unemployed.[9] At one point Bennett thought that Dr. Morand was a closet socialist! Perhaps our attitudes had a great deal to do with the city we lived in, where a few large industries employed most of the workers, who forced

9 Series of letters between R. B. Bennett and R. D. Morand, R. B. Bennett Papers (p. 305354 ff.), PAC.

their politicians, aspiring or elected, to take strong steps to put
people back to work.

Before long, the situation confronted us starkly. The unemployed who had been sent to work in the Windsor wood yard went
on strike. Although the municipal council was opposed to forcing
men to work for relief, the provincial relief administrator had said
that they had been employed cutting wood for six months, during
which time they had not produced enough to earn their keep. As a
disciplinary measure, they had been given one-and-a-half days
work — with crosscut saws in the hot sun — for every day they did
not cut enough wood to support themselves. As soon as they went
on strike, their relief vouchers were stopped. The whole business —
reminiscent of a slave camp whose inmates were forced to do
unproductive work — distressed me greatly and increased my
resolve to try to do something about it.

The basic premise of my campaign — both for the nomination
and for the election — was the need for reform. First of all, I argued
that unless the Liberal Party carefully examined the economic
structure of society and adjusted its programs to meet people's
needs, it would disappear within ten years. This did not mean that
the party must adopt a totally new set of principles, but "the
application of old principles to new situations that would ensure
the greatest freedom, security and happiness for the greatest
number." In effect, I wanted to restrain "initiative that runs wild
to such an extent that it preys upon individuals."[10]

Since I had already staked out my territory, the announcement
of a reform program by R. B. Bennett in early January 1935 did
not disturb my course. Bennett's new deal promised huge state
intervention in the economy; he went on the radio and announced
plans to bring in legislation to provide unemployment insurance, a
minimum wage and set hours of work. Responding to these proposals, I told the voters of Essex East that it was too much to expect an old free enterprise dog to learn such new tricks. If he had
been sincere, I asked, why did he wait until just before an election

10 *Border Cities Star*, 6 December 1934. Report of a speech at Chatham.

for such a dramatic conversion? "I subscribe absolutely to Mr. Bennett's statement that capitalism has to be reformed," I said, but measures like unemployment insurance, while necessary, were on too small a scale to cope with the million and a quarter unemployed:

> The machinery of government today is not adequate to meet current needs. The division of governmental responsibility between the provinces and the Dominion illustrates this. . . . Social legislation was a matter definitely left to the provinces so that the Dominion Government has no power to deal with unemployment insurance and old age pensions and we therefore must remodel our government machinery in such a way that we can meet the problems of our day.[11]

My contention was that by raising tariffs, the federal government was creating unemployment. It therefore should enforce national standards for other programs, such as a universal minimum wage and pensions, through an amendment of the British North America Act.

In 1930, Bennett had said that he would provide work for everyone; by 1935 he had obviously failed to do this. In my opinion, "full employment," as conceived by Keynes and Beveridge — another British economist — was of paramount importance, and I set forth proposals to assist the aged, children and other dependent groups. Certainly recent recessions, including those of 1948, 1960 and the early 1980s, would have been unendurable if there had been no unemployment insurance, family allowances or old-age security. None of these excited when I put my name forward as the Liberal candidate for Essex East in the mid-1930s. It was my assertion then, as it is now, that social security benefits would not destroy incentives or make people less enterprising, and I emphasized the weakness of Bennett's plan, which was clearly contrary to the BNA Act. Earlier, Mackenzie King had maintained that Bennett's measures, correct in principle,

---

11 *Border Cities Star*, 19 January 1935.

could not see the light of day because they were unconstitutional. I further argued that the prime minister would have assured the Canadian people of the sincerity of his proposals if he had taken steps to make them constitutionally effective. "The people are tired of the old-time politics and politicians...and want their representatives to get down to earth and solve the problems of the day." As far as the Liberals were concerned, "criticism of Prime Minister Bennett and the Conservatives is not enough.... No party has the right to go into office only because it criticizes the party in power."[12]

My views on domestic and foreign affairs were linked, and I took pains to explain that one was an extension of the other, recalling the decline of the British Liberal Party, which had failed to adapt to the changed conditions of the early twentieth century. The world had become more complex and interdependent; not all nineteenth-century programs were relevant in the 1930s, and the Liberal Party of Mackenzie King would have to don the cloak of modernity and learn the international game of give-and-take in an interdependent world economy.

International relations assumed the spotlight when Mussolini ordered an invasion of Abyssinia ten days before the election. Even before this, I had always defended the League of Nations by telling audiences that although it would be criticized, "it is our only hope for peace." If the League failed and war came, I knew that Canadians would not be interested in shedding their blood for a cause far removed from them. After the Abyssinian invasion, my fellow countrymen grew increasingly nervous about Canadian participation in any conflict. While Mackenzie King argued that parliament should decide, I still believed that strong sanctions against Italy could avoid another war. I pledged that I would resign my seat rather than agree to a war, unless those who had to do the fighting were given the chance to decide the nation's course.[13] My argument was that an act of parliament could affirm

12 *Border Cities Star*, 7 June 1935.
13 *Border Cities Star*, 15 April 1935; *WDS*, 27 August 1935; ibid., 24 September 1935.

that Canada was not automatically at war when another part of the British Empire had been called to arms; if possible, the Canadian people should express their wishes in a plebiscite before any declaration of hostilities. It was very difficult for me to choose a course that would satisfy my own beliefs, the wishes of the voters, and the program of the Liberal Party.

Even though I mentioned foreign policy in most of my speeches, it was (and is) rarely an issue in election campaigns. But it was important for the voters of Essex East to know that foreign affairs had a high place on my personal agenda. Dr. Morand contented himself with accusing me of taking advantage of the popular and natural aversion to war in an effort to make that the issue.[14]

Voters in Essex East were concerned less with foreign problems than with industrial relations — the vital political issue in Windsor throughout the 1930s. In my student days in Toronto, I had read Mackenzie King's *Industry and Humanity* to learn about the background of the emerging industrial strife. The author believed that "in the cooperation of the parties to Industry along intelligent lines, they may yet be led to an application of principles which governing in all human relations, will best promote the wellbeing of mankind."[15] It is a rather pedantic book, but it did highlight the important thesis that each of the partners — labour, management and government — had its rights and obligations. No one could ignore the dangers of industrial friction and the economic paralysis and suffering that conflict could cause.

At this time, great changes were taking place in the trade union movement, particularly in Windsor, Toronto and Oshawa. Windsor was the home of the Ford Motor Company and other car manufacturers, and it was here, more than elsewhere, that the CCF aspired to become labour's political arm. I supported the unionization of those who worked in the car factories, but the United Auto Workers had not yet organized the Windsor plants.

14 *WDS*, 28 August 1935.
15 W. L. M. King, *Industry and Humanity: A Study in the Principles Underlying Industrial Reconstruction* (Boston: Houghton Mifflin, 1918), p. 28.

The unions' big test lay ahead: the Oshawa strike of 1937 confirmed the strength of trade unionism in a modern industrial democracy. Before this, though, the industrial unions, such as the Auto Workers, who wanted to represent all employees — skilled and unskilled — in the industry, had to push to gain recognition from the craft unions, who represented members of a single skilled trade. The main concern of the individual trade unionist in the 1930s was acquiring a job and a secure income, and I wondered how much the ordinary worker knew about the rivalry at the top of his union. From its founding, the CCF received increasing local support from union leadership. What the party did not get in Windsor was the backing of the rank and file.

In my speeches, I was at pains to emphasize that industry should be compelled to ensure that labour receive a fair return and secure employment.[16] Repeating my belief in the partnership of management and labour, a partnership which the working man had a right to share, it was painful to know deep down that I was expressing concepts that most people could not accept. Even some of the socialists who had things in common with me regarded me as a man with rather advanced political views.

There were both advantages and disadvantages in my stance. Many people were questioning as never before the validity of the free enterprise system, and more liberal ideas were gaining ground; Canadians were no longer satisfied with the status quo. I gained considerable support from young people, who thought that I somehow represented their fight against the Depression.[17] At a meeting in London, Ontario, King spoke of the participation of young men in political life and then mentioned my name. The cheer that followed gave me a big lift, although when I think about it now, it is clear that my name was used as a rather empty symbol. The older generation of that period was less accommodating towards youth than the elders of today, and I was one of very few young men selected as a Liberal candidate. My candidacy was my

16 *Border Cities Star*, 1 June 1935; *WDS*, 22 July 1935
17 J. W. Dafoe welcomed the participation of younger, active Liberals as "men of promise" (J. W. Dafoe to R. J. Cromie, 26 April 1935, Dafoe Papers (reel M77), PAC.

way of encouraging change, but it was so dispiriting that the Liberal Party was a little sluggish to move with the times. A lot of people regarded my views as dangerous, and many, both in the Liberal Party and outside it, treated me a little suspiciously. Even in Windsor, senior Liberals (including Norman McLarty) cautioned me that the private enterprise system was sacrosanct. Since any speech I made would be reported throughout the Windsor area, some of the other Liberal candidates objected to my views and told me that what I was saying was hurting them. Windsor, I used to explain, was an industrial island in this relatively wealthy rural region, and it was necessary for me to take industrial concerns into account.

Sometimes I wonder whether I would have lost a considerable amount of my rural following had I not had such great support from the French population of Essex East — with whom I shared a cultural affinity. My opponents, knowing that the sentiments I expressed were in advance of my party's position, delighted in pointing out this divergence at public meetings. About two months before the election, I was disheartened to find that our party had made no plans for a platform that espoused economic reform. I went to Ottawa and saw Mackenzie King to tell him that I hoped he would make strong speeches indicating that the Liberals supported an employment program and emergency measures to relieve the situation. When the campaign began, there was still no indication that the party felt any urgency to campaign on this platform. So I made another journey to Ottawa and reiterated my position to Claire Moyer, a sometime secretary to King and a man who had his ear. "You know," I said, "the speeches he is making are not going to do the trick; they're not going to satisfy my voters and they're not going to satisfy me. We have to announce programs to put people to work." Shortly after, Moyer told me that King would do something soon.

It pleased me greatly that Mackenzie King's radio broadcast early in August spelled out many of the ideas I had been promulgating. He told Canadians that the first priority of the Liberal Party was the provision of unemployment insurance. Credit, he stated, was a public matter of direct concern to the average citizen, and the party would support a properly constituted national central bank. My leader further pledged a plan for industrial reconstruction that would seek to give the workers and consumers a larger share in the government of industry and would contrive to effect a more equitable distribution of income. Nevertheless, I was irked that King's traditional adherence to balanced budgets overlooked the Keynesian solution to mitigating the consequences of high unemployment.

I addressed myself as well to my rural constituents. Essex County was a cash crop farm area (mainly corn and sugar beets) and provided higher income returns than other parts of the country. Charlie O'Brien, an active member of the Corn Growers' Association, helped me understand the problems of the corn grower, particularly the trade pacts of 1932 that allowed corn to enter Canada from South Africa duty free. I made much of the fact that the Bennett government not only had imported five million bushels of corn from South Africa but also had subsidized that country's corn growers to the tune of $500,000.[18]

Among the highlights of the campaign were two debates between Dr. Morand and me. The first took place at the Gordon McGregor School in the heart of East Windsor. The place was packed, and we had a spirited war of words, chaired by the mayor of the city, Colonel Wigle, who told me later that he thought the debate had helped establish me as a political personality in the community. Dr. Morand and I discussed unemployment and what the government was or was not doing about it, and also talked about the growth of combines and the low price of corn since the Conservatives had taken office. The hecklers were out in force and pushed Dr. Morand and me to new heights of quick response and rebuttal.

It was my impression that I had the debate well in hand, and from the applause it seemed as if I might have bested the master. But then I made a gaffe — one I have never forgotten. Sitting in

18 *WDS*, 13 September 1935.

the front row was a Morand supporter who began to question my statements with persistent and irritating grunts. At one point he shouted out, "I don't follow your argument." Furious, I yelled back, "What I am trying to point out, if your thick skull can take it in..." Bedlam broke out. There was tremendous revulsion in the audience, and they reacted very strongly against me. It sounded somehow as though I had accused them all of stupidity.[19] The incident taught me the virtues of patience and prudence, and I have never been quite so impetuous again. The soft touch is much more effective than an *ad hominem* attack. In general, I think that Dr. Morand and I had a very objective discussion of the issues throughout the campaign. We both were "students" of the times, and I remember feeling proud about some of the things we spoke about.

Shortly after my second debate with Dr. Morand, in Belle River, Vincent Massey came to Windsor to speak on my behalf. I had invited him down because I knew I was trailing my Tory opponent very badly in Walkerville. My feeling was that this prosperous community, the home of most of the city's business executives, would be impressed by Massey's presence. Although he was not a riveting speaker, his endorsement would benefit my cause.[20] "King or Chaos!" — the slogan that Massey helped devise — formed the substance of his speech to a packed Walkerville Collegiate.[21] Massey was not helped in his delivery by the unrelenting efforts of the *Windsor Star*'s photographer, who kept setting off his flash in Massey's face. My discouraging and frantic gestures at the photographer did not ingratiate me with the *Star*'s editorial chief, Ellison Young.

Before the meeting, the Masseys were dinner guests of the leading Liberals in the three ridings of Essex County. It was an occasion long remembered. Windsor's Simon Meretsky's speech

19 *WDS*, 17 October 1935.
20 With characteristic generosity, Massey also gave me a cheque for $1,500 to help cover my election expenses.
21 *WDS*, 11 October 1935.

was the *pièce de résistance* and a discourse that Massey enjoyed —
belying his undeserved reputation for stuffiness. Simon was one of
the city's most loveable and original characters. His delightfully
imperfect English, winsome accent and charming smile, which
showed up his many gold teeth, made him a most popular figure.
In certain parts of Essex East, no platform speaker was in greater
demand. I can see him yet, illustrating the evils of high tariffs.
From a black grip, he withdrew one article after another, with
suitably derisory comments, provoking his audience into uncon-
trollable laughter. A roll of toilet paper came last. Was the level of
the tariff on such an article appreciated? Simon asked, as the roll
slowly unfolded off the stage into the rows of clapping and approving listeners.

During the campaign, I made extensive use of the radio, giving
about twelve talks in all. Ted Campeau, the manager of the
CKLW station, taught me whatever broadcasting skills I was able
to develop. Radio technique was so different from that for the
platform. Whereas one talked quietly over the microphone, voice
inflection and a varying pace were effective in getting one's message across at a public meeting.

Early in the campaign, on 16 August, Mackenzie King spoke at
a large open-air meeting in London; all the Liberal candidates
from the region shared the platform. Before the proceedings
began, I sought out the party leader and told him that he must
reiterate the Liberals' concern about measures to alleviate unemployment. Unsympathetically, he told me that he intended to talk
about farm problems because southwestern Ontario was an important farming district. "Well," I said, "voters in London, Windsor,
St. Thomas, Sarnia and Stratford will be disheartened if you just
talk about farm problems. You must not overlook the tremendous
difficulties faced in urban centres." Although King appeared to be
unconvinced, he did make a pitch along the lines I had suggested.
It was the kind of forum where King excelled, and I told him that I
hoped he could arrange to visit Windsor before election day. To
my delight, a week before the big day, King came to speak to a

large audience in the Windsor Arena. The three candidates in the county spoke before the leader, and I took the opportunity to get off my chest some of the frustrations that had been building up gradually over the previous months. During the campaign, I said repeatedly that although I believed in the Liberal Party, I would not be a rubber stamp; I would exercise the liberal principle of private judgment and, if necessary, would criticize my own party.

With Mackenzie King sitting on the platform, I repeated my profession of independence, making it clear that "above my party I will place the interests of my country and my constituency, and to this end I will speak my mind in parliament or out." My remarks hit their target. Some months later, when I was taking a pretty independent stand on foreign policy in the Commons, the prime minister took me aside and said, "Martin, I always remember that speech you made about being independent. Let me give you some advice. You can be too independent."

Mackenzie King spoke of the third parties in his Windsor address. Although he tore apart the CCF platform, he was full of praise for J. S. Woodsworth's idealism. King said that the CCF could jeopardize national unity by postulating the class struggle but that they were just Liberals in a hurry in their proposals for social reform. He dubbed the Reconstruction Party "an outcrop of the Tories" and emphasized that the Liberal reforms had a lasting quality that the election would prove. If King had not addressed himself to the need for change in the economic system, I am convinced that my chances for success would have been uncertain at best.

As election day approached, tensions mounted. I stepped up the pace of canvassing and public speaking and tried to show that Dr. Morand was jumping on my bandwagon and making free with my ideas. In one radio broadcast, I noted that "at a recent meeting, Dr. Morand said he was in favour of state medicine in limited terms, to include hospital and medical insurance, something I advocated last February." The doctor was not as interested as he made out, I maintained. Two years previously, he had opposed such a scheme, saying that it savoured of communism. Just before election day, I had a terrible scare. Three months previously, under the supervision of David Croll, residents of the town of Walkerville had strenuously opposed the amalgamation of their affluent municipality with the bankrupt city of Windsor. Feelings ran so high against Croll that I felt my chances were doomed when a card was shoved into every Walkerville house proclaiming boldly, "A vote for Paul Martin is a vote for David Croll." Alf Morell, who headed my workers in Walkerville, was very despondent: results in Walkerville would have been adverse enough in any event, but with this he could see disaster looming. Another of my workers, the energetic Joe Delaney, saved the day. He got together a group of boys, and during the dead of night they took every card they could find from the doors of the houses in Walkerville.

On the morning of election day, I visited the city polling booths, going on in the afternoon to those in the rural townships. There was not much I could do but be seen and give an encouraging word as I moved through the constituency during the long, nerve-wracking day.

By the evening I was back in our headquarters on Ellrose Avenue to listen to the returns. Unconfirmed early reports were not good, in spite of the cheers that went up when it was announced that I had won two of the four votes cast in the advance poll and was in front by one vote. When Walkerville reported, Dr. Morand had a substantial lead, but as the returns came in from Tecumseh and Sandwich East, I went ahead. The first returns from Windsor favored Ben Levert. This startled me, but Bill Tubman said he would rather lose votes to the CCF than to the Tories. At this point, Tubman and Ernie Chauvin, who were calculating the outcome, told me that I had won. Pessimistic until the last, I found their self-assurance premature, particularly when my plurality dwindled to twenty-one votes a bit later. When more rural returns arrived and my lead was 940, everyone began to celebrate, threatening to throw me out of the committee room if I did not cheer up. The final count left me 1,163 votes in front of Dr.

Morand.[22] Norman McLarty and Murray Clark won too, and a large Liberal majority was elected to Ottawa.

Before we left the committee room, I called my mother to tell her the news. She hoped that I would thank God — and my workers — for a job well done. Then our troupe moved to the *Windsor Star* offices, where, according to custom, the gladiators went either to enjoy success or to concede defeat. Mr. Herman and his staff were obviously well pleased with the results. At my next stop, CKLW, Ted Campeau and his crew welcomed me like a hero. I gave a brief radio speech, thanking the voters for their confidence in me. It occurred to me that I was perhaps lucky to have won; my majority was not something to boast about. Nevertheless, it pleased me later to receive a telegram of congratulation from my leader.

The night's festivities were far from over. Now began a ritual that was repeated at each successive election night — a cavalcade through the riding. The first stop was in Remington Park, where I recalled events in the long campaign. Then on to Walkerville, our headquarters in East Windsor, and our rooms in Riverside and Tecumseh. The parade grew with each stop. After one in the morning, on the main street in Belle River, the scene of my nomination, several hundred people met the cars from the city, carrying the torch of celebration. Then on to Pointe Aux Roches, and the home of Raoul Chauvin. An endless line of lighted automobiles moved along the long dirt road and on to St. Joachim, where I spoke in French: "La victoire, c'est à vous. C'est vous qui avez gagné aujourd'hui." Our final stop, the Maidstone home of Tom and Alice Shanahan, was engulfed by the friendly invasion of happy well-wishers.

22 The final count was:

Martin	— 7,579
Morand	— 6,416
Levert	— 4,167
McPharlin	— 1,110

VI

Warming the Bench

"**Y**OUR REPRESENTATIVE," said Edmund Burke to his Bristol constituents in 1774, "owes you, not his industry only, but his judgment. . . ."[1] Strongly influenced by the British parliamentary tradition, I tried to follow this precept throughout my time as an elected representative — and no more so that in my first five years on the Hill, when I worked as assiduously as a backbencher could to further the cause of world peace and to promote measures that would ameliorate the lives of Canadians hurt by the Depression. If I had it to do all over again, I wonder if I would have gone into politics as early as I did. I feel that a member of parliament who has spent most of his life in the House can get stale and may at times be regarded as an institution. The voters often get so used to him that they forget what he has achieved over the years on their behalf. This occasional thought, however, did not persist. Public life was my *métier* and my vocation.

From the early days of my political life, I was a liberal, committed to effecting human betterment and security, even if that meant

---

1 B. W. Hill, (ed.), *Edmund Burke on Government, Politics and Society* (New York: International Publications Service, 1976), p. 157.

disagreeing with fellow party members. At perhaps the third meeting of caucus after the 1935 election, I spoke about the need for partnership in industry. My purpose was to appeal directly to Mackenzie King, but he studiedly avoided any reference to my remarks in his summing-up. Shortly afterwards, though, he took me aside and said, "Martin, don't worry. What you advocate is admirable and will stand you in good stead in time. A Liberal must always be a reformer."

When I entered the House of Commons in 1935, the progressive stamp of my liberalism, the nature of the industrial constituency I represented, my youth and educational background all set me apart from many of my caucus colleagues. Although I did not know every member of the cabinet announced by Prime Minister King on 23 October — nine days after the election — their reputations did not leave me optimistic that the party leadership was about to adopt the views I espoused.

As I got to know the new ministers, many of them men of exceptional talent, my impression was confirmed. Norman Rogers, who was assigned the labour portfolio, was the only one who generally shared my reformist beliefs. Charles Dunning, the minister of finance, represented the voice of big business and economic orthodoxy in the cabinet. Long-time Kitchener MP, W. D. Euler, and C. D. Howe — respectively heads of the department of trade and commerce and of the department of the marine — shared Dunning's more conservative outlook. The durable T. A. Crerar, the minister of mines and of immigration, remained a defender of nineteenth-century laissez-faire liberalism and seemed blind to the problems of industrial society. If ever there was a generation gap in politics, it was between Crerar and me. I greatly admired Ernest Lapointe, the minister of justice and a towering figure, for his efforts to build a country where two cultures could coexist happily; but he, too, was far from a radical. James Lorimer Ilsley, the minister of national revenue, who became a great friend and my mentor, never shared my sympathy towards modern industrial unionism. Chubby Power, the popular and jocular minister of pensions and national health, was an able spokesman, but only after the war did I realize the depth of his concern for human rights. Another influential member of cabinet, J. G. Gardiner, the minister of agriculture, was a doughty champion of the farming community, particularly the wheatgrowers of the West.

Mackenzie King had some doubts about who should be the cabinet member from southwestern Ontario. My suspicion that he would choose J. C. Elliott, from London, was confirmed when the cabinet list was posted. Elliott, who was certainly not going to set the world alight no matter what ministry he was given,[2] became postmaster general. Murray Clark and I had momentary hopes for Norman McLarty; he would have been an asset to the new administration, and his WASP background and Presbyterianism blended well with our region's political tradition. We also thought the prime minister might have brought in the Liberal whip, Ross Gray, from Lambton West, but Gray's friendship with Mitch Hepburn probably deterred King. Even before the cabinet was announced, Hepburn had tried to influence the prime minister's selection. George McCullaugh, the publisher of *The Globe and Mail* and a Hepburn adviser, put on a dinner for the Ontario members of the new parliament to press for the appointment of Arthur Slaght, a leading Toronto lawyer who was coming into the House for the first time. I supported King's rejection of Slaght, perhaps because of his veto of me in 1934 as assistant counsel to him on an important probe established by the Liberal provincial government.

In early November, before the House assembled, Murray Clark and I came to Ottawa to be sworn in and to take the oath of allegiance. The clerk of the House of Commons, Dr. Arthur Beauchesne, who held this office for many years, was in charge of the

2 H. Blair Neatby, *William Lyon Mackenzie King*, Vol. III, *1932-1939: The Prism of Unity* (Toronto: University of Toronto Press, 1976), pp. 132-33. Elliott became a member of the Liberal cabinet on 8 March 1926, serving as minister of labour and minister of soldier's civil re-establishment until the ministry resigned for the short-lived Meighen government. He then took over as minister of public works from 25 September 1926 until 6 August 1930. Elliott was again appointed postmaster general on 23 October 1935, a position he held until 22 January 1939, when he was asked to resign.

proceedings. The indispensable Beauchesne, self-satisfied and devious, took custody of parliament's procedures from his long table on the floor of the House. Clad in his black robes and tricorn hat, he reminded me of a Machiavellian cleric.

During this first session, I shared an office on the fifth floor with Tom Farquhar, from Algoma East, a much older man than me; he was the MP who resigned this safe seat in 1948 to give Mike Pearson a chance to enter parliament. Most of our neighbours on the corridor were from the West or the Maritimes; I was the only member on that floor with a French Canadian background. Office accommodation and facilities in those days were less than ideal; only senior MPs had a private secretary. Tom Farquhar and I had one stenographer between us, and it was very difficult to work while the other was dictating. Dozens of MPs did not know how to dictate a letter easily and would tie up a secretary for hours while their officemate sat there fuming. Recalling Lord Morley's advice to the new parliamentarian — "Use the library" — I took to going down there to work. On the whole, our offices were better than the pokey little rooms in Westminster but were not as commodious and well-furnished as those in the United States Congress. How much easier our job would have been if we had had the same facilities as members of parliament today — research and secretarial staff on hand and decent constituency offices.

There were several receptions following the opening day of my first parliament, 6 February 1936.[3] I had hoped that both my parents would come to Ottawa for the occasion, but my father preferred to stay at work — he was a little shy, I think. My mother travelled down from Pembroke; it was her day, too, and she wore an elegant long dress for the first time in her life. She and the family had worked so unselfishly to help qualify me for my new duties, and it

---

3 After the clerk of the House announced that the chief justice and deputy governor general, Sir Lyman P. Duff, would open parliament in the afternoon, the MPs had to choose a Speaker. King proposed Pierre François Casgrain, the member for Charlevoix-Saguenay. R. B. Bennett objected that Casgrain, the previous Liberal whip, would not be impartial, but he was elected on division (House of Commons, *Debates*, 6 February 1936, p. 2 ff.).

was with great pride that I introduced her to some of the personalities on Canada's parliamentary stage. The sight of a small number of privy councillors — Ernest Lapointe was one dressed in Windsor unfiorms — made me take a second look, although I cannot recall any of them wearing that garb again.

The three members for Essex County were assigned seats in the back row of the Liberal benches, on Mr. Speaker's right. I shared a desk with a former classmate at Osgoode Hall, Lionel Chevrier, the new member for Stormont; thus began our long parliamentary association — Lionel and I joined the cabinet at the same time in 1945.

In the following weeks, as I came to know my fellow back-benchers, I discovered that very few of them felt as I did about the direction the government should take. Most of the young members from Québec were essentially generalists, expressing little interest in long-term policy. Malcolm Mclean, of Melfort, Saskatchewan, whose office was next to mine, used to stretch out on his couch reading; usually Thomas Carlyle or Matthew Arnold — seldom anything to do with current party programs. Gerry McGeer, of Vancouver, something of a demagogue, fancied himself as a monetary reformer. He was a powerful speaker and always had the attention of Mackenzie King, who feared that McGeer, with his great bellowing voice, would single out the prime minister for some caustic remark. Lionel Chevrier was very caught up promoting the St. Lawrence seaway, admittedly a great project.

It was a shock to find that the party's emphasis was on political activities and not on social and economic programs. When they got together, members frequently talked solely about political tactics and how to gain party advantage. There was an interest in public questions, but my fellow Liberals' pursuit of larger issues frequently had too partisan a slant; I was not free from this myself. A member would stand up in caucus to raise a grievance and would complain about this particular policy or that, generally arguing that if no change occurred, the government, the party and he would suffer. When I left the House in 1968, the members of the House of

Commons were better informed and less political than their predecessors. This, perhaps, reflects the times. But I believe their greater
competence and tempered partisanship grew in part out of Pierre
Trudeau's emphasis on participatory democracy when he assumed
the prime ministership. In the Liberal caucus of the 1960s, MPs
were, on the whole, better educated than their predecessors; they
tended to look more for solutions to problems than for temporary
political advantage.

I attribute the earlier concentration on political manoeuvre
partly to the small extent to which the ordinary member had an
opportunity to shape policy. When I was elected, my expectation
was that I would not only represent my constituency but would
also help devise responses to the great issues of the day. Committee
work was much more restricted than it is now: government bills
were not presented to caucus ahead of time, there were no caucus
committees to investigate policies, and few backbenchers made
special efforts to have government matters brought before caucus
— which was basically a gripe session. We were therefore called
upon in parliament to approve measures without having had an
opportunity to amend or influence them. In the late 1960s, the
practice was changed: caucus insisted on greater participation in
government legislation, which was outlined to it before being
presented to parliament and the public. Whether this system
works well and gives the backbenchers a greater say is another
question, but the special caucuses to inform members of the
government's plans were a major innovation. This was the type of
thing that I had hoped to find when I first went into the House.
Disappointed when I discovered there was no such consultation, I
began to agitate for improved communication between the
cabinet and the private member. Government MPs, I argued,
should perhaps be assigned to particular ministers to perform roles
in the department.

In our caucus in the 1930s we would discuss the general desirability of a particular measure (unemployment insurance, for
example) but would never hash over a specific plan beforehand.

Mackenzie King — and parliamentary practice and tradition — was against it. The expanded role of the backbencher has led to the establishment of active caucus committees; the full meeting of caucus usually lasts a couple of hours — far too short a time for a review of complex measures. The intention when the committees were set up was that they could pronounce on policy before it was finally approved by the executive. The original idea was that such a system would help to make parliament more than a rubber stamp, but, unhappily, this has not proven to be the case.

In my first caucus, I was amazed to hear such a babble of voices claiming attention from the ministers. Members from industrial areas were demanding more assistance for the unemployed. But this problem did not mean as much to prairie representatives, who kept up a steady barrage about farm incomes and overseas markets for Canadian grain. I remember the members from western Canada as more active in caucus, at the time, than any other sectional group and found it hard to see how the Liberal Party could possibly be sustained in the face of such diverse and conflicting grumbles from all parts of the country. But, before long, I realized that the nature of Canada would inspire similar divisions in any national party.

Mackenzie King was the master of the caucus, listening attentively to whoever had the floor. I can hear the voices even now — Walter Tucker, of Rosthern, Dr. A. M. Young, of Saskatoon, and Malcolm Mclean, westerners competing against people like me, Gerry McGeer, and some of the Quebec members, who were so preoccupied with the widespread unemployment. At the close of a caucus meeting, King would always speak at some length (Louis St. Laurent and Mike Pearson talked for only a couple of minutes, while Pierre Trudeau was the briefest of all), taking into account every argument to weave together the threads of difference and pointing out how difficult it was to run Canada and how fortunate it was that there was a Liberal Party to take charge. We would finish with much cheering and gratitude that God Almighty had selected such a great man to be our leader. Some of King's best speeches were made in caucus; he used it to keep the party together, and powerful oratory was his instrument.

In my first session, Ross Gray, the Liberal whip, did not encourage members to study or to think up new programs — and asking too many questions of ministers in the House was frowned upon. Bill Golding, who chaired the caucus, was chosen by Mackenzie King for his reliability, moderation and admiration of the leader, and he once cautioned me not to become too outspoken.

It took a while to learn that a backbencher could pursue a matter quietly. One could not count too often on putting an oral question to a minister — apart from the scrictures of party discipline, fair opportunity for the opposition restricted government members — but the carefully written question frequently proved potent. In theory, these questions could be asked in unlimited numbers, and if they were on an important subject, the press would likely give coverage to both the question and the reply.

Mackenzie King liked opposition from his own side no more than any party leader, but I always felt that a member could simultaneously fulfil his obligations to his constituents and remain loyal to his party; it was important for the parliamentarian to address issues that he or she considered important. For me, this meant agitating for measures to protect Essex County corn growers or speaking on foreign policy, perhaps more than cabinet ministers would have liked. There were some MPs who merely approved everything the government did, never taking an independent stand; they got along, but they did not usually leave their mark in parliament. Generally, if a backbencher felt strongly about a matter and stated his case effectively, no exception was taken.

However, I was not absolutely alone as a Liberal advocating a progressive position. Brooke Claxton, a Montreal lawyer, felt very much the same way, but he did not join me in parliament until 1940, and for the first five years, only Normal Rogers seemed to share my reformist views. I had known Rogers slightly before I went to Ottawa — he was at gatherings of groups interested in international affairs and also at the Port Hope conference in 1933 — and had found him more prepared to adopt a "new deal" liberalism than any other leading member of the party. Norman was an intellectual who belonged neither to management nor to labour, but yet had strong sympathy for the oppressed. I came to see a good deal of him and would often go up to his office to have a chat. At one point he asked the prime minister whether I could act as his parliamentary assistant; King was unwilling to sanction it and said that if Rogers kept pressing for an assistant or let it be known that I was helping him, other members would become annoyed. So Norman arranged for me to work for him on the quiet, lending a hand with speeches on unemployment and on social questions. I devilled away quite happily.

Although at first I found few soulmates among the members, before long I began to develop a community of interest with a number of departmental officials. I had no quarrel with the bureaucracy — indeed I always found its officers obliging — but I was not satisfied with the liaison between the members of parliament and the public service. I felt that improvements could be made in keeping MPs better informed about particular departments; for example, a House committee on estimates should examine officials directly. In the public service at that time, it was fairly easy to separate the wheat from the chaff, and the abler public servants shared my interest in international affairs and economic and social questions. Occasionally I went along to the Chateau Laurier cafeteria, where many senior public servants had lunch. No other MP joined the group until Brooke Claxton came along in 1940. One of those who held court at the Chateau luncheons was Norman Robertson, a first secretary in the department of external affairs and one of Dr. Skelton's brightest protégés. I greatly enjoyed these midday discussions and learned a good deal from them.

Of the mandarins, I grew quite close to W. A. (Bill) Mackintosh, who had come to Ottawa from Queen's University to work on the National Employment Commission, which answered to Norman Rogers. Bill was a strong proponent of a system of unemployment insurance. Through him, I got to know Clifford Clark, the deputy minister of finance, whom I used to phone up and say, "Well, you don't have a budget to prepare. Can I come over for a chat?" Even before coming to Ottawa, I had met the undersecretary of state for external affairs, Dr. O. D. Skelton, at League of Nations Society meetings.[4] Knowing of my interest in foreign affairs, Skelton wondered during my first year in parliament whether I might like to join his department, but of course it was out of the question.

Despite King's reassurance about my independence of mind, I believe that my so-called "left-wing" propensity did eventually hurt me with certain senior figures in the party. They perhaps saw me as being too close to the CCF — a view my constituents did not endorse. Sometimes I perhaps went too far even for Mackenzie King, but I believe he saw my views as an asset to the party — certainly the CCF would have made more gains in Windsor and in other industrial cities if I had not taken the positions that I did. My progressivism likely induced King to appoint me parliamentary assistant to the minister of labour in 1943 and then to the national health and welfare portfolio three years later. But in 1958, when the party came to consider who should succeed Louis St. Laurent as leader, many delegates thought that my outlook was too close to the CCF's, even though no other minister had been so hounded by that party.

During my first session, I did have a lot of sympathy with the CCF point of view and could find a sort of common ground in some of the measures they were proposing. Perhaps I got a certain thrill out of considering myself more modern than most of my party. Yet although I accepted social democracy, I could never sanction the idea that the state should own the instruments of production. That was the basic philosophy of the CCF's Regina Manifesto and a view propounded by the British socialist Harold Laski, who was a great influence on many of the intellectuals in the

---

4 Skelton had strong reservations about the League of Nations; but, as the deputy minister responsible for foreign affairs, he felt constrained to attend the meetings of the Society.

CCF. After reading Laski's book, *Faith, Reason and Civilization*,[5] I knew that he was a Marxist. He wrote of a system in which the state controlled all economic activity and where there was no room for religious faith or for the questioning of socialist doctrine.

I had very little time for the doctrinaire position of CCFers and felt that many left-wing MPs themselves did not really understand socialism. Abe Heaps, who had represented Winnipeg North, believed in the cause of trade unionism and labour, in a nineteenth-century sort of way. When we were in London together in 1945, Heaps, who had left politics, came with me to meet Laski, who, as I remembered from my student days, held regular evening discussions in his home. At one point, Abe asked Laski a question, and the great socialist theoretician tore him apart. It hurt Abe beyond words. Turning to me with tears in his eyes, he said, "I have fought for the ordinary man and woman more than Laski ever has or ever will. I do not belong to these people."

Undoubtedly Heaps was correct, since he and most others in his party fought for social legislation, not socialism. Unemployment insurance, for instance, was not necessarily a socialist measure; it was an assurance to working people of their right to human dignity. When the CCF MPs Grant MacNeil, Abe Heaps and Angus MacInnis advocated it, I was right behind them. In the House committees, I frequently argued the same case as the CCF members and sometimes voted with them; they performed a very necessary function by talking at length — sometimes like broken records — about social needs. I do not think the CCF has ever had more attractive or abler representatives than in this eighteenth parliament.

Most CCFers admired the idealism of their leader, J. S. Woodsworth, although not everyone knew the extent to which he practised what he preached. On one occasion, when I was on my way to Windsor, I saw Woodsworth get on the same train as me; but when I looked for him in the club car, he was nowhere to be found. The conductor told me that he always sat in a coach. I bought Woodsworth a ticket for the club car and went to fetch him, but he

5 Harold Laski, *Faith, Reason and Civilization* (New York: The Viking Press, 1944).

would not change seats, telling me he would rather see the dollar and fifty cents go to help the poor. On another occasion, he came clandestinely to my apartment in Windsor to spend the night. He had been speaking to the CCF workers in the city and did not want them to know that he was staying with a Liberal. There was nothing shameful in it, he explained, but it had to do with the party's esprit de corps.

During my first session, the sole member of the Reconstruction Party, H. H. Stevens, sat by himself on the opposition benches. In the heat of the election campaign, it had looked as if Stevens might return to parliament with the makings of a third party, but that did not happen. Despite his abilities, Stevens demonstrated that it was not easy for a party to survive against the two major groups unless, like the CCF, it was backed by a following with a strong ideology. Stevens was not the champion of a new social order; he was a pragmatist who wanted to correct abuses in the economic system. Once back in the House, he lacked the loftiness and thrust of the reformer who had captivated the electorate during the first weeks of the campaign. He rejoined the Conservatives in 1938 but did not run again in 1940. At several points in my career, there were occasions when fundamental disagreements with cabinet policy made me contemplate resignation. But Stevens's ultimate fate gave me second thoughts, and so I was able to avoid the same error. It has been my observation that impulse often plays a great part in resignations. I do not deny that a minister sometimes has no course but to quit; however, those who act hastily may find that further public service is denied them.

The leader of the opposition, R. B. Bennett, was one of the most fascinating men in the House. Immaculately dressed in a short black coat, starched wing collar and cuffs, he sat at his desk on the front bench, listening to whoever had the floor or writing busily. There were few, if any, better parliamentary debaters, but he had a tendency to prolixity. Jimmy Gardiner once had a field day ridiculing Bennett's long-windedness by quipping that if a member mentioned the name of a British ship, the leader of the opposition would reel off the names of every vessel in the navy; he went on to say that if there was a suggestion that a few words of French might be incorporated on the Bank of Canada's paper money, Bennett would recite the history of Canada!

One of the most hilarious episodes concerning Bennett occurred when Ernest Lapointe was piloting the RCMP estimates through the House in 1936. General Sir James MacBrien, the force's commissioner, sat at the table on the floor of the House and had to listen to Agnes Macphail, the sharp-tongued CCF member, attack his salary as exorbitant, given the hardship of many Canadians. Naturally, General MacBrien could not answer her. Before Mr. Lapointe could respond, Bennett caught the Speaker's eye. "Some thirty years ago in western Canada," intoned R. B., as he began a windy peregrination through the past, "there was a constable in the Northwest Mounted Police whose name was James H. Mac-Brien...." Bennett was as impassioned in MacBrien's defence as Macphail had been in her attack. In fact, his adjectives were so excessive that the address began to sound like a panegyric. Jean François Pouliot, the member for Témiscouata and the stormy petrel of the Liberal Party — and no admirer of MacBrien — cried out, "Is he dead? This sounds like a funeral oration." Amid the resulting hoots of laughter, the Speaker called it six o'clock and adjourned the House.[6]

Bennett's knowledge was indeed prodigious, although he was capable of a little bluff, as I soon ascertained. In full flight on the opening day of my first session, Bennett, looking directly at me, made some reference to a House address by Sir Wilfrid Laurier. Doubtful that Laurier had ever thus expressed himself, I sent for the relevant Hansard. Looking at the named page, I found that the debate concerned a completely different subject, during which Laurier had said not a word. Bennett must have taken immediate advantage of the opportunity given to members to "set the record straight" by making a change to the Hansard "blues" before it

6 House of Commons, *Debates*, 22 June 1936, pp. 4074-76.

went to press. This would not have been the first time a member rewrote Hansard, contrary to the rules of the House.

After the 1935 election, Bennett was a little stiff with me and replied rather formally to my letter of congratulation on his personal victory in Calgary.[7] When I met him later, he shook my hand and said, "I suppose now that you are a member of parliament, you think you are the most important man in Canada. Well you are, I suppose, in one sense. But I want you to know that as a backbencher in the party of Mackenzie King, you are nothing more than a rubber stamp." Yet, having delivered this warning, he was always very kind to me and occasionally invited me up to his apartment in the Chateau Laurier; he even came over to our side of the House to sit and chat. When Bennett left Ottawa on his retirement, he departed a lonely and unappreciated man; I was one of the very few to see him off at Ottawa's railway station.

Unlike Bennett, Mackenzie King was not regarded as a consistently effective House of Commons debater. I have heard him deliver powerful addresses outside the Chamber, but I cannot recall many great speeches by King inside the House. I was particularly disappointed with his first speech of the 1935 session and generally found that he relied overmuch on prepared texts. In my view, there is a good deal to be said for departing from a written address. Nevertheless, King's speeches read well in Hansard and leave a better record to posterity than many others. My view of King's parliamentary oratory, however, should perhaps be considered in the light of his consummate skill in the Commons; the prime minister can make his authority felt without being on his feet all the time. King knew exactly when to intervene. John Diefenbaker, on the other hand, was not as shrewd when he was prime minister, and although he was a talented debater, his interventions often had less impact because he was on his feet all the time.

7 Martin to Bennett, 2 November 1935, R. B. Bennett Papers (p. 519745), PAC; Martin to Bennett, 20 November 1935, ibid. (p. 519746).

From the beginning of my parliamentary life, I was determined to express my ideas on foreign policy, but several factors inhibited my contribution: the House's interest in agriculture and King's attitude about private members speaking out on international affairs.

Parliament's interests depend greatly on the character of the party in power and on the regions of the country strongly represented in the governing party. In my first session, the strength of Liberal representation from the prairie provinces ensured that agriculture, and not international issues, would be one of the major topics for discussion within caucus. In addition, members of the House did not see Canada as an important industrial power but regarded the country as a community sustained by agriculture; they therefore downplayed issues relating to industry.

The fact that Jimmy Gardiner, the agriculture minister, came from Saskatchewan (he had been lured into his federal portfolio from the premier's office) increased the attention given to grain and the grain trade. Likewise, the presence of a large contingent of Social Credit members from rural Alberta made it absolutely certain that the problems faced by Canada's farmers would be spoken about *ad nauseam*. Between 1935 and 1940, we heard far too much about Social Credit monetary policy. Wheat was another obsession. One of the House manoeuvres at this time was to find some way of stopping the Social Credit leader, John Blackmore, from taking up time repeating Major Douglas's theorems.[8] This was not easy to do, but the minister of finance, Charles Dunning, would make approaches to convince Blackmore that the speech would go over better at a later date. When that moment arrived, another effort would be made to postpone Blackmore's expositions.

A few years later, Cyrus MacMillan, chairman of the English department at McGill University and MP from Prince Edward Island, wrote a poem, every stanza of which ended with the lines:

8 Major Clifford Hugh Douglas, a British "economist," originated the theory of social credit. In 1935, he became chief reconstruction adviser to the Alberta government, but he soon resigned.

"But the damndest word/I ever heard/Was that word/Wheat, wheat, wheat!" Many of us from eastern Canada memorized the couplet and would mouth it to one another in the House whenever westerners started in on one of their two pet topics.

Mackenzie King did not encourage private members to speak out on international relations. As the weeks wore on, I grew more and more frustrated because I had not yet addressed the House. So I resolved to ask my first question. At question period on 27 February 1936, I inquired whether the prime minister would be prepared to make a statement about the assassination of a prominent Japanese statesman during an uprising of young army officers in Tokyo the previous day. It was unusual for a Liberal backbencher to ask a question on foreign policy, and King replied curtly that he had nothing to add to the press reports. Actually, the question had been suggested to me by Norman Robertson when we had lunched together a few hours before in the Chateau Laurier. My impression was that King thought the question presumptuous. Earl Lawson, a Tory friend sitting near Bennett in the front row of the Conservative benches, sent a note across the aisle telling me that it was clear from the look on King's face that I had pulled a boner. In spite of my strong belief that what I had done was dutiful and designed to encourage greater interest in foreign affairs, this was far from a moment of triumph. Ross Gray later told me at dinner that backbenchers with little experience were not in the habit of asking such questions of their leader.

I got no support from King the following year when I advocated that the House establish a committee to deal specifically with external affairs instead of continuing to lump them together with industrial relations. So determined was the prime minister to retain sole grasp of foreign policy that a separate committee was not established until 1949.

I am pleased that by the time I left parliament, committees of the House of Commons had far more latitude than in the 1930s. This came about partly because recent governments have needed to spend considerably more hours discussing matters in the House than earlier administrations. When I was first elected, backbenchers used to have time on two days a week to bring in resolutions and two hours for private members' bills. Now, in order that the government may deal adequately with its program, back-benchers have about four hours a week of House time, apart from question period. Members agitated for more opportunity to air their views on various subjects, and the committees provided such a vehicle.

Nevertheless, all this early discouragement did not prevent me from closely following the international situation. The Italian invasion of Abyssinia gave rise to a major crisis about the time of the 1935 election. Like Scott Macdonald, Mike Pearson and Norman Robertson in the department of external affairs, I was a strong proponent of the view that collective security was a prerequisite of peace. Just before the 1935 election, the League of Nations Assembly convened to consider Article XVI of the covenant, which empowered the League's members to impose sanctions on aggressors. Using his own discretion, Howard Ferguson, the head of Canada's delegation and our high commissioner to Britain, voted with the majority of League members to affirm that the Italians had contravened the covenant. It was cheering that Ferguson showed such initiative; his action prevented Canada from undermining the League.

Before and after the Liberal victory, despite King's and Skelton's reservations, W. A. Riddell, our man in Geneva, served on the League's committee that was considering economic sanctions against Italy. There, he pressed for additions to a proposed list of embargoed goods and, early in November, suggested appending petroleum, as well as iron and steel, to the commodities that Italy would not receive. Since the Canadian government had not responded to his telegram asking for instructions, Riddell, assuming that Ottawa had consented, began discussions with the French and the British. The sanctions committee endorsed his proposal. Italy declared that this meant war. To my dismay, the King government repudiated Riddell's initiative a month later. Mackenzie King, like most Canadians at that time, was disposed to limit the activities of the League. He saw it as a forum for debate and discussion and a place to reach accommodation, but he had no faith in the institution's capacity for collective action and security. Despite the contrary opinions of Norman Rogers, King's view of the situation was supported by Dr. Skelton and held the day. Yet the government did take care to explain that this was not by itself a rejection of the principle of economic sanctions. The effort to contain Italian aggression collapsed and weakened the League immeasurably.

As someone who wanted the League of Nations to succeed, the outcome of the Abyssinian affair upset my illusions of international order; in my opinion, "the law" was for nations as much as for individuals. I did not subscribe to King's theory that Canada's backing down helped avert a European war. Who can deny that the hesitancy and failure of the member states of the League of Nations to confront the aggressor in 1935 encouraged Hitler four years later? Nonetheless, I think that what the prime minister was concerned about was clear: that our membership in the League could involve us in international situations that might bring about divisions at home, notably between French and English Canadians who remembered the schism over Canada's participation in the Great War. But this should not have absolved Canada from taking an independent stand, since League membership created problems for other countries too. Peace among the nations was a vital national consideration. If, as seemed obvious, the various governments were cutting the ground out from under the League, what then could we do? I supposed that I must support the principle of collective security with all my might, but recognize reality in a situation that was becoming a question of *sauve qui peut.*

The first debate on sanctions in the parliamentary session did not take place until mid-June 1936. A supply motion to approve the estimates of the department of external affairs — specifically, the salaries and expenses of the Canadian office in Geneva — provided the occasion. In his avuncular way, R. B. Bennett had spoken to me previously about waiting for the right opportunity to make my maiden speech. When the estimates were called, his secretary phoned to say that the leader of the opposition had suggested that the time was now ripe. I wondered why my own chief had not encouraged me in the same way.

That I had not spoken in the House, except for a few inconsequential questions, bothered me. My public utterances during the election campaign and afterwards, I assumed, had indicated to the voters of Essex East that I would be on my feet early in this first parliamentary session. One Saturday, after parliament had been sitting for several months, a man stopped me on the street in Windsor and asked, "How are things in Toronto?" Perplexed, I explained that I had not been to that city for months. "Were you ill?" "No, I have been in Ottawa." "But I thought you were a member of the Ontario legislature," he declared. Could it be that my constituents were not as interested as I had supposed? Certainly, the fellow who thought I was at Queen's Park knew me by sight, but it rankled that he was that indifferent to my activities.

Now the time for me to speak had come. Proposing the motion, Mackenzie King defended his government's policy on sanctions against Italy, asserting that he did not look upon the League of Nations as an ineffective body; he drew an analogy with Christianity, which should not be regarded as a failure, even though it had failed time and time again. J. S. Woodsworth supported the government's backing down on sanctions but complained about its lack of interest in foreign policy and the fact that it had taken nearly five months to call the present debate. I was the only private member to participate on the government side. This in itself confirmed Woodsworth's comment, and in my speech on 18 June I pointed out the desirability of greater discussion of international affairs, which in my mind were inevitably linked with domestic issues. Furthermore, I spoke of the importance of having well-briefed delegates at international conferences and suggested that the department of external affairs be reorganized into divisions representing geographical and functional interests.

I told the House that I did not then fully agree with the economic sanctions against Italy; Canada had only nine million people, was thousands of miles from Europe, and had no direct regional or local interest in the situation. Events since the autumn of 1935 had put the prime minister's stance in a better light since there were "circumstances which pro-League people like myself were not in a position to know." There were, I suggested, a number of ways of strengthening the League of Nations and improving the international climate. Summing up, I stressed that there was no conflict between a healthy nationalism and a strong internationalism. I realized that in some ways I was publicly hedging my strong private support for the League; but the international situation was confused and potentially explosive, and I felt I could not be too categorical.

R. B. Bennett arose and complimented me warmly on my speech. Mackenzie King, too, seemed pleased and sent me a note to say so. My friend Denton Massey, from the Conservative benches, teasingly acknowledged that I had "made the best of the wrong end of an argument," while Tommy Douglas, the CCF member for Weyburn, waggishly remarked that my speech was convincing and "sounded very CCF." Despite these flattering remarks, I was not totally happy with my maiden effort. My intention had been to strike a balance. I did not want to take too strong a position, caught as I was between Mackenzie King's foreign policy and my belief in internationalism — positions that conflicted to some extent. This speech was my best shot at putting forward a number of constructive suggestions and at reconciling differing viewpoints.

Outside the House of Commons, I kept alive my interest in international affairs by reading, studying, public speaking, and by collaborating with others in the Canadian Institute of International Affairs.[9] In the spring of 1936, the Windsor League of Nations Society chose me as a delegate to the Canadian Youth Congress in Toronto, and when the League of Nations Societies, under the auspices of the federation of League Societies, decided to

9 In 1936, I served on the national council of the Institute. The next year I was selected as a member of the executive committee, and participated in studying the formation of a parliamentary branch of the CIIA; but I decided that an all-party study group would serve the purpose better.

take an active part in a World Youth Congress to be held later that summer in Geneva, I was sent as a delegate of the Liberal Party. As I recall, the participating Canadian groups asked Mackenzie King and the leaders of the Conservative and CCF parties to name one delegate each to represent their parties at the meeting. The Conservatives chose Denton Massey, and the CCF picked Tommy Douglas. On 8 July I was voted chairman of the Canadian delegation, comprising twenty-seven representatives of church groups, YMCAs, and similar interested bodies. Twenty of us set sail on *The Aurania* on 21 August. It was a good delegation, and we met regularly during the voyage to prepare for the congress. Although the group decided to take a strong stand in support of the League of Nations and collective security, we agreed that the primary consideration of Canadian foreign policy was the welfare of Canada and that this did not preclude maintaining a neutral position. Practical considerations made it necessary to take national interests into account, as well as to express our support for the League. It was not an easy task.

A rather troubled Tommy Douglas spoke to me at one point on the voyage about the strength of communist representation in our delegation. The CP contingent included William Kashtan, secretary of the Young Communist League, and we also suspected Reg Davis, a journalist and a contributor to B. K. Sandwell's *Saturday Night*. Neither Tommy nor I opposed their presence, since the peace movement inevitably included communists, but we did not want them to take over. When we docked at Cherbourg, I was upset to find that we were being welcomed by many well-known French communists and A. A. MacLeod, a leading light in the Canadian League against War and Fascism, a communist front.

Tommy's concern proved to be well founded in the light of later efforts to prove that the delegation was controlled by communists. The "evidence" was a photograph taken on board ship and published for propaganda purposes during the 1945 general election; it was dragged out again in 1965 by the Canadian Intelligence Service, a fanatical right-wing organization. Although the photo included everyone on the delegation except me, the caption named me as its chairman. Tommy claims he was not embarrassed, but the slander certainly bothered me in 1945 because at that time communism was anathema to many Canadians. Curiously enough, when the photograph was used again during the 1965 election, I did not care; people had become more discriminating and recognized what a crude smear it was. No one thought Tommy — an ordained Baptist minister — was a communist either. When I was leader of the government in the Senate in the early 1970s, Pierre Trudeau handed me a clipping from a Detroit newspaper that claimed that Canada was governed by communists — including himself, Bob Bryce (a former deputy minister of finance) and that "old-time communist" Paul Martin. Later, when a reporter asked me for my reaction, I said that I strongly objected to being characterized as "old-time."

Once in Geneva, the delegation rallied to help elect Emmanuel Mounier president of the congress; the editor of the influential French lay Catholic publication *Esprit* defeated a young candidate from the Soviet Union.[10] The World Youth Congress provided an opportunity for young people from all over the world to demonstrate their opposition to war. We adopted resolutions that supported disarmament, whether Germany would agree to accept this proposition or not. Few delegates thought that the League's sanctions against Italy — by this time jettisoned — would have prompted Mussolini to go to war. I have often wondered whether Mackenzie King's limited support for that body would have been attacked if the congress had been sitting a month later, during the September session of the League. Among those on our delegation who complained of Canada's reservations towards the League was Arnold Smith, a future Canadian ambassador and distinguished secretary general of the commonwealth.

An outpouring of idealistic fervour came from the World Youth Congress. How surprising had it been otherwise. But I was not the

---

10 Mounier founded *Esprit* in 1932 with the advice and help of Jacques Maritain. See Bernard E. Doering, *Jacques Maritain and the French Catholic Intellectuals* (Notre Dame: University of Notre Dame Press, 1983).

only one whose faith in the League of Nations was shaken by the failure of the first attempt to apply the principles of collective security and by the abandonment of sanctions against Italy.

I stayed on in Geneva for part of the eighteenth session of the League of Nations Assembly. Just before the meetings convened, the· threat of military might in Europe came home to me when I visited Rome with Denton Massey in October. During this visit, we saw the frightening spectacle of a never-ending parade of young Fascists marching past a bemedalled Mussolini, who strutted with great bravado to the reviewing stand. Mackenzie King had decided to head our delegation to the assembly to make certain that Canada maintained a distance from efforts at coercion. I met the prime minister at the Hôtel de la Paix one morning, and we strolled in the fine park that lies close to the university. From my student days, I remembered the impressive monument there to the Protestant reformers Knox, Calvin, Farel, Beza and others. Mackenzie King walked towards it with a sure eye, and I readily understood why when I saw this son of Ottawa's St. Andrew's Presbyterian Church bowing before the statue of John Knox. The prime minister then looked at me, glowering a little, and remarked "Oh! *You* wouldn't understand."

Although King knew that despite the shortcomings of the League, I was still a supporter of collective security, he invited me to his hotel room to review his address to the assembly. The entire delegation was there to listen to the prime minister reading his prepared speech, in which he outlined his view that the purpose of the League should be conciliation rather than coercion; he objected to committing members to maintaining the status quo. King further pointed out that the League had failed to achieve universal membership and, therefore, could not coerce its members; he rejected collective security out of hand. When he had finished, I questioned the prime minister's rationale, pointing out that given the right conditions and the support of the major powers, collective security could be made to work. Did a commitment to collective security really mean that the decision to go to

war would be taken away from Canada's parliament and handed
to the League at Geneva? I asked rhetorically. While acknowledging the League's imperfections, I still saw it as a potentially useful
instrument for peace and as a forum for the airing and resolution of
international problems.

My comments, I was told, gave the prime minister cause to
wonder whether I was as intelligent as touted. Yet King thanked
me, in a note, for my "helpful cooperation" that contributed to his
"feeling of confidence" over the content of his speech. "Opinion,"
he acknowledged, "will of course vary and change. I believe,
however, it will be seen that, having regard to Canada's present
and future position in inter-imperial and international affairs,
what I said was right and that it was said at the right time and in
the right place."[11] While I was critical of the prime minister's
stand, I defended him from the editorial condemnation of
J. W. Dafoe, who claimed that King's remarks were tantamount
to a repudiation of the League.[12] After reading this editorial, I
wrote to Dafoe to say that his analysis would have been different if
he had been in Geneva. "Mr. King's speech," I wrote, "in terms of
the current European scene, seems unanswerable. As to the long
future...a reorganized League of Nations...must be based on
the certain willingness of the great powers particularly to abide by
the dictates of collective action." On this point, Dafoe and I were
as one. Nevertheless, I confessed to him that I would have preferred it if the prime minister had dealt with the "more positive
side, indicating what we were prepared to do to bolster a machinery not now functioning."[13]

On my way home by sea, I shared a cabin with Georges Vanier.
What a delightful man he was! When he removed his long artifi-
cial leg at one of the two beds in our cabin, I understood better the
nature of Georges' public service; he had lost his limb during the

11 King to Martin, 5 October 1936, W. L. Mackenzie King Papers (J1 series,
    p. 191216), PAC.
12 *Winnipeg Free Press*, 1 October 1936.
13 Martin to Dafoe, 28 October 1936, J. W. Dafoe Papers (reel M77), PAC.

Great War. In our cabin, night after night, we talked about religion, God and the afterlife. Although he did not try to dampen my exhilaration with life, Vanier gave me good advice: do not become too satisfied.

After settling in back home, I undertook to talk to local groups in Windsor and then to tour the Maritimes for the League of Nations Association to speak about what I had done and seen in Europe. Frankly, I was not optimistic about world events and told the *Windsor Daily Star* that a conflict of serious proportions appeared inevitable if the arms race continued. "Perhaps it may not come for a year, possibly even two years, but Europe is headed in the direction of war."[14] Miss Constance Hayward, a member of the League of Nations Society executive, accompanied me on most of my tour of eastern Canada. From Chatham, New Brunswick, I moved along to Newcastle and Saint John, where I was impressed by the large audience and pleased by an editorial in the *Saint John Telegraph* on my speech. A bright young man thanked me for my address when I spoke to the students at Mount Allison University in Sackville; years later, I discovered that he was A. E. Ritchie, who by then had become an undersecretary of state for external affairs. In Wolfville, Nova Scotia, I competed for an audience one night with Sergei Rachmaninoff, the famous composer and pianist. He won.

My speeches urged a realistic approach to the complex European situation. The League, I acknowledged, had faltered under the circumstances, but its principles had not failed. Criticism, therefore, should be directed not at the international organization but at those governments that had refused to support it. In particular, I blamed the worsening situation on the great powers for not recognizing the emptiness of victory in 1919 and for refusing to treat the vanquished nations more magnanimously. In part, they were the authors of the current situation since Hitler would not have had the same opportunity if Germany's economy had not been beleaguered by demands for reparations.[15]

On 10 December, as I was about to leave the Atlantic provinces, I heard the moving abdication speech of Edward VIII. Whatever one's views of his relationship with Mrs. Simpson, the young king was such a part of the times that his decision to step down provoked a powerful emotional reaction. I recalled seeing him first in 1920 when, as a youth of nineteen, he was wildly cheered by the people of Ottawa at Lansdowne Park. I saw him again in the summer of 1926 when he opened the Prince's Gates and the Canadian National Exhibition in Toronto; on that same visit, he came to Hart House to play squash with Professor Coventry. The young prince captured the world's fancy.

Nevertheless, Edward's marital plans concerned me less than my own aspirations in that regard. I had been reading relaxedly in my apartment on the eve of my departure for Europe to attend the World Youth Congress. Then, as now, I enjoyed a book after my evening meal, and usually smoked a cigar, my favourite ten-cent punch panatella. Not having one on this particular evening, I drove to a drugstore at the corner of Tecumseh and Windermere. As I walked in, a young woman behind the counter glanced my way while saying to another customer, "Well, you know, I'll never get married." For some extraordinary reason, I found myself saying, "Oh yes you will, for some day you will marry me." We laughed merrily. When she gave me my cigar, I had a full view of a beautiful Irish face and rich blue eyes.

Back in my apartment I decided I could not leave for Europe without finding out more about this entrancing colleen. Not being able to recall the name of the drugstore, I rang a pharmacist friend,

15 *WDS*, 26 November 1926.

Fred Holmes, who identified my cigar salesgirl as Eleanor Adams, popularly known as Nellie. She, like her sister Roxalana, was a druggist, and they ran two family-owned stores. I telephoned her. Did she know who was speaking? Yes, she recognized my voice but did not know my name. Presumptuous as I was, I assumed that everyone would know the member of parliament for Essex East and that most young women would accept my invitation to go out at short notice. She said that she knew nothing about politics and could not see me that night, even after I told her that I was leaving the next day for Geneva.

While abroad, I thought of Nell often and sent her postcards to remind her of my interest. As soon as I got home, a courtship began. I quickly discovered that she was not only lovely and animated but was also a very accomplished woman. She had graduated from St. Mary's Academy in Windsor but, too young to attend university, had spent the next year at Walkerville Collegiate as well as studying music and earning a diploma from the Toronto Conservatory. Nell loved sports and was an agile tennis player — she had once finished runner-up in the ladies singles in the Ontario junior championships. Their mother had prescribed that Nell and Roxalana must acquire the practical skills to get along in the world, and so she sent them both to study pharmacy at the University of Toronto before arranging for them to manage the two Adams drugstores.

Nell's father, Edgar Adams, had been a bank teller and was not a wealthy man. Her mother was Amelia McManamy, a school-teacher, and Nell was the youngest of their five children. Mrs. Adams ran the family with a tight rein, as I soon learned. She was a true-blue Tory and did not take to Mackenzie King; whenever we argued about politics, she would mischievously try to change the subject, snowing me under by quoting verse after verse of poetry. Her Irish background had made her prone to dislike the British, and she constantly brought up Ireland's troubled history. She was an avid reader and also an amateur financier who had made a considerable amount of money on the stock market. For a while,

Mrs. Adams ran the largest store in the area around the crossroads of McGregor. A remarkable woman indeed.

The tempo of my life disturbed Nell. Was there no time for pursuits other than those connected with politics? she asked. From what she could see, my life was all work — engagements every day of the week; even on Sundays there were church dinners and functions. Nell, ten years younger than me, was overawed by the responsibilities of the life I led and that I was now urging upon her. She continued to see other beaux. One of them was in the next chair when I went one day to the barber's for a haircut and a shave. He turned to me and said, "If you're not going to marry Nellie Adams, I am!" I knew I had to move fast.

One day, after we had been seeing each other for several months, Nell came down to my law office — I rather suspect her mother had something to do with this — and said, "Are we going to get married or not? I'm too young to spend my life waiting for you to make up your mind. If we're not going to get married, I want to go dancing with other young men and enjoy myself. If we are getting married, set the date right now!" And that is how we got engaged. My father happened to be visiting me in Windsor, and I asked him to come down to the office. When he arrived, I said, "Dad, Nell and I are going to get married. Is it all right?" He was overjoyed, put his arms around Nell and said "Welcome!" Nell and I were married at Immaculate Conception Church on 8 September 1937 by my former professor, Father McCorkell.

Nell imprinted her own informal, friendly style on every aspect of my life. My parents loved her, although I think Mother gave up her son with great reluctance. As the wife of an MP, Nell assumed some social engagements, but that did not change her. She arrived at one of her first political teas, given by some proper Walkerville ladies, in unconventional style — sitting on the front seat of a delivery truck. Her car had broken down, but the driver, whom she knew, had picked her up and deposited her at the correct address! One of our first dinner guests was Rabbi Leon Fram of Detroit. Nell fussed over the menu, setting the table with all the appropriate accoutrements. We have often laughingly recalled how her delightful roast pork sat untouched on the polite rabbi's plate.

Shortly after our wedding, Mackenzie King invited Nell and me to a dinner he was hosting for three recently married Liberal members. It was the first time I had visited Laurier House as a guest of the prime minister, and I was a little nervous. Coaching Nell a bit beforehand, I explained that this man was my boss and that much of my career would depend on him. Nell told me not to worry. When we arrived at the door, the prime minister laid on all his charm for her. "How do you do, Mr. Prime Minister?" began Nell. "My husband thinks you're a very great man." "And what do you think, Mrs. Martin?" "Well," said she, "I'm going to need some convincing." I just about dropped from embarrassment and fidgeted for the rest of the meal. King seemed to take it in good form, though. At about four o'clock the next afternoon, there was a knock at the door of our little flat on Delaware Avenue. I was in the back of the apartment and heard Nell say, "Hello, Mr. King." It was the prime minister, who had been so taken with Nell that he had come to invite her out for an afternoon stroll. I did not dare make an appearance. When Nell returned, she quipped, "Well, Paul, you're made now!" This was her sweet revenge for my fretting.

My second session of parliament opened on 14 January 1937. The speech from the throne was read by the governor general, Lord Tweedsmuir, better known to Canadians as John Buchan, author of *The Thirty-Nine Steps* and *Greenmantle*. We, the commoners, stood outside the bar of the Senate but could scarcely hear what was being read because the members insisted on catching up on gossip. Norman McLarty, my colleague from Essex West, was chosen by the prime minister to move the adoption of the address. He did well, opening with an expression of loyalty and homage to the new king and queen, George VI and his wife, Elizabeth.

The question of Canadian rearmament and neutrality agitated the House once more. Early in the session, J. S. Woodsworth and the CCF protested about the Canadian government's rubber-stamping decisions of the United Kingdom government.[16] The issue arose again a month later, when the House discussed the government's increased defence estimates.[17] During this debate, the CCF members continually tried to embarrass the government by telling the House that Canada was committed to going to war at Britain's side. Tommy Douglas hit the nail squarely on the head when he said that there was a difference between neutrality and isolation, and that the time had come when we had to work collectively or risk world war. Grant MacNeil, the CCF member for Vancouver North, wheeled out the "guns-and-butter" argument — in his view, voting more money for defence was depriving Canadians of social security measures. I did not find that position very practical because Canada surely had to be committed to its own defence. At the same time, I objected to the case put by the minister of national defence, Ian Mackenzie, who identified social security measures with socialism.

Within the Liberal parliamentary group, some members voiced their own doubts about the increased allocation for defence. But the wily prime minister raised the matter in the first caucus, when many members were not prepared to discuss the issue; King's appeal for party and national unity carried the day. Nobody had forgotten the crisis of 1917, and King had to present the estimates cautiously, stressing Canada's inability to defend itself. Most Liberals did not like their role as the sole party in the House to advocate rearmament — the Conservatives were pointedly keeping quiet. Certainly I did not relish the idea of rearming, but, given the lack of support for collective security, I saw no alternative and urged the House to set up a separate Commons committee to give private members a grasp of foreign policy. J. S. Woodsworth supported me, but my own leader, bolstered by R. B. Bennett, rejected the proposition. Several of my caucus colleagues, including

16 House of Commons, *Debates*, 15 January 1937, p. 14.
17 The government proposed to increase the amount spent for defence from $20 million in 1936 to $36 million the following year.

J. T. Thorson, the MP for Selkirk, and over a dozen French Canadian MPs, led by Maxime Raymond, also declared their opposition.

When the prime minister spoke in the debate on 19 February, he sought to quell the obvious dissension in his party's ranks. He stated emphatically that Canada would not participate in an overseas war except with the consent of the Canadian parliament. King obviously implied that Canada had accepted no commitments to join Britain in a war when he said that the Imperial Conference, scheduled for later that year, was not a policy-making instrument and that it could not bind Canada in any way without the knowledge and consent of parliament. I was not present to vote on the measure, but it was remarkable that even those Liberals who had criticized the government ultimately voted to pass the defence estimates.

Mackenzie King departed for Europe in April 1937 to attend both the coronation of King George VI and the commonwealth prime ministers' conference that opened in mid-May. At this meeting, the government was true to its word: Ian Mackenzie repeated the Canadian policy of no commitments and refused to contribute to plans for imperial defence. He made it clear that further increases in defence expenditure would create difficulties at home. But whatever King maintained in public, he believed that aggression by Hitler would rally Canadians to Britain's side. This he said privately to Chamberlain and Eden, but he refrained from declaring it publicly in Canada until the hour of decision in 1939. While this was not a formal commitment, it was an assurance that verged on one, and King should have told the Canadian parliament. He repeated his pledge during his meeting with Hitler in the *Reichskanzlei* in Berlin at the end of June 1937. This was much further than he had gone in the debate on the defence estimates a few months earlier.[18]

---

18 Diary, 15 June 1937, King Papers (J13 series), PAC; diary, 29 June 1937, ibid. See James Eayrs, *In Defence of Canada*, Vol. II, *Appeasement and Rearmament* (Toronto: University of Toronto Press, 1965), pp. 45-46.

The international situation worsened throughout 1937 and the early months of 1938. Japan invaded China in July 1937, and the Germans took over and proclaimed *Anschluss* with Austria the following March. Many who had questioned the government's swingeing increase in defence spending in 1937 were not quite as prepared to question it a year later. King, however, kept the lid on things and did not raise the 1938 estimates beyond the amount approved the year before. The debate began on 24 March, two months after the House resumed sitting. Grant MacNeil insisted that the prime minister should specify the exact nature, implied or specified, of Canada's commitments; he had found that the department of defence plans and acquisitions were not for local or coastal defence but for an expeditionary force. I questioned his assertion that Canada would be automatically at war when Britain was at war because of the nature of the military relationship between the two countries; my suggestion was to accept the assurances of the prime minister and the minister of national defence.

On 1 April 1938, I spoke at great length to the House about my disappointment that the League of Nations was impotent to deal with the disturbances in Europe or in any other part of the world. Despite my conviction that collective security was the best means of keeping the peace, I was forced to recognize that this instrument was ineffective in current circumstances. No greater disillusionment could have come to one of my particular opinion. Denton Massey equated nationhood with military strength, a notion which I strongly disputed. The mere fact of preparing to defend ourselves, I remonstrated, contradicting Grant MacNeil, did not commit us to any particular course of action; however, I did support MacNeil's contention that Canada should have the right to assert its neutrality, although I opposed declaring this in advance of any outbreak of war. At the end of my speech, I outlined what I felt should be the principles of Canadian foreign policy in the light of the confused international situation.

First of all was the maintenance of national unity. This was followed by the proper consideration of our ties with Britain and the United States. Our taking a less active role at the League of

Nations did not, I emphasized, arise from anything but the need to bow to current circumstances. I did not support this in principle. The situation dictated, however, that Canada was under no obligation to participate either in the League's economic and military sanctions or in the defence of any other part of the commonwealth. Finally, I asserted that Canada should specify its willingness to participate in international inquiries into economic grievances.

I told the House that I would vote for the military estimates, but as one who consents to an amputation: "not because I believe we are defending our homes [I fully thought the war would be fought in Europe]. If war comes, whether of aggression or defence, it can only mean destruction." Before going back to negotiate at the League, we would have to adopt a program of conciliation that should include:

1 the renunciation of economic warfare
2 military disarmament
3 positive international cooperation
   (a) improved standards of living as promoted by the International Labour Office
   (b) fair access to raw materials
   (c) freer access to markets
   (d) international trade based on equality
   (e) stabilization of currency
   (f) the extension of mandates
   (g) provision in the international system for peaceful change
   (h) readoption, if possible, of the system of collective security.[19]

Weekend visits to Windsor reinforced my stand: it was clear that the public was worked up about Hitler's challenge. In the spring of 1938, I found that the middle way followed by King was acceptable to most people to whom I spoke. At the end of April, I

19 House of Commons, *Debates*, 1 April 1938, pp. 1728-37, 1922-30.

addressed the Twentieth Century Liberal Clubs (the young Liberals) in western Ontario. They agreed with my statement, "If war comes, it will face us with no commitments made to any country, to any group, or to any nation." Youth did not want war, and many wondered why Canada could not remain neutral in a European conflict. Most Canadians, however, were growing to understand the seriousness of the situation in Europe and the need, at some stage, to take a stand.

At the close of the parliamentary session, I went home to Windsor and stayed at the Adams's family cottage in Colchester, on the shores of Lake Erie. I drove about thirty miles each morning to my law office in the city, where constituents awaited me, along with clients seeking help and advice. The summer was always a happy period in Essex County, and the many church picnics I attended were a pleasant way to meet those who lived in my riding.

Several months previously, I had agreed to join the Canadian group at the Commonwealth Relations Conference in Canberra that September. Edgar Tarr of Winnipeg and Stanley McLean of Toronto were also going to Australia, and I looked forward to what would have been my first visit to the South Pacific. The relations between Canada and the commonwealth had been such an important point of discussion in the previous two parliamentary sessions that I was eager to attend the conference.

Mackenzie King, however, had other plans. In mid-July, just before our scheduled departure for Australia, my secretary was startled to hear the long distance operator announce that the prime minister was on the line. He wanted me to attend the League of Nations Assembly; it would convene in Geneva on 12 September 1938, and Ernest Lapointe was to lead the Canadian delegation. Hesitating, I told King of my plans for Australia, saying that I would have to discuss this with the organizers of the Canadian contingent. When I explained the situation to them, though, there was general agreement that I should accept the prime minister's invitation. So it was arranged, and King expressed his hope that the visit would "prove an experience of much value to you in your public life."[20] When the prime minister announced the rest of the delegation on 17 August, I found that Mr. Lapointe and I were to be accompanied by Nellie McClung, a prominent member of the Canadian women's movement, and Joe Thorson, a fellow Liberal MP. The press noted that I was the youngest member of parliament ever to be appointed a delegate to the League.

My trip was a great worry because Nell was expecting our first child about the time I was due to leave. Her physician, Dr. Trottier, alone could give a clue about whether the baby would be born before I had to go. Towards the end of the month, he decided to encourage the birth, and Paul Edgar Philippe Martin was born in Windsor's Hotel Dieu Hospital on 28 August.[21] Impatiently, I awaited the moment when I could visit Nell and my new son; immediately after seeing them, I had to take the train to Montreal and sail for Britain on 2 September on *The Empress of Australia*. It was not easy to leave them; but after a wrenching goodbye, I went on a mission of which my wife fully approved.

My fellow delegates and I dined together on board. Joe Thorson, an able constitutional lawyer, took advantage of the presence of Ernest Lapointe to discuss complicated legal questions, but I could see that this irritated the minister of justice. After our first dinner, Lapointe called me into his cabin. "Now, Paul, we have seven days together on this boat, and it could be very pleasant. But if that man Thorson talks at me every time he sees me, I will not leave my cabin. It may be an interesting academic

20 Martin to King, 29 July 1938, King Papers (J2 series, vol. 172, file L-150, part 14), PAC; King to Martin, 2 August 1938, ibid.
21 I did not know it at the time but Mackenzie King was taking a considerable interest in our family. I suppose he thought the birth might upset his plans, but I also know how fond he was of Nell (Memo, King to H. R. L. Henry, 3 August 1938, ibid.).

exercise for him to discuss constitutional law, but it makes me tired." He then asked me to let Joe know discreetly that shoptalk was unwelcome at the dinner table. Thorson never took the hint. After the third meal, Mr. Lapointe stayed in his cabin.

Also on board was the recently retired R. B. Bennett, with whom I shared a compartment on the train from Liverpool. Looking out of the train window when we got to London, I could see Georges Vanier on the platform, and I wondered if he knew that Bennett was arriving. Georges had already made arrangements to meet me at the station, and I suspected that he was unaware of R. B.'s presence. I deliberately got off the train behind the former prime minister so that Vanier could greet him properly. The next thing I heard was "Now, Georges, I know you didn't come to meet me." With his typical aplomb, Vanier recovered and made the right diplomatic response.

Mike Pearson was also in London, serving at Canada's High Commission, and I spent an afternoon with him at a soccer match. He told me that Hitler's pressure on Czechoslovakia had moved Europe closer to war and that a conflict was very probable. When I saw Vincent Massey immediately after his return from a visit to Lord Halifax, Britain's foreign secretary, he told me that Hitler was determined to recover the Sudeten portions of Czechoslovakia, by force if necessary. The questions were to what extent Britain would support France, in view of the Franco-Czech alliance, and whether France would fight if Hitler seized the Sudetenland.

The Czech crisis was part of the background when the president of the Assembly of the League of Nations, Eamon de Valera, prime minister of Eire, opened the session in Geneva on 12 September. The increasingly tense situation in Europe dominated our discussions. This meeting was the first in the League's new home, the Palais des Nations, but it was clear to me that it was the beginning of the end for this great body. As I looked around the assembly, most of the personalities whom I recognized from previous sojourns in Geneva were in their places. A sure guarantee that this was so was seeing Lady Diana Cooper in the gallery.

There was a feeling among the delegates that we were accomplishing little of real importance. This sense of helplessness I blamed not on the League's structure but on the attitudes of its member governments. Even the work of the economic and social agencies had begun to falter, as I noticed when I sat on the economic committee. Here, Lou Rasminsky, a friend from the University of Toronto and a member of the League secretariat's economic division, spoke of the change. The committees now directed their aim not at governments but at the problems of the individual and the family. One positive decision was that non-member states would be allowed to voice an opinion on the future economic and social program of the League in order to encourage international cooperation in these fields.

I made my first address at the League of Nations in the economic committee on 20 September, where I prescribed an international convention to regulate oil transport and to guard against the possibility of pollution. In a later discussion about exchange controls, I advocated international action to relieve economic depressions, since single governments usually acted to protect themselves and hence damaged the trade of other countries. Retaliation would only make the hard times worse.

In view of the broadened scope of League activities in social and technical questions requiring international collaboration, it was decided to set up a new committee to deal with a number of non-political subjects that had previously been referred to the second (economic questions) and fifth (social questions) committees. Nellie McClung and I represented Canada when this seventh committee met, and I expressed our country's concern about the opium trade in the Far East. The assembly of the League subsequently adopted the resolution that I had presented to the committee and asked Japan, China and other concerned countries for their observations.

The problem of Spain was one of the dominant issues of the 1938 assembly. Despite the active role of Juan Negrin, the Spanish prime minister, and his foreign minister, Julio Alvarez Del Vayo, there was little that the League could do to stop the bloodshed on the Iberian peninsula. If only the League's nations had been steadfast in upholding the cause in Abyssinia, China and Spain! No wonder that in the autumn of 1938, member after member announced that they were no longer bound by those parts of the covenant that proscribed aggression.

Maxim Litvinov of the Soviet Union had been a strong supporter of the League; but, naturally, this stand had served his country's interests. In 1938, his last appearance in Geneva, Litvinov was the only foreign minister of a great power to attend. On 21 September, he made a speech declaring his country's intention to stand by Czechoslovakia. Mr. Lapointe and I were invited with other delegates to a private showing of a film, *The Fall of the Romanov Dynasty*. Litvinov sat a couple of places away as we watched this vivid portrayal of the end of the last czar and his family. I kept looking at Litvinov from time to time, and he seemed a little unnerved. He must have known that the undiplomatic choice of film would anger some of his guests. On the way out, I said to Mr. Lapointe, "Aren't you going to thank Litvinov for his hospitality?" He snapped, "I certainly will not."

Stories of what might happen circulated constantly during the session. Nonetheless, the important events appeared to happen outside the League; the chief British delegate, Earl de la Warr, made eight flying trips to London, and it became evident that the organization was playing only a small role in the growing crisis. On 14 September, at a dinner given by the British government, everything was going well until a member of the foreign office hurriedly approached the earl, who immediately became quite grave. We soon found out that the British prime minister, Neville Chamberlain, had suggested meeting Hitler on German soil. Everyone realized what failure could mean, and there was a general feeling that Chamberlain had taken a courageous step. de Valera invited Ernest Lapointe and me to his rooms to discuss the telegrams sent by Chamberlain to commonwealth heads of government. Chamberlain wanted to know the attitude of the commonwealth prime ministers towards his proposed visit to Hitler for a series of talks. We told de Valera that Mackenzie King strongly endorsed Chamberlain's efforts to encourage Hitler to back down. I fully shared that view. de Valera, too, was in favour of Chamberlain's proposed visit and told us that he regarded him as Britain's greatest prime minister and a man who really understood the Irish problem. The bitterest opponents of Chamberlain's casting aside the diplomatic channels were those who feared that the German demands would be met. What we all felt was that meeting these demands was inevitable in view of the alternative, for which neither Britain nor France was prepared.

At his second talk with Hitler at Bad Godesberg, Chamberlain rejected the *Führer*'s terms and began preparations for war. The suspense at Geneva was dreadful, particularly when we learned that all that remained was for Chamberlain to take his leave of Hitler.

In order to escape the increasingly cheerless situation, I left Geneva one weekend to visit Lou Rasminsky and his wife, Lila, at their villa near Gstaad. But even in that peaceful mountain setting, we could not escape the radio, and we heard Hitler's speech on 26 September from the *Sportsplatz* in Berlin. I remember the Rasminskys' fear after that ranting speech, in which Hitler shouted that his patience was running out and that he would invade Czechoslovakia unless Germany's legitimate claims to the Sudetenland were recognized. The Nazis, prepared to leave the whole matter to the judgment of one man, cheered hysterically. Hitler did not equivocate — 1 October was the deadline. Never had one head of state spoken of another as Hitler did of the Czech leader, Eduard Beneš — he called him stupid, a liar, and a democratic ass. Switzerland placed areas under military supervision, Czechoslovakia began to mobilize, France called up reservists, and Londoners prepared to evacuate. Afterwards, Lou and I quietly walked down the mountain road. Neither of us had to speak. It was impossible to get a reservation on a boat, and I even volunteered to take the Rasminskys' baby home with me.

In the midst of the gloom came a bolt out of the blue. Late that Thursday afternoon, a courier advised us, as we sat in session in the economic committee, that Chamberlain had announced that he would fly to Munich to meet Hitler, Mussolini and Premier

Daladier of France. We adjourned immediately, realizing that there was still hope for peace. I went to a brief service in a nearby Catholic church and saw tears of joy on the faces in the congregation. That same day, 27 September, Mr. Lapointe received instructions from Mackenzie King to return home to bring the prime minister up-to-date on his talks with various European statesmen. Two days later we drove Lapointe to the train station in Geneva. The city was black, all its lights out — a grim harbinger of things to come.

On the day before the assembly adjourned, it passed a resolution condemning the use of force in the European débâcle. That night, however, the Munich Pact was signed, and Hitler secured all he had demanded. Chamberlain returned home, proud of the piece of paper signed by the German chancellor. Canada's prime minister shared this pride. For him, the threat of war had passed.

Aga Mohamed Khan, the Moslem leader and previous president of the general assembly, gave a sumptuous dinner for the delegates to wind up the session. I found myself with de Valera, Lady Diana Cooper, Luis Padilla-Nervo of Mexico, Euan Wallace from Britain and the eminent Joseph Paul-Boncour of France. Everyone seemed to concur that the Munich Pact had removed the threat of war. No one dared say that the peace was precarious.

On my way to catch *The Empress of Britain*, I stopped in Paris and was standing on the street when Premier Edouard Daladier's motorcade drove past. Crowds cheered him as he waved his hat in greeting, but I shook my head. The League of Nations had been shorn of its powers to avert war by the very nations who strove so feverishly to avoid catastrophe.

Anxiously, I awaited my return home. After such a traumatic time in Europe, I wanted to see my wife and new son. Early on 8 October, I climbed out of my berth just after the train arrived in Windsor's station. The porter showed me to Nell, sitting in a coach that was hooked onto my train. My heart melted when I saw her frail form; I realized that she too had lived all those anxious moments at Geneva, not knowing whether we would be reunited and wondering what our future together would bring. Eleven months later, the nations were at war.

VII

Life of the Party

W HEN I WAS ON MY WAY home from Geneva in October 1938, the governor general, Lord Tweedsmuir, happened to be a fellow passenger on the boat. One day, as we were both walking around the deck, he told me in confidence, and a little indiscreetly, that preparations for the first tour of North America by a reigning British monarch were under way; the king and queen would be coming to Canada and the USA for six weeks. Afterwards, when I learned that Windsor probably would not be included in the itinerary, I immediately took up the matter with the undersecretary of state, Dr. E. H. Coleman. But to my great disappointment, when the preliminary schedule was announced, Windsor indeed did not make the list. The only explanation I could get for the omission was that the city's railway terminal facilities were inadequate and that the RCMP could not guarantee the safety of the king and queen; visions of an influx of hoodlums from Detroit and Chicago loomed in the minds of the Ottawa bureaucrats. It was crystal clear to me that the tour would create political and other problems for us local MPs if Windsor was not part of the royal itinerary.

Mayor David Croll and other municipal officials began to chide the three Essex County MPs for our supposed lack of concern. The *Windsor Daily Star* issued its own blast, warning that if the king and queen did not come to Windsor, Norman McLarty, Paul Martin and Murray Clark would shortly be hanging up their coats in another corridor. Until then, Norman had downplayed any likelihood of political repercussions over the visit. Very concerned about the newspaper's jeremiad, I phoned Norman at his office — but he was not there. So I rang him at home and asked if he had read that morning's *Star*. "At this hour, Paul? I never read papers so early in the day. You know that." "Well," I said, "you'd better read this one." I went right over to Norman's house to discuss the story. Unused to editorial chastisement, he got as red as a beet; not only had he been lambasted — the newspaper was predicting his political demise.

Norman and I knew we had to reverse the situation and to work for a revised itinerary. We got together right away with Mr. Herman and Mayor Croll, and soon afterwards the city council appointed one of its controllers, Frank Begley, and Alderman Norman Eansor to travel up to Ottawa to make representations at the highest level. I went with them, knowing full well that Mackenzie King would not make himself available, but Begley seemed impressed with the rigour of the position my fellow MPs and I had taken. Despite the prime minister's refusal to see the delegation, our lobbying eventually had an effect, and Norman McLarty announced at the end of February that the king and queen would come to Windsor for a day (initially, this was to have been a free day for them in the Muskokas). The critics quickly changed their tune and began singing the praises of the Essex County members.

On 6 June 1939, a train carrying King George VI and Queen Elizabeth rolled into Windsor's station. People from all over southwestern Ontario and even from faraway places in the United States came in their thousands to greet the royal couple. Crowds of schoolchildren were on hand to cheer them, and they were entertained everywhere they went by brass bands, many of them

American, effusively blowing and banging their respective interpretations of "God Save the King." At the end of their afternoon
visit, and just as they were about to leave, a tardy Mayor Richard
Reading[1] of Detroit rushed into the railway station for an unscheduled presentation. Word was passed, and the king and queen held
up their departure to meet him. Strutting onto the platform and
backed up by his own musical ensemble, Reading was formally
presented to their majesties . . . and curtsied! After he had taken his
leave and a rather weary king was boarding his train, the Detroit
band again blared forth the royal anthem. Standing close by, I
heard King George mutter to his queen, "There's that song
again!"[2]

The royal tour was an event of great importance. The world
situation had been deteriorating steadily; even after the announcement of the visit, there were hints in the speech from the throne on 12
January 1939 that the visit might have to be cancelled. For Mackenzie King, the tour was an auspicious one, presenting him with an
opportunity to publicly affirm Canada's loyalty to the crown.

The three days that the king and queen spent in Ottawa in
mid-May left a lasting impression on the thousands who turned
out to see them and was an unrivalled demonstration of the esteem
that the Canadian people felt for the monarchy. In the Senate, the
king gave royal assent to various bills; later, he laid the cornerstone
of the new Supreme Court of Canada building and dedicated the
imposing memorial on Confederation Square to the dead of the
Great War. Nell accompanied me to the state functions, and on
every invitation made a careful note of the appropriate dress to be
worn — for me, striped trousers and a short morning coat. During
the ceremony at the War Memorial on 21 May, I filmed the events
with my new 8 mm movie camera, creeping up quite close to the

---

1 Reading was mayor of Detroit from 1937 to 1939. Later he was sent to prison for
  allegedly shielding some racketeers.
2 I mentioned this incident to Queen Elizabeth II during one of her visits to Canada.
  Mike Pearson was very annoyed with me because he thought it was not the type of
  anecdote to recount. Later, when I was high commissioner to the Court of St.
  James and told the story to the Queen Mother, she said she did not remember the
  remark but nevertheless found it very amusing.

king as he was laying the wreath. A little later, not knowing me
from Adam, the queen said, "You certainly take a lot of photos."
The following issue of *Time* magazine contained a picture of
William Tomlinson, a fellow Liberal member, and me with the
caption, "The royal photographers."

The struggle to get the government to include Windsor in the royal
tour was indicative of the duty that I always felt I owed my
constituency and my adopted city. This attention to Windsor
quickly resulted in my local nickname "Oom Paul," a soubriquet
that has followed me for the rest of my life.[3] Since I had been living
in Windsor only five years when I was first sent to parliament, it
was obvious that if I did not work hard, re-election could prove
uncertain at best.

I soon learned that a member is regarded differently in his
constituency than he is by those outside the riding. Many voters
think that a member is there for them alone, and it is often true
that MPs do not gain great political advantage by spending time
on national or international issues. The electorate may respect an
MP for his endeavours on weighty matters of state, but most
members solidify their position by the relationship they establish
with their own constituency. Work for community improvements
and services does tell in the long run, and it is frequently the small
things that make a member appreciated. Apart from this, the
concerns of Essex East frequently reflected the wider interests of
the nation. If I was not elected, obviously I would be unable to do
the things that I wanted to do.

In the early 1950s, I was at the United Nations General Assembly to participate in the resumption of disarmament negotiations.
The Western powers had suggested that on their behalf I should
carry on discussions with the Soviet Union regarding the terms of

3 Paulus Kruger (1825 - 1904), the original "Oom Paul," was an Afrikaans general
   and statesman, a founder of the Transvaal state. By his care of his people, he
   became a symbol of the entire Afrikaaner nation.

reference of the talks. These negotiations succeeded and stories about them appeared in the press all over the world. When I returned to Windsor for the weekend, I was met by a battery of reporters at the airport. Foreign affairs do not always excite the same interest with local folks as some purely domestic issue. Remembering that, after a long struggle, I had been able to persuade the postmaster general to build a small post office in Belle River, I put aside the issue with which I had been seized in New York and inquired about work on the new post office building. That did the trick. The *Star*'s front page equated Paul Martin's UN achievement with the Belle River post office.

I wrote innumerable letters to constituents and always answered those who took the trouble to write to me. My secretary, Anne Rozek, and I read the newspapers every day and would then prepare a list of individuals to whom we should send a letter concerning a birth, a graduation, a marriage, or a bereavement. When I was driving around the riding, I would often stop and give a lift to someone standing on a corner; this way, I met the voters and found out what they were thinking. Every Saturday morning, I used to see people to discuss their problems — some wanted pensions, many were looking for jobs, others even wanted advice on marital troubles. Generally, when I was in Windsor, I ate lunch at the counter in the downtown Kresge's, where I met dozens of people and heard what was on their minds. Most Saturday evenings Nell and I would go to a church supper, a concert put on by one of the city's immigrant groups, or a sports event. My efforts to meet the people were unstinting and at times, I felt, almost a form of slavery.

Despite the very tiring nature of my schedule, I derived a great deal of satisfaction from getting to know my constituents and took a genuine interest in their affairs. It was particularly pleasant for me to meet the "ordinary Joes," and I felt far more comfortable with them than with many who ranked higher on the local social scale. One day in January 1937, I met Tom Fitzgerald on the church steps in Woodslee. Locally renowned for his knowledge of Hansard, Tom could quote from memory the parliamentary speeches of Sir Wilfred Laurier. His support for me began with my nomination campaign, but I soon learned that his backing did not involve a blind acceptance of all my pronouncements — I had no more vigilant critic. As we were chatting on this particular Sunday, I suggested that he come to Ottawa to stay with me — his first visit to the capital. In no time, the word spread that Woodslee's seventy-four-year-old student of politics was off to Ottawa with the young member. On our tour of the Parliament Buildings, I made certain that Tom met the MPs on my floor and introduced him to the great Ernest Lapointe. From my seat on the back benches of the Commons chamber, I remember looking up with pride at Tom Fitzgerald, the sage of Woodslee, folding his long legs in the cramped members' gallery.

In order that I could carry out my constituency obligations, I made a regular weekend train journey between Ottawa and Windsor that formed a very tiring part of my life. I used to get on board in Ottawa at four o'clock on a Thursday or Friday afternoon and arrive in Toronto about ten. Then I would change trains, waiting an hour before setting off for Windsor, where we pulled in at seven the following morning. Sometimes, after a busy week in the House, I left Ottawa later in the evening and went overnight to Toronto. For thirteen years, when parliament was sitting, I made this weekly rail trip almost without fail; it took a long time for MPs to be given air passes — that was like extracting a tooth from a reluctant gum. Even with a berth it was frequently not a pleasant trip: the train was cold and steamy in the winter and stifling in hot weather. The cars usually would be full of members of parliament returning home to constituencies along Lake Ontario, in Toronto or in southwestern Ontario. From time to time, I saw Arthur Meighen, then Conservative leader in the Senate, travelling in a sleeper. Although he was well off, the frugal Meighen always took an upper berth, clambering up into it with one of the railway's brass spittoons. When I asked a porter about this ritual, he replied, "If you were his age, you might need one too!"

Many historians and political scientists mistakenly equate patronage with a political machine as the means by which a politician retains office. Strictly speaking, there was no patronage that could have been called consequential for an MP to administer at this time. There had been some in earlier days, when an MP could have some effect on the granting of government contracts, but that practice was petering out when I first entered the House. Yet it was possible sometimes for members to influence the appointments of janitors in federal buildings or make recommendations on the selection of government prosecutors. In fact, many MPs used to complain that there was not enough patronage; if there was going to be any, they would say, it might as well be substantial. I often thanked God that backbenchers had such limited influence, for I quickly discovered that for every favour done on behalf of a constituent, an MP could end up with a hundred enemies.

The one matter on which I had some say was over the distribution of contracts for rural mail delivery; it took up far too much time, though, and gave me plenty of headaches. When a contract was about to expire, the post office department would advise the local MP, asking him whether he wanted it renewed. If he demurred, the department would call for tenders. That was the signal for a barrage of letters petitioning the member for an endorsement. I always advised applicants that the government would award the contract to the person with the lowest tender; sometimes, upon request, I would write a letter of reference to the post office department. If someone I had recommended did not receive the contract, I could ask the department to investigate the competence of the lowest bidder. But, in the end, the post office made the final choice unless there was a tie, in which case they might ask me to break it.

Like many MPs, I did not want to have anything to do with the dispensing of favours. Liberal vied against Liberal to get a contract, and the unsuccessful applicant often turned his wrath on me. To prevent myself from always being in the firing line, I argued that appointments should not be at the sole discretion of the MP. I wanted the township Liberal associations to make recommendations and the riding executive to pass upon them. But sometimes there was no escape. Those who had worked hard for the party often wondered what their reward would be. In our political system, many party workers were not satisfied unless they received some return; occasionally they got it — perhaps wrongly. Going around the riding to discuss everyone's gripes took up hours of my time, but no one can be an effective member of parliament unless he listens sympathetically to the grouses of his constituents and does something about them. Nevertheless, I concurred with my friend Mrs. Beatrice Emerson, a formidable Liberal, who once said caustically, "Some think because they cast a vote, they must have a job out of it."

Vastly more important in gaining support than any amount of patronage I was able to dispense was the work I did to look after the interests of Windsor and Essex East. Dr. Morand's comment on my maiden speech in the House provided an appropriate warning when he said that

> as a new member, one would have thought it better had he tried to do something for his riding. And yet, if I were in his place, I would probably have talked about Geneva and the League of Nations too. For it was his party . . . which brought down a tariff which allows more automobile parts to be imported here, which has closed up some automobile factories and which has allowed vegetables to come into Canada without our getting similar concessions on the other side.

I took these remarks to heart and began to do all I could for my constituents.

When I was first elected, much of my work dealt with the fundamental changes then taking place in Canada's trade union movement. In 1935, the Committee for Industrial Organization (CIO) decided to move north of the American border to establish industrial unions. Previously, the Canadian labour movement outside Québec had been dominated by the craft unions that made up the Trades and Labour Congress. The unions composing the TLC were organized according to individual trades, such as carpentry and plumbing, with a local representing the appropriate skill in a particular factory. The new movement wanted to organize all the workers of a particular industry into one union, regardless of their individual skill; I often heard labour leaders in Windsor say that in a factory organized for mass production there should be just one union. Within the next decade, this view would affect the factory workers in Windsor and substantially alter the structure of Canadian unionism. I was concerned not only about the improvements that unions could bring to workers in Essex County but also about their effect on the local political structure.

After settling in Windsor, I became acquainted with a number of the members of the Essex and Kent Trades and Labour Council. Some were active Liberals, others transferred their allegiance to the CCF before the 1935 election, and a number — including some of the more influential labour organizers — were communists. The attraction of the CCF for the labour unions could not be denied; I soon realized that if I was not alert in party organization and in parliament, I would not be able to hold my position in the political arena in a city where sixty-five percent of the workforce was employed in the automobile industry or its parts plants.[4] David Croll recognized this too. It was fairly obvious that the executives of the car plants could influence only a tiny number of voters. My recognition of this and my work with constituents are two of the reasons why the CCF was shut out of Windsor's representation in the House of Commons. The Liberals won other seats as well because of my advocacy of labour. Perhaps this was one of the reasons Mackenzie King tolerated — perhaps more than he otherwise would have — my prodding for improved social legislation.

Although it intrigued me in my first days there to see the apparent profitability of Windsor's car industry — the workers

4 In my first year as a member of parliament, there were seven car manufacturers in Essex East. The Canadian branch of the Ford Motor Company was the largest automobile manufacturer in Canada. In addition, thirty plants in my riding manufactured automobile parts and accessories.

seemed to be making pretty good money — I soon discovered that this was not the case. The Depression had changed things utterly. While the hourly wage appeared to be high, the average earnings of the car worker had diminished considerably — from $33.00 for 44 hours in 1928 to $19.60 in the 1930s.[5] In fact, the annual wage was always low because of the inevitable seasonal layoffs. Unskilled auto workers laboured on monotonous assembly lines, and the turnover in manpower was high. It was difficult for older workers to retain their jobs: many men were fired after fifteen to twenty years in a plant, and faithful service did not guarantee keeping a job. Discharges were frequently given without notice. The companies used to call men to work but then would send them home as soon as they arrived, making them pay the expense of their trip. If a man was thirty seconds late, a minimum of a half-hour was deducted from his pay.

When the United Automobile Workers (UAW) tried to move into Windsor from the US, I came to know its Canadian organizer, Charlie Millard, and helped him overcome some opposition from the local labour council. I was foursquare behind the union in its fight for higher and more certain wages, better working conditions, job security and the rooting out of favouritism. During the election campaign, I emphasized my support for these legitimate demands and am proud to think that I championed the workers in their struggle. In justice, one must recognize that what big business often did at this period of my life big unions sometimes do today.

Of the three Essex members, I was the main agitator for the workers' cause. Norman McLarty had too close a personal tie with Wallace Campbell, the Ford president, to appear convincing in supporting unionization, and the essentially rural character of Murray Clark's riding did not oblige him to spend time explaining the lot of the industrial worker. My speeches emphasized the responsibility of industry towards labour and a desire to avoid the antediluvian attitudes of the 1920s.

5   L. J. Veres, "A History of the United Automobile Workers in Windsor 1936-1955" (Master's thesis, University of Western Ontario, 1956), p. 8.

Norman McLarty not only enjoyed socializing with the Windsor magnates but also loved the social life in Ottawa. I remember one afternoon he turned to me on the backbenches and commented on what a "delightful place" the national capital was, asking me why I made the long trip home every weekend. Some weeks later — on a quiet Thursday afternoon in the House — I saw Norman sitting at his place, probably thinking of his weekend social engagements. I called a page boy over and gave him a dollar to tell Norman that Lady Tweedsmuir wished to speak to him on the telephone. Naturally, when he got there the line was dead. A few minutes later, I asked my secretary to call McLarty, pretending that she was a member of the staff at Government House, and invite him to tea on Saturday. He returned with his "invitation," sat down beside me and said, "Paul, are you going home this weekend? You should stay here and sample Ottawa's social life. For instance, I'm going over to see Lady Tweedsmuir on Saturday." "Gosh, isn't that nice," I remarked, chuckling to myself.

I fully intended to "disinvite" Norman before I left for Windsor, but it went clean out of my mind. At mass the following Sunday, as I was contemplating "mes péchés mortelles," I remembered my practical joke, but there was nothing to do. As soon as I returned to Ottawa, I went to see McLarty. "Well, Norm, did you have a busy weekend?" "Oh yes, Paul, I had a wonderful time at Government House. Lady Tweedsmuir was so gracious."

Stumped, I left his office, and for a couple of days could not figure out what had happened. After a few discreet inquiries, I found out that Lady Tweedsmuir had been holding a tea party for the Imperial Order of the Daughters of the Empire, when in walked Norman. Not knowing what to do with this misplaced member of parliament, the governor general's wife and her staff said nothing and served tea for him — the only thorn among the roses.

As soon as I entered the House of Commons, I urged Norman Rogers, the minister of labour, to introduce legislation like the

Wagner Act, an act obliging employers to bargain with the representatives of their employees, passed by the United States government in 1935. Norman expressed his understanding of the new demands of industrial workers, but perhaps because of other pressures he did not always have a sympathetic hearing from Mackenzie King. My supporters began to grumble that the government and Rogers were "more academic than practical"; I had to defend King, although I too felt that his administration was not as alert and go-ahead as I would have liked.

The established labour movement and the TLC leaders, Tom Moore and Percy Bengough, were adamantly opposed to the UAW and to industrial unionism. But it was clear that this new grouping in the Oshawa and Windsor auto industries was very much part of the growing influence of the industrial union movement in North America.

Many were hostile to the UAW because of its reported communist influence. Although some of the union's organizers were Marxists, they exercised varying but not necessarily decisive sway. The Communist Party paper, the *Daily Clarion*, continually harangued the auto workers to organize, and it was obvious that the communists had penetrated the union leadership. Oscar Kogan, the communists' representative, was an active figure in Windsor in the early UAW period, and William Kashtan, who directed the Young Communist League, often came to the city to agitate.

During the late 1930s, the aspirations of the UAW led to political strife. The new UAW objective was not to take over the car plants but to gain recognition as the workers' legitimate agent, an essential ingredient in collective bargaining. The big automobile companies feared control and interference from the unions and fought them tooth and nail. In 1936, local 195 of the UAW began to organize Kelsey Wheel, a small parts plant in Windsor. I knew Jimmy Napier, one of the activists, quite well, as I did the later directors of the union, Earl Watson and Charlie Brooks; Watson was a political supporter of mine, while Brooks had Marxist leanings. Local 195 pioneered the union cause in Windsor, and five workers at the Kelsey Wheel plant were dismissed because of their union membership. Malcolm Campbell, the president of Kelsey Wheel and the brother of the chief executive of Ford of Canada, refused to have anything to do with the union. He had once been president of the Essex West Conservative Association, and the champions of labour were infrequently found in the Tory camp. After the dismissal of the five men, some workers picketed the plant; fighting broke out and the police had to intervene. Once the issue went to conciliation, an informal agreement enabled the men to work, but the management still refused to recognize the UAW as the workers' bargaining agent.

Although these developments had occasioned little interest in Ottawa, the UAW-inspired strike of General Motors workers in Oshawa made Canadians aware of the aspirations of industrial unions. Premier Mitch Hepburn, who backed the company against the UAW, claimed that the settlement of the twelve-day strike had effectively shut the UAW-CIO out of Canada; but the events were not interpreted that way either by the population at large or by two of Hepburn's colleagues, the attorney general, Arthur Roebuck, and the public welfare minister, David Croll, who were dismissed from the cabinet. The contract settlement between the company and the workers did not mention the union or give it status as the bargaining agent for the workers. However, the inclusion of many items that formed part of the UAW contract in the United States and the public declaration of the workers that they considered themselves affiliated with the union were landmarks, and I applauded them wholeheartedly.[6]

It pleased me that throughout the Oshawa strike, Norman Rogers and Mackenzie King had issued statements confirming the

6 For the story of the strike see I. M. Abella, (ed.), *On Strike: Six Key Labour Struggles in Canada 1919-1949* (Toronto: James, Lewis and Samuel, 1974), pp. 93-128. The strikers won an agreement that included a forty-four-hour week, wage increases, the seniority system, a grievance committee, a minimum wage and the promise never to discriminate against an employee engaged in union activity.

federal government's advocacy of collective bargaining. I strongly supported the position taken by Roebuck and Croll. It was outrageous that the premier of a Liberal government could challenge the right of a group of workers to choose their bargaining agent. In Windsor, I publicly welcomed the UAW's growing strength, while regretting that the union's toughness was frequently associated in the popular mind with threats of violence. The increased militancy of the industrial unions caused considerable dislocation in the Windsor labour organizations. For example, the Essex County Trades and Labour Council refused to recognize the CIO as a legitimate voice of labour. The *Windsor Daily Star*, spooked by the unwarranted reputation for lawlessness of the UAW-CIO, did not support the attempts of the union to gain adherents in the city and spoke about efforts "to force the will of an organized minority on the majority."[7]

During the first days of the parliamentary session in January 1938, I eagerly followed the progress of a private bill introduced by J. S. Woodsworth that sought to guarantee to labour the right to organize.[8] The bill's purpose was to prevent employers from refusing to hire, from dismissing workers, and from conspiring with others to deny employment to members of a trade union. The minister of justice, Ernest Lapointe, advised the House that the measure did not lie within federal jurisdiction because it dealt with property and civil rights, which under the British North America Act were the responsibilities of provincial governments. However, both Lapointe and Norman Rogers affirmed that they believed in the right of workers to form and join trade unions.

When I spoke, I reminded the House that no one had objected to the principle of the bill and pointed out the keen interest of my constituents in the proposed legislation. Repeating what I had said

7 *WDS*, 12 August 1937; ibid., 10 November 1937; ibid., 18 October 1938, editorial. The Committee for Industrial Organization was distributing pamphlets at a Ford plant in Windsor when several sticks of dynamite were found nearby.
8 House of Commons, *Debates*, 31 January 1938, p. 16; ibid., 15 February 1938, p. 482 ff.

earlier on a radio broadcast, I maintained that

> it is not enough for a man to be able to think freely. . . . A man must be free to associate with his fellow men for joint action in realms where there is a community of interest. The difficulty arises, not so much with the denial of this right of association as with the measure óf control which the state is entitled to use over voluntary associations. . . . Liberty must reside within the context of this restrictive basis, but this restriction must be defined. . . . A government is not justified in suppressing an association, the mere beliefs of which are subversive of the existing order. The occasion for governmental interference must be when the association has moved . . . to bring about an overthrow of the established order.[9]

To deny the freedom of association to workers in any organization of their choice, I argued, would play into the hand of extremists, who would then be able to attack collective bargaining as a course of action. Nobody questioned the right of employees to organize for lawful purposes. If these matters were recognized only as a declaration of government policy and not as a statutory right, it was because the matter rested outside the constitutional powers of parliament; the exception had to do with public servants, and I was in favour of making the bill applicable to them. The effective way to enforce labour's right to the freedom it should have lay in the compulsion that came from liberal attitudes, and not in legislation. With that civilized influence and outlook, I asserted, Canada would not have witnessed the disgraceful treatment meted out to labour during the Oshawa strike.

R. B. Bennett, the next speaker, dared me to vote for Woodsworth's bill as a demonstration of my beliefs. He claimed that he would not otherwise be convinced that the bill was *ultra vires*; in his view, the courts could determine its validity once it had been passed. Time ran out on the measure, and the bill was not voted on before parliament was prorogued on 1 July.

The right of workers to organize collectively formed only a part of some of the policies I was advocating for the wage earner.

9 House of Commons, *Debates*, 17 June 1938, p. 3,992 ff.

During my first session, in the House of Commons Committee on Industrial and International Relations, I sparked a revolt against the practice that this committee was allowed to consider only measures referred to it by the government. I raised the question of the need to discuss means of providing employment and, when this was not permitted, told the committee that "I, for one, was elected on the understanding that I would do all that I could to solve the problem of unemployment." When other members spoke in a similar vein, the committee chairman, C. R. McIntosh, tried to put down the revolt by saying that the minister of labour would probably be happy to discuss the matter later.

My convictions would not allow me to sit there and say nothing. Another reason I pressed forward so publicly with proposals that the government was unwilling to adopt was the fear that my constituents would associate me with the cutback in direct relief that the Liberal government had made in 1936. I received reports from Windsor that the municipal relief officers did not know how they would cope with the demand, since their grants from the province had been reduced as a result of the federal government's retrenchment. Norman McLarty and I had to meet representatives of the Essex County municipalities to explain the situation. During the meeting I spoke out about the needs of the unemployed; I knew the municipalities had to get the money from Queen's Park, which had limited sources of revenue.[10]

One of the priorities I urged on caucus was the implementation of a comprehensive system of unemployment relief, including unemployment insurance. I knew that the latter measure could not be considered until the government had secured an amendment to the British North America Act that would allow the federal government to pass the necessary legislation. At least three provinces asked to see the federal government's proposed legislation before consenting to an amendment. While Mackenzie King had declared himself in favour of the amendment and had referred it to

10 *WDS*, 14 April 1936.

the premiers in November 1937, he would not move until there was unanimity among the provincial governments.[11]

It suited Mackenzie King's interests to be able to rely on the unconstitutionality of the federal government's proceeding on its own to enact unemployment insurance. Without doubt, his enthusiasm for the measure was dampened by the cost involved, and yet it would be difficult for him to oppose the program publicly.[12] Unemployment insurance obviously would not have the same impact in Brandon, Manitoba, as in Windsor. In the West, the number of workers affected would be very small, and the large contingent of western Liberal members assigned this proposal a much lower priority than agricultural issues.

At one point during my first term in parliament, I felt obliged to plead for the sympathetic understanding of the western members for the problems of industrial areas. It was, I pointed out

> . . . not going to do my honourable friends from the west any good
> to suggest to those of us who live in the east that we are unmindful
> of the problems of the west or that under our economy we are
> causing those in the west to be continually subordinated to our
> interests. . . . Undoubtedly we have conflicting economic interests
> and the task of government in this country is to reconcile and
> compromise those interests [for the benefit] of all.

It would have made me a very popular man in Essex East and in the rest of Ontario if I had opposed wheat subsidies or the Prairie Farm Rehabilitation Act. But I refused "to stoop to that kind of

11 The Employment and Social Insurance Act had been passed by the Bennett government in 1935. Although it was a step that I approved in principle, it had been declared *ultra vires* by the Judicial Committee of the Privy Council in 1937. Mackenzie King subsequently decided in October of that year to establish a national system of unemployment insurance. In November, he announced to the House that he had communicated with the provinces to secure approval for a constitutional amendment. Premiers Aberhart of Alberta, Duplessis of Québec and Dysart of New Brunswick had asked to see the proposed legislation before they sanctioned it.

12 H. Blair Neatby, *William Lyon Mackenzie King*, Vol. III, *1932-1939: The Prism of Unity* (Toronto: University of Toronto Press, 1976), pp. 243, 247-48.

practice." In an appeal to those from the West — who had great problems — I made it plain that easterners had difficulties as well:

> Come to my own city of Windsor, go up street after street and you will find men and women living under the most difficult economic circumstances, just as difficult as those experienced by the unfortunate drought areas of the west. . . . We too have our problems and we are not going to get anywhere in this House by putting our sectional and political interests against the interest of Canada generally.[13]

The report of the National Employment Commission that had been set up in May 1936 to investigate the unemployment system gave me heart that others shared my views. Norman Rogers had asked me to agitate in caucus for a study of unemployment, such as the one the commission had begun in March 1936. Mackenzie King accepted the idea of a study because it was one way of sloughing off the problem. The chairman of the commission, Arthur Purvis, was a leading and progressive industrialist who was determined to make a serious examination of the whole question. Bill Mackintosh, a brilliant political economist from Queen's University, was also a member. I met both of them when the commission held hearings in Toronto. As they moved around the country, I could see that most members of the commission were coming to share my point of view that separate systems of relief were needed for industrial and agricultural workers.

The commission's final report was tabled in the Commons in April 1938. It proposed that since direct relief was wasteful, the government ought to undertake a large public works program to stimulate the construction industry and to put into effect youth training programs in a nationally coordinated scheme. It had been recognized that the needs of Canadians had gone beyond the lower tariffs proposed by the western Liberals and the balanced budget sought by King and his finance minister, Charles Dunning. In fact, the commission advocated an active government role in

13 House of Commons, *Debates*, 23 March 1939, p. 2,192 ff.

devising fiscal policy by which public spending would expand or contract, as required, to moderate economic swings between depression and prosperity.[14]

The delay in implementing any of these schemes made me more and more frustrated. In the House on 3 May, I spoke determinedly in favour of unemployment insurance, referring to the demoralizing consequences of unemployment in my own constituency. When CCFer Abe Heaps interrupted me to ask how we could best proceed, my response was that the federal government could develop a scheme of unemployment insurance with those provinces that had shown a willingness to cooperate and that the others would soon follow. I knew my suggestion would not be well received by the government, but I was resolved to do all I could to see that unemployment insurance was put on the statute books.[15]

Yet the government still dragged its feet. In February 1939, I supported a resolution introduced by A. W. Neill, the independent member from Comox-Alberni, that the government should act immediately to introduce unemployment insurance. Under the existing economic system, I pointed out, neither reciprocity treaties nor trade policy in general could cure the blight of unemployment. I urged the government to recognize this and to take immediate steps to provide a contributory unemployment insurance scheme. I spoke in the House of Commons on 20 February, pointing out that

> ... the answer to all these difficulties, we are told, is a constitutional
> one. We are told that we all want a system of unemployment
> insurance in Canada, but that because of the judgments of the

14 The National Employment Commission reported to Norman Rogers. The prime minister originally hoped that the commission would reduce relief costs as a means of balancing the budget. Its terms of reference included bringing some order into the administration of relief, collecting data and advising the minister on cooperation with relief agencies. It also recommended programs and projects that would stimulate employment (House of Commons, *Debates*, 30 March 1936, p. 1,570). The report was not one Mackenzie King enjoyed receiving, since it envisaged objectives contrary to his hopes (National Employment Commission, *Final Report* (Ottawa: King's Printer, 1938)).

15 House of Commons, *Debates*, 3 May 1938, pp. 2,499-2,502.

judicial committee, this is not possible. Well of course, we have to recognize the findings of the judicial committee, and nothing will be gained by disagreeing with these decisions. At this point, however, I believe I should say that *this parliament would clearly have the power, without resorting to the provinces, to bring about the amendment to our constitution in order to clearly and unmistakedly endow this parliament with the authority now lacking.* [My italics]

I added that I was aware that this course would occasion dissent among the provinces, six of whom were in favour of a national system of unemployment insurance. The government agreed with the desirability of unemployment insurance but was not prepared to act immediately. The philosophy of laissez-faire, I claimed, was opposed to any overall method of planning and could not ameliorate the causes of unemployment: seasonal fluctuations, cyclical depressions, technological developments, the decay and merger of industrial firms, and disputes. Of the proposed nostrums, only unemployment insurance would be effective. I pointed to the British scheme as the means by which that country had been saved from social disaster during the Depression. In my view, a similar nationwide system in Canada would ensure the most equitable distribution of costs among employer, employee and state. The government could shift a considerable share of the burden to the wealthy by income and inheritance taxes. I again implored the government to proceed unilaterally if provincial consent was not forthcoming.

In response to the arguments in favour, Norman Rogers recognized the validity of my arguments but pointed out that the antagonistic attitude of Premier Duplessis of Québec made federal action difficult. Rogers contended that the government was rendering a great service in not creating disharmony by riding roughshod over the provinces. Despite the arguments of A. W. Neill and me, other speakers supported unemployment insurance but were reluctant to enlist in a vigorous campaign;[16] small wonder that the legislation was so long delayed.

16 House of Commons, *Debates*, 20 February 1939, p. 1,108 ff.

Although I considered relief works to be mainly a palliative measure, I was pleased when, in May 1938, the government undertook to provide employment through public works. Norman Rogers, who had come to espouse a truly Keynesian approach to improving the economic and employment situation, had a tough fight in cabinet, but he finally pried $50 million out of Mackenzie King and Charles Dunning.[17] The Municipal Improvements Assistance Act[18] provided for federal loans to municipalities for works projects of a self-liquidating nature. This new departure involved the federal government in direct financial dealings with municipalities; instead of relief, work might be offered to the unemployed. The legislation carefully avoided antagonizing the provinces, which were ultimately responsible for the municipalities, by requesting provincial approval for all proposed subsidies.

On 2 June, I inquired of the minister of finance if the city transportation system in Windsor could expand and modernize by taking advantage of the new money available. While Charles Dunning did not rule out the possibility, he indicated that Windsor's proposal did not appear to be a self-liquidating project and that he was not anxious to broaden the scheme.[19] I had known full well what Dunning would reply but felt that I had to keep on poking and prodding. After all, "faint heart never won fair lady!" Apparently, the new program would operate under such strict conditions that the provision of created work instead of direct relief was not to be a major contribution to solving the problem of unemployment in Canada.

The scheme eventually provided some work: the building of an airport to serve the Windsor area. This project was the culmination of considerable pressure from the Windsor MPs to get the

17 H. Blair Neatby, *William Lyon Mackenzie King*, Vol. III, *1932-1939: The Prism of Unity*, pp. 253-55.
18 2 George VI, C. 33.
19 House of Commons, *Debates*, 2 June 1938, p. 3,474.

My father, Philippe Martin

My mother, Lumina Martin, née Chouinard

My Uncle Isidore's grocery store in Pembroke, 1907. My aproned father is leaning nonchalantly on the counter. Uncle Isidore stands behind him.

With a school chum at St
Alexandre, Ironside, Québec.

*In our garden at Isabella Street, Pembroke,
about 1920. Back row (left to right): Lucille,
Aline, Marie. Front row (left to right): Claire,
Paul, Anita.*

*The grade seven class at Pembroke Separate School, 1915. I am third from the right in the
middle row, with arms folded. John Stoqua is immediately in front of the door at the back.
Two places to my right is Vera Chaput.*

Manager (third from the right of the bottom row) of the football team at St. Michael's College, University of Toronto, 1924. Above me and a little to the right is Morley Callaghan.

Notre Dame cathedral, Easter 1930. Frank Mallon is facing the photographer (probably Wynne Plumptre), while Jack Beer looks over the parapet.

At Cambridge, 1929-30. I am second from the left in the middle row, Wynne Plumptre is on the far left of the back row.

At La Grande Boissière during the Zimmern International Summer School in Geneva, summer 1930.

My parents on the path in front of their Isabella Street home, about 1937.

DETROIT NEWS

Shaking hands with Franklin Delano Roosevelt at the Book Cadillac Hotel, Detroit, during the presidential election campaign 1932. Mrs Eleanor Roosevelt and their son Jim, my classmate at the Harvard Law School, are beside the future president.

Windsor in the 1930s. Looking down Ouellette Avenue to the Detroit River and skyline.

Campaigning during the 1930s in front of the town hall in Belle River. John D. Renaud, the village policeman and undertaker, is beside me.

With my mother at the opening of my first parliament, February 1936.

An earnest young lawyer in Windsor, about 1934.

In Rome in October 1936 with Mrs Denton Massey. Her husband, the Conservative MP, took the photograph.

On the steps of Immaculate Conception Church, Windsor, 8 September 1937. Nell's sister, Roxalana, and my partner, Keith Laird, are behind us. Lionel Chevrier is on the top step.

The start of our honeymoon. On the boat in New York, just before setting sail for Bermuda.

Nell about the time of our marriage.

At the League of Nations — the entrance to Le Bâtiment Electoral. Left to right: J.T. Thorson, MP for Selkirk; myself; Ernest Lapointe, minister of justice; Philippe Picard, Mr Lapointe's private secretary and, later, Canada's ambassador to the Argentine.

The Royal Visit June 1939. Queen Elizabeth accepts a bouquet from a Windsor girl.

Three cheers for Winston Churchill, just before he made his famous "Some chicken; some neck" speech in the House of Commons, 30 December 1941.

Dad's army: the 30th Reconnaissance (Reserve) Battalion of the Essex Regiment. Closest to the camera is John Chick, a Windsor businessman; on my right is an apprehensive Harold Vaughan, editor of The Windsor Daily Star.

*Wyndham Lewis's celebrated portrait
of Nell, painted in 1945.*

*In the office of the secretary of state as I was taking over that portfolio from
my long-time colleague, Norman McLarty, April 1945.*

Canadian delegates to the meetings of the United Nations in London, January-February 1946. Front row (left to right): Vincent Massey, J.G. Gardiner, Louis St Laurent, myself, Hume Wrong. Back row (left to right): Stanley Knowles, Dana Wilgress, Louis Rasminsky, Gordon Graydon, Alfred Rive, John Read, Escott Reid, Charles Ritchie.

After I had passed the loving-cup to Ernest Bevin at the Guildhall banquet, London, February 1946. Peter Fraser, the New Zealand prime minister, is reading the menu.

The United States delegation at the United Nations meetings in London. Seated in the front, from left to right, are Edward Stettinius, Secretary of State James Byrnes, Senator Tom Connally, and Eleanor Roosevelt.

Ernest Bevin, Britain's foreign secretary, is surrounded by Canadians at the United Nations meetings in London, January-February 1946. Seated on his left with a copy of Life *is M.J. Coldwell, while John Bracken is chatting to me.*

Walking along Fifth Avenue, New York, during the meetings of the United Nations, September 1946. M.J. Coldwell is beside me. Between him and Louis St Laurent, is Mrs Mathieu Samson, Mr St Laurent's daughter.

At the United Nations meetings, Flushing Meadow, New York, in the fall of 1946. Next to me is New York's mayor, Fiorello La Guardia. Adlai Stevenson and Helen Gahagan Douglas make up the party.

With Louis St Laurent, Canada's minister of external affairs at Hyde Park, the home of Mrs Eleanor Roosevelt, 3 November 1946.

At the ceremony to present certificates to the first Canadian citizens, 3 January 1947. With me at the Supreme Court of Canada building are Colin Gibson, who succeeded me as secretary of state, and the prime minister, W.L. Mackenzie King.

A Tory view of the Citizenship Act, by cartoonist Harry Hall.

Nell and young Paul, photographed about 1946.

Our daughter, Mary Anne, aged four.

minister of transport, C. D. Howe, to provide such a facility.[20] A site was selected in Sandwich East, a township in my constituency. The federal administration agreed to contribute $100,000 towards an airport if the city provided the site, and Mitch Hepburn also approved loans for the project on behalf of the Ontario government. At the same time, Ottawa contributed a small amount to help pay for Windsor's share in the Detroit River waterfront development scheme, which employed relief labour. The assistance of the two senior governments could be spent only on labour costs. Here again, plans to put the unemployed to work looked better on paper than they did in practice.

My support for federal scholarships for young people also grew out of a concern that they were suffering from a severe lack of opportunity heightened by the Depression. When I was living at Assumption College during the early 1930s, I had been struck by how few students were sons or daughters of workers in the car factories. It also disturbed me that hardly any trade union organizers had received higher education. So I began to speak publicly about the need for scholarships for those who could not afford to attend post-secondary institutions. When I went to Ottawa, I looked into the possibility of doing something about this problem, speaking to a number of people, including Tom Moore, president of the Trades and Labour Congress and one of the most respected labour leaders in Canada. He told me that he deplored not having a formal education and gave me some literature on scholarship schemes that had been put in place in Europe. Dr. H. M. Tory of the National Research Council also pressed me to agitate for more

20 House of Commons, *Debates*, 24 February 1938, pp. 783-84. When Howe had
     visited Windsor in the summer of 1937, he had given an assurance that the city
     would participate in the air transportation network.

federal money for students. With this encouragement, I planned to find a public forum for my proposal that the government should establish scholarships for students to proceed beyond high school.

My first session in the House of Commons had taught me that a bill standing in the name of a member was not a sure method of pushing the government to adopt a particular policy. Very often, it would not even be debated. On rare occasions, a private member's bill might be acceptable to the government and so would be reintroduced as government legislation. Only in that event was its passage secured. An effective method of importuning the government on an issue was to table a resolution in the name of a private member.[21] In my time, these resolutions were debated on Wednesdays and Thursdays; towards the end of the session, the Thursday discussion was dropped in order to secure the passage of government legislation.

I rose in the House on 24 February 1937 to propose that provision be made for the academic and technical training of outstanding students who were financially unable to continue their education.[22] Reflecting on my own experience as a boy whose parents could not afford to pay for his education, I thought the resolution would publicly acknowledge the help that I had received from my benefactors. To me, it was self-evident that many young people were similarly hindered in paying for their education.

More intervention by the state was inevitable in the evolving industrial society, and this committed the government to provide educational facilities for its citizens. I proposed that this obligation be further extended so that the state would ensure that deserving students were able to fulfil their capacities. I cited the British example, where the government provided scholarships for merit and to ensure a measure of equal opportunity. Germany, Japan,

21 A private member's bill was less likely to be discussed than a resolution.
22 I had tabled the resolution too late in the 1936 session for it to be debated. In framing the resolution, I had to couch it in terms that did not commit the government to spending; I therefore proposed that the government "investigate the desirability of scholarships for undergraduate or postgraduate training."

the USSR, Australia and New Zealand had provided funds for this purpose. I told the House that in the rural parts of Essex East, only three students in fifteen years had gone to an agricultural college; this astonishingly low figure meant that we were failing to develop talent that could improve our agriculture. Since education is a provincial matter under the British North America Act, I had to argue that this did not necessarily impede federal assistance; the national government already provided help under the National Research Council scholarships.[23]

Conservative and CCF members supported my resolution, but when Norman Rogers stood up, he raised several caveats. In his opinion, the question of provincial jurisdiction could not be altogether avoided, although he admitted that there was no insuperable constitutional obstacle. Nevertheless, he said that the federal government would have to discuss the priority of this scheme with the different governments of Canada and must determine who would administer the scholarships. The minister stressed the obligation of individuals and corporations to provide university endowments for scholarships and pointed out that employment assistance to the young must take precedence over any far-reaching scholarship program. To my disappointment, time ran out before the House could vote on my proposal. The success of the initiative lay not in achieving an affirmative vote but in airing the proposition and in stimulating public debate.

In fact, the resolution set off a campaign for national scholarships in which I allied myself with teachers and students. I spoke in various universities and over the radio, urging that the measure be adopted. The Canadian Student Assembly, chaired by Neil Morrison — the secretary of the Royal Commission on Bilingualism and Biculturalism in the 1960s — took up the cause. School boards, municipalities, university students clubs and the Ontario Secondary School Teachers Federation circulated a petition to support a second resolution that I proposed to table in 1939.

Although the outbreak of war made it difficult for me to continue

23 House of Commons, *Debates*, 24 February 1937, pp. 1,188-95.

the discussion — many thought this question was irrelevant — by that time the government had moved at least partway. The National Employment Commission had recommended a youth training program and in 1938 Norman Rogers introduced a measure to provide assistance to unemployed youth. The scheme would train young people in jobs allied to forestry and mining, as well as provide occupational and agricultural apprenticeships for urban and rural youth. Speaking on the measure, I noted that the government program would be one of the best in the industrial world and that it partly accepted the principle of national scholarships. The department of labour had proposed student aid in the form of scholarships on a contributory basis with the provinces — 300 in the first year, 500 in the second and 700 in the third. The real difficulty with this program again grew out of the divided jurisdiction under the BNA Act and the inability of the central authority to set up the program I had proposed.[24] This federal plan was a modified form of the larger grant that I had in mind.

Obviously, the problem of Canada's constitution had come to nettle me. In my opinion, the provinces were showing too much autonomy, and I blamed the BNA Act, which, as I told one audience, had been "framed in the horse and buggy days." I had begun to feel that Canadians should not let the act prevent the country from providing relief for those who needed it and the federal government from passing the necessary social legislation. The federal government should be granted the power to equalize conditions across the country.[25] The economic difficulties of the various levels of government and their inability to enact beneficial social legislation, unemployment insurance, for example, would

24 House of Commons, *Debates*, 1938, pp. 3,310-26; ibid., 15 May 1939, pp. 4,104-05. Rogers announced that the terms would provide for provincial proposals for scholarships based on a fixed percentage of the total Dominion allocation to each province under the youth training measure. The percentage would increase in each of the three years. In specific terms, it meant providing $25 a month for eight months to the students, for a total of $200 each.

25 *WDS*, 30 March 1936.

require amendments to reallocate powers between the federal and the provincial governments.

One means of promoting constitutional change, I argued, was the abolition of appeals to the Judicial Committee of the Privy Council. During my student days in Britain, I followed the practice of many budding lawyers and dropped in to hear the arguments in the Judicial Committee on Whitehall. In an informal court, the best judicial minds of Britain and the commonwealth discussed the law. My admiration for the court in no way abridged my conviction that Canada should not accept the committee's jurisdiction. By its decisions, this British tribunal had undermined the intentions of the fathers of confederation and had placed unforeseen restrictions on the ability of the federal government to meet changing conditions by taking powers from the federal government and giving them to the provinces. The Supreme Court of Canada, in my view, could competently serve as the final court of appeal, could protect the rights of racial and religious minorities, and could undertake the interpretation of the Canadian constitution capably and with due regard for and understanding of national conditions.[26] As I have mentioned, my growing frustration with constitutional impediments to unemployment insurance that grew out of Canada's federal nature led me to insist that the federal government had the power to unilaterally recommend amendments to the BNA Act despite provincial opposition.

Many times throughout the past five decades, the question of constitutional amendment has agitated the Canadian public and parliament. In the years after 1935, both Mackenzie King and R. B. Bennett agreed that constitutional changes were necessary to render our system of government more able to deal with current circumstances. The means of achieving constitutional amendment

26 House of Commons, *Debates*, 8 April 1938, pp. 2,193-96. I spoke in favour of a private member's bill, introduced by Conservative MP C. H. Cahan, to abolish appeals.

challenged the prime minister and the leader of the opposition in 1937, as it did until 1981-82. Under the guidance of Louis St. Laurent, the federal parliament asked Westminster to amend the British North America Act respecting the federal government's powers, without provincial consent.

In 1978-79, Pierre Trudeau was on the verge of similar action in the absence of desirable agreement with the provinces. While I was high commissioner and he was in London on one of his visits, I urged him to move unilaterally. It would be preferable for an amendment to be preceded by an agreement, I said, but it was not essential.

Despite my similar agitation in the late 1930s, Mackenzie King's caution would never have allowed him, even in frustration, to ruffle provincial feathers. Apart from this, not until the end of World War II did the British government, led at that time by Clement Attlee, recognize the sole authority of Canada's government to petition for constitutional change. When I was in London at the first General Assembly of the United Nations, I raised the constitutional question with Attlee. The solicitor in him caused the British prime minister to observe crisply that if Canada was a sovereign power under international law, the British government had no course open to it but to act on a petition by the federal government for constitutional change.

The Depression had imposed considerable strains on the Canadian federal system, and yet the government was slow to act. When Saskatchewan and Manitoba faced bankruptcy in early 1937, Mackenzie King decided to appoint a Royal Commission on Dominion-Provincial Relations to investigate the federal system, particularly the economic and fiscal relationships between the federal government and the provinces. The Rowell-Sirois Commission,[27] as it became known, held hearings across the country

27 The first chairman was Ontario's chief justice, N. W. Rowell, appointed in mid-August 1937. He suffered a stroke and was succeeded in October 1938 by commission member Joseph Sirois, a professor of constitutional law at Université Laval. Other members were H. F. Angus, of the University of British Columbia, R. A. McKay, of Dalhousie University, and J. W. Dafoe.

but was not expected to make a report quickly (it was not received until 30 May 1940). This delay did little to ease my feeling of impotence: my contact with some of the commissioners led me to believe that they shared my frustration and were prepared to recommend changes that would strengthen the central government.

Along with my support for collective bargaining, my advocacy of unemployment insurance, relief works and national scholarships stood me in good stead with the workers in the Windsor factories. They had a member of parliament who would fight for their interests and who believed strongly in what he was doing. In part, this commitment grew out of my own experience as a boy in Pembroke who had depended substantially on the goodwill and assistance of others for his education and whose father had suffered many of the privations that became so widespread during the Depression.

I did not speak only on industrial questions but often addressed the problems faced by the farming community. During my last years in parliament, people would make joking references to my catholicity of interests and cite as "proof" my "profound" knowledge of agricultural problems. On 15 July 1958, when the Liberals were in opposition, Mike Pearson tried to make his first speech on agriculture as leader of the opposition. The speaker, however, ruled that Mike had exhausted his right to speak — since he had already spoken in the debate for the House to go into the Committee of Supply. There sat Pearson with all his notes in front of him and no opportunity to make a statement of the Liberal policy on agriculture. I caught the Speaker's eye and rose to make the speech. The shouts of the Tories reverberated throughout the House — "Another farmer." "A horse trader." "I-love-hogs Martin." As Pearson furiously passed me his speech notes, I fended off the sarcasm and launched into *his* address.[28] I have heard it described as one of my great performances.

28 House of Commons, *Debates*, 15 July 1958, p. 2,237 ff.

The fact was that agricultural production and marketing had always been an important interest to my constituents, particularly the sugarbeet growers and corn growers. The situation of farmers during the Depression was as difficult as that of city folk. They lost their livelihood as surely as industrial workers lost their jobs. There was little the farmers of southwestern Ontario could do when the prices of agricultural commodities dropped, and I kept on promoting strong farm organizations that would function in much the same way as unions and that would deal with the large food processors.

Farmers worried about gaining a secure income either through getting better prices for crops or by increasing their share of the market. In the case of sugarbeet growers, the issue centred on the extent to which they should cooperate with the sugar companies in petitioning the government to drop the tax of one cent per pound on all sugar; the growers hoped that the companies would pass the reduced cost on to the farmers in the form of higher prices. For their part, the corn growers were concerned about the imports of South African corn duty free under the trade pacts of 1932 and the extent of imported corn in the Canadian market. However, southwestern Ontario's corn was inferior because of its high moisture content — a consequence of the lack of proper drying facilities. The local farmers had formed various organizations — the beet growers, the corn growers and *l'Union des cultivateurs d'Essex et Kent* — to further their objectives. To the tomato growers, who did not belong to an organized group, I always pointed out that there was strength in numbers.[29]

During this period, the *Windsor Daily Star* was full of reports from various farmers' meetings; agriculture was certainly a very powerful but necessary lobby. The beet growers, backed by the local member of the Ontario legislature and federal MPs from the

29 *WDS*, 6 January 1936; ibid., 14 January 1936; ibid., 7 February 1936. J. H. Grisdale, the former federal deputy minister of agriculture, had prepared a report on the corn situation, urging the farmers to make a cooperative effort to establish corn driers. Undried corn "heated" while it was being transported, and that was why Essex corn had a bad reputation; ibid., 4 March 1936; ibid., 6 August 1936.

Windsor area, organized delegations to come to Ottawa to petition the federal government for help.

Five hundred corn growers met and passed a resolution asking the government to consider building a corn elevator and drying facilities for Essex County. Along with Murray Clark, I presented their request to the minister of agriculture, Jimmy Gardiner, and convinced him to make a tour of the corngrowing area later in the year. When, on 24 September 1936, the government eliminated the duty of 20 cents per bushel on corn imported from the United States and Argentina, the farmers were up in arms and passed resolutions condemning the change. Responding to pressure and the fact that the growers had produced a bumper crop, the government reimposed the tariff on imported corn. The inconsistency of the policy upset both me and my constituents, particularly when the large elevator companies in Toronto used the temporary lapse of duties to import millions of bushels of cheap corn, which they then sold for higher prices that included the cost of duties that had not been collected.[30]

The pressure from the Windsor area began to pay off, and early in February 1937, following a meeting with the Essex County members of parliament, Jimmy Gardiner announced that the government would help pay for a corn drier at Chatham.[31] The minister also agreed to send an official to Windsor to look into the commercial wisdom of building an elevator in the city. The city's chamber of commerce and board of control quickly endorsed the project.[32] The Toronto Elevator Company, which owned a corn elevator in Sarnia, opposed the proposal and incited other municipalities to join in decrying the expenditure of any public money in Windsor. I found Jimmy Gardiner to be an able minister who responded to representations such as mine.

When little further progress was made on the issue, I forwarded a resolution to the Clerk of the House of Commons early in 1938,

30 *WDS*, 5 March 1936. There were two meetings, one on 4 March and another on 12 March; ibid., 3 and 4 October 1936; ibid., 19 January 1937.
31 ibid., 5 February 1937.
32 ibid., 1 June 1937.

entreating the government to consider the need for improved marketing, drying, grading, inspection and storage facilities for corn in the Windsor area. Support for this action came from both my CCF opponent, Ben Levert, and from a former Conservative MP, Eccles Gott, popularly known as "The Onion King." Although the Essex County Council approved my resolution, one councillor did not think I would get very far in pushing the government since there was no election on the horizon. Lum Clark commented sarcastically, "We know the home folk expect you to make your elevator speech, Paul, old man, so you had better get it off your chest while the members of the House of Commons are having supper."

The House *did* hear my speech on the resolution in March, when I pleaded the cause of the rehabilitation of agriculture and the case for giving our producers subventions to help fight foreign competition.[33] Our corn growers, I argued, deserved help because they produced the highest corn yields per acre of any of the major nations. With financial assistance, they could clearly meet domestic demands.[34]

The resolution received unanimous support from the House, and W. D. Euler, the minister of trade and commerce, agreed that his department would study the matter with a view to taking some action. The elevator proposal did not materialize, but I derived some satisfaction from the government's agreement to help supply drying facilities, inspection, and grading services. My success in lobbying for support in the farmers' cause led to considerable praise from both my rural constituents and from the *Windsor Daily Star*[35] and shows what continual pressure from a backbencher can achieve.

33 Cabinet had agreed in January to allow me to proceed with my corn resolution, and this meant that it would pass in the House (E. A. Pickering to Ross Gray, 29 January 1938, W. L. Mackenzie King Papers (J2 series, file P-569), PAC).
34 House of Commons, *Debates*, 16 March 1938, p. 1,383 ff.
35 *WDS*, 17 March 1938.

One factor that threatened to disturb my relations with my constituents was the growing feud between the federal and provincial wings of the Liberal Party. More accurately, perhaps, the fight was between Mackenzie King and Mitch Hepburn. Since his election in 1934, I had grown increasingly disenchanted with the premier of Ontario. His attempt to break the UAW and his disdain for the rights of labour during the Oshawa strike further reinforced my disillusionment. Hepburn's dismissal of his two most progressive ministers, David Croll and Arthur Roebuck, left him more exposed than ever to the influence of his cronies, mostly mining magnates, who, unhappily, reinforced his illiberal tendencies.

The animosity of Ontario's premier to the federal Liberals threatened party unity and its national standing. When Norman Rogers lowered federal relief grants to Ontario in 1936, Mitch took great umbrage, refusing to attend the National Liberal Federation meeting and severing the provincial party from its federal counterpart. One consequence of this arbitrary decision was to remove a key supplier of financial assistance from the federal party, since Hepburn controlled the major sources of party funds in Ontario.

I determined that Hepburn's split would not discourage me from maintaining close relations with the provincial MLA, Dr. Trottier, whose riding overlapped mine. It was plain that he did not support Hepburn's confrontation with Ottawa, and I decided that we could work amicably together; after all, our political organizations were composed mostly of the same people. Norman Lambert of the National Liberal Federation badgered me to speak to those who could put some sense into Mitch's head. At his behest, I spoke, but in vain, with another member from the Windsor area, James H. Clark, the Speaker of the Ontario legislature, who resented what he called the high and mighty Ottawa crowd. After discussing the situation with Harry Johnston, the Ontario organizer, and with Frank O'Connor, another of Mitch's pals, it looked to be a lost cause. Since there was little to do at the top, common sense had to prevail in the ridings, and the provincial and federal MLAs and MPs in Essex County decided not to allow Mitch's quarrel to prevent cooperation among ourselves.

When rumours of a provincial election became rife, I decided I would live up to my assurance to support Dr. Trottier, in part because I knew the doctor did not approve of Mitch's attacks on the King government. Hepburn, however, was too wily to carry on his vendetta during an election campaign, and King was chary of bringing the spat into the open. We all knew that the public had approved of Mitch's anti-union stand during the Oshawa strike, and he was still popular with the voters. Lum Clark had often expressed the view that I might find it difficult to support the provincial party as a result of Hepburn's feud. The prime minister wisely took the position that his Ontario followers should each decide whom to support. By doing this and by announcing that he desired Hepburn's re-election, King minimized the evident disunity in the party.

Although Hepburn fought the election on an anti-union platform, that was but one issue. It may well be wondered how I found it possible to support the provincial party if I felt so keenly about the rights of labour. I was not alone. But the provincial leader dominated his party, all of whom looked on the Oshawa strike from different perspectives and as only one item in the campaign. The desire to keep out the fragmented and reactionary Tories and to assist individual candidates formed the basis of Liberal support for Hepburn during the election. This situation involved the contradictory attitudes and illogical positions that are frequently the very stuff of the electoral process. In any event, the provincial Liberals carried the Essex seats yet again in the provincial election on 6 October 1937.

Following Hepburn's victory, his continued intransigence over the export of power to the United States again aroused Mackenzie King's ire. I saw the divisions reappearing among the Liberals of Essex East. Miss A. D. L. Robinson, an anti-Hepburn member of my riding association, had to be restrained from putting a motion to the 1938 annual meeting of the constituency, deploring the premier's posture. However, I could not stop her from introducing a resolution of censure at a meeting of the Essex County Federation of Women Liberals, where some of the wounds surfaced again, and the pro-Hepburn ladies defeated her motion. On an optimistic note, she wrote to Mackenzie King explaining her action and prophesying, correctly, that "most people will vote for the party at each election, provincial or federal, and that in the next federal election, their loyalty will return to the federal government."[36]

36 A. D. L. Robinson to King, 31 January 1939, King Papers (J2 series, vol. 287, file P-305, part 10) PAC. I had sent on to King her letter to me protesting Hepburn's actions as one means of keeping the prime minister informed and of trying to coddle a very strong-willed local pillar of the party.

VIII

For "King" and Country

O N 7 SEPTEMBER 1939, the parliament that had been prorogued three months before was hurriedly called into a special session to deal with Canada's role in Hitler's war. After the members of the House of Commons and the Senate had gathered, the governor general, Lord Tweedsmuir, solemnly told us what we already knew — that Britain was at war with Germany. We had been summoned, he said, "at the earliest possible moment in order that the government may seek authority for the measures necessary for the defence of Canada . . . to resist further aggression and to prevent the appeal to force instead of to pacific means in the settlement of international disputes."[1] The government had already mobilized the armed forces and proclaimed the War Measures Act to put the country on a war footing. Our task as legislators was to commit Canada formally to the conflict.

The events of the special session reinforced my view that Mackenzie King had acted cautiously and wisely when he

---

1 House of Commons, *Debates*, 7 September 1939, p. 1.

brought Canada into the hostilities as a united nation.[2] The prime minister told the House he had no doubt that when the moment of decision arrived, the Canadian people would wish to defend freedom. But, King explained, "the supreme endeavour of my leadership is to let no hasty or premature threat or pronouncement create mistrust or divisions between the different elements that compose the population."[3] That statement I fully upheld. King expressed his confidence that he had the support of parliament in declaring war, although he recalled that in 1937 and 1938 he had made it clear to the House that no commitment for such a proclamation had been made to the British. When I heard him say this, I felt that the prime minister had misled us, although it could be argued that he had assured Chamberlain and Eden only that in his judgment the Canadian people would wish to be at Britain's side.[4] Certainly what he told the British earlier verged on a commitment to go to war. Despite my reservations on this point, I still believe that no one could have prepared Canada for the decision to declare war with greater care than Mackenzie King. His long service as prime minister had been marked by a punctilious attention to detail. This was the hallmark of his extraordinary leadership, needed now as never before.

In his address, Mackenzie King insisted on the voluntary nature of the decision of Canada's parliament to authorize war. We were not subservient to Britain: Canada was a nation in the fullest sense. Hansard did not record my "Hear, hear," but I gave it full voice. In 1939 I did not share the orthodox Tory position that when

2 Before the debate on the address from the throne had begun, Maxime Raymond of Beauharnois-Laprairie tabled a petition, signed by thousands of his compatriots, protesting against participation by Canada in any extraterritorial war.

3 House of Commons, *Debates*, 8 September 1939, p. 25 ff.

4 ibid., p. 32. I disagree with J. W. Pickersgill's observations in *The Mackenzie King Record*, Vol. I, *1939-1944* (Toronto: University of Toronto Press, 1960), pp. 11-12, which imply that King faced the situation in September 1939 as a completely free agent. There was no signed commitment, to be sure, but a sort of assurance had been given to Chamberlain and his foreign minister, Anthony Eden.

Britain was at war, we were automatically at war; parliament had brought Canada into the struggle and rightfully so.[5] Certainly, in law, Canada could have pursued a policy of neutrality, although that would have been difficult when the British were mobilizing. I could not have supported neutrality. The representatives of the Canadian people took the only honourable course when they confirmed the government's policy of joining Britain in a call to arms to preserve freedom.

The prime minister repeated an undertaking he had given at the end of March 1939 that he would not introduce conscription for overseas service. The leader of the opposition, R. J. Manion,[6] and most members of parliament supported this position. Given the memory of the disunity between French and English Canada in the Great War, parliamentarians felt that no other course could have been taken. My own memory of the Great War convinced me that it would be very unwise to introduce compulsory military service, so divisive in 1917. There was but one sort of conscription that I would support: "conscription of all the wealth of this country"[7] so that no one would profit from war.

Winding up the debate, the prime minister began to recite

> *When a deed is done for Freedom, through*
> *the broad earth's aching breast,*
> *Runs a thrill of joy prophetic,*
> *trembling on from east to west.*

He did not stop before he had droned through the full fourteen stanzas from "The Present Crisis," by the nineteenth-century American poet James Russell Lowell. Although Lowell's poem speaks about the opposite of all that Hitler stood for, King's

---

5 I had defended King's actions in advance, pointing out that "despite what critics . . . have to say, it is not for Mr. King to decide. . . . That is for Parliament to say." (*WDS*, 24 August 1939).

6 Bob Manion was elected leader of the Conservative Party at a national convention in Ottawa on 3 July 1938. He was elected to the House of Commons as the member for London, Ontario, on 14 November of that year.

7 *WDS*, 24 August 1939.

long-spun quotation had a certain remoteness from the crisis of 1939. It was, I suppose, a confirmation of Mackenzie King's peculiarity.

The prime minister's speech was comprehensive and tactful but in no way as inspirational as the words of Ernest Lapointe. Speaking particularly to many in Québec and to some western Canadians, Lapointe showed how impossible it would have been for Canada to remain neutral. "I hate war," said Lapointe, "with all my heart and conscience, but devotion to peace does not mean ignorance or blindness. . . . By doing nothing, and by being neutral, we actually would be taking the side of Adolf Hitler." Lapointe eloquently challenged both the extreme Québec nationalists who espoused neutrality and the gung ho English Canadians who had already begun to agitate for conscription. "Is it not worthwhile to the Canadian nation, when the nation is at war, to preserve unity . . . ?"[8]

When the House voted, only J. S. Woodsworth called out "nay" to a declaration of war. Speaking earlier to a hushed chamber, he had shown that he had the courage of his pacifist convictions. In my many years in the House, it never loomed so great as when its members listened quietly to this man of conscience, even though some of us felt his words might increase the frictions among Canadians.

Lord Tweedsmuir prorogued the special session on 19 September and said that "the days of stress and strain which lie ahead cannot fail to prove a supreme test of national determination and endurance." After hearing this, I contemplated what we had done as I walked from the Senate chamber to my office on the fifth floor. We had assembled to authorize Canada's participation in a war that inevitably would engender waste, destruction and death. My generation had dreamed of a world where the occasions for war would be minimized by the League of Nations. But the statesmen who had failed to make the League work were now making war work, and I was part of all this. I had told my constituency

8 House of Commons, *Debates*, 9 September 1939, p. 65 ff.

association just two weeks previously that "war is not of our making. War is not in our blood; not in our tradition."[9] Yet I knew that it was right to give my backing to a declaration of war — there was no other way.

Nevertheless, Canada's decision to join battle with Nazi Germany raised questions in my mind. There had been talk of equality of sacrifice — I was thirty-six years of age and therefore qualified for active service. What was I to do? My contemporaries had already begun to flock to the recruiting stations, but I was torn in two. I suppose there was some selfishness in my brooding; others might not know of my physical disability, and that worried me. But conscience, as Herbert Asquith once observed, is a faithful barometer. Since the president of the National Research Council, General A. G. L. McNaughton, was an acquaintance, I went to see him at his office on Sussex Street and told him of my dilemma. McNaughton, who was soon to take on the command of the first overseas contingent of the armed forces, readily understood my feelings but said that my duty was to stay at my parliamentary post.

Before returning to Windsor, I called at the offices of the new minister of labour, my mentor and friend, Norman McLarty.[10] On 19 September, he had relinquished his position as postmaster general to take over a new portfolio.[11] Foreseeing that his task

9 *WDS*, 24 August 1939.
10 Before McLarty first joined the government as postmaster general nine months earlier, King canvassed the Ontario members about the appointment (Martin to King, n. d. January 1939, King Papers (J1 series, vol. 274, p. 231503 ff) PAC). Along with most, I welcomed the decision and felt he would be a worthy successor to J. C. Elliott.
11 In his cabinet reorganization, King had appointed J. L. Ralston minister of finance on 5 September to replace Charles Dunning, who had resigned. Then, on 19 September, he appointed Norman Rogers to national defence, made Chubby Power postmaster general, and moved McLarty to labour and Ian MacKenzie to pensions and national health.

would be a doubly difficult one in wartime, he had told me of his uncertainty about how the trade unions would regard him. Assuring him that labour leaders knew him to be a just man, I offered to help in any way I could to make industrial relations in Windsor as untroubled as possible.

On the afternoon of my first day back home after the declaration of war, I strolled along Windsor's Ouellette Avenue, chatting with anyone I met. Some asked about what the war meant; they were anxious to learn how parliament had reached the decision to summon Canadians to arms. Others wanted to know why we had not opted for neutrality. As we talked, I was heartened to find out that most of those I spoke to approved of the decision and also declared themselves in favour of the no-conscription pledge.

One day I paid a surprise visit to the recruiting centre of the Essex Scottish Regiment, where I received a warm greeting from Kenneth McIntyre, a junior officer. I told him I had come to enlist. Amazed, he blurted out, "But Paul . . . ." As I was led to a table in a nearby room, the colonel of the regiment, Arthur Pearson, asked me to come to his quarters. When I told him what I had told McNaughton, Arthur proffered the same advice. After a medical examination, I was assigned to the "E" category, designating me unfit for active service. As I was leaving, the colonel laughingly observed that it would have pleased the enemy if the army had taken me on strength. But the gesture — and it was no more than that — greatly relieved my conscience.

The fighting in Poland soon ended, and the "phoney war" that lasted until the spring of 1940 gave the government and Canadians a chance to make ready. The war caused a few ripples in the Windsor area. Shortly after the declaration, the local communists, tarnished by Soviet-German collaboration, were purged from the Windsor delegation of the CIO just before it went to Ottawa to present its views to the new minister of labour. I sympathized with the unions' contention that the labour department should have their interests as its major objective, but I warned the delegation that the government would prefer to see labour and management as partners in industry. To my annoyance, as the problems multiplied, so did bureaucratic miscalculation. The Ontario government set the cat among the pigeons with its order-in-council cutting off relief to resident aliens who had not taken an oath of allegiance. Since no court authorized to hear oaths could be held in Windsor before the following March, only 75 out of 300 aliens were entitled to relief, and I had Russians, Czechs, and even Americans on my doorstep, imploring me to intercede on their behalf.

To help solve problems before they grew serious and to inspire cooperation and support, I urged the government to take Canadians into its confidence and explain how it was conducting the country's war effort. My reasoning was that the press, if properly informed, could be trusted not to publish anything harmful to the cause. In a plea for tolerance towards both the immigrant groups and French Canada, I told the Windsor Kiwanis Club in late November 1939 that the government and ordinary Canadians must keep in mind the nation's multiracial character — no single group or region should be allowed to force its views on the rest of the country.

These remarks were prompted by my awareness of the trouble the national government had experienced during the recent Québec election campaign. Premier Maurice Duplessis was a calculating politician, content to stay within the Canadian family but not prepared to go out of his way to strengthen its unity. It was clear that in announcing an October election, Duplessis wanted to take advantage of the uncertainty occasioned by the war. It was an irresponsible and opportunistic political act. Québec's lack of enthusiasm for the war had prompted Duplessis to believe that he could fan a conscription scare that would reawaken memories of 1917. He told the electors that under the guise of war, Mackenzie King, Ernest Lapointe and the federal government wanted to assimilate Québecois and to push for a greater centralization that would usurp the power of the country's only French-dominated government.

It was clear to me that the gloves were off. If Québec had supported Duplessis, it would have been catastrophic. Chubby

Power convinced Lapointe that a Duplessis victory would amount
to a repudiation of the federal Québec ministers, who might feel
compelled to resign; in consequence, Chubby urged them to take
an active part in the provincial election, set for 25 October. But
King was leery about members of his cabinet taking the gamble
and putting their jobs on the line. I felt so strongly about the
Québec premier's unconscionable tactics that I threw myself into
the campaign. On the radio and at five meetings in the province, I
reminded the electorate that Duplessis was jeopardizing Canadian
unity at a time when a concerted national effort was needed.[12]
Canadians were engaged in a common task — to preserve the
ideals without which the social and cultural life of French Canada
would be meaningless. At one public meeting, the single mention
of Hitler's name brought forth a chorus of boos, but these changed
to cheers when I spoke of the liberty of speech guaranteed by our
free society.

Few election results pleased me more than the defeat of the
Duplessis administration by Adélard Godbout's Liberals. I cred-
ited the victory in large part to the efforts of Ernest Lapointe, who
had acted as a dispassionate Canadian and not as a blinkered
partisan. The result was a demonstration by the citizens of
Québec, ever tenacious of their own traditions, that they were not
prepared to champion them at the expense of national unity.[13]

Duplessis' defeat heartened me for other reasons, too. I knew
that his removal from office would make it easier to introduce
unemployment insurance since the Québec premier's opposition
had been one of the major obstacles to a constitutional amendment

12 I spoke to two large meetings in Montreal (in Laurier and St. Jacques ridings) and at
    rallies in Berthier, Arthabasca and Trois Rivières.
13 In 1966 when my former colleague Jean Lesage took an extreme course as premier of
    Québec in advancing Québec's international role, I told a national Liberal confer-
    ence that he had embarked on a dangerous path. If Lesage had pursued his course to
    its end, I felt that it might have been necessary for Québec ministers to challenge his
    strategy, as Lapointe and Power had challenged Duplessis years before. Trudeau,
    Jean Marchand and their ministerial colleagues, I hope, would have had no hesita-
    tion in doing what their predecessors had done. But before things reached that point,
    the able but impulsive Lesage lost an election.

authorizing the scheme. But I quickly learned that this resistance had not been the only hurdle: some federal ministers believed that the measure could be a financial strain in wartime. I went to see Norman McLarty, who, as minister of labour, held responsibility for the issue, and told him that the Liberal Party would suffer in public esteem if it failed to enact such a vital piece of legislation once the way had been cleared by the provinces.

After the Québec election, I took advantage of the parliamentary recess to practise law again, mostly as counsel, and this kept me in the courts for close to two months. I wondered occasionally if the courtroom would not give me the occupational satisfaction I sought; but I always concluded that it would not, because my ultimate hopes went beyond the legal profession. Practising law was my *métier*, but the problems of Canada and its relations with other countries, the question of international organization and the achievement of world peace — these were part of my vocation.

During my first years on the Hill, the two careers did not conflict to any great extent. The parliamentary sessions were not long, and because the salary of $4,000 was not enough to raise a family and meet the upkeep of a couple of houses,[14] I would try to practise law for two or three days each week while parliament sat, and I used to miss the odd day in the House. When I became parliamentary secretary to the minister of labour in April 1943, my law practice had to be curtailed drastically. As a member of parliament, there was no restriction on the type of cases I could take on. For example, an MP could bring the government to court on behalf of his client, and I once acted for a man who unsuccessfully sued the minister of national revenue. When I dealt with J. L. Ilsley, the minister, concerning the case, my regard for him grew stronger. How he wrestled with the point of law at issue, not just taking his officials'

14 From the start of my working life, I made it a policy to put aside ten percent of my earnings each week.

advice! He argued the law with me as though he were a lawyer retained by the Crown. There were cases that I would and could not countenance; one client, a Tory naturally, wanted me to prosecute a case that involved the prime minister, but I refused point blank.

On 25 January 1940, I was cross-examining a witness in an important trial before the Supreme Court of Ontario, when Mr. Justice McFarlane interrupted me — destroying my cross-examination — adjourned the court and asked me to go with him to his chambers. Was there a problem in my presentation? I asked, trying to control my irritation. No, the judge assured me with a smile on his face. But he took me aback by asking if I knew that a federal election had just been called for March. Mackenzie King had decided on a dissolution of parliament and had written the announcement into Lord Tweedsmuir's speech from the throne on the opening day of the new session.

Bob Manion, the leader of the opposition, was understandably furious, even though dissolution was the prime minister's prerogative. Looking back on the incident, I find it difficult to accept that there was so little explanation from King. The following day, anticipating Mitch Hepburn's efforts to influence federal candidates, the prime minister told the caucus that he would recognize as Liberal candidates only those who supported him personally; he expected others to withdraw. This I questioned in principle. In our parliamentary democracy, should standing as a candidate for a political party ever — even in time of war — depend upon acceptance of a particular person as leader? Not in my opinion, but most of my fellow Liberals were not displeased with the prime minister's stand. I never felt that Hepburn would replace King. Few Canadians did.

My court cases were bound to last for some weeks, and there was little I could do about getting into the fray. I had already missed the opening of parliament, but it would not have entered my head to leave my client in untried hands. The critical work — the nomination and the organization of the election in Essex East — would have to be undertaken by the constituency executive. I followed events closely but did not enter the campaign until the trial was over.

The reason for King's sudden election call was his determination to confront the anti-government agitation being fomented by Hepburn and his unlikely ally, George Drew, the leader of the provincial Conservatives. When the Ontario legislature opened its session on 10 January, both men had spoken critically of the war effort and had attacked Mackenzie King for what they claimed was lack of leadership. Eight days later, as Drew was yet again berating Ottawa's anaemic stewardship, Hepburn — to everyone's amazement — introduced a hastily conceived resolution regretting that "the federal government at Ottawa has made so little effort to prosecute Canada's duty in the war in the vigorous manner the people of Canada desire to see."[15] Several Liberal members of the House told me later of their embarrassment about this, but Hepburn was not going to give his legislative colleagues an opportunity to evade a recorded vote.

Mitch was a bully. It appalled me that at such a critical time he was able to dominate so many Liberals at Queen's Park, especially his cabinet. The pettiness of ministers like T. B. McQuesten, of Hamilton, who was forever backbiting about the federal leader, disturbed and disillusioned me. In any event, when the division bells rang, twenty-two Liberals ignored the summons, and ten voted against Hepburn. The motion was passed, however, because Mitch's entire cabinet joined the Conservatives to produce a 44-vote majority. In few other situations have politicians lowered themselves to such a level. That night, after I had returned from court, I phoned Harry Nixon, Hepburn's right-hand man. It was just as well that I did not reach him.

Hepburn's resolution provided King with the excuse he needed to call a snap election. The prime minister must have had it in the back of his mind that it would be advantageous to go to the country before the war took a more serious turn. Although I was

15 Mackenzie King had read the motion to the House (House of Commons, *Debates*, 25 January 1940, pp. 4-5).

jolted by the announcement, I was ready to run. My riding association had begun to gear up in August 1939 for a possible election; as I told its members then, "The Conservative Party is essentially a party of reaction. . . . They are not offering anything that they have not offered the people in the past." I predicted, mistakenly, that in Essex East the real contest would lie between the Liberals and the CCF.[16]

As soon as parliament was prorogued, my team of workers began to make ready for battle, but I was still defending my clients in the Supreme Court of Ontario. What kept me so busy were two major criminal conspiracy cases, each of which went on for well over three weeks. One of my clients was Rocco Perri, a notorious Hamiltonian charged with bribing certain customs officials. I was eventually able to get him an acquittal.[17] With a lot of effort, I managed to get a new trial for Sam Motruk, the other defendant, but he thought he would try his luck with another lawyer; he was convicted, although the facts were identical to those in the Perri case.

My chief electoral organizer in 1940 was Angus Buchanan, who had previously worked for the YMCA. Among those helping him at party headquarters were Isabelle Quenneville, Russell Farrow, George Scott, Frank Hoolihan and Cliff Chauvin, and they set about rounding up the poll captains and canvassers. With forty-eight electioneering days left, they assured me on 30 January that the organization for the nomination was well underway. Despite their confidence that we would win, I was far from certain. In the many elections I have contested, I was never able to assess my own chances accurately and always preferred to "run scared." In the 1958 election, Stanley Knowles, the long-time member for Winnipeg North Centre, debated with me before a large audience in Windsor. Afterwards, he said, "Paul, you're going to lose your seat," leaving no doubt that he would win his own seat with a

16 *WDS*, 24 August 1939.
17 It was rumoured years later that Perri had been found in Hamilton Harbour, with a cement block tied around his neck.

substantial majority. In the event, Stanley was defeated, while I was one of a handful of Liberal survivors in Ontario.

When the second conspiracy case finished on 9 February, all was ready for the nomination meeting the following day at the St. Jean-Baptiste Hall in Tecumseh. Albert Wallace, the Essex East Liberal Association president, chaired an overflowing gathering; Norman McLarty, Murray Clark and Senator Gustave Lacasse were also on the platform. What a contrast to five years before! This meeting was unanimous from the outset. The mayor of Tecumseh, Fred Bouteillier, put forward my name. Murray Clark spoke of the party standing foursquare behind Mackenzie King, and Norman McLarty declared that the outrageous acts of Duplessis and Hepburn had obviously rallied our supporters.

In my acceptance speech, I laid out my campaign platform in French and English (bilingualism was not merely token in Essex East, and I spoke in both official languages at all election meetings except those in the totally English communities of Walkerville, Maidstone and Sandwich South). Saying that two years before I had seen certain conflict unless the Nazi dictator was stopped, I reiterated that the best way to halt aggression was not through war but through international organization. (Winston Churchill's remark that "jaw, jaw, jaw" is better than "war, war, war" strikes a sympathetic chord in me.) The League of Nations was not an institution to be abandoned, I said, but was the ultimate hope for the maintenance of peace once hostilities had ceased. An unemployment insurance scheme and improved agricultural facilities were important elements in my electoral platform, and I spoke of my great worry about the number of jobless and about the legitimacy of trade union organization.

The Conservative campaign was based on the proposition that what was required in wartime was an administration of all talents — in effect, a national government. The Tories had adopted Sir Robert Borden's 1917 concept of union government under another name. Bob Manion, however, tried to avoid drawing too many parallels because the union government had implemented the unpopular measure. Instead, he tried to stimulate public disquiet over political partisanship at a time of war and ran his candidates under the National Government label. Manion's chief difficulty was in specifying the people he had in mind to constitute his proposed national government. The Liberals had made it clear that they would not have any part of such an administration, and without them the government could not be a true coalition. From the start, the proposal for a national government was dead in the water. At Norman McLarty's nomination meeting on 21 February, I addressed the issue. After lauding Norman's record as both backbencher and minister, I called on the leader of the opposition to report on the composition of his proposed government. Who, I asked with a sense of imminent triumph, would join a national government? "Art Reaume," cried out a voice in the audience. The hall broke into hilarious laughter. Reaume, an insouciant wag, was McLarty's Conservative opponent. There are umpteen tales about Reaume's jests. One evening during the campaign, Norman retired to his office for a chat and a drink with his law partner, Gordon Fraser. The phone rang. Norman answered and a voice said, "You're a minister and a candidate for re-election; put that glass down." The caller hung up, but from then on every time Norman lifted his glass, the phone would ring with the same message. Afterwards, he told me about it with considerable bewilderment. Years later, when Art Reaume was a Liberal MLA at Queen's Park (he had seen the light) he confessed that *he* had been the practical joker. Reaume's headquarters were in the Norton Palmer Hotel, right across from McLarty's office, and from there Reaume could see everything that was happening across the way. He had decided to have a little fun and had rung Norman himself.

Manion's call for a united opposition to the Liberals fell on deaf ears in Essex East. In the fall of 1939, the Conservatives had picked as their candidate Dr. Raymond Morand, my 1935 opponent. Earlier, Roy Hicks, a prominent member of that party, had left the Tories and secured a nomination as an Independent Conservative. His charge was that the Tories' nominating meeting was a put-up

job and that their closed convention did not reflect the opinions of
all Conservatives in Essex East. Hicks later changed his appella-
tion to Labour-Conservative, one of the most bizarre combinations in Canadian political history. At the beginning of February,
Dr. Morand announced that he would run as a National Government candidate in accordance with Manion's directive. This episode left the local Tories disunited and confused, and throughout
the campaign, Hicks kept calling on Dr. Morand to withdraw.

Politics can be a tough business and occasionally leads to bitterness. The 1940 campaign was a little strange at the beginning; for
the first time, I had to defend my own record instead of attacking
somebody else's. Dr. Morand blamed the Liberal government for
rejecting unemployment and health insurance schemes that the
Tories had drafted. Speaking in Windsor in mid-March, Bob
Manion called the minister of national defence, Norman Rogers,
"that irresponsible little falsifier"; a few days before, on the stage of
the Walkerville Collegiate, George Drew had called Rogers a liar.
All of this I refuted emphatically. My CCF opponent, again Ben
Levert, complained that I was wooing the communist vote, but
this was denied by Thane Campbell, the premier of Prince
Edward Island, who was in Essex East to speak on my behalf.
Although political differences can be sharp and public debate
strenuous, it is a mistake to let one's emotions get the better of one.
Certainly, Dr. Morand, Ben Levert and I managed to run a
basically civilized contest, and we retained reciprocal feelings of
respect.

The 1940 election was Nell's first political campaign, and her
part in it was imprinted with her own inimitable style. She refused
to set foot on the platform at any public meeting, but when I
introduced her she would always wave her hellos from her seat in
the audience. Her greatest thrill was touring the countryside with
Buster Riberdy to put up posters. Buster had borrowed a truck
with a loudspeaker on top, through which he would boom out the
Liberal slogan: "We don't care who you vote for, as long as you
vote for Paul Martin." Nell still talks with the greatest of glee about
that loudspeaker, particularly about the time she and Buster went

up the Byrne line and the loudspeaker alerted certain Tory residents of North Woodslee to their presence. The truck left under a barrage of rotten eggs and tomatoes.

My workers loved Nell, even though she did not take to the activities traditionally expected of politicians' wives. She never did like teas and tried to avoid them if she could; but she went along to certain Liberal soirées and was always the liveliest person in the room. Nell was popular because she was always herself; when she came to a meeting, she was as likely to take a high step over her chair as to sit on it. When I was out on the stump, I used to phone in to the central committee room every so often to see how things were going. Whoever answered was always full of reassurance. Once I called back unexpectedly and found nobody there   the entire campaign staff were across the street in the pub, having an impromptu party with Nell. Whoever had answered the phone ran over and alerted them, "He's comin' in and he's barkin'." Needless to say, all hell broke loose. But I always knew that my wife provided the spirit, warmth and spontaneity that added sparkle to this and subsequent campaigns for me and my workers.

Despite Hepburn's strictures against King, both federal and provincial Liberals gradually united behind the prime minister. Ross Gray, the MP from Sarnia and a good friend of Hepburn, was nominated as a King supporter in Lambton West. And the provincial attorney general, Gordon Conant, who had backed Hepburn to the hilt, let it be known that he would support W. E. N. Sinclair, the federal Liberal candidate in Ontario riding. In Essex East, Dr. Trottier helped boost my campaign. Hepburn had little alternative but to declare that he would not punish the provincial MLAs for supporting the federal Liberals. Harry Nixon, Hepburn's senior minister, resigned from the cabinet on 11 March, explaining that he had voted for the premier's January resolution to deny Hepburn an excuse for calling his own election; he made it clear that he still supported King's leadership. Two days later, Nixon returned to the provincial cabinet, apparently on the understanding that the premier would keep his nose out of the federal campaign.

As in 1935, my days were not spent in the committee rooms —
those I was happy to leave to Angus Buchanan's care. One of my
most vigorous workers was Don Emerson, who took charge of
organizing the younger Liberals. This was Don's second venture
on my behalf and a forerunner to his diligent years as my private
secretary and long-time political organizer. Satisfied that the fight
was in good hands, I spent each day talking with the voters. I have
always somehow established an easy rapport with people and
made friends on the streets. I never relied on public speeches to win
adherents to my cause.

There was not the slightest doubt during the campaign that the
King government would be returned. The speech Harry Nixon
made at Massey Hall on 15 March, endorsing the prime minister,
had clinched it. My friend Milton Gregg, on leave from his job as
the House of Commons's sergeant at arms, remembered my pet
concerns during the previous five years and wrote to me: "You will
win (to the entire disgust of a few colleagues from the prairies)."
On election day, I drove from one poll to another to cheer on my
workers and to chat to the electors. My circuit took in the urban
areas in the forenoon, the rural communities in the early afternoon, and the city polling stations again at the end of the day-shifts
in the car factories. As the thousands of workers left the Ford and
Chrysler plants during the afternoon, we knew that the heaviest
voting would begin then and would last until the polls closed.

Before going to the committee rooms, I followed what was to
become a practice — I would wait anxiously in the car for the
returns from two stations on Monmouth Road in Walkerville. If
the results were satisfactory, I knew — but never accepted until the
last minute — that the final returns would be too. The pattern did
not fail in 1940 — nor in my nine subsequent elections. When I
reached our headquarters on Ellrose Avenue, I received a noisy
welcome from Angus Buchanan and a crowd of well-wishers. By
nine o'clock it was evident that I had been elected, and the other
candidates conceded defeat. Dr. Morand was particularly gracious. I had triumphed for a second time over a worthy and
distinguished man. After extending congratulations at the *Star*'s

offices to McLarty and Clark, who had both been re-elected, my parade took off to the various committee rooms scattered around the riding. Hundreds of cars streamed down the concession roads until we reached the Shanahan farm in Maidstone, our last stop.

The final tally gave me a plurality of 1,776, a better margin than in 1935.[18] But if the results in Essex County turned out well, King's national victory was a triumph. The Liberals won 181 seats. Bob Manion lost in Fort William, and only forty Conservative or National Government candidates were successful. Mackenzie King had achieved an unprecedented majority of 117 in the House of Commons and had won more than 50 percent of the popular vote. Perhaps the factor that contributed most to the victory was King's circumspection. His shrewdness, understanding of the Canadian scene, and balancing of interests, had demonstrated what an adroit and effective leader he was.

After the election, I felt as limp as a rag and in need of a break. Not since our honeymoon in Bermuda had Nell and I been on holiday together. Meanwhile, I had been pursuing the hectic life that parliamentary obligations enforce. Paul, now two-and-a-half, was a great joy. Nell's mother agreed to look after him for about ten days so that we could visit the east coast of Florida, where neither of us had been before. We went by train — a good way to see the United States. Since we could not afford the big and expensive hotels in Palm Beach, we looked for a tourist home and found one with a friendly landlady. On our rented bicycles, Nell and I peddled past the great houses of the Dodges and the Kennedys and the home of Barbara Hutton. The holiday was one to remember and greatly refreshed our spirits.

As parliamentarians came to Ottawa for the opening of the session on 16 May, the corridors were abuzz with the happy

18 The results were Paul Martin 9,274; R. D. Morand 7,998; Ben Levert 2,924; Roy Hicks 392.

greetings of returning Liberal members, marvelling at Mackenzie King's sagacity in calling the election when he did. We all knew that if the *blitzkrieg*, which began with German attacks on Denmark and Norway in early April, had been going on during the campaign, Manion's call for a national government might have had a greater public appeal.

It was an especial delight for me to welcome two new members to Ottawa, Brooke Claxton and Doug Abbott. Claxton, the Liberal MP for the Montreal riding of St. Lawrence-St. George, had beaten the veteran Conservative C. H. Cahan. I had come to know Brooke through our association with the Institute of International Affairs. We had many interests in common: liberalism itself, the Liberal Party and foreign affairs. For a year before the election, I had been urging him to join me in the Commons. Brooke's voice and influence in the party caucus would make me feel less isolated than I had felt in my first parliament. Doug Abbott I had not met before, but I knew he was a man of promise. A delightful and sunny personality helped to give Doug an impressive start in public life.

When Claxton and Abbott took their seats, theirs were but two places that had changed as a result of the election. After losing in Fort William,[19] Bob Manion had resigned as Tory chief; R. B. Hanson, the long-serving member for York Sunbury, agreed to step in as interim leader. But rumours quickly spread that the party was thinking of asking its former head, Senator Arthur Meighen, to take the helm again. A good House leader, Hanson showed more subtlety in debate than Manion, but he did not have the prowess or presence of R. B. Bennett or Meighen, who always intimidated King.[20]

19 Manion had represented Fort William until 1935. When he was chosen leader, he won a byelection in London, Ontario, but in the 1940 general election, he again was a candidate in the Lakehead.
20 That Meighen and King were resistible to one another was well known. A gathering in June 1941 at Cataraqui outside Kingston, on the fiftieth anniversary of Sir John A. Macdonald's death, attracted many public figures. Indicating that the governor general would lead the procession, Mackenzie King turned to his long-standing rival and said, "You will follow me." Just afterwards, I heard Meighen say *sotto voce* to his neighbour, "Now, why should I follow him?"

The opening weeks of the 1940 session were full of uncertainty as the German army swept into the Low Countries and invaded France. After the unexpected Nazi occupation of Denmark and Norway, Neville Chamberlain, Britain's prime minister, had resigned to make way for Winston Churchill. The war worsened, and I grew more and more concerned about a possible hysterical reaction to the string of Allied defeats. We had to "remember [that] the war will not be won by undisciplined emotion," I wrote to Nell. Mackenzie King quickly announced that a second division would proceed to Europe under the command of General Victor Odlum; he also declared that the government would undertake other measures to speed up the war effort and increase armaments production. These initiatives — particularly the heavy financial commitments — were proof, as I told my wife, that "the government is not guilty of inactivity."

Despite our frequent letters to each other, I missed Nell terribly as the news from France got bleaker. It was proving difficult for me to visit Windsor as often as I wished. The atmosphere in Ottawa grew tense when we heard that Hitler had apparently abandoned his Paris objective and that his armies were beginning to fight their way to the English Channel. At the end of May, the unpardonable capitulation of Leopold III, King of the Belgians, outraged Canadians; he had left the British and French generals isolated, and it was probable that the French, too, would have to surrender. One thing was certain, I wrote to Nell: "Faith, determination and hope must never fail." The following week, the miracle of Dunkirk caught the imagination of a Canada starved for good news. While I felt that the withdrawal of British troops was brilliant, I told Nell that "it must not be forgotten that the retreat was a defeat for us." On 10 June, Mussolini, who had hovered like a bird of prey, invaded France; the House approved a resolution, without demurral, declaring war on Italy. Four days later, the Germans entered Paris; and on 16 June Paul Reynaud resigned and made way for Marshal Pétain. Thus began the final act, which concluded six days later with the armistice between France and Germany.

Throughout the developing crisis, Mackenzie King demonstrated yet again his mastery of the Canadian political arena. At our caucus on 23 May, he repeated his warning that the federal Tories and Hepburn were likely to renew their demands for a national coalition government. Challengingly, the prime minister told us that he did not want to cling to office, and he volunteered to step down. This was out of the question, but King's tactic served to disarm party criticism. The nimble prime minister later revealed that he had asked Grote Sterling, the Conservative MP from Okanagan Boundary, and Jim Macdonnell, president of the National Trust Company and Vincent Massey's brother-in-law, to join his administration. Neither offer was taken up. Not long afterwards, Macdonnell told me that King had tried to cajole him by promising him the new department of national war services. Macdonnell felt he had no special competence for that ministry, but he suggested to me that his response would have been different had he been offered the department of finance.

The prime minister dominated the caucus, telling us just enough to underline the grave perils of the war. Most Québec members did not approve of proposals for any form of national government — nor did a majority in the Liberal Party. But the continuing agitation in English Canada could not escape association in the minds of French Canadians with the imposition of conscription in 1917. By his skill in 1940, King managed to discredit the idea of national government for the remainder of the war.

As Bismarck said, politics is the art of the possible. This Mackenzie King understood, and he continued to practise the art throughout the war. He held the Canadian ship afloat as no other leader could have. Caught as he was between the desire of French Canada to avoid conscription for overseas and the intense pressure from English Canada for urgent action, King introduced the National Resources Mobilization Bill on 18 June 1940. This measure authorized the registration of every available worker and made provision for the conscription of all unmarried Canadians between the ages of twenty-one and forty-five. Some of the Québec members felt uneasy about the bill, but Ernest Lapointe and the prime minister emphasized that it did not modify the stand against conscription for overseas and would have the effect of minimizing party dissension.

Certain elements in the Conservative Party, however, sought every opportunity to attack the prime minister. "Calling Canada," an advertisement in the *Toronto Telegram* by an anonymous group of Tories, referred to the government's lack of preparation for evacuating British children to Canada to protect them and accused Mackenzie King of obstructing this humanitarian objective. I raised the issue in the House on 27 June, pointing out that the advertisement went beyond the standards of public comment and criticism. My intervention gave the prime minister a chance to outline the government's plans to take British children into Canada, far from the Nazi bombs.[21]

At about the same time, I became entangled in a dispute with M. J. Coldwell, the acting leader of the CCF,[22] who had lambasted Ford of Canada over a statement by Henry Ford that he would not allow the American company to make engines for nations of the British empire who might use them in the war effort. Coldwell argued that Canada should retaliate by cancelling provisions in the Special War Revenue Bill that gave certain advantages to manufacturers of low-priced automobiles; his view was that the Ford Company of Canada should be nationalized. He further objected to Ford's publicity, which boasted of what the firm had done for the British empire.[23]

C. D. Howe, the minister of munitions and supply, R. B. Hanson and I took issue with Coldwell's remarks. None of us in

21 *WDS*, 28 June 1940.
22 J. S. Woodsworth had suffered a stroke and was away from the House.
23 Wallace Campbell, the president of Ford of Canada, had served for a while as chairman of the War Supply Board. From my own dealings with him, I was tempted to agree with Mackenzie King's private assessment that he was "an old-fashioned, hard industrialist . . . unsympathetic with labour organization. . . . That type is to the industrial world what dictators are in the political world" (Pickersgill, *The Mackenzie King Record*, Vol. I, *1939-1944*, p. 27). This incident provided me with an opportunity to meet Henry Ford, who asked to see me. When I went to his home in Detroit, he appeared more interested in playing the piano. For my remarks, see the House of Commons, *Debates*, 26 June 1940, pp. 1,166-67.

any way condoned what Henry Ford had said, but as I told the House, his personal opinions should not permit unmerited criticism against Ford of Canada. I did in fact agree with Coldwell's censure of Ford but pointed out that the firm was more Canadian than any other car-manufacturing company. Wallace Campbell and Ford of Canada had done as much as any other Canadian company to further the country's war production; more than fifty percent of the vehicles built in the Windsor plant were destined for military use by Canada and her allies. Of course I was justifying the actions not only of the company's Canadian management but also of the 8,000 workers from Essex County who laboured in the various Ford plants.[24]

Despite the preoccupation of all MPs with the war, we still had more mundane matters to attend to. During the opening months of the session, I spoke in favour of appointing local residents as customs collectors. On the question of the pay of members of the armed forces, I urged the minister of finance to exempt it from taxation. I asked C. D. Howe, the minister of transport, when the airport at Windsor would open for business. On 22 July, I took issue with the government's refusal to allow appeals from boards of review under the Farmers' Creditors Arrangement Act. Prompted by my administrative law course with Felix Frankfurter, I condemned the fact that without recourse to the courts, decisions could be made that affected property and civil rights.[25]

When Norman McLarty moved, on 16 July, that the House go into committee on the resolution to introduce unemployment insurance, I felt proud that I had helped to bring about this important social measure. It had taken such a long time for it to become law in Canada.[26] It was somewhat ironic that after my

24 House of Commons, *Debates*, 26 June 1940, pp. 1,164-65.
25 ibid., 4 June 1940, pp. 497-98; ibid., 27 May 1940, p. 217; ibid., 29 May 1940, pp. 334-35; ibid., 22 July 1940, pp. 1,815-16.
26 The Liberal convention that had selected Mackenzie King as party leader in 1919 had adopted a resolution that "in so far as may be practicable, having regard to

having fought for this measure since 1935, it was left to Norman, who was ideologically much less sympathetic to it than I was, to introduce it. I minded particularly keenly that I was not appointed to the parliamentary committee to study the matter. But the unfortunate tradition was that a committee should not contain two members from the same geographic area; naturally McLarty, the minister, was on it, and I could not serve. It could also be that I had prodded the government too forcefully and had been almost sent to Coventry. It would have pleased me to have had my name publicly associated with this measure. But the provinces had finally agreed to the constitutional amendment that would enable Ottawa to put the scheme in place.

Many people were opposed to the enactment of unemployment insurance in time of war. Certain employers in Essex East took this view, but provision for the unemployed was for me a part of the war effort and a means of preparing for the post-war period.[27] In my speech on second reading, I warned against making exaggerated claims for unemployment insurance but affirmed its importance and the absolute necessity for it. It was to be expected that with fluctuating rates of employment, the proposed Unemployment Insurance Commission occasionally would have to draw on the federal treasury for funds to pay to claimants. But unemployment insurance had already been amply studied, and I called for its quick passage into law. The principle was clear, and opposition from groups such as the Canadian Manufacturers' Association should not be allowed to delay the bill's enactment. To ensure the widest distribution of the risk and an equitable sharing of the cost among employer, employee and the state, I argued for a

---

Canada's financial position, an adequate system of insurance against unemployment, sickness, dependence, old age and other disability should be instituted by the federal government in conjunction with the governments of the several provinces." The conditions attached to the resolution had, I felt, delayed progress for too long.

27 House of Commons, *Debates*, 19 July 1940, pp. 1,776-86.

compulsory scheme. Government participation with money from graduated income and inheritance taxes would allocate the burden among those financially able to contribute. A national scheme was necessary to take into account the mobility of labour between provinces and to spread the costs equally among the various regions.

On 19 July, near the end of the session, the House passed the act, and after being voted on in the Senate, it became law. Norman McLarty handled the measure with great tact and ability. No one was happier than me to see the measure through. What would we have done subsequently had this insurance not been in place? Anyone who went through the Depression can understand the anguish of widespread unemployment and knows that much suffering would have been eliminated if it had been operating then. Despite the undoubted abuses, the need for it is as real today as it was in the past.

Tragedy had forced the prime minister to make changes in his government in the middle of the parliamentary session. On 10 June, Norman Rogers was killed in an air crash on his way to speak in Toronto. His death was a loss both to the government, of which he had been a key member, and to me personally. Since 1935, we had shared the same desire to make the nation a better place for ordinary citizens. Norman was one of the government's most knowledgeable personalities in federal-provincial relations. In my view, he might have succeeded Mackenzie King, to whom he was very close. To replace him as minister for national defence, King chose Colonel J. L. Ralston, a greatly respected figure whose appointment assured the country that the war effort would remain in good hands. I was very pleased that King appointed J. L. Ilsley to fill Ralston's shoes in finance. This was the beginning of Ilsley's greatest hour, one that marked him as a gifted and dedicated statesman. On the day of his appointment, I rose to

congratulate him as "my pet minister," only to be greeted by
R. B. Hanson's jibe, "What are you looking for?"[28] After he assumed his new position, Jim asked me to go with him on a speaking
tour for the victory loan campaign. In his speeches, he asked people
to make sacrifices, and it occurred to me how he himself symbolized
what he was asking them to do. He did not own an automobile.
Once, when Mackenzie King was about to climb into his big black
car, he said to me, "Look, there's Ilsley." The minister of finance
was getting into a streetcar to go home.

On 14 June, King made Angus Macdonald, my friend from
Harvard Law School days, minister of national defence for naval
services. To join the government, he left the premiership of Nova
Scotia and, as I learned shortly, quickly had his differences with
Mackenzie King. Angus had come from a province where he was
easily the most popular public figure — almost a legend. When he
walked into a room, Nova Scotians would practically genuflect.
But in Ottawa, he found another prime minister, over whom
people did not fawn but who commanded great power and
respect. Angus was a little jealous and showed it unnecessarily.
Nonetheless, his presence certainly strengthened the government.

Two other newcomers entered the cabinet at this time; Bill
Mulock of York North became postmaster general and Colin
Gibson assumed the post of minister of national revenue. To Nell, I
wrote a short "no comment" about both these choices. Mulock, the
grandson of Mackenzie King's patron, Sir William Mulock, never
really stood out; nor did Gibson, whom I suspected of being the
protégé of the prime minister's friend, Lily Hendrie.

As a backbencher, one could do little more than follow the
course laid out by the government. The end of the session on
7 August was a great relief; I was a bit frustrated and thought that I
might be of more help to the war effort outside the House. This
meant encouraging Windsor citizens to contribute to salvage campaigns — everything from toothpaste tubes to jam jars could help

28 House of Commons, *Debates*, 8 July 1940, p. 1,433.

raise revenue for the war. At Windsor theatres, I joined popular singer Ella Logan to plead for the purchase of war savings stamps. Canada, I told the audience, had become a prize of conquest for Hitler, and the stamps would not only help fight the war but could prove to be good investment. "Britain is now fighting alone, but not only for herself. . . . France, regardless of the Pétains, will again live." In trying to raise the spirits of my fellow countrymen, I suppose I sometimes got carried away by hyperbole, but these were abnormal times and demanded the utmost in response. My speeches emphasized the need for sacrifice, lest the Canadian way of life go down before the onslaught of evil gangsters. "We in this country can't take this thing lying down. We must mobilize all resources . . . so that those who come after us . . . will be able to enjoy the freedom without which the life we love could not be lived."[29] In the fall of 1940, I warned an audience in London, Ontario, that Canada's part in the war would vastly increase the government's financial burden and that of all Canadians. "To achieve our aims," I stressed, "we must offer more than mere expressions of sympathy."[30]

Subversion was an issue that had to be confronted in wartime. Given the circumstances of 1940, it is hardly surprising that this should concern both the government and the general public. There probably were excesses in the attempts to place controls on suspected German or Italian enemy aliens — this was not an easy matter to work out. In Windsor, the police carried on a purge of the Italian population that led to the arrest of scores of heads of households suspected — after the seizure of firearms and a large quantity of propaganda literature — of being pro-Mussolini. Without doubt, there were injustices and false arrests, but the vast majority of the Italian population remained loyal to Canada. This was a very difficult situation for me because many of them were friends and supporters whose families came to ask me to intercede

29 *WDS*, 16 July 1940; speech to the Ukrainian Catholic Youth League.
30 *London Free Press*, 4 October 1940; speech to London Kiwanis Club.

on their behalf. I greatly admired the way they reacted; there was little complaining and no lingering bitterness.

In August 1965, when I was secretary of state for external affairs, I joined Averell Harriman to commemorate the signing of the Ogdensburg Agreement. In this upstate New York town on the St. Lawrence, Mackenzie King and Franklin Roosevelt met on 17 August 1940 and signed an agreement that immediately brought into being a board that would plan the defence of North America. The Permanent Joint Board on Defence comprised representatives from both countries who would study defence matters and make recommendations to the two governments. The agreement involved a country at war and a defence pact with a friendly non-belligerent. Canada, in effect, was assured of the protection of the United States at a time when Britain was in no position to help in case of attack. What struck me at the time was the spontaneous nature of the agreement; it had not been the subject of much preliminary consideration or preparation.[31] Shortly after this meeting, Roosevelt arranged with Churchill to exchange fifty aging US destroyers for leases on British bases. Mackenzie King had played a significant role in the negotiations leading to this deal.

The first opportunity to say my piece on all these developments arose during the debate on the address after the opening of parliament on 7 November.[32] I took part in the debate later that month, to defend the government from the attacks of R. B. Hanson and to

---

31 The first Canadian chairman was O. M. Biggar of Ottawa. The members included representatives from the three armed services, with Hugh Keenleyside as secretary. Fiorello La Guardia, the mayor of New York, served as the US chairman. The first meeting was held in Ottawa on 26 August 1940.

32 Brooke Claxton proposed the motion on the address. I have always remembered his statement that "Canada, next to Britain, is the strongest power facing the enemy today" (House of Commons, *Debates*, 8 November, 1940, p. 4).

insist that the talks with the United States were of great importance for the present and the future. Defence and economic policies were inseparable, I argued, and a joint defence arrangement
would open new markets for Canada; our country's best guarantee
of maintaining her national existence was to administer its own
defence, in cooperation with the United States. This was not to
dismiss the importance of Britain, which still served as Canada's
first line of defence, and these arrangements would be pursued in
consultation with the United Kingdom government.[33] Drawing
further conclusions from Ogdensburg, I used the agreement to
bolster the case for Canada's entry into the Pan-American Union.
This would strengthen hemispheric defence even further and provide scientific planning for the threat from the Axis powers. In my
concluding remarks on the Ogdensburg agreement to a university
audience, I forecast that Canada

> must realize that time will make the Ogdensburg agreement more
> complex. The United States is a much stronger power than we
> are. As a consequence, we will want to protect ourselves against
> decisions executed without reference to us; we will not want to be
> dragged into embroilments automatically. There is a guarantee
> against this and it is simply a clear understanding and a definite
> foreign policy of our own — one that will reflect *our* minds....
> ... we have only begun to chart the courses our foreign policy
> must assume. To stop here would be to temporize as we have
> temporized in the past. It would be a false security that could
> only end in more disaster and destruction....[34]

The other issue that interested me in the first months of the
session was the evolution of federal-provincial relations. The
Rowell-Sirois report, advocating the assumption of greater power
by the federal government, had been tabled in May 1940, but the
European crisis had caused the government to delay consideration

33 House of Commons, *Debates*, November 1940, pp. 412-17.
34 *WDS*, 17 March 1941. Report of a speech at the University of Ottawa the day before.

of it. Mackenzie King now indicated that he would call a federal-provincial meeting in January 1941 to discuss the report. After reading it, I urged the various levels of government to pull together to help win the war. "No man can afford to think in terms of city, district or province in Canada at the present time. . . . We must avoid all needless overlapping. We must centralize the collection of all kinds of taxes. Provincial politicians, no matter what their political opinions might be, will receive nothing but condemnation . . . unless they dispense with their party views and work together for unity."[35] I was, of course, thinking of the expected opposition of Premiers Aberhart and Hepburn to the federal government's decision to push ahead and implement the Rowell-Sirois recommendations.

As we approached the conference, Bill Mackintosh, a special adviser to the deputy minister of finance, spoke to me of the urgent need to organize the nation's finances to meet the exigencies of war. Mackenzie King was concerned that Mitch Hepburn would take advantage of the forum provided by the conference to launch another attack on him and his government's conduct of the war. The cabinet, we all knew, was divided on holding the conference. Ilsley, for one, believed it was necessary, but not right then. Later on, I found out that King never liked federal-provincial conferences; they unsettled him and, he felt, disturbed the political structure and the nation as well.

Although I was not directly involved in the conference, I went along to the opening meeting. J. L. Ilsley did not mince his words and told the provincial governments that the Rowell-Sirois report had to be adopted. I felt like cheering him on when he emphasized the need for a national standard of decency and justice, reminding all those present of the importance of preparing for post-war reconstruction. The minister of finance proposed that the federal government collect the provinces' share of income and corporation taxes and succession duties in return for a fixed rental payment. At

35 *WDS*, 13 December 1940; speech to the warden's banquet of the Essex County Council.

this point Hepburn exploded, blustering that he would not sell Ontario down the river and allow social services to remain the victim of a dictatorial federal bureaucracy.

Although most observers considered the conference a failure, Mackenzie King believed that it was a considerable achievement to have secured the agreement of the provinces to invade their fields of taxation, if this was necessary. The government proceeded along this course when Ilsley presented the second wartime budget at the end of April. Using its wartime powers, the federal government proposed to take over all income and corporation taxes, as well as succession duties, and to compensate the provinces for vacating the field. Speaking on the taxation system, I said in the House that the fiasco described by the Rowell-Sirois report should not be allowed to continue, and I supported the government's proposition that it was unsound for Ottawa and the nine provinces to tax in the same field.[36] If we were to carry on with the war, money had to be found. Nevertheless, I did question the federal government's taking over the excise tax on gasoline without providing adequate compensation to the provinces.[37]

By 1941, my public life seemed fragmented, and I had begun to feel a little underemployed. Excluded from the armed forces, I tried to act creditably on General McNaughton's advice to carry on with my duties as an MP, but for a while I did so without much enthusiasm. In my speech to the House on the address in reply to the speech from the throne, I gave vent to some of my frustrations and suggested that the government ought to put private members to more productive use. The committees of the House, for example, could consider legislative measures that did not require the immediate decision of the executive; this would produce better informed private members.[38]

36 House of Commons, *Debates*, 28 May 1941, pp. 3,254-55.
37 ibid., 20 May 1941, pp. 3,008-14.
38 ibid., 26 November 1940, pp. 412-17.

At this time, my letters to Nell reflect the ennui of separation from her and my young son. I would try to cajole her into coming to Ottawa to stay with me for a few days and then would often close with the request to "kiss the baby for me and remind him that he has a father." Sometimes I would drop her a note as I sat in the House; once I pointed out that "as I write I sit between two very doubtful people, the Minister of Trade and Commerce and the member for Selkirk.[39] I see no indication that this propinquity will in any way be profitable. It is one of the things that must simply be accepted." I would ask Nell a little enviously about her busy and happy life in Windsor, while listening to much talk that seemed to me to have little value. Even Mackenzie King came under my critical eye: "If he would only speak and not read his speeches." Less than a day after returning from a visit to Windsor, I always felt lonely and frustrated. There was, I believed, "not much likelihood of anything unusual taking place. . . . How effective we could all be if only there was some encouragement. All I can do is wait the opportunity — if ever it will come."

There was still, of course, some satisfaction in helping my constituents. The corn growers of Essex County lobbied for the provision of adequate drying, grading and marketing facilities, and I did my best to help them, despite criticisms that "Paul Martin does not know anything about the corn business." The growers, however, were appreciative of my efforts.[40] When Windsor businessmen objected that a new customs form for American visitors would discourage tourism, I took up the cudgels with the minister of national revenue, Colin Gibson, with great relish. Gibson eventually backed down and made completing the form voluntary, but I still felt that if the bureaucrats had done without this information for years, "surely they can do without it now, in the midst of war."[41]

39 Respectively James A. MacKinnon and J. T. Thorson.
40 *WDS*, 6 June 1941; House of Commons, *Debates*, 4 June 1941, pp. 3,498-3,502; *WDS*, 25 June 1941; ibid., 5 July 1941; ibid., 26 July 1941; ibid., 16 September 1941.
41 ibid., 3 April 1941; ibid., 5 April 1941; ibid., 8 April 1941; ibid., 10 April 1941; ibid., 1 May 1941; ibid., 3 May 1941; ibid., 8 May 1941.

Odd incidents enlivened life considerably in those dark days. One in Windsor centred on the question of housing. As minister of munitions and supply, C. D. Howe was responsible for the construction of housing units for wartime plant workers. Towards the end of 1941, 125 of the projected 500 homes in Windsor were completed, though unoccupied. Coincidentally, the city was having difficulty providing accommodation for the dependants of servicemen overseas. Mayor Art Reaume was chafed to see empty houses while the city faced severe shortages and, with typical impetuosity, commandeered some of the houses and even used his car to help the families move in. C. D. Howe, en route from California with Colonel Ralston, called it "hijacking" and peppered us with angry comments when he was forced to break his trip back to Ottawa to stop in Windsor. During the rancorous meeting with Howe and Reaume, I had to confess that I supported the mayor. Finally, Howe agreed to let the soldiers' families stay in the houses until the spring.[42]

The inability of the federal government to find housing, coupled with Howe's bullheaded attitude, did as much to undermine morale in Windsor as any other single issue at the time. It was no coincidence that in a week in April 1942 chosen to build up both active and reserve forces, the city's board of control sent a telegram to Howe and Norman McLarty (the innocent victim in this affair) complaining that the federal government was planning to evict the dependants of men serving overseas. The situation provided no incentive to recruiting or to an affirmative vote in the plebiscite eventually held to release the government from its pledge not to introduce conscription.

Conscription dominated discussion both in and outside parliament when the new session began on 3 November 1941. For a few

42 *WDS*, 1 October 1941.

weeks before the members were called back to Ottawa, the Canadian Legion had been tub-thumping for compulsory military service. I myself had seen manifestations of the strong wish for conscription in the Windsor business community, particularly among the Conservatives, who were using it to provide "proof" of Mackenzie King's alleged lack of zeal for the war. Trying to head off the pro-conscription voices in the caucus, King reiterated his stand against the measure at one of our first caucuses and for the first time raised the possibility of a plebiscite on the issue.

The pressure on the government grew after the Conservatives elected Arthur Meighen as their leader at a meeting in Ottawa on 12 November. The resurrection of the former prime minister left little doubt that the Tories would espouse conscription and advocate a national government that excluded Mackenzie King. Caucus agreed with the prime minister that selective service registration in Canada was all that was required. But King suffered a setback when Ernest Lapointe, his closest colleague and one of Canada's most noble statesmen, died on 26 November. King's role in unifying Canada's many elements had been fortified by the collaboration of his ranking minister and friend from Québec. On the day of Lapointe's funeral, I was arguing a case in court; at one point everything stopped so that the magistrate and members of the bar could pay their tributes to the late minister of justice. I spoke of Lapointe as a great man, "a French Canadian loyal to the traditions of his race and to his church."[43]

Mackenzie King wasted little time in appointing a successor. Louis St. Laurent had never sat in parliament and remained an unknown political quantity. He struck me as a great legal mind, but I do not think anyone would have said for certain that he would prove to be as strong and worthy a minister of justice as he turned out to be. Shortly after his appointment, however, we lunched together, and I told Nell that he was "most charming . . . able and genuine. You would like him very much."

43 *WDS*, 29 November 1941.

A dramatic change in the nature and pace of the war affected the campaign of the pro-conscriptionists. The United States joined the conflict on 7 December after the attack on Pearl Harbor, but the Canadian government decided not to recall parliament to declare war on Japan. Mackenzie King took the position that a formal meeting was unnecessary since parliament had authorized the government to join Britain in resisting aggression. I questioned King's judgment; the decision seemed to me to be much the same in principle as in September 1939. A war in the Far East as well as in Europe increased pressures on the government to amend the National Resources Mobilization Act to permit compulsory service for overseas. I was aware that the cabinet was struggling over the issue. Canadians, I told my constituents, should not give in and belittle the war effort of the previous two years. It was their democratic duty to follow the leaders they had chosen, despite the sterner days and greater regimentation that lay ahead.[44] Throughout December, hints that the government would call a referendum on the conscription question appeared regularly in the press.

On 30 December 1941, both Canada and the House of Commons played host to Winston Churchill. I had not planned to be in Ottawa until the New Year, but I could not miss seeing and hearing this remarkable man. Nell came to the House with me. Several MPs waited to see him and Mackenzie King leave the Senate Speaker's chambers and cross the corridor leading to the House of Commons. I gave him a rousing cheer. Churchill's address to parliament could not offend any party in the conscription debate, and I found it truly uplifting. "When I warned [the French]," he intoned, "that Britain would fight on alone whatever they did, their generals told their prime minister and his divided cabinet, 'In three weeks England will have her neck wrung like a chicken.' Some chicken; some neck!" This indeed was the speech of a great warrior, whose words of defiance inspired free men to fight irrevocably.

44 *WDS,* 10 December 1941; speech to the Essex County Automobile Club.

There had been so much talk and rumour that it was not surprising to hear in the speech from the throne on 22 January 1942 that the government had decided to "seek from the people, by means of a plebiscite, release from any obligation arising out of any past commitments restricting methods of raising men for military service." As King told the caucus later, a positive vote in the plebiscite would not decide the issue but would enable the government to proceed with conscription, if that course was deemed necessary. More than ever, King showed his continuing reliance on the party caucus to support his leadership, and we were given a full account of cabinet opinion, a very unusual occurrence. Senator Bill Euler, a former cabinet colleague of King, told me afterwards that he took exception to the prime minister's frankness.

The government's announcement compelled me to re-evaluate my stance. I had voiced my opposition to conscription when war broke out, and while I had not been against conscription for home duty, I had continued to speak out against ordering involuntary recruits overseas. But there I was. First of all, I had to accept that the plebiscite would draw off the dangers of excess from both the pro-conscriptionists and the anti-conscriptionists. As I understood King's motives, he wanted to reduce tensions by turning the focus of debate towards the plebiscite. It was an ingenious, though unorthodox, way of avoiding the conscription issue. Not all Liberals, or even all cabinet ministers, fully understood the Canadian dilemma of satisfying the aspirations of the two founding races; few had the vision to see that strict allegiance to one view without regard for the other would result in the denial of a consensus. The one man who did see was the prime minister. For all his quirks, King remained tireless and patient in his patchwork missions to hold together government and party. Had his gamble not succeeded, political turmoil would have engulfed parliament and the nation.

The evening of 9 February provided heartening news for government members worried about the plebiscite. That day, voters in four ridings had gone to the polls in byelections. In

Québec East, Louis St. Laurent was elected; he soon took his seat in the House of Commons. The new minister of labour, Humphrey Mitchell, was returned in Welland (Norman McLarty had moved to become secretary of state on 15 December 1941). Even though St. Laurent was under pressure during the byelection to take a definite stance against conscription and Mitchell was under a similar strain to support it, neither gave in, and the government's view prevailed.

The greatest triumph for the government, however, was the defeat of the new Conservative leader, Arthur Meighen, in York South by an unknown schoolteacher, Joe Noseworthy, the CCF candidate. Even the opportunistic support of Mitch Hepburn did not pull Meighen through.[45] The loss of their leader left the conscriptionist forces reeling.

Mackenzie King reacted badly to particular personalities who might become leaders of the opposition. Arthur Meighen, able and caustic, disturbed King from the beginning. His political views were certainly not mine, and I can think of no leading Conservative for whose philosophy I had less sympathy. But my estimate of Meighen was not entirely negative. He was friendly to me, and I was attracted by his intellect and literary leanings. In my first year in parliament, I was invited to a luncheon at the Chateau Laurier with Meighen and Norman Armour, the United States minister in Ottawa. Meighen greatly impressed me as he and the ambassador, in a brilliant exchange of Shakespearean quotations, dazzled their fellow diners.

I was in the House when I was told the results of the four byelections. Knowing that the prime minister would be pleased to hear that his old adversary would not be returning to the Commons, I phoned King at Laurier House. To my surprise, he had not yet heard the news. He could hardly mask his glee and hurried

---

45 For the full story on the York South byelection, see J. L. Granatstein, *The Politics of Survival: The Conservative Party of Canada, 1939-1945* (Toronto: University of Toronto Press, 1967), p. 96 ff. The Liberals, following their tradition of not opposing a party leader in a byelection, had not contested York South.

down to the House to make an appearance and to be applauded by the Liberal members.

After final reading of the bill authorizing the plebiscite for 27 April, campaigning for the vote began. I was aware that not all would be smooth sailing in Essex East and had received a warning of what we might expect. An issue of *La Feuille d'Erable*, published in Tecumseh by the Liberal senator Gustave Lacasse, contained an open letter to me informing readers that I was on record as opposing conscription. It claimed that "the constituency you have the honour and the responsibility to represent is also opposed" and concluded with an appeal to me to "remain faithful to those who have put their trust in you on two solemn occasions, for the sake of Canada, your country and ours. God Save the King!"[46]

Despite this storm signal, I helped Mayor Reaume to organize a citywide campaign with federal and provincial members of parliament to promote a result that would release the prime minister from his pledge. This urban "yes" campaign was similar to an organization set up in the rural areas under Essex County warden W. McCormick. Striving to ensure a loud "yes" vote, I spoke with Norman McLarty at a large rally of ethnic groups in East Windsor. At one of these meetings, I introduced McLarty after I had spoken. "Nothing," Norman began, "could give me greater pleasure than to speak to the Polish people of this area." The audience became fidgety — they were mainly Czechs!

Curious to know whether the French communities were disposed to release the government from its commitment, I was at pains to show them that setting it free did not mean that conscription would occur. The issue, I told my audiences, was to show a united front to the enemy and then go forward to fight the battle together. I deplored those who went around saying that in Québec there was a desire to do less in the fight than there was in other parts of the country. "Let us stop smearing each other," I begged.

46 *La Feuille d'Erable*, 15 January 1942. This statement, originally printed in French, was translated into English and distributed as a pamphlet.

"Let us try to understand each other's point of view." The leaders of all major political parties were asking Canadians to vote "yes" and the issue was therefore not a vote either in favour of or against the government. "The world is in flames. And one does not tie the hands of firemen fighting a three-alarm fire. That, simply, is what a 'no' vote would do to the government."[47]

On 27 April, when Canadians voiced their opinions, French Canada voted overwhelmingly "no" and English Canada re-soundingly "yes."[48] The split confirmed that more than ever the Liberal Party should endeavour to keep Canada united. Significantly, in Essex East, where about thirty percent of the population was French speaking, the "no" vote was of the same proportion. The "yes" vote in Riverside, East Windsor and Walkerville was large enough to carry the day. In my own riding, I faced the same problem that confronted the government nationally and knew that I had to tread warily.

Unfortunately, the plebiscite did not settle the issue — even within cabinet. Colonel Ralston, the minister of national defence, wanted to pass legislation at once instituting conscription for overseas service. He regarded the plebiscite as a signal for all-out action. Dedicated though Ralston was, I believed him to be wrong; shortly after the vote I told him so in an unpleasant exchange that I have always regretted. King decided that in view of the conscriptionist sentiment, something had to be done; he proposed deleting the provision restricting the conscripts' service to Canada from the National Resources Mobilization Act. If conscription was required for overseas reinforcements, the prime minister believed the government should ask parliament to vote confidence in it before putting this further extension into effect. King tried to convince J. P. A. Cardin, the senior Québec minister, that the proposed amendment to the Mobilization Act did not change government policy and that all the proposed legislation

47 *WDS*, 11 April 1942.
48 In Ontario, 82.3 percent of the voters favoured releasing the government from its pledge. In Quebec, 78.3 percent refused.

would do was make the government's legal position consistent with the result of the plebiscite. But on 11 May, Cardin resigned from the cabinet. When I met Angus Macdonald on his way into the Commons chamber that day, I told him that it must be clear that no action by the cabinet could ignore parliament's wishes. Cardin could have been discouraged from resigning if certain ministers had agreed that if the time for applying conscription for overseas ever arrived, parliamentary approval for it would have to be sought. Angus, one of the most strongly conscriptionist ministers, curtly said, "You and I do not have the time to discuss that now."

Given the difficulties with any other course, I supported the introduction of Bill 80, the government amendment permitting conscription of men for overseas. McLarty had taken the same position, as I explained to Nell. After Cardin's resignation, I spoke to King, although I was much concerned at the failure of the prime minister to say that there would be a chance to debate any extension of conscription legislation to include overseas service. The prime minister told me that the discussion would not come up in the House for at least two weeks and that he was hoping things would have calmed down by then. King's talk with me was far more inspiring than his speech on Bill 80 in the House, which was too long and not as effective as those he had delivered in caucus. The speech merely repeated his view that the legislation was an extension of the plebiscite result. I engaged in considerable soul-searching over whether I should speak in the debate myself but eventually decided to keep my peace; anything I might say would only split the French and English in Essex East. When the legislation reached third reading in the House on 23 July, only two French-speaking Liberal members from Québec supported it, although the vote went in favour: 141 for to 45 against.

After this vote, some of us eavesdropped on quite a carry-on. Liguori Lacombe, an independent Liberal and MP for Laval-Deux Montagnes, had opposed the motion with all his strength and after the vote had retired to his office to console himself. We all knew that when he had a drop too much, all kinds of things would go on in there, and we would gather around his door trying to decipher them. This time we heard chairs being tossed, pictures being ripped off the walls, and at one point he shouted, "And you can take this, Laurier!" There was a crash. In his frustration and anger, he had had a quarrel with his plaster bust of Laurier and had shattered it to pieces.

In the House of Commons, the Speaker sometimes calls on members to preside during his temporary absence. On 19 June 1942, I sat in the Speaker's chair for the first and only time in my career when the Deputy Speaker, Thomas Vien, who was busy, asked me to take his place. Several rumours sprang up as a result of this harmless episode. One was that Vien was likely to be promoted to the cabinet — he was one of four French-speaking Liberals whose ridings had returned a majority of "yes" votes in the plebiscite. In such an event, the fantasy had me replacing Vien. Such an assignment would not have interested me — rarely did anyone go from the Speaker's chair to the cabinet.[49]

In July, however, I did begin a new part-time career — that of private in the 30th Reconnaissance (Reserve) Battalion of the Essex Regiment. The regiment needed recruits, and I decided that if I joined up, it might provide an impetus for others to seek service in the reserve army. The head of the regiment was Colonel Stuart, the city clerk of Windsor and a good friend, and with his help and that of the department of national defence, I got into the unit as a trooper, despite my physical disabilities. Once in, I tried to get to as many of the drill practices on Tuesday and Thursday nights as possible. We gathered together quite a group of raw recruits,

---

49 In 1940, I had received a letter from Colonel Milton Gregg, the former sergeant-at-arms of the House and at that time the officer commanding the Royal Canadian Regiment. A beloved friend of Nell and mine, Milton had suggested that I ought to look for the appointment as Speaker.

including Harold Vaughan, the editor of the *Windsor Daily Star*, and John Chick, a well-padded local businessman.

Soldiering was a very enjoyable experience for me. As I told Nell, "My uniform has come . . . and it seems to be a good fit, although it will take more than a uniform to make a good soldier out of me." The camaraderie among the boys made me feel that the regiment appreciated my effort. In the summer, when the time came for more extensive training, I went along with the others to the Thames Valley military camp. I had to make a point of keeping out of the way of officers; because of my childhood ailment, I could not salute properly with my right arm or engage in rifle drill. One day I had a toothache and had to go into London to see the dentist. As I was walking along the street, I suddenly came face-to-face with an officer, whom I promptly saluted with my left hand. He responded with a very proper and effective salute. When I was a few feet past him, he turned and said, "Hey, trooper, come here. Who the hell taught you to salute?" Not wishing to explain that I simply could not do it well, I said, "That's the way I was taught, sir." He demanded my name and number. As he walked stiffly away, he said threateningly, "You certainly will hear about this!" but I never did.

The possibility of another new job opened up on 22 October: Mitch Hepburn unexpectedly resigned as premier of Ontario. The attorney general, Gordon Conant, was sworn in as interim leader and premier. Why had Hepburn quit? With Mitch, motivation was sometimes difficult to understand. Certainly he had had differences with his colleagues over his overtures to the Communist Party, and his health had not been good. The rumour mill began its search for a successor. My name had been bruited in 1940, and Lum Clark brought it up again in his column in the *Star*, giving my francophone background as an asset — when in fact it was not. The "news" spread across the Canadian Press wires.[50] The Liberal Party of Ontario would never have accepted as leader anyone with

50 *Montreal Star*, 28 October 1942.

my credentials. A group of young Liberals approached me about running, but I told them my background disqualified me; in any case, my interests lay elsewhere. I wondered, however, when my leader in Ottawa would move to recognize some of the hard work I had done as a private member.[51]

51 I wrote to Nell in June 1942 that "I will relate an hour's chat I had with the Prime Minister. He sent for me and wanted my views (nothing to do about the cabinet—no such luck)."

IX

Off to Philadelphia

ARLY IN MAY 1943, I received a copy of an order-in-council[1]
confirming my appointment as parliamentary assistant to
the minister of labour. This ended several months of speculation and began a new and exciting phase of my parliamentary
career.

For many years, there had been talk in Canadian political
circles about the need for MPs to serve as assistants to ministers,
taking over some of the duties of the busiest members of the
cabinet; as I have already mentioned, I had worked informally for
a while with Norman Rogers when he was minister of labour. The
expansion of government activities occasioned by the war had
increased ministers' responsibilities, and in cabinet on 12 January
1943, Mackenzie King therefore raised the question of appointing
fellow members of parliament to help them. The prime minister
spoke of "the necessity of bringing in younger men," partly, I
suppose, so that those who, like me, had begun to mutter a little for
want of a challenge would not get too impatient. King went ahead
with his suggestion, and in the speech from the throne on 27

1 P. C. 3796, 7 May 1943.

January, the governor general announced that provision would be made for the appointment of parliamentary assistants.

Naturally, rumours about which members would receive the assignments were rife. The *Windsor Daily Star* began boosting me for one of the jobs and suggested that I ought to serve as parliamentary assistant to the prime minister in his capacity as minister of external affairs.[2] I did not know it at the time, but the prime minister had indeed placed my name on the list as a possible aide to himself, and I was also a candidate for the labour department.[3]

When he submitted a measure asking the House to make an appropriation to authorize the appointments, King outlined the nature of the jobs. The new appointees were to help ministers both inside and outside the House. As someone acceptable to the minister, the assistant would be in close contact with departmental officials as well as the government. The minister would have final responsibility for the official acts and utterances of the assistant, who might be given access to confidential material and occasionally even attend cabinet meetings. King emphasized that being made a parliamentary assistant (he expected there would be ten such positions)[4] was not necessarily a stepping-stone to the cabinet.

When the first four appointments were announced on 1 May, my name was not among them.[5] I could not help thinking of the prime minister's remarks to Norman Rogers when King had discouraged my assisting him in 1936. Individual ministers, King had pointed out, would be jealous of their authority and not want a political rival in their own department; furthermore, he warned, geography, race and religion would not be easily surmounted.

2 *WDS*, 12 February 1943.
3 Handwritten note, W. L. Mackenzie King Papers (J4 series, p. C218,517), PAC.
4 House of Commons, *Debates*, 20 April 1943, pp. 2,345-46. Assistants would serve ministers in the departments of the president of the council (the prime minister), finance, national defence (three assistants for the various branches), munitions and supply, labour, justice, agriculture, and pensions and national health. The last two positions and one of the defence portfolios were not filled in 1943.
5 Those getting preferment were Douglas Abbott to finance, Lionel Chevrier to munitions and supply, W. C. MacDonald to national defence, and Cyrus MacMillan to national defence for air.

When I learned that Lionel Chevrier had been given an assistant-
ship, I thought it unlikely that I would make the grade. King
would be loath to appoint two MPs from Ontario who had a
French background.

It was then that I came to appreciate fully the handicap that
racial origin and religion could impose on someone in public life. I
had set off in my political career hoping to make it to the top.
Perhaps I was franker in my ambition than most men in the same
position, but many of my contemporaries had similar aspirations.
Some of them, however, dissembled about their intentions, not
acknowledging that the secret wish of most politicians was to
become prime minister. Given the work I had done, it should have
been my time for recognition and promotion. I was sure that I had
more interest in the bigger problems than most ministers, but
knew that it would not be possible for me to enter the cabinet as
long as Norman McLarty remained in it. After all, he was the
member of parliament for the riding next to mine. Nevertheless, I
did not like excessive attention to geography; racial and religious
restrictions I abhorred. It hurt and offended me to think that, on
those grounds, the Liberal Party could ignore the work I had done,
and it angered me to conclude that Liberals would discriminate in
a manner that contravened the essence of liberalism.

But I knew what the reservations were: as a Catholic member of
parliament with a French background, I was an anomaly in
southwestern Ontario. Looking back on it now, I think that if I had
ever consciously planned a public career, I might have had second
thoughts about moving to that region; it was very Protestant, very
Anglo-Saxon and very rural. But on the other hand, Windsor was
my type of place: a community of many cultures, including the
French, and a city with a rich and impressive history. I could see
why Mackenzie King was concerned about appointing me: that
part of Ontario did not reflect Windsor — or me. It had been the
domain of George Brown and still harboured many who were
repelled by the French and the "Church of Rome." This is certainly no longer the case, but at that time I was a stranger in the
land.

Yet a public life was what I had carved out for myself. I was a "parliament man," and that was the life I wanted. But even if I had not received advancement, I think I would have stayed on as a member of the House of Commons.

Three or four days after the first appointments, the prime minister's office called to ask me to come to see Mackenzie King. Angus Macdonald had told me on the quiet that I would be offered the job of parliamentary assistant to Humphrey Mitchell, the minister of labour. I had no reason to doubt Angus, but Mitchell never so much as hinted to me of the possibility. Years later, I discovered that he had indicated to King that he would have preferred Gray Turgeon. Turgeon, the MP for Cariboo, was then sixty-four and a bit long in the tooth; in effect, Mitchell was saying that he wanted no assistant at all. King overrode the minister's demurral, contradicting his public assertion that he would not foist an assistant on an unwilling minister.[6]

This circumstance must have affected King and explains the line he took during our talk. One of the reasons for choosing me, he said, was his feeling that I shared his views on labour. As he spoke, it became obvious to me that he thought there were large sections of the labour movement that the minister did not understand and to which he was unsympathetic. As an electrician who had belonged to a craft union, Mitchell had little time for the growing industrial union movement. Mackenzie King implied that one of my functions would be to supply the knowledge and understanding to offset the minister's blind spots. When he asked me to keep him quietly informed, it became obvious to me that the prime minister was not totally happy with Mitchell. I told him that I could not allow myself to be a stool pigeon and left his office with a feeling of great unease.[7]

6 Arnold Heeney to King, 30 April 1943, King Papers, (J4 series, p. C218,542), PAC.

7 The others appointed at the same time were Brooke Claxton to the prime minister's office, and Joseph Jean to justice.

Whatever my initial doubts about Mitchell's modernity, he was managing a sensitive portfolio at a difficult time and doing it creditably. When I called on him shortly after seeing King, I could tell that he was not overly enthusiastic about it all. Although I found his attitude discouraging, it was much easier for me to understand his misgivings when I became a minister two years later. The successful parliamentary assistant is one who is eager to make himself useful and productive; he initiates work and does not depend everlastingly on instructions from a busy minister. Luckily for me, I found this out early and quickly made the rounds in the department to make myself known. Mitchell and I got along reasonably well as a result.

Any direction I received in discharging my new duties came from Arthur MacNamara, the deputy minister of labour, who became a trusted colleague and mentor. MacNamara was perhaps the most efficient administrator I have ever known. He saved the government and Humphrey Mitchell from all kinds of embarrassment and in many respects was effectively the minister of labour. I discussed with him the predicament of establishing myself, particularly Mitchell's unwillingness to have me around. "Well," he said, "you'll just have to accommodate yourself to it." What would I do about going to departmental meetings, I wondered. "Just walk in," MacNamara replied. "You are the parliamentary assistant." He was right and we became allies. Many on the Hill felt that MacNamara loved power; I was able to discount such suspicion and to pass along many of his useful suggestions to members of the prime minister's staff—Jack Pickersgill in particular.

MacNamara was not close to Mackenzie King — his interests and rough-and-tumble education would not have appealed to the prime minister — but King recognized that he was a valuable and reliable public servant, always as cool as a cucumber. During a crisis, the unperturbable MacNamara would sit in his office, smoking a cigar and placidly negotiating with the parties in dispute. Whatever the issue, it was usually settled by the end of the day.

※—※

After I moved into my new office in the Confederation Building, I realized that there was much to learn about the functioning of the department. My task was made somewhat easier by my keen interest in labour matters.

Some of my methods were slighty unorthodox. On a trip to northern Ontario, I was waiting on the station platform at North Bay and decided to conduct a brief investigation into working conditions among railway employees. After donning a porter's cap and jacket, I stuck around for the next train. Out of it stepped an elderly lady who handed me her suitcase; like a model porter, I carried her bags to a taxi. She placed a dime in my hand for my services, and I showed off that ten-cent piece for years as a memento of a brief career.

Right after my appointment, I became fully involved in the work of the department of labour. The officers gave me information on various issues for study and for comment. Sometimes these consisted of general studies to do with the relationship between labour and management in a particular industry. At other times, my work dealt with specific cases — usually the efforts of a company to prevent the unionization of its workers. It fell to my lot to maintain contact with other members of parliament regarding labour matters. I would suggest to Liberal members that they ask the minister a question in order that the department might make its policy clear on an issue.[8] I also would negotiate with opposition MPs about their requests for government documents to be tabled in the House as orders for return.

In February 1944, at the prime minister's request, I chaired a caucus committee on labour problems and invited twenty-one other Liberal members to attend its meetings. Initially, we had planned meetings every Tuesday and Thursday in order to inform the members so that they could defend the government's labour

8 In May 1944, for example, I suggested to Ross Macdonald, MP for Brant, that he put a question regarding the employment of conscientious objectors in Alberta and British Columbia.

policy in the House. Unfortunately, interest quickly waned, and the committe fizzled out within a short time.

My ideas about the role of labour did not change, founded as they were on the view that industry should be a partnership among the state, management and the workers. For me, this meant labour's participating in the operation of industry more than as a mere cog — and never more so than during the dark days of the 1940s, when the war demanded the mobilization of all talents. These views were buttressed by a conviction that labour should have the right to collective bargaining and to choose its own bargaining agent.

In 1939 the government had to start mobilizing manpower to satisfy both civilian and military demands. The premise was that every person must contribute to the war effort and people should be put in positions where their training and ability would be used to greatest effect. These were the aims of the government's labour policies. At first, there was a plentiful supply of labour — jobs went to those who had been unemployed during the Depression — and men could be recruited for the armed forces or hired for expanding war industries without causing shortages.

Because of our free society, Canadians do not take well to regulations — even those invoked during national emergencies. Realizing this, the King government tried to rely largely on voluntary cooperation and persuasion. The very nature of the labour question demanded that the cabinet take no position that was fixed in stone: policy should evolve as conditions changed and as the government acquired the ability to assure efficient and humanitarian management of manpower in time of war.

It was as a direct consequence of the war's deterioration in 1940 that the government embarked on the second phase of its manpower policy — partial regulation of the availability for military service and civilian employment. That summer, a registration drive had provided an inventory of available talent, and a special wartime training program was established to place skilled workers where they were needed. By the end of 1941, when Humphrey

Mitchell took over as minister of labour, it had become apparent that trained personnel would have to be recruited for the industrial war effort. Employers were prohibited from soliciting workers already engaged in war industry, and the government agreed to defray the workers' expenses if they had to move to do work essential to the war.

With the rise in prices in 1941, organized labour grew restless; there were strikes, and dissaffection was widespread. At first, the Wartime Prices and Trade Board did not try to control wages and prices too rigidly. But on 19 October, the prime minister broadcast to the nation that a strict enforcement of the wage and price freeze would be put into effect immediately; it would be policed by the board, functioning under the authority of the minister of finance.[9] The replacement for Hector Mackinnon as the head of the agency would be Donald Gordon, deputy governor of the Bank of Canada. King's speech pleased me because he had taken steps to ensure that labour would not be unduly antagonized.[10] This decision provoked plenty of discussion in ridings such as Essex East, and members of parliament once more found themselves in the position of intermediaries between the government and the workers.

Coupled with the wage and price freeze was the demand for increased production in all sectors of the economy. This required the most effective deployment of labour. Voluntary measures were encouraged to reduce growing shortages; however, on occasion, the government was compelled to resort to direct control. The administration of manpower measures, previously divided among several ministries, became centralized in the department of labour. A series of orders-in-council passed in March 1942 were

9 Until this time, the Wartime Prices and Trade Board had been the responsibility of the minister of labour. P. C. 7440, 18 December 1940, had set up a formula for establishing maximum and minimum wages based on 1926 to 1929 rates as the maximum allowed, plus a provision for cost-of-living bonuses to provide for increases. The freeze and enforcement measures were put into effect by P. C. 8253 of 24 October 1941.

10 The government proposed that after 15 November all employers would be required to pay a cost-of-living bonus.

later amended and consolidated into the National Selective Regulations of January 1943.

Shortly after the wage and price freeze, I argued that it was an experiment almost without precedent and should be given a chance. Workers had legitimate grievances that must be recognized if labour disputes and strikes were to be avoided.[11] To labour groups, I pleaded for tolerance and a common understanding with industrial management, even though "from the point of view of organized labour, the actual practice has not been consistent with the declaration of government policy."[12]

During this period, when the freedom of trade unions was being increasingly circumscribed by government regulations, I took up the theme of organized labour and spoke out strongly in favour of representation by labour on government boards.[13] Asserting that it was essential to trust labour, I noted that "at the present time, my own father is engaged in making munitions of war. Am I to say I do not trust him? And he is no different from the thousands of men who are engaged in the war factories of this country." The government should make industry a true partner by giving labour full representation on government agencies. The "so-called radical groups," I believed, would not take advantage of the situation.[14] After all, the Soviet Union had been our ally in June 1941.

One other subject on which I spoke disapprovingly of the government was its reluctance to enact mandatory collective bargaining in a measure that contained enforcement provisions. Moreover, I felt that the criminal code provisions[15] barring discrimination against union members by anti-union employers were

11 *WDS*, 28 October 1941.
12 Speech to Montreal bank clerks, November 1941.
13 Pickersgill to King, 24 November 1943, King Papers (J4 series, p. C250,231), PAC. Pickersgill had prepared a list of union grievances for the prime minister. This particular demand led all the rest.
14 House of Commons, *Debates*, 26 March 1942, pp. 1,679-80.
15 The government had passed an order-in-council (P. C. 2685, 19 June 1940) that provided moral support for collective bargaining; but it lacked teeth. Speech to the Office and Professional Workers Organizing Committee in Montreal in November 1941.

not adequate. Although the government had suggested that employers establish measures for collective bargaining, very few had done so voluntarily, and this foot-dragging was greatly resented by workers and union leaders. In March 1942, I told the House of Commons that collective bargaining was "a technique that is older than any member of this House, and it has kept the industrial peace of more countries than one could count on one's ten fingers. The preservation of the industrial peace [in Britain] has been maintained largely because the British government and industry and labour . . . have fostered the development of a tradition" of collective bargaining that dissuaded employees and employers from any other means of negotiation. A few months afterwards,I rose in the House to declare that labour's right to collective bargaining should also apply to industries that were controlled, operated or owned by the government itself.[16]

If events in Essex County were any indication, labour's support for collective bargaining could not long be gainsaid. Despite claims that the workers were surrendering to professional organizers their right to manage their own affairs, the Ford workers voted 4,455 against to 6,853 in favour of having the UAW-CIO represent them in negotiations with the company. On 26 November 1941, the UAW began its first set of negotiations as the agent of all Ford of Canada workers in Windsor. Encouraged by this success, 750 workers attended a meeting, under UAW auspices, the following day and called upon the federal government to conduct a vote in the Windsor Chrysler plants to determine the wishes of the workers for an exclusive bargaining agent.[17]

Chrysler workers received a further stimulus when the UAW and Ford reached an agreement after just six weeks of negotiations.[18] But Chrysler was not as easy a nut to crack, and despite a

16 ibid., 1 August 1942, pp. 5,173-74.
17 *WDS*, 10 November 1941, editorial. At this stage in the UAW's development, I felt that the *Star* maintained an unsupportable position regarding the union's claims (ibid., 14 November 1941). The alternative to the UAW was an association of employees at the Ford plant (ibid., 27 November 1941).
18 ibid., 12 November 1941.
19 ibid., 22 May 1942; ibid., 28 May 1942. The vote was 2,856 for and 707 against.

conciliation board report favouring the UAW as the bargaining agent of the workers, the company would not budge. The conciliation board, headed by Mr. Justice Gillanders, recommended that the UAW not be recognized as the exclusive bargaining agent of all 2,596 hourly rated employees, as the union desired, but that the UAW be allowed to negotiate with the company for those employees who were members of the union. On 22 May 1942, I issued a statement supporting the UAW in its efforts to bargain with Chrysler and urging the company to accept the report. In full-page advertisements in the *Windsor Daily Star*, the union printed my remarks and asked: "Why does Chrysler Corporation defy our Government and democratic principles while a world struggle for democracy rages?" Six days later, voting began in the Chrysler plants to ascertain whether the workers favoured the UAW as their bargaining agent. The union scored a resounding victory, and on 1 September the Chrysler Corporation signed an agreement recognizing the United Automobile Workers.[19]

After my appointment as parliamentary assistant, I continued to support the rights of labour to choose their bargaining representatives. In my first public statement, at a meeting of the Knights of Columbus, I claimed that the recognition of labour's rights was based on Christian charity. I hoped to minimize the opposition of Catholics to the secular industrial union; I went on to say that the church, in a declaration of Leo XIII, had sanctioned this right.[20] About this time, too, I tried to help the workers at the Dominion Arsenals factories in Québec to set up a local union to bargain on their behalf. However, the department of justice ruled that as employees of a crown corporation, they were in the same position as civil servants and, therefore, could not enter a collective agreement.

When I made my first speech as parliamentary assistant in the House of Commons (it was my fortieth birthday), I emphasized that we were dealing with a very difficult problem — the question of the proper allocation of manpower. The opposition had criticized the government for not having a master scheme, but in fact

20 *WDS*, 17 May 1943.

there was a day-to-day policy that could meet particular contin-
gencies. Any other course, I contended, amounted to copying the
methods of totalitarian regimes. Only where it was necessary had
the Canadian government applied compulsory powers to channel
skills to the place of greatest need. The opposition were so obsessed
with the question of recruiting men for the army that they had
forgotten that the country needed men and women for industry
and agriculture too. "We are a democratic country," I argued,

> . . . a people deep-rooted in the desire to be left alone. We do not
> like to be moved out of our jobs; we do not like to do things that
> disturb our family attachments or our community interests. But our
> people . . . [have acquiesced in these very things]. . . . The
> government has pursued its course with vigour, with understanding
> and with results. I submit to you, sir, that nothing else counts.[21]

Political controversy swirled around the labour department for the
first few months after my appointment. In February 1943, the
government had restructured the national wartime labour board; its
new chairman was C. P. McTague, then a justice of the Ontario
Appeal Court, and its members included Léon Lalande, who had
worked as a junior with me in the McTague firm, and J. L. Cohen,
the well-known labour lawyer. Cohen was not an easy person to
work with, as McTague and Lalande soon discovered. The board
quickly agreed to establish an inquiry to enable it to advise the
government on labour relations. I saw Cohen frequently; I suppose
he intended me to keep the minister of labour informed of his views
on government policy. There was not much love lost between
Humphrey Mitchell and J. L. Cohen, who was overly critical of
the minister in exchanges with his trade union clients. Cohen was
an able counsel but proved very difficult when his point of view
was questioned. He complained to me about the secrecy of the

21   House of Commons, *Debates*, 23 June 1943, pp. 4,113-18.

board's deliberations and about the length of time it took the government to act on its recommendations.

The dispute became public in August 1943, when Cohen released a letter complaining about the scope of the board's activities; he decided not to participate in its hearings until the government had implemented certain reforms. McTague was on the other side of the fence: in his view, the board's function was not to express an opinion about policy but to administer it fairly under the law.[22] To further publicize his opinions, Cohen spoke to the Trades and Labour Congress in Québec City on 1 September, claiming that the results of the inquiry had led the board to write reports critical of the existing labour laws and the way they were administered. He was angry that the government had not made the majority and minority reports public. While not quarrelling with Cohen's contention that the National Labour Relations Board should strive to modify an unsatisfacory labour policy, I could see that making public observations on the reports before the government had commented on them would get him and the government into hot water. Because of Cohen's outspokenness, which went beyond the bounds of acceptable behaviour by a member of a government-appointed board, the cabinet agreed with Mackenzie King's recommendation to pass an order-in-council dismissing him.

Many members of the government, including the prime minister, thought that Cohen had contrived to produce the maximum embarrassment for the Liberals and the greatest benefit for his own party, the CCF, which had become the official opposition in Ontario after the August 1943 provincial election. Cohen's behaviour certainly strengthened the hand of Aaron Mosher, president

---

22 J. L. Cohen to C. P. McTague, 18 August 1943; McTague to Cohen, 19 August 1943, King Papers (J4 series, pp. C165,310-14), PAC.

of the Canadian Congress of Labour (CCL) and an avowed CCF supporter. I had known Mosher, an ex-railwayman, from the beginning of the war; he was a hard-fisted and redoubtable champion of labour, and I had developed much respect for him. I had known Pat Conroy, the secretary-treasurer of the CCL, since my early days in parliament. Pat was thought to be the most accomplished trade unionist in Canada; he was certainly the best informed. The Trades and Labour Congress, the organization of craft unions, remained far less influenced by the CCF, and Percy Bengough, its president, was both personally and politically more amenable than Mosher.

When he asked me to take on the job of parliamentary assistant, King said that labour's attitude to the government was a major obstacle to the Liberals winning the next election. I agreed, although I did not add that some of the government's responses to labour were often singularly unhelpful. Not the least of these deficiencies was Humphrey Mitchell's antagonism towards the industrial union leaders. While I had the greatest respect for the minister of munitions and supply, C. D. Howe, his opinions on trade unions were politically disturbing;[23] indeed, Howe's aversion was shared by most of the cabinet in 1942, and he greatly influenced Humphrey Mitchell. Too much, I thought. Howe's view was that the government must not give in to labour's excessive demands. Brooke Claxton and I felt that what was required was a sympathetic understanding of labour's general needs.

Unrest in the ranks of labour paralleled swelling support for the CCF. In the national Gallup polls, great numbers of respondents indicated that they were prepared to vote for the socialists. The rout of the Liberal Party in Ontario in the 1943 election[24] shocked federal Liberals, even though they knew that the party had been in a muddle long before Hepburn's resignation. At a convention in

23 Howe suspected that even the advice given to him by his department's own industrial relations advisor, Carl Goldenberg, tended to favour labour too much.
24 The Conservatives, led by George Drew, elected thirty-eight members; the CCF, under E. B. Jolliffe, thirty-four, and the Liberals, fifteen.

March 1943, Harry Nixon had been chosen leader and led the provincial Liberals back into good relations with their federal counterparts. But Nixon was not a strong leader and could not overcome the handicaps he had inherited from Hepburn. More alarming than the defeat by the Tories, however, was the election of the thirty-four CCF members and the cementing of an alliance between that party and the various components of the Canadian Congress of Labour.[25] A Gallup poll taken in September 1943 contained even gloomier news for federal Liberals: it showed that the CCF had the largest measure of public support of any national party.[26]

In spite of my own concern over the loss of Liberal support, particularly in such industrial areas as Windsor, I was firm in my resolve that the rights of labour had to be respected. A. Nelson Alles, the member-elect for the CCF in Essex North, was dismissed from his job at Ford's for attending caucus meetings of his party. Locals 200 and 240 of the UAW, representing 10,000 of his fellow workers, were immediately up in arms. I made it plain that a matter of principle was involved and that I was prepared to fight. It was a negation of democracy for the Ford Motor Company to dismiss an employee who was absent on official public duties.[27]

A mass meeting was held in Windsor on 2 October to protest against curtailed industrial production. I went along to explain that the cutback was merely temporary — the result of a shortage of materials — and again took the opportunity to assert my support for labour's legitimate demands. Although I had urged my fellow MPs from Essex County to join me, both had demurred. That was the party's difficulty: were we liberals or were we not? It was not hard to see why the government had lost favour. Referring to Nelson Alles, I told the audience of three thousand that he had a

25 The September 1942 convention of the Canadian Congress of Labour had endorsed the CCF as its political arm. By mid-1943, forty union locals had affiliated with the party. See Chapter X for a longer discussion of this question.
26 Twenty-nine percent expressed support for the CCF and twenty-eight percent for the Liberals and for the Conservatives.
27 *WDS*, 25 September 1943.

right to attend to his duties and that "we're not going to stand for any discrimination against any class or race or political group . . . ." I also expressed my belief in labour-management councils and hoped that they would soon be established in Windsor. Once again I affirmed my strong faith in collective bargaining, hinting that while it was not for me to disclose government policy, I was certain that collective bargaining would soon become the law of the land.[28]

What I knew was that cabinet had already approved in principle the application of compulsory collective bargaining and the sanctions to make it work. On 5 and 6 November, cabinet had considered and approved a draft submitted by the department of labour that would enact a wartime labour relations code to embody the arrangement.[29] I had worked with Humphrey Mitchell in his presentation of the proposals to cabinet; they also included the setting up of a revised labour relations board as well as some form of compulsory arbitration of disputes.[30]

On 27 October, Mitchell announced that a labour conference between the federal and provincial governments would be convened on 8 November. Ottawa had full authority to carry out these provisions under the War Measures Act but was holding the conference to secure the provinces' cooperation about all parts of the code over which they would have peacetime jurisdiction.[31]

At the two-day conference, a rather *pro forma* affair, I did little but sit at the table and observe. Mitchell was looking for accommodation with the provinces in the short and in the long term. Many of the visiting representatives took the position that legislation already in effect in their provinces should be the model for the federal proposals. Although the provincial governments did not

28 *WDS*, 4 October 1943.
29 Memorandum for file by A. D. P. Heeney, 6 November 1943, and attachments, King Papers (J4 series, pp. C250,200-12), PAC.
30 Mackenzie King's notation, "approved by council, 16 ix, 43," King Papers, ibid., (pp. C250,148-56).
31 Draft of remarks of welcome, 6 November 1943, King Papers, ibid., (p. C250,188).

disagree with the principle of compulsory collective bargaining, they were apprehensive lest their voluntary acceptance of it in wartime should prejudice their position when labour matters returned to their jurisdiction after hostilities had ceased and the War Measures Act no longer superceded their responsibility under the BNA Act.

The new labour policy announced in early December greatly troubled the unions. Aaron Mosher, president of the Canadian Congress of Labour, complained that there was no provision in the new wage order[32] to meet an increase in the cost of living. He was wrong: it was quite clear that adjustments would be made if the cost of living rose. Mosher also complained that organized labour would have only one designated representative (as would employers) on the new labour relations board and grumbled that the two public representatives would be opposed to working people and would vote consistently with "the big interests." He grudgingly approved the government's decision to make the cost-of-living bonus a part of the basic wage rate.[33] Unlike Mosher, Percy Bengough, the president of the Trades and Labour Congress, made a helpful statement during the annual meeting of the congress and the government on 25 February 1944.

In order to assure that the new labour code received the most favourable publicity, I had convinced Jack Pickersgill that it should be announced separately from modifications to the wage order. It would have been impossible to satisfy labour entirely on the wage order and to retain the strict anti-inflation aspect of wage controls. And yet I knew that the labour leaders would be far less critical of the new labour code.[34] Despite my advice, the unions still linked the two issues in their submissions to the government.

The labour code came into force on 17 February as P.C. 1003; it became organized labour's Magna Carta. Now there could be no

32 P. C. 9384.
33 *WDS*,13 December 1943.
34 Pickersgill to King, 8 February 1944, King Papers (J4 series, p. C250,267), PAC.

obstacle to the right of employees to establish and join unions. The code outlawed unfair practices and established a method for identifying and certifying bargaining units. Provision was made for compulsory collective bargaining and conciliation, and it was affirmed that labour had the right to strike; no longer could the unions be brushed off as they had been in the Ford and Chrysler plants. P.C. 1003, I thought, would do much to reverse the political advances of the CCF.

On 14 February, Norman McLarty and I met representatives of organized labour in Windsor to listen to their protests about the new wage order. They also wanted company unions to be outlawed. There was no question in my mind that unions must be independent if they were to represent the wishes of workers, but I thought it was up to individual men and women to decide which union they wished to join. The government, I told the delegation, was not hostile to labour, as both the new labour code and even the wage order had shown. But McLarty and I agreed to examine the case against purported inequality of application of the cost-of-living bonus. W. C. Riggs, the CCF provincial member for Windsor-Sandwich, blamed the unrest on the delays in arbitration proceedings established by the government, but I pointed out that labour had been given a voice in the new legislation. It gave me great satisfaction to emphasize that the new provisions embodied in the order-in-council represented official recognition by cabinet of labour's rights and obligations.[35]

The year 1944 was an eventful one. It opened happily with the birth of our daughter, Mary Anne Eleanor, on 22 January. Our son, Paul, had given us such pleasure that Nell had decided that we should have another child. A little earlier, Nell had gone back to manage one of the family drugstores. Out of the blue, her formidable mother had called one evening and informed Nell,

35 *WDS*, 4 February 1944.

"You will open up the store at nine tomorrow morning." I think Mrs. Adams was a little resentful of the fact that Nell had only worked for about a year after she had completed her professional training. Although Nell enjoyed her second stint in the drugstore, she did not change her mind about wanting another child. My preoccupations in the constituency, the law office and parliament by no means reduced the importance of our family life and my ever-growing love for my wife and son. We were thrilled when Mary Anne joined us — she was born at Hôtel Dieu Hospital, on Windsor's Ouellette Avenue.

We regretted that while my father had been able to hold Paul in his arms, that important pleasure was not there for Mary Anne; Father had died in October 1913. I was greatly shaken by his death and by my mother's night-time grief as she tried to sleep in one of her home's two small bedrooms while my father lay in his coffin in our little parlour.

The day after his death, I thought much of what my father had meant to me. I was very thankful that I had been in Ottawa and close to home so that throughout the previous eight years I had been able to spend some time with him. On one excursion we had motored to Thurso, where he had spent his boyhood. He showed me his house, as well as the church where he had served mass, and introduced me to people whom he had not seen for thirty-five years.

My sisters and brother tried to ease Mother's sorrow. By that time, Anita had graduated from St. Joseph's College at Varsity and was working in Ottawa. Marie had come from Hamilton, where she worked for Silverwood's Dairy. Claire and her new husband, Mel Guay, had come from the military camp at Peta-wawa, where she had worked for the army engineers. Lucille, as always the mainstay of the family, was there in Pembroke to help Mother through those first difficult hours until we arrived.

The day Father was buried, his bier was taken out of the house in pouring rain. Because of the bad weather, not many mourners accompanied the funeral procession to the church. One figure, however, remains indelibly in my mind — Senator Gerald White,

a Pembroke Conservative; my father had referred to him as
"Dummy" White. He could hardly be called a friend of the family
— he was a Tory and my father a Grit. It was with great amazement that I saw him standing in the rain, on the wet grass, hat off,
paying his last respects. His presence touched me.

My mother's situation after my father's death made me aware of
how precarious life can be for older people with few means. Since
Dad had left a very small amount of life insurance, Emile and I
would help Mother out financially, but her main provider was
Lucille, who lived at home with her. If our family arrangements
had not existed, life could have been very difficult. In retrospect, it
is amazing how little provision the government had for those, like
my mother, who could receive a pension only if they had no family
and were practically penniless.

The International Labour Organization had played an important
part in my devotion to international cooperation since my student
days in Geneva. Albert Thomas, the former French statesman and
a socialist whom I greatly admired, had been one of the architects
of the ILO after the Versailles conference.[36] My friend Wilfred
Jenks had continued his association with the ILO and was now one
of the right-hand men of the director general, E. J. Phelan. The
ILO's mandate was to achieve, by agreement among the nations
and by the vast sweep of international collaboration and purpose,
the betterment of living and working conditions for labour
throughout the world. It had no means of creating a binding
authority over governments but was rather a medium through
which agreement could be reached on desirable labour standards.
Its governing body appointed the director general and supervised

---

36 From 1919 until his death in 1932, he was director of the International Labour
    Bureau of the League of Nations.

the work of the permanent secretariat;[37] policy was decided upon at international conferences. In very many ways, the ideals of the organization paralleled those for which I was striving in Canada. For example, at its assemblies, workers and employers were represented as well as governments. The ILO obviously had practised the partnership in industry that I favoured.

To measure the organization's achievements, it was interesting to note some of the objectives that were considered "of urgent importance" in 1919 by the framers of the ILO's constitution: freedom of association, reasonable minimum wages, an eight-hour day and a forty-eight-hour week, one day's rest in seven, the abolition of child labour, and equal pay for women and men doing the same work As I noted in 1944:

> In spite of the ILO's efforts, it cannot be said that all of [these
> ideals] have been attained in all countries. Nevertheless a great
> deal of progress has been made, and the existence of international
> standards has inspired many countries to make improvements in
> their legislation that might otherwise not have been made. The
> extent of the progress may also be measured in our mental
> attitude to these early principles, which, revolutionary as they
> were in their day, now seem almost conservative.[38]

From the outbreak of war, the work of the ILO had been carried on under trying conditions. In 1940, the secretariat evacuated most of its personnel from Geneva and, at the invitation of the Canadian government, set up a temporary office at McGill University in Montreal. Despite the problems of operating in "exile," the ILO began to grow steadily in influence. As nations turned their attention to considering a post-war world, they discovered that this body, through its voluminous store of studies and

37 The governing body comprised sixteen government delegates, eight employers and eight employees.
38 Paul Martin, "Canada and the International Labour Organization," *Public Affairs* 7, no. 4 (1944): 196.

research, could help them prepare for the future. In Canada, the government had taken advantage of the expert technical assistance of the ILO in devising unemployment insurance legislation. Some of our wartime labour measures and reports on various social problems had benefited in the same way.

Yet the ILO was neither well known in Canada nor well supported by the government. One person to whom the organization mattered was Dr. Margaret Mackintosh, of the department of labour, but unfortunately, Humphrey Mitchell did not share her enthusiasm or belief in the ILO's importance. Mitchell was also out of tune with the thinking of President Roosevelt, who had suggested to Winston Churchill, when they met at Québec in August 1943, the possibility of holding a general labour conference. There had been no such meeting since a conference in New York and Washington in 1941. Discussions continued when E. J. Phelan and Carter Goodrich, the chairman of the governing body, came to Ottawa in November 1943 to meet Norman Robertson and Hume Wrong. Although none of the pre-war international organizations had enjoyed as wide a membership as the ILO, the institution's advantages were dissipating. Robertson and Wrong maintained that this was because Phelan was not an effective and crusading head;[39] I did not share their view.

It was felt that the proposed conference should strive to influence social policy in liberated Europe, especially by stressing the importance of full employment. Specific recommendations for governments were required. Canadian officials believed that the conference needed the inspiration of a missionary spirit. Because the proposed date of the conference — April 1944 — came in the middle of a parliamentary session, the federal government preferred that the meeting not be held in Canada.[40] In the end, it was decided to meet in Philadelphia. In December 1943 the governing body approved an agenda that included a discussion of future

39 Robertson to King, 2 December 1943, King Papers (J4 series, p. C193,821), PAC; Wrong to file, 18 November 1943, ibid. (p. C193,981).
40 Robertson to King, 11 November 1943, ibid. (p. C193,979).

policy and the status of the ILO, recommendations for present and post-war policy, the organization of employment in the transition from war to peace, and social security and minimum labour standards for dependent territories. I was very pleased to receive an invitation to attend the conference as one of the government delegates, along with Humphrey Mitchell and Brooke Claxton.[41] (Humphrey Mitchell attended *ex officio* as minister of labour.) Neither stayed long in Philadelphia, and for most of the time I was in charge.

Delegates from over forty nations gathered at Temple University in Philadelphia on 20 April 1944. It was widely believed that the ILO would expand its activities, but in the Canadian government's opinion, it would have to have features in common with other proposed international bodies, such as the World Bank and the Food and Agriculture Organization. Speaking at the plenary session of the conference, I stated that a number of separate institutions for international cooperation would be created, each covering a particular phase of economic or social affairs, such as monetary and exchange policy, commercial policy, food and agriculture. "These organizations must eventually be brought together in an international framework," I said; "if we are to avoid overlapping and confusion, we must discourage any tendency to take on vague general purposes." I could therefore not subscribe to the statement in the proposed declaration of aims and purposes that would give the ILO the authority to scrutinize all international economic policies and measures and otherwise broaden its scope of operations to include matters that were the purview of other organizations. After talking it over with my friend Wilfred Jenks, I had decided to speak in this vein because of my wish to see the ILO carry on its important work. I did not want to see it lose its identity by overreaching itself at the end of the war.[42]

41 Canada sent a large delegation that included officials from the federal departments of labour and external affairs, provincial legislators and officials, representatives of the employers and employees, and technical advisors.
42 *WDS*, 26 April 1944.

My proposal was that the ILO should set up a committee, with headquarters in Montreal, and give it the task of "fitting the organization into its proper and rightful place . . . ." Accordingly, our delegation submitted a resolution to the effect that the committee examine and report on the relationship of the organization to other international bodies; the constitutional practice of the ILO and its clarification and codification; the status, immunities and other facilities to be accorded to the organization by governments for the efficient discharge of the responsibilities of the organization; and the method of financing it.

These proposals were criticized by trade unionists at the conference. Led by Joseph Hallsworth, one of Britain's leading labour leaders and the chairman of the group representing all the workers' delegates, they accused us of stalling and of dodging our responsibility. The Canadian workers' representative, Percy Bengough, agreed; he thought that the future of the ILO should be settled there and then. On 29 April, three days after I had introduced Canada's resolution, the delegation felt obliged to issue a statement to the effect that we hoped that final decisions would be reached wherever possible and that there was no difference of opinion between the Canadian government delegates and those who represented the workers.[43] We all wanted the ILO to face the post-war world in as strong a position as possible.

A compromise was eventually reached that allowed our resolution to be referred to one of the conference's sitting committees; it was understood that should this committee be unable to submit definite recommendations before the conference ended, a special committee would have to be established to undertake the study we had proposed. In the end, the conference committee reached a stalemate, and the special committee was established to report to the governing body at a meeting in London set for the following January. Our views on the relationship of the ILO to other international bodies proved to be a wise course that came to get wide commendation. I did not know that within twelve months, I

43 *The Globe and Mail*, 30 April 1944.

would have a further opportunity to help settle the relationship of the organization to the United Nations.

In addition to presenting the resolution about the future of the ILO, I was named chairman of the committee on employment. Delegates to this committee were asked to consider and to make recommendations on post-war social policy, and particularly on the means by which full employment would be achieved in countries no longer at war. The conference urged governments and organizations of employers and workers to formulate programs suited to the particular needs of their countries. But the committee recognized that the difficult period of reconstruction would demand international cooperation as well as efforts by individual nations.

The final report of the committee, a draft of which had been prepared in advance by the ILO's office in Montreal, was presented after eleven sittings. We asked signatory countries to accept these recommendations as guiding principles. For example, our report set out the techniques to be used during the demobilization of the armed forces and the winding down of war industries; described sound employment service and vocational guidance methods; and discussed training programs geared to post-war economic requirements, as well as the problems of the young, the disabled, and women in industry, who, we said, should be given equality of opportunity and wages. We thought it unsound to recommend that war industries be kept in operation when they were no longer needed, just to keep workers employed.

In submitting the committee's conclusions, I expressed the view that the objective of full employment could not be attained unless proper national and international economic and political measures were adopted. But if member countries tackled the problem with the same energy with which they had pursued the war, I was certain that full employment would be achieved.[44] Jobs for all who were fit to work and security for those who could not were, I told the plenary sitting on 11 May, among the highest aims to which

44 *Montreal Gazette*, 29 April 1944.

the ILO gave expression. These and other recommendations pointed the way to a solution of our economic and social ills, without which there could be no peace. "Our deliberations," I concluded,

> were predicated upon the assumption on which not only human dignity but the peace of the world depends; that in determining the character of the peace, there shall not be forgotten those important human considerations which were perhaps neglected twenty years ago.

The conference adopted the report by eight-eight votes to none.

As its most important achievement, the conference issued the Philadelphia Declaration. In light of changing conditions, it restated the aims and purposes of the ILO, affirming that "lasting peace can be established only if it is based on social justice" and that "poverty anywhere constitutes a danger to prosperity everywhere." The obligation of the organization, the eloquent declaration asserted, included furthering, among the nations of the world, programs that would achieve full employment and the raising of standards of living; social security; protection of the life and health of workers; effective recognition of the right of collective bargaining; and equality of educational and vocational opportunity. I believe that when we adopted the Philadelphia Declaration, we endorsed an historic formulation. At the time, it was widely felt that it would help us improve the welfare of mankind.

Shortly after I left the conference, I told the annual meeting of the League of Nations Society in Montreal on 20 May that the Philadelphia Declaration was a benchmark: it constituted agreement on principles "that a quarter of a century ago would have been labelled as revolutionary — labelled by the beneficiaries of privilege as political, economic and social disaster."[45]

Throughout the conference, I was constantly reminded of the contrast between the principles we were enunciating and the

45 *WDS*, 27 May 1944.

extent to which they were so often disregarded. A confrontation between labour and management at the Ford plant in Essex East led to a strike, and so I had to return to Windsor and Ottawa several times during the course of the conference. As I journeyed back and forth, I reflected on the irony of the situation: the parties in the Ford dispute were oblivious of what was going on a few hundred miles away. On 19 April, UAW local 200 at Ford went on strike in protest over the company's interpretation of the collective bargaining agreement. The specific question was the operation of the grievance procedure. Under the contract, shop stewards were entitled to take off two hours in any one day or three hours in any two days to investigate grievances against the company. Management at Ford was not happy with this provision; when no agreement was reached at a meeting with the national wartime labour relations board on 17 April and the stewards were dismissed, 14,000 workers downed tools.

When I arrived in Ottawa towards the end of April, I had to do my best to be in three places at once and was happy when the workers began to return to their jobs on 1 May. My relief was short-lived; the workers went out again on 3 May and closed the plants even to management. Although both company and union had agreed to negotiate a new contract, there were still misunderstandings about the operation of the grievance procedure.

The resumption of the strike meant that my commuting schedule continued to be hectic. As the old song had it, I was always "off to Philadelphia in the morning." I was pleased that Louis St. Laurent, the minister of justice, heeded my advice and refused to allow Ford to use the RCMP to keep the plants open. He felt, as I did, that the attitude of the Ford workers was "very satisfactory," that the company had brought on the situation, and that the use of the police was unjustifiable. Finally, at the invitation of both parties to the dispute, Mr. Justice G. B. O'Connor, the new chairman of the national wartime labour relations board,[46] agreed

---

46 C. P. McTague had resigned in February, ostensibly to resume his judicial work (see p. 365).

to come to Windsor; in the meantime, the workers allowed officials and administrators into the plant. After the hearing about the grievance procedure, members of local 200 agreed to go back to work when the board informed them that the strike was illegal and that no clarification of the grievance issue would be made before they returned to the workplace. I was kept busy conferring both with the union's representative, J. L. Cohen, and with officers of the board. Cohen and I got along very well, and I believe that our activities helped to convince the men to return to work.

The incongruity of this contretemps and the work of the ILO at Philadelphia did not escape me, and I worried that the progress made for labour at the international level would be regarded as visionary but of little applicability. The drive behind Canadian participation in the organization was left to a small parliamentary group and a few officials in the department of labour. Because the jurisdiction over labour affairs was divided between federal and provincial governments, Canada had ratified only a few international labour conventions. Federal legislation had often been modified to conform to ILO standards, but formal ratification was impossible without provincial assent. Clearly, what was needed was some form of federal-provincial cooperation that would enable Canada to put the ILO conventions into effect to assure minimum national labour standards and give the country credibility in the operation of the international organization.[47]

After Philadelphia, Margaret Mackintosh, Eric Stangroom (special assistant to the deputy minister) and I decided to push for greater recognition of the work of the organization. We wanted the conventions and recommendations of the ILO to be formally transmitted to the provincial governments and informal discussion between federal and provincial ministers of labour to consider provincial action on those proposals that fell within their jurisdiction. We also recommended that the reports of international

47 Paul Martin, "Canada and the International Labour Organization," p. 197.

labour conferences be tabled in the House of Commons to provide an opportunity for debate and public education.

Despite our efforts, we found Arthur MacNamara rather uninterested in the work of the ILO. Like Humphrey Mitchell, he was too preoccupied with the more immediate concerns of his department. Although I believed that the prime minister would be interested, I did not wish to go over the head of the minister of labour to reach King. Instead, I suggested that we ought to get Mitchell to make a statement on the Philadelphia conference in the debates in the House on the estimates for either the department of external affairs or the department of labour. To my exasperation, he chose to do nothing. The minister's only comment came during the Philadelphia conference itself, when he told the House that "I do not know . . . nor do I think any member of this House knows, what kind of world we shall live in when the war is over." "You," suggested R. B. Hanson, the Conservative House leader, "ought to ask Paul Martin."[48]

48 Reported in *WDS*, 2 May 1944.

X

Towards a People's World

Partisan politics seemed far removed when, on 6 June 1944, Mackenzie King told the House of Commons that Allied troops had begun to land on the northern coast of France. Members of the House reacted with the solemnity that such an historic announcement was bound to evoke. Canadian forces were taking part in the long-awaited Normandy landings, which we all hoped would be the beginning of the end in the war against Germany. On that day, parliament and Canada were as one. The lack of enthusiasm of some Québec members for Canada's war policies momentarily evaporated as Maurice Lalonde led the House in paying tribute to France's hour of liberation, launching into "God Save the King" and "La Marseillaise." A ragtag parliamentary chorus struggled its way through both anthems.[1]

Another moment — seemingly unrelated and far less dramatic — took place in the House in the last ten days of the month when the government introduced legislation to establish three new departments: reconstruction, veterans' affairs, and national health

1 House of Commons, *Debates*, 6 June 1944, p. 3,564.

312

and welfare. The governor general had previously declared the government's intention to create these ministries in the speech from the throne on 27 January 1944, when he had also announced that a system of universal children's allowances was to be set up.

Both D-day and the bills tabled that same month constituted major steps towards realizing the post-war world for which we all longed.

Consideration of a better life after the war had begun for me neither with the government's legislative proposals nor with my appointment as parliamentary assistant; it had been a preoccupation since September 1939, when I supported national scholarships and unemployment insurance because they would bring about desirable social change for Canadians. The fact that most of our energies had to be focussed on the war did not mean that the government should not prepare for the post-war period. In my judgment, the objectives of the war and the subsequent peace were two sides of the same coin, and I frequently repeated that

> Our aim in this war may be simply stated, if not easy to achieve. It is to defeat Hitler and his associates, and more particularly to remove the instincts of which these dictators are the products, and having succeeded in the prosecution of this assignment to set about at social reconstruction and at the establishment of a sounder basis for the peace of the world.[2]

It was unfortunate that many Canadians did not see the connection between the kind of peacetime world we wanted to live in and the ideals for which we were fighting. The country, I contended, was not in the struggle just to preserve the imperfections of past decades but was striving to achieve a more equitable and decent

2 Paul Martin, "War Aims and Peace Aims," *The Canadian Spokesman*, April 1941, pp. 14-17.

society. The social and economic research being carried out in Canada and elsewhere should consist of realistic and precise proposals for a richer and more secure life for all when peace came.

It was my opinion that Canadians would not countenance a return to the economic injustices of the pre-war years. Reconstruction, therefore, meant examining proposals covering the spectrum of Canada's political, economic and social life. The Atlantic Charter of August 1941, which reaffirmed aims that looked to the world's eventual liberation from fascist tyranny, linked the principles for battle to the objectives of a post-war world. When Roosevelt and Churchill drew up the charter on the British battleship *Prince of Wales* and the American warship *Augusta* in Placentia Bay, Newfoundland, they urged nations at war with Germany and Italy to collaborate "with the object of securing for all, improved labour standards, economic advancement and social security." They made it plain that the end of the conflict ought to bring "freedom from fear and want." The charter, although little more than an exercise in exhortation, thereby accepted an important principle: war is tolerable only when it is associated with reform.

Some of us in the Liberal Party in 1942 recognized the importance of post-war economic cooperation, but we also knew that more than high-flown promises of reform were required. An enormous reallocation of manpower had taken place in Canada, and the government had provided significant financial assistance to essential manufacturing industries. This commitment had already had an enormous effect on the country's infrastructure. If plants were shut down after the war, the argument went, and returning soldiers were left to fend for themselves, wholesale disaster would ensue. Canada's peacetime requirements would demand an immense effort to constructively convert wartime industries. Expanded markets for agriculture, the building of railways and highways, modernization of transport and civil aviation, public and private works, and new housing — all should form part of a vast public program to transform the country from war to peace. The often-put question would have to be answered: why could the government not do in peace what it had done in war?

Largely at the instigation of Ian Mackenzie, the minister of pensions and national health, the government began to act on several fronts. Mackenzie chaired the cabinet committee on demobilization and re-establishment that had been set up in December 1939 — charged with the task of integrating ex-servicemen into civilian society. After a lot of wrangling in cabinet, Mackenzie finally won approval early in 1941 to establish an advisory committee on reconstruction, composed of prominent academics, businessmen and labour leaders and headed by F. Cyril James.[3] The committee was to recommend ways by which the government could institute effective policies for reconstruction, and it began by setting up a research program under the direction of Leonard Marsh, a British trained economist who was teaching at McGill. I had met Marsh often and knew that his sympathies lay with the CCF.[4] Although this impaired his credibility with some Ottawa stuffed-shirts, it certainly did not with me.

The House of Commons embarked on its own study of post-war requirements by forming the special committee on reconstruction and re-establishment in March 1942. The thirty-four members of this committee, to which I belonged,[5] carried out their own analysis of what was needed, calling expert witnesses and listening to interested parties, including members of the James committee, with whom we had considerable contact. The publication in December 1942 of Sir William Beveridge's report on social insurance and allied services in Britain excited considerable interest, certainly among those of us studying reconstruction in Canada, and we eagerly read his comprehensive recommendations.[6] To

---

3 He called together Principal F. Cyril James, of McGill University (as chairman); Principal R. C. Wallace, of Queen's University; Tom Moore, of the Trades and Labour Congress; J. S. McLean, of Canada Packers; and Edouard Montpetit, of the Université de Montréal.

4 He had played an active role in establishing the League for Social Reconstruction.

5 House of Commons, *Debates*, 24 March 1942, p. 1,573. The committee was established on a motion of Ian Mackenzie. Its chairman was J. G. Turgeon, the member for Cariboo.

6 Beveridge visited Ottawa in May 1943; to my dismay, I found him much less impressive than I had expected.

combat poverty and mass unemployment, Beveridge proposed that one weekly contribution provide for social and unemployment assistance as well as a national health plan and family allowances. Cyril James agreed to set Leonard Marsh to work at once preparing a report on social security for Canada. Marsh had known Beveridge at the London School of Economics, where they had examined various social problems together.

When the government re-established the special committee on reconstruction for the 1943 parliamentary session, I lost no time in airing my views on post-war planning. The fundamental question, I argued, was what kind of world we hoped to bring about at the end of the war; to my mind, the war's prosecution must go hand in hand with plans for its aftermath. But to say that we had taken up arms only to build a better world was to ignore the evil perpetrated by Hitler. Surely, however, we would have proceeded with what had become known as our "peace aims" even if the war had not taken place. Yet there is no doubt that the struggle hastened the realization of the urgency of planning for new social security programs. I supported Clarie Gillis's proposal that the parliamentary committee needed its own research staff, and I tried to awaken its members' interest in proposals for collective security; it was my belief that they ought to address such important matters.

In *Conditions of Peace*, E. H. Carr had written that

> The war has brought the final proof of the bankruptcy of the political, economic and moral system which did duty in the prosperous days of the nineteenth century. It has also provided . . . a moral purpose which has revived the national will. . . . But it is essential to recognise in all humility that this purpose is the product of war. . . . There is no guarantee that out of it will grow a more permanent purpose to create in time of peace a new world . . . the crisis cannot be explained — and much less solved — in constitutional, or even in economic terms. The fundamental issue is moral.[7]

One of the first ways of arriving at this political and economic system would be to ensure the reintegration of the armed forces

7 E. H. Carr, *Conditions of Peace* (London: Macmillan, 1942), pp. 124-25.

into the economic life of Canada. The department of pensions and national health, I pointed out, had developed a program that would go some way towards meeting Carr's aspirations and would provide minimum requirements for adequate health standards, nutrition and educational opportunities. Although I was all in favour of an economic and social program, I warned against any scheme that would lead to built-in rigidity. My ultimate aim was to eliminate the extremes of poverty and wealth in Canada and abroad.[8]

My views on the reforms that ought to be undertaken by the Liberal Party were contained in a speech delivered in February 1943 to the Montreal Young Men's Canadian Club. Convinced that only Liberalism could effect humane social change, I proposed that government eat away at big incomes that derived from monopoly and inefficient markets, where the ignorant and the poor were at a disadvantage. Compulsory collective bargaining was, to my mind, a cornerstone of any reform program. Capital should be encouraged to be mobile, not to become entrenched in favoured corporate structures. The limited liability corporation had to be stripped of the right to retain and invest profits at the discretion of individual managers instead of according to the determination of the market. I also urged the party to guard against the expansion of the holding company, which was nothing more than an agency by which large corporations could control the management of other corporations, resulting in the establishment of huge industrial empires within which executive discretion often supercedes the free market as the regulator of output. This type of organization represented a form of collectivism, a principle against which big business habitually railed.

Farmers had to be taken care of as well; those with perishable crops had less bargaining power than ones whose products could be stored. Liberalism, I stressed, should ensure that differences in the workings of divergent markets were kept to a minimum. Land

8 House of Commons, *Debates*, 26 February 1943, pp. 729-31; ibid., 26 February 1943, pp. 739-42.

and natural resources had to be conserved, and all rights of private property in these domains should be made subject to the condition that there would be no waste or destruction.[9]

Just as the Beveridge Report had focussed the debate in Britain, so too did the Marsh Report in Canada.[10] It was supposed to be released only after it had been studied by the government, but Marsh jumped the gun and made the report public on 16 March. He had told some of us that he feared the government might tinker with his work, and so the report was released ahead of schedule. There was an exceptionally favourable public reaction. It outlined current social legislation and suggested many improvements, postulating schemes to combat unemployment as the first requirement. As war production slackened, it would be necessary to ensure the continuation of the community's purchasing power and its ability to contribute to social security programs. Marsh called for planning to reconvert industry, to maintain jobs and to retrain the workforce. Public employment schemes and a well-financed works program would counteract the expected post-war recession. The report went on to recommend a national health program based on universal health insurance and with levels of assistance that depended on individual income. Sickness, maternity and cash benefits would be provided for all female workers. The Marsh Report also recommended both children's allowances and a universal, contributory old-age pension of $45 a month for married couples as a clear part of the policy of providing a national minimum standard of living.

The cost of these changes disturbed some in the cabinet, including C. D. Howe and the conscientious keeper of the public purse, Jim Ilsley. Ilsley's objection was that the report, having been released prematurely, did not carry the official sanction of government and therefore could not be accepted as the basis for legislation. While Ilsley might have based his official objections to the proposals on these grounds, I knew that philosophically he did not

9 *WDS*, 13 February 1943.
10 *Report on Social Security for Canada* (Ottawa: King's Printer, 1943).

favour spending the government's money in this manner. One night he and I talked long into the wee hours arguing the pros and cons of state measures for social security. He honestly felt that the government could not afford these measures and that some of them should be undertaken by the family, the church or the provinces. Ilsley kept asking me, "Why do you want to saddle us with these things?" My answer was "Because of my liberalism." All ministers of finance eventually succumb to Ilsley's type of thinking — and so do prime ministers. The need for revenue appears to be unlimited, and as they undertake their juggling act, they do not like to see costly schemes come forward.

Ilsley applied identical criticism to a plan for health insurance that was released at the same time by Ian Mackenzie, who was very anxious that his work not be overshadowed. Mackenzie's amended scheme was finally presented for study to the House of Commons social security committee a year later, in March 1944; it called for contributions at a flat rate, as well as a graduated scale of benefits. The plan would cover all necessary medical, hospital, surgical, nursing and dental services, plus the provision of drugs and medical appliances. The provinces were to take responsibility for the total administrative costs, and the federal government would cover any charges over and above the amount collected from those who were insured.[11]

In principle, I welcomed the Marsh Report and Mackenzie's proposals. Sooner or later, I told the caucus, Liberals must advocate a comprehensive social security program. I did not know then that, after the war, I would come to play a significant role in that process. At the same meeting of caucus, I was unhappy to hear Mackenzie King say that he would oppose an appeal to the people on social security measures while the country was at war. He wanted Canadians to be informed of the value of the proposals and to defer outlays of money until the war was over.

The concepts of social security outlined by Beveridge and Marsh were right up my alley at the time — I would not subscribe

11 *WDS*, 2 March 1944.

to all of them today, nor perhaps would the authors themselves. I am not certain what effect my agitation had on a reluctant government, but I have often wondered whether it impeded my appointment to the cabinet. Nonetheless, I always followed John Stuart Mill's dictum. "Nothing is more certain," he observed, "than that improvement in human affairs is wholly the work of uncontented characters."[12] But I never liked the journalistic description of social security proposals as "cradle-to-the-grave"; this was too simple a rubric, one that would polarize opinion to the detriment of good ideas. Although I never liked the term "welfare state," its concept was acceptable to me, providing that this meant a society where the emphasis was on welfare and not on the state. This conviction certainly differentiated me from the CCF. For me, liberalism has always remained a belief in the value of the human personality and a conviction that the source of all progress lies in the free exercise of individual energy. Liberalism produces an eagerness to emancipate the individual to exercise his powers in so far as this can be done without injury to others. In order to achieve this end, the liberal must be ready

> to use the power of the state for the purpose of creating the conditions within which individual energy can thrive, of preventing all abuses of power, of affording every citizen the means of acquiring mastery of his own capacities and of establishing a real equality of opportunity for all.

These aims are compatible with a very active policy of social reorganization, involving a great enlargement of the state. But they are not compatible with socialism which, strictly speaking, would banish individual initiative and responsibility from the economic sphere.[13]

Although I was all for proceeding with social security measures, I agreed with Marsh's contention that the first concern must be

12 J. S. Mill, *Considerations on Representative Government*, Ch. 3.
13 Speech to the 1944 annual meeting of the Lincoln Liberal Association.

jobs. The prospect of unemployed workers and ex-servicemen in the streets was a grim one. Members of the House committee remembered the civil disturbances in 1919 and were resolved not to allow such a situation to develop again. Afraid that labour and agriculture might not have the full ear of the committee, I urged that we make a special effort to call all interested parties before us. Experts could provide the plans, but those who were affected should have an opportunity to state their views.[14]

Witness after witness who appeared before us emphasized that jobs were the priority: there should be no return to the system that had prevailed during the Depression. This sentiment was echoed by voluntary organizations, provincial governments and private industry, as well as by the trade unions. The submission of the Canadian Legion summed up the universal response:

> A type of economy must be developed that, while providing for individual liberty, ensures employment and a decent standard of living for all, including those who, through no fault of their own, are physically unable to accept employment. To this end we should be prepared to accept whatever type of controls may be necessary, either through the retention of those now in effect or through new ones which must be created to cope with postwar conditions. Freedom and control are not incompatible when control is exercised to prevent or restrain harmful actions or conditions harmful to the public generally. . . . Without restraint there can be no economic freedom; that is, freedom to consume as well as to produce.[15]

This brief, like many others, implied a degree of state intervention in the economy, and the debate focussed on the extent to which the government should be responsible for controlling economic life. My own feelings were much the same as those expressed by Clarie Gillis, who claimed that for seventy-five years private

14 *WDS*, 14 April 1943.
15 House of Commons, special committee on reconstruction and re-establishment, *Minutes of Proceedings and Evidence*, 23 (2 July 1943), p. 615. Submission to the parliamentary committee on reconstruction and re-establishment by the Canadian Legion of the British Empire Service League, presented 2 July 1943.

enterprise had been so private that a large majority of the country's working people had never even received an invitation into the field of employment.[16] On the other hand, a witness like union leader Percy Bengough placed full responsibility for post-war employment on the state. For me, the major responsibility for creating jobs did lie with the private sector. The government must ensure that workers were not exploited and should strive to create an economic climate that would stimulate the creation of jobs.[17] Every wage earner was entitled to the necessities of life — by that, I did not mean the bare necessities. Although the government had repeatedly urged industry to provide adequate remuneration, I wanted the government to set a good example by reforming the working conditions of civil servants.

Industry also looked to the government for help in preparing its own plans for the post-war period. For example, the Canadian Construction Association proposed that the government encourage private enterprise by planning large-scale engineering projects. Their brief, however, cautioned that the construction industry should not function as a relief agency, as it had done during the last years of the Depression. Financing should be provided through crown corporations to stimulate such measures as house building.[18]

My view was that the choice did not lie between free enterprise and collectivism; I supported a mixed economy. The government should not interfere with business activity that contributed "its proper share of social profit." But I believed that industry had to assume some responsibility for shaping the economic future, particularly in the auto industry, where workers had always suffered from seasonal layoffs and uncertainty. Responding to those who believed that the post-war world should return free enterprise to a condition of no restraint, I felt that "to the extent that [public and

16 Special Committee, *Minutes*, 18 (28 May 1943), p. 469.
17 ibid., 24 (7 July 1943), p. 661.
18 Brief submitted by the Canadian Construction Association to the special committee on reconstruction and re-establishment, 12 November 1943.

private welfare] are synonymous, there would be no restraint from the government, but . . . the public welfare must come first."[19] I was encouraged to see that the views I had been promoting for the past ten years had gained such wide currency.

The debate over government participation also brought into focus the division of powers between federal and provincial governments. One of the best presentations made to the committee was that of Premier Stuart Garson of Manitoba. His contention was that since unemployment was nationwide, it should be tackled by policies that were uniformly applicable throughout the country — as should the question of social security. Nine uncoordinated provincial solutions would not suffice. I was delighted to note that Garson was willing to continue to abandon provincial income and corporation taxes in return for tax rental cash payments from the federal government. Garson's position was that Ottawa should assume the burden of providing reconstruction measures. I also agreed with his criticism of Ian Mackenzie's submission to the committee on 16 March, when the minister had spoken about the advantages of national standards of social services while concluding that they were impractical. Garson pointed out that Manitoba thought the problem could be solved either by a constitutional amendment or by adjustment grants paid to the poorer provinces in order to achieve a national health insurance scheme and other essential reforms. The British North America Act had placed limits on provincial resources; at the same time, many reconstruction projects fell within provincial jurisdiction, and the provinces simply would be unable to pay for them.[20]

In sum, I was fully behind the Ontario Teachers' Council, which argued before the committee that "the greatest political absurdity of our Dominion is that every facility has been carefully provided for the growth of national industrial and financial centres and every

19 *The Globe and Mail*, 30 November 1943.
20 "Manitoba brief presented by Premier Stuart Garson to the House of Commons committee on postwar reconstruction," 2 June 1943 (Special Committee, *Minutes*, 19 (2 June 1943), p. 485 ff.)

obstacle has been carefully maintained to prevent the redistribution of the national surplus into roads, hospitals and schools."[21]

The federal government was fully aware that not only the provinces but also municipalities were waiting for it to move and were only too willing to blame it for not giving a lead. The public, too, was feeling uncertain and critical because it did not see action in the area of post-war reconstruction. Voters, however, had a most effective way of showing their feelings.

In the York South byelection of 1942, Joe Noseworthy had talked of the need for improved social security. He had won. Arthur Meighen had emphasized national government and conscription. He had lost. At their Port Hope conference in September 1942, the Conservatives seemed to have absorbed the lessons of this defeat and included social security as a major objective in their reformulated platform. J. M. Macdonnell said that it would be the government's responsibility to give everyone a job at a wage that would enable them to live a decent life. These recommendations were included in the Tory platform and hammered out at their convention in Winnipeg at the end of that year. It all seemed to fit in with the party's new name, which included the designation "Progressive" at the insistence of the freshly recruited leader, John Bracken, the former Manitoba premier.[22]

This whole exercise on the part of the Conservatives struck me as too late and opportunistic to be believable, but I did not as easily dismiss the CCF's threat. After the death of J. S. Woodsworth in March 1942, the CCF selected M. J. Coldwell as its new leader. Coldwell was an effective parliamentary speaker, a man who I thought could have become a good member of the cabinet, or even

21 "Federal Aid to Education: A brief presented by the Ontario Teachers' Council," found in Paul Martin Papers (vol. 1, Federal aid for education file), PAC.

22 J. L. Granatstein, *The Politics of Survival: The Conservative Party of Canada, 1939-1945* (Toronto: University of Toronto Press, 1967), p. 126 ff.

prime minister, if he had been a Liberal. We were very close friends, and he was one of the first MPs that Nell and I entertained at home after our marriage. Coldwell was fond of Nell, and she loved to tease him. One day when we were having lunch in the parliamentary restaurant, Coldwell walked by. My irrepressible wife called out in a rather loud voice, "M. J., I must remember to return your pyjamas." (Coldwell and I had been at the UN together in New York. I had forgotten to pack my pyjamas and had borrowed a spare pair of his. When I got home, Nell had washed and laundered them.) She delighted in the double entendre and chortled at the raised eyebrows and chuckles of those who had overheard her remark.

Shortly after Coldwell assumed the leadership, support for the CCF began to climb. Since its inception, the party had always emphasized organization and had established cadres across the country. It also had greater access to funds as an increasing number of union locals affiliated with the party. No one could deny that the major strength of the CCF was the crusading spirit of its workers. Asked by the prime minister for our analysis of the increasing popularity of the CCF, my fellow parliamentary assistants and I worked on a report for King that told him that

> . . . its support has been won almost entirely at our expense and it is important that we should know why the CCF has succeeded. In the forefront of the minds of the people to whom the CCF appeals is the vivid memory of the Depression. They identify what they went through then with the Conservative party which was in power until 1935 and with the Liberal government which took office that year. They see today full employment at the highest wages . . . and they ask "if in war, why not in peace?" . . . Many who support the CCF just don't want the Depression to happen again.

We also realized that by its campaigning zeal, the CCF had identified itself with all progressive causes. Through effective propaganda, the party had made it appear as if reform and progress were solely its prerogative; it had been able to take advantage of the Liberal government's preoccupation with the war. In our report, we noted that "whenever possible at a meeting of a local school board, a trade union or a citizens' forum, the CCF will have a long table covered with books and pamphlets on politics, economics and social questions." Canadians had begun to identify the CCF with the expression of all progressive ideas, whether they were expounded by a member of that party or not.[23]

A series of Liberal political reversals demonstrated that the CCF's appeal was not a chimera. The Ontario Conservatives, under George Drew, had defeated Harry Nixon's Liberals in August 1943; despite the revivification of the provincial Liberal Party after Mitch Hepburn's resignation,[24] his chickens had come home to roost. The Liberals had won only 15 seats, compared to the CCF's 34 and 38 for the Conservatives. In Essex County, the CCF won three of the four seats.[25] On 9 August, the federal Liberals lost the four byelections,[26] and a month later the Gallup poll showed that the party was less popular than the CCF and was tied with the Conservatives.

Fear of the CCF finally led the prime minister to mobilize his staff and to reorganize the party to meet the challenge. He called a full caucus for 27 September and revived the moribund National Liberal Federation for a meeting three days later. The last meeting had been a decade previously and, apart from the regular get-togethers of young Liberals, the party had no national gatherings. Mackenzie King constantly complained about this situation, but I feel that it was due to him. The leader must stimulate others.

23 Memo, "The political parties today," prepared by the parliamentary assistants and read to caucus by Mackenzie King on 14 March 1944, W. L. Mackenzie King Papers (J4 series, pp. C161,493-512), PAC.

24 Martin to King, n.d. May 1943, after the convention that elected Nixon. "There is no heart-burning. The interest in the party and its future was manifested by the great number in attendance. . . . An undoubted enthusiasm for Liberalism was recorded . . . ." ibid. (J1 series, pp. 298,058-9).

25 Essex East comprised two provincial seats, Essex North and Windsor-Walkerville. The two respective members, Dr. Trottier and David Croll, were defeated.

26 The Montreal riding of Cartier was won by the Labour-Progressive Party, Stanstead by the Bloc Populaire, and Selkirk and Humboldt by the CCF.

No one expects the party leader to undertake the task of organizing, but it is his job to see that there is a functioning national executive. When I left parliament, Pierre Trudeau met with the party president and, at least four times per year, the cabinet held "political meetings," where we discussed certain organizational issues.

I was among those at the caucus who wanted social security measures prepared for enactment as soon as possible. At the meeting of the Federation, King returned to his perennial theme — how weak the party's organization was — and pointed out that improving it was more important than the implementation of policy in regaining lost support. Gently disagreeing with my leader, I reminded caucus of the great success the CCF had achieved in penetrating the trade unions. As Liberals, we could not be fully satisfied until we had not only improved our organization but also set out policies and programs that would inspire labour to support our party. My three months as parliamentary assistant had convinced me of this. After the meeting, I felt that the party had espoused a commitment to a social welfare policy. P.C. 1003 provided one example of what I was working for. But was that enough?

Two of the most influential men in the reorganization of the Liberal Party were Jack Pickersgill, who worked in King's office, and Brooke Claxton, who served as the prime minister's parliamentary assistant. Both of them shared my outlook and point of view — that our party must again become the party of reform. I had known Pickersgill in early 1938, in his first days as assistant to the prime minister. To be sure, he was not King's right-bower. Walter Turnbull was. But Turnbull, the prime minister's principal secretary, was not an orthodox King helpmate: he did not have the impressive academic credentials that the prime minister liked. Pickersgill as assistant secretary to King may not have had the official status of Turnbull, but his mental acuity and political savvy quickly established him in King's esteem. As I got to know Jack, I found that he not only had good ideas but also loved to express them at length. Most members were intimidated by him because he had the ear of Mackenzie King, but it is always in the interest of MPs to be in the good graces of the prime minister's doorkeepers.

As Pickersgill himself has pointed out, he soon became involved in planning political activities and working on behalf of the Liberal Party which he wholeheartedly supported. He took to political strategy as a duck takes to water.[27] Very soon after he went to work for the prime minister, he began to bend his will to looking after his master's interests. I suppose Mackenzie King, and later Louis St. Laurent, often did not realize the extent to which they were following through on Pickersgill's plans. The Liberal Party owes Jack Pickersgill a great deal. I have never doubted the contribution he has made to the party, but I worried occasionally about the tremendous power he wielded by virtue of his position. Jack had all kinds of subtle ways of suggesting that such and such a person should get a particular appointment. I have a hunch it was he who was really responsible for my becoming parliamentary assistant to the minister of labour. Labour-management relations were obviously troubled, and Pickersgill, I suspect, had managed to convince King that a younger, progressive man attached to the department might help the government regain some of its lost support among the workers.

It was obvious that Humphrey Mitchell was quite lost in setting up the department to deal with the post-war period. In some ways, perhaps the minister was pressed by Arthur MacNamara to overreach himself, so he tried to expand the department by proposing that it should take over the administration of family allowances and unemployment assistance schemes.[28]

---

27 J. W. Pickersgill, *My Years with Louis St. Laurent: A Political Memoir* (Toronto: University of Toronto Press, 1975), pp. 9-10, 12.
28 Mitchell to King, 18 January 1944, King Papers (J1 series, pp. 318,246-48) PAC.

As soon as he had assessed the political situation in 1943, Pickersgill began drafting memoranda embodying many of the ideas that some of us in the party had been pushing. In these notes to Mackenzie King, he made it clear that the government had protected the position of the less fortunate members of society but now should try to remove the fears about the future by implementing family allowances. In his own fashion, Pickersgill promoted the proposal not as a social measure but as a way of removing some of labour's grievances about wages.[29] I took issue with any argument such as this for relieving industry of its responsibility to pay an adequate wage to its workers. For me, family allowances remained purely a matter of social justice. Surprisingly, labour leaders did not object strenuously to the family allowance proposal. Pickersgill also advocated a floor for farm prices, a housing policy and more public works. "Parties in opposition," he told King, "can afford to rest on their promises; that is really all they have to offer.... The voters know that a government in office has the power to act and they are going to judge it largely on the concrete evidences of action."[30]

Once the war had been won, voters would not credit the political party that had organized the victory but would look to those who could provide a better future. That was the lesson that the Churchill Conservatives did not learn in 1945, when they suffered a drubbing at the polls.

Brooke Claxton was the other man to whom the Liberal Party owed much during this period. He was a most capable organizer and used to bombard the prime minister with suggestions for presenting Liberal policies more persuasively. Brooke helped devise new means of reaching the public through modern advertizing techniques and public opinion polling. Perhaps he glorified the

29 This view of family allowances was put forth in the memorandum to cabinet prepared by Clifford Clark, the deputy minister of finance (Clark's memo to council, n. d. 1943, King Papers (J4 series, p. C187,895) PAC).

30 Quoted in J. W. Pickersgill, *The Liberal Party* (Toronto: McClelland and Stewart, 1962), p. 32 ff.

body politic too much, and I sometimes thought he believed that the way to win elections was mainly by devising a good chart. But he had a sound grasp of policies and was one of us who pushed the prime minister to give more thought to the post-war world. Brooke would isolate problems and analyze them methodically. We shared the same views on the development of social and welfare programs; yet in some ways he was as different from me as chalk is from cheese. Like Vincent Massey, he felt most at home with his classmates from private schools and shone among the cognoscenti and patrons of the arts. Despite his enlightened social ideas, I often wondered how much he really understood of the lives of working people in places like East Windsor.

Pickersgill and Claxton were close enough to Mackenzie King to be able to reinforce his interest in the needs of the post-war period. The speech from the throne on 27 January 1944 confirmed the government's commitment. It was music to my ears when I heard the governor general say that "the establishment of a national minimum of social security and human welfare should be advanced as rapidly as possible." The Liberal government was finally pledging itself to provide jobs for all who were willing to work, to upgrade housing and to provide social insurance. The central pillars of the program were the rehabilitation of former servicemen, the reconstruction of the economy, and health and social insurance. For this, three new departments would be created. Family allowances would be introduced, a more generous contributory old-age pension scheme put in place, and floor prices for farm products instituted.[31]

This was the program that I had been urging on the government for some time, and I continued to do so right up to the week before it was announced.[32] Once it was public, I set about promoting it like a true zealot. It was my view that the new department of reconstruction would develop policies to help industry protect and create jobs. I envisaged a greater democratization of industry;

31 House of Commons, *Debates*, 27 January 1944, pp. 1-3.
32 *Winnipeg Free Press*, 20 January 1944.

although industry existed to make profits, I thought it right that it should involve the workers more directly in its operations. Members of the House of Commons heard my view that the responsibilities of the new ministry would include providing workers with new jobs as war industries were dismantled or reconverted and layoffs began. The department should gather information regarding job openings due to retirements and should also encourage the transfer of surplus labour and the relocation of industry in order to guarantee work and minimize layoffs. As far as servicemen were concerned, the department ought to assess their individual occupational backgrounds and skills to plan for their efficient reintegration into peacetime jobs. In addition, special training and employment facilities should assist disabled veterans.[33]

I spoke on the second reading of the bill to establish family allowances, describing it as part of a more comprehensive future social security program. The allowances could not but be regarded as the basic means of assuring an income, regardless of what may happen to the breadwinner and, as such, of helping maintain family income. I was confident the measures would not depress wages, especially if labour was well organized. In fact, I pointed out that the bill would be of benefit to labour — for instance in the event of a strike, when the loss of income would deleteriously affect the family as a whole. Furthermore, wages were based on work, not on the number of dependent children.[34]

As far as veterans were concerned, I maintained that Canada's broad rehabilitation program for the armed forces was not as well known as it should have been. The measures included reinstatement of veterans in their former jobs, vocational and educational training, and assistance in setting up a business or a farm, as well as financial aid in buying a home. Veterans could be assured of

33 House of Commons, *Debates*, 20 June 1944, pp. 4,010-20.
34 ibid., 26 July 1944, pp. 5,402-06. The allowances involved a payment of $5 per month for children to 5 years; $6 for those from 6 to 9; $7 for those from 10 to 12; and $8 for those from 13 to 15. The rates would be reduced by $1 per month for the fifth child, $2 for the sixth and seventh, and $3 for the eighth and additional.

preference in employment, medical treatment and unemployment insurance benefits to help them resume civilian life.[35]

By the end of the year, I could say with confidence that "we mean to see to it that our people will have work to do, a good home to live in, food to eat, schools for our children, and all the conditions that make for a good life."[36] Criticism by the Tory *Ottawa Journal* that my figures on poverty in Canada were inaccurate or by the then-reactionary *Globe and Mail* that I was too left-leaning were like praise to me.[37]

There was no doubt in my mind that the Conservative opposition had committed a major political error by taking a stand against certain parts of the government's program, particularly the family allowance scheme. They realized this during the debate on second reading, and in the end all but Dr. Herbert Bruce, MP for Parkdale, voted for the bill. There was resistance to the measure in the Liberal caucus. Some representatives from rural areas questioned the bill and George Fulford, the wealthy MP from Brockville, discussed his opposition with me. I cautioned him not to broach the subject in caucus, but he disregarded my warning. When he spoke out, the prime minister squelched him by pointing out his privileged upbringing. Liberal divisions were kept quiet and the public remembered the Conservatives' initial reluctance to support family allowances, not their final vote in the House of Commons.

Apart from giving full vocal support to the government's reconstruction legislation, my own role involved working fairly closely with the other parliamentary assistants to suggest new means of organizing the Liberal Party. Brooke Claxton took the lead in the report prepared for King, in which the assistants lauded the government's decision to embody a reform program in the speech from the throne — "the best ever given in this country." We also noted the decentralization of party organization under various

35 *WDS*, 28 September 1944.
36 ibid., 4 November 1944.
37 *Ottawa Journal*, 3 April 1944; *The Globe and Mail*, 20 June 1944.

ministers who were responsible for particular regions of the country and pointed out that

> within a few months of the most crucial election in the history of
> Canada, the party has no publicity program, no expert on publicity,
> no expert in radio, no research workers and not very much in the
> way of organization geared up for a real campaign.

Once this situation was rectified, we thought that we should aim our sights at the twenty percent of the people who had not committed themselves to any political party. For our next target, we singled out the Conservative supporters who most feared the CCF. If the Liberal Party could convince them that we had the best chance of shutting the CCF out of the government, we could get a lot of votes from those who abhorred the so-called "socialist menace." Finally, the Liberals could gain votes from the CCF by convincing its supporters that our party could achieve their fundamental social objectives without an economic revolution or a radical upheaval. The Liberals could, in fact, capitalize on fears of the consequences of a CCF victory. The electorate that we wanted to reach, the

> . . . seventy per cent who would now vote other than Liberal, will
> be reached best through the positive appeal of practical and progres-
> sive policies and because of confidence in the administration. We
> must show them how much better off they are than before and per-
> suade them that we mean to go forward from where we are, not
> back . . . . Our dominant theme should connect war achievements
> with postwar prospects.[38]

While I saw the CCF as a political threat, these were years when I spent a lot of time in the company of some of its members of parliament. I lived in a boarding house on Cobourg Street in

---

38 "The Political Parties Today," read to caucus 14 March 1944, King Papers (J4
series, pp. C161,493-512), PAC.

Ottawa run by two spinsters, ironically both staunch Tories. Four CCF members lived in the house: Clarence ("Clarie") Gillis; G. H. ("Cas") Castleden, from Yorkton, Saskatchewan; Sandy Nicholson, from Mackenzie, Saskatchewan; and Joe Noseworthy. The rather more than rotund, outgoing John Turner, from Springfield, Manitoba, and I made up the Liberal duo. I became fast friends with all my fellow lodgers, especially Clarie Gillis, a former coal miner, who was the most effective speaker in the party after Coldwell. The CCFers and I would often walk home together following late-night sittings in the House, arguing like mad, all of them against me, except sometimes for Clarie. He once said, "Paul speaks my language. Sometimes I think he's more of a reformer than any of us." When he said that, he was looking right at the "saintly" Stanley Knowles, who had joined us that night.

Clarie had a special affection for C. D. Howe. Apparently Howe had quietly helped a member of Gillis's family who had been in trouble. I still remember Knowles going after Howe in the House and Gillis standing up and defending the minister. Friendship, I think, can make stranger bedfellows than politics.

When the parliamentary assistants met to discuss their recommendations regarding the party's reorganization, I tried to make it clear that we were dealing essentially with the national party, as opposed to the party in each constituency. To my mind, the latter was perhaps the more important. Of course, it could be greatly influenced by what was done in Ottawa, but my experience was that the constituency organization, the member of parliament and his rapport with the electorate were overwhelmingly influential. In most cases, what the member contributed to victory or defeat depended substantially on what he did between elections, his relationship with the riding and its voters, and the work that he performed at home and in parliament. After thirty-three years in the House of Commons and ten successful elections, I would not amend my assessment one jot.

This, certainly, was one of the considerations in my mind as I struggled for a wartime and a postwar program for labour as parliamentary assistant to Humphrey Mitchell. P.C. 1003, the labour code for which I had agitated for so long, removed all obstructions by employers to the rights of their workers to join and establish unions. But it also tended to retard the advances of the CCF within the ranks of labour. In effect, we had implemented the CCF's labour program as formulated at a special conference at Regina in the first days of 1944.[39]

From the time the UAW was formed in Windsor, I was sure that its regional directors, Charlie Millard and — later — George Burt, might endeavour to use the union for political purposes. Actually, I was more worried that they might attempt to make the evolving CCF the arm of the Canadian Congress of Labour. I did all I could to prevent this from happening. Naturally, I was concerned for political reasons; but that was not all. It was wrong for labour to become affiliated with a political party, and such an association could harm the legitimate aims of the union movement (I soon came to believe that trade unions were by their nature more conservative than political parties, certainly more so than the CCF was in its midwar heyday). The two were incompatible. When Philip Murray, the head of the CIO, came to Windsor in January 1943 to receive the Christian Culture award,[40] I spoke to him about the identification of the unions with the CCF, but he said that it was none of my business. He was right.

It was clear to me that the CCF was going to get the support of the leaders of the Canadian Congress of Labour. But although the party increased its following among trade union leaders, it did not earn the backing of the rank and file. I used to go to the plants and knew very well that the CCF would not get widespread support on the shop floor. I visited union halls — not to go to meetings but to talk to the members. Some trade unionists spoke publicly of my

39 *WDS*, 3 January 1944.
40 I had something to do with Murray getting this distinction, because I wanted labour to be given some public recognition.

championship of labour and progressive social policies. At the CIO convention in Québec City, Thomas MacLean of the Windsor UAW opposed the affiliation of the unions with any political party. He lost, but the point was made. Michael McClosky, an active member of local 200 of the UAW, was elected president of one of the Liberal associations in Windsor shortly thereafter. As the *Windsor Daily Star* pointed out, "the CCF doesn't have all the UAW votes in the bag."[41] My appeals to the workers, over the heads of the union leaders, were beginning to pay off. This was not done by avoiding theoretical discussions and concentrating on practical politics. I would discuss with my constituents the notion of partnership in industry and would not shy away from discussions of international affairs and interdependence. I hardly hid my work at the ILO under a bushel.

Even though most of the labour leaders decided to support the CCF, I did not shun them. I liked them: they talked my language, and I could appreciate what they wanted. I understood what they were getting at long before the UAW was officially established in Canada and was hurt when these men did not support me politically. But I did not stop working for labour, nor was I unsympathetic to the aspirations and requests of its leaders. When I think of the exploitive conditions that prevailed in the automobile factories and compare them with the current situation, the benefits that the unions effected are inescapable. It is true to say that often the unions created their own abuses — unnecessary strikes that fuelled inflation, for example. Despite these excesses, I always supported the unions. Sometimes, I despised the irresponsibility of the leaders who were jockeying for power within their organizations. But I recognized that the industrial union movement was new, and it would take time for it to mature. Some observers tend to blame communists for much of the labour troubles during this period. The communists may have had something to do with the situation, but if it were not for the approval of a majority in a particular plant, there would not be a strike. The communists' influence is

41 *WDS*, 2 August 1944; ibid., 20 October 1944; ibid., 27 October 1944.

exaggerated, and it must be remembered that they were in a minority. I do not know what society would have done without the unions. Except for their militancy, the benefits would not exist today. In the Liberal Party during World War II, there were not many who felt as keenly about the rights of labour as I did.[42]

The question in my mind, however, remained whether I would be given the opportunity to participate fully in the decisions regarding post-war Canada. Would I be able to translate my words into deeds? We all knew that Mackenzie King was planning cabinet changes. On 13 October 1944, when the new appointments were made, my name was not on the list.[43] My friend Brooke Claxton, who shared many of my attitudes, moved into the cabinet and now had the occasion, as minister of the new department of national health and welfare, to promote our common views. He replied to my telephone call of congratulation with a note that ended, "I hope that this is just cutting the ice for you." His final comment — "It should have been you anyway" — was the response of a friend to what he knew must have been a disappointment for me.

42 I. M. Abella, *Nationalism, Communism and Canadian Labour: The CIO, the Communist Party and the Canadian Congress of Labour, 1935-1956* (Toronto: University of Toronto Press, 1973), p. 146.

43 C. D. Howe became minister of the new department of reconstruction; Ian Mackenzie moved from pensions and national health to veterans' affairs.

XI

The Viper's Den

NINETEEN FORTY-FIVE was a year of change — perhaps one of the most important years of my life. It signalled the end of an exhausting war and the establishment of an international organization to preserve the peace. That year, I made a trip to Britain to help bring about what we hoped would be a new world order. In Canada, the Liberal Party was re-elected with a mandate to continue its program for reconstruction. Mackenzie King gave me a larger role in this great undertaking when he brought me into his cabinet as secretary of state and asked me to take part in the first meetings of the United Nations.

As the year began, however, the nation was still recovering slowly from the trauma of another conscription crisis. In the early fall of 1944, the government had thought that there were adequate military reserves on duty overseas. In the limited sphere of Essex East and the caucus, it looked as though events had happily conspired to remove the need for conscription. But working in the department of labour, I was keenly aware of the weaknesses of our

338

selective service program. Industry needed manpower, and it was clear that the standing army of men conscripted for home service was doing little productive work in the camps around the country; in fact, sometimes it hampered meeting our industrial needs. However, once J. L. Ralston, the minister of national defence, returned on 18 October from his trip to the Canadian forces in Europe, the situation began to change. Reinforcements for overseas became his major preoccupation, and a crisis was precipitated.

It worried me greatly when newspapers and some of my constituents began to take up Ralston's theme. Relatives of servicemen overseas joined a large section of the Canadian public in arguing forcefully that more troops were needed at the front and that those conscripted for home defence should be sent to Europe. Ontario's George Drew was especially relentless in his calls for full conscription.

Ralston, too, pursued his theme with stolid single-mindedness. Reinforcements, he told the prime minister, were needed urgently; the reserves were less than estimated and casualties had been heavy. Mackenzie King disagreed with his minister, feeling that the war was being won and that an eleventh-hour conscription call was unnecessary. Had King persisted in his course, a major cabinet crisis would have been likely, since it was assumed that Ralston, Angus Macdonald and Jim Ilsley would resign. Parliament was not in session, and from our constituencies, my fellow members and I anxiously followed events. My talks with Norman McLarty caused me to think that he, C. D. Howe, Humphrey Mitchell, Colin Gibson and Bill Mulock would also throw in the towel if King did not act.

To my mind there was only one option: if need be, the cabinet must hold together without Ralston. Any other course would lead to confusion and the crippling of a strong government. The question was: would the conscriptionist ministers, especially his fellow Nova Scotians, Ilsley and Macdonald, allow Ralston to leave the cabinet on his own? No one could question Ralston's integrity or candour — that was the difficulty. But, like Ilsley, he did not fully understand the compromises that both the French and the English had to make to ensure good government. It was about this time that I told Ilsley that his lack of understanding of the Québec position meant that the leadership of the Liberal Party was not within his reach.

On 1 November, Mackenzie King accepted the resignation that Ralston had submitted two years earlier — and which had not been accepted at that time. It had been held in reserve — a canny and cold-blooded act. In my view, the prime minister had little choice. No one who knew Ralston could help feeling sympathy for him, as I did when I learned what had happened. Everyone admired Ralston, who was a very honourable and able but unimaginative man. The appointment of the former commander of the armed forces, General A. G. L. McNaughton, to replace him minimized the damage to the government and reassured me that conscription would not be imposed.

Yet feeling against the prime minister continued to run high in many places. In my own constituency, it was obvious that many believed that the government had acted wisely; but in Walkerville and Riverside, I expected condemnation for King's failure to introduce conscription — and I got it. Certainly some of my close friends in the armed forces told me in no uncertain manner of their disapproval, as did others at home. Even Nell questioned the government's reluctance. In Branch 12 of the Canadian Legion,[1] the resentment was especially strong; but this was to be expected. What bothered me most were the jibes and sneers against Québec and the refusal to note that not all of the conscripts for home defence who refused to volunteer for overseas service were French-speaking.

The House of Commons was recalled on 22 November. Cabinet discussions on the reinforcement issue had been prolonged, and the Liberal private members were growing restless. I thought it was high time for King — his cabinet divided — to speak to us and

---

1 Shortly after the war, the branch made me its honorary president, a position I still hold.

explain what was going on. Caucus met the morning before the opening of parliament. The prime minister was given a rousing reception and then spoke about Ralston's resignation (the former minister was present), pleading that there be no recrimination. At one point, I thought of asking for a show of hands, knowing that the conscriptionists in the room were not in the majority. It would reveal where everyone stood before the confrontation in parliament that afternoon. Although I did not go through with it, it was still my belief at the end of the meeting that the majority of the caucus supported the government's stand.

But that night King changed his mind. In a telephone call, General McNaughton told him that the latest reports indicated that reinforcements were needed. This news convinced King that some of those conscripted for home defence, under the provisions of the National Resource Mobilization Act, should be sent overseas. The prime minister informed caucus of the new policy the next morning. When King urged party solidarity, Chubby Power rose to say that he could not stay in office with the change of policy.[2] The prime minister made another eloquent appeal to caucus and issued a daring challenge: he would step down if caucus did not support him. He warned that any administration that followed his would implement full conscription and would send soldiers to the Far East as well as to Europe.

My own opposition to conscription was bedrock. I suspect that if I had represented a Québec riding, I would have been against it as vociferously as Maxime Raymond. I had had some misgivings about the plebiscite in 1942 but soon saw that it was an effective way of getting the government out of a mess. Yet I never spoke publicly against conscription; it made no sense to come to Windsor to make speeches that would only antagonize some of my constituents. I am not yet convinced that the Liberal Party was divided as evenly as the cabinet over conscription. In Ontario, practically every minister favoured it at this time. The sentiments, I believe, were almost reversed within the party itself. Although we

2 He resigned that day.

all knew the dangers and remembered 1917, we allowed ourselves to trust the judgment of the prime minister. My technique was to downplay the issue, and it seemed to work well. Despite King's *volte-face*, I accepted his argument. It was clear to me that he and General McNaughton had exhausted all other possible courses. Mackenzie King had to humiliate himself before his party and before his colleagues, knowing the dangers of divisions that he faced. We knew that the military hated and distrusted King[3] for not bringing in conscription, and understood that he had withstood the pressure as long as he could. The Conservatives would certainly not have treated the issue with the same sympathy for French Canada. After Ralston attacked the government in the House on 28 November, I went to see the prime minister to show him that Ralston had contradicted statements he had made earlier as minister of defence. King calmed me down and rightly convinced me to let sleeping dogs lie. The crisis passed on 7 December when the House voted confidence in the government by 143 votes to 70. King had triumphed.

After this worrying episode, I turned my thoughts once more to the international arena. The January meeting of the governing body of the International Labour Organization was drawing nearer, but it was evident that the meeting was not a priority in the department of labour. I began to agitate for adequate Canadian representation at the conference and proposed that Humphrey Mitchell, Arthur MacNamara and I should make every effort to see that Canada pushed to maintain the course that the ILO had set at the Philadelphia conference in April 1943.

My speeches on reconstruction were not restricted to Canada. Canadians had to consider the kind of world as well as the kind of country in which they wanted to live. In my view, the only

---

3 Some of the survivors from this period, C. P. Stacey, for example, have not forgiven him yet.

guarantee of true reconstruction in Canada was successful international political and economic collaboration. At the food conference in Virginia in 1942, at the United Nations Relief and Rehabilitation conference in Montreal the next year, and at the ILO conference in Philadelphia, the Canadian government supported the policy of helping the developing nations achieve the social security desired in Canada itself.[4]

The organization of the peace was one of the matters the commonwealth prime ministers had discussed at their meeting in Westminster in May 1944. Reporting to parliament on the meeting, Mackenzie King had said that the cooperation of the great powers was essential to the maintenance of peace. But to remove the fear that more powerful nations would reach settlements at their expense, the smaller countries must be allowed to participate. Apprising parliament for the first time of the structure of the emerging United Nations, King said that it would be different from the League of Nations. The "functional principle" should determine the composition of the permanent members of a council responsible for enforcing security provisions.[5] He emphasized that in addition to political matters and world security, the new organization must be prepared to take action in many fields: social welfare, trade, technical progress, transportation and economic development.

In my contribution to the debate, I emphasized that unless nations collaborated to achieve social and economic justice, any projected world organization would be frustrated in its attempts to maintain peace.[6] It was my belief that an international organization to preserve world peace must be based on universal obligations: justice, the prevention of aggression, the control of arms, economic and social cooperation, human rights, and colonial trusteeship. As I told the Ottawa League of Nations Society early in 1944, a post-war international organization should be universal,

---

4 House of Commons, *Debates*, 20 June 1944, p. 4,010 ff.
5 For a fuller description of the "functional principle," see p. 360.
6 House of Commons, *Debates*, 4 August 1944, pp. 5,931-36.

and

> . . . aggression should be made a crime against mankind, and all
> nations must be obligated to settle their disputes peacefully. Aggres-
> sion should be prevented by nations functioning through the interna-
> tional organization and agreeing to employ the necessary means,
> including armed force . . .

An international police force, recruited from volunteers, would serve as a deterrent and would be ready to act in case of emergency. All this should be stipulated by law, and the power to adjudicate disputes should rest with the international organization itself and the International Court of Justice. The new central body should include the ILO, as well as agencies responsible for food, relief and rehabilitation, economic and social welfare, health and culture.[7] My advocacy of international order was founded on a steadfast belief that "peace cannot come through an undisciplined competition among sovereign states." It could come about only through a "limit on national authority in the interest of international liberty and order."[8]

Because I felt that Canada had reached a point where it could reach understandings on world affairs with other nations, I was disappointed by Humphrey Mitchell's seeming lack of concern for international labour measures; to my mind, they formed part of the economic foundation of any long-term multinational cooperation. Without the various governments' strong backing for such arrangements, there was a distinct likelihood that the nations of the world would repeat the ineffectual attempts to secure peace that had followed the formation of the League. At the end of the Great War, Canada had taken the position that the terms of the conference called to design the post-war structure included only political matters and not economic ones. By 1944 many, myself among them, had become convinced of the importance of pursuing a policy of international economic cooperation instead of one of political and economic isolation. In his speech on the estimates of the department of external affairs in August 1944, Mackenzie

7 *The Ottawa Journal*, 21 February 1944.
8 League of Nations Society in Canada, *News Bulletin*, July 1943.

King had recognized this but only in a rather vague way. Of course, it would not have been possible for the prime minister to make a commitment in advance, but he could have gone further in setting out Canada's thinking about the kind of post-war world for which we should strive. Naturally, I was anxious to see progress on the work that had begun in Philadelphia, and after the conference, I spoke to many audiences about my hopes for a new world order.

When the House of Commons recessed after the conscription debate on 7 December, no decision had been made about the composition of the Canadian delegation to the ILO meeting in London the next month. Another memo went down the hall of the Confederation Building from Martin to MacNamara to Mitchell, suggesting the appointment of a delegation made up not only of those from external affairs but also of representatives from our department. I made it plain that a high-level group would indicate to the ILO that Canada regarded its work and objectives to be of the utmost importance. I also suggested that Eric Stangroom, a talented officer in the department, be asked to go along. The answer to these recommendations — not long in coming from Mitchell to MacNamara to Martin — stated that the minister was "inclined to the view that the Right Honourable Vincent Massey [already in London as Canadian High Commissioner] and someone from External Affairs is all [*sic*] that is necessary."

On Boxing Day, three weeks before the conference, MacNamara wired me in Windsor: he was willing to recommend to the minister that Eric Stangroom and I attend the meetings, along with Abe Heaps, a former CCF member of parliament, then with the Unemployment Insurance Commission. MacNamara's telegram summarized the minister's view. Mitchell was "of the opinion that you would be quite sufficient. He sees no need for Stangroom but is willing if you insist."[9]

This last-minute decision left little time for briefing, and I was instructed to be in Montreal on 10 January for a departure the

9 Percy Bengough, president of the Trades and Labour Congress, was also on the delegation, as the workers' delegate.

next morning. At Brooke Claxton's for dinner that night, my discomfort about the flight turned to outright fear as Leonard Brockington delighted in telling us about his narrow escapes when flying across the Atlantic in winter. When I arrived at Dorval airport the following morning, I was relieved that the severe weather had caused the flight's postponement. But relief soon turned to frustration; we waited in Montreal for six days before winter relented and the plane took off.

Our pilot, a Shropshire lad, gave me some comfort as we boarded the Liberator aircraft, but the twelve-hour flight lived up to all my expectations. The heating system, if such there was, had failed, and the plane was bitterly cold in spite of the heavy woollen blankets in which we wrapped ourselves. I saw flames shooting out of the exhaust and, like most novices, thought the plane was on fire. The Mexican government's representative in Ottawa, also on his way to the ILO meeting, proved to be a diverting travelling companion. He regaled us with amusing stories, not all of them consistent with high standards of morality. When my Mexican friend was in the middle of a particularly risqué anecdote, the plane would lurch violently; he would stop in mid-sentence and began saying his rosary. When the flight got smoother, he quickly dropped the beads and returned to his racy tales.

My last visit to London had been in 1938, so it was hard for me to imagine what war would have done to that great city. How could it have survived the intense and continual bombardment? The destruction of the House of Commons in May 1941 had shocked us all. What was the blackout like? Was it cold for those who slept in London's tubes? We knew from radio broadcasts that Germany's "secret weapon," the buzz bombs, did not seem to provoke any pronounced terror in ordinary Londoners.

At Northolt Airport, an RAF installation outside London, John Holmes greeted us.[10] We drove to the Park Lane Hotel, passing

---

10 John Holmes, then a junior external affairs officer in the Canadian High Commission, is now Canada's most respected foreign affairs specialist.

scores of buildings reduced to rubble. I could not wait to walk about London, although the ground was covered with more snow than I had ever seen there. During the first few days this heavy snow hid some of the worst of the damage, but later, in East Ham, I saw what war could do — acres and acres of devastated houses.

Abe Heaps was the only one of us to admit that he was nervous about being alone during a bombing raid, so we began to share a room. This really tickled Percy Bengough. The morning after a night's bombing, Percy would complacently ask me, "How did Abe get along last night?" One particularly noisy night, there was a loud knock on the door that jolted us more than the bombs. There stood the president of the Trades and Labour Congress in his long johns, scared stiff. He pleaded to be let in, and all three of us shared the room — Percy on the floor.

The meetings of the ILO committee on constitutional questions began on 18 January at Britain's ministry of labour and national service and continued beyond the opening session of the governing body a week later. As one of those who had drawn up the resolution at Philadelphia that had recommended establishing this committee, I was asked to serve as chairman. Our terms of reference covered two sets of questions. First, we were asked to indicate the principles that should guide the ILO's negotiating delegation before it was asked to consult on the Organization's place in the developing international structure. Second, we also had to deal with a whole series of constitutional questions referred to us by the terms of the resolution adopted at Philadelphia. The points on which the committee could express a final opinion depended on external circumstances. Since the previous meeting, the course of the war had changed.

By January 1945, France and Belgium were almost liberated, and the end to the war was in sight. While no final agreement had been reached, the "Big Four" — the United States, the Soviet Union, Britain and China — had met at Dumbarton Oaks, near Washington, in the early fall of 1944 to discuss the structure of the proposed United Nations Organization, especially the character of the Security Council and its relationship to the League of Nations. As a result, the ILO had already appointed to the body representatives deputed to draw up proposals for the creation of new international institutions.

The onus was clearly on our committee to enunciate definitively and expeditiously not only guidelines for the negotiating delegation but also principles upon which the post-war ILO could build. Papers had been submitted on the various questions within the committee's terms of reference, and Wilfred Jenks had supplied a voluminous legal memorandum dealing with the future development and constitutional practices of the Organization. Jenks had played a major role at Philadelphia, and his contributions at the London meetings were no less important. More than anyone else, he had worked out what the relationship should be between the ILO and the future United Nations. We worked very closely together, and much of my contribution was determined by the help Wilfred gave me. I have many reasons to remember my Cambridge contemporary; his services to peace through international organization were revealed in his work at the ILO and in his notable writings, which have delineated a rich store of knowledge of the problems facing mankind in its search for peace.

The relationship between the ILO and other international bodies raised two broad issues. The first centred on the constitutional connection between the ILO and the League of Nations, and the second had to do with the degree of latitude to be given the negotiating delegation.

The ILO's future was clouded by speculation about the fate of the now-discredited League. There was no doubt that the League would undergo severe changes if it was not replaced and that the ILO must be prepared for this contingency. I therefore urged the committee to consider the consequences for the ILO of the Dumbarton Oaks proposals. Once complete and adopted, these suggestions would contain, for example, provision for the registration of treaties. The problem would then be, what would become of the clauses in the constitution of the ILO providing for the registration of international labour conventions by the secretary general of the League of Nations? In this same vein, a member of the League automatically became a member of the ILO. This procedure had unfortunate consequences when states remained members of the ILO after resigning their membership in the League. The divergence between the composition of the two institutions seriously complicated financial arrangements for the ILO. If the Dumbarton Oaks recommendations perpetuated this difference, there could be financial repercussions. I believed that matters of constitutional reform were extremely delicate and should not be undertaken in haste. Paradoxically, however, they were tending to absorb too much of the committee's time and were not allowing us to prepare the guidelines for the delegation that would negotiate the Organization's future.

It had been suggested the the ILO might work under the aegis of a proposed Economic and Social Council. On the other hand, it was thought preferable, especially by the British delegates, for the ILO and the Economic and Social Council to be established as equals. This was acceptable to the committee members, but the key proviso was that the ILO be given the same direct access to the assembly that it had under the League. No decisions concerning the ILO could then be taken without the Organization having an opportunity to put forward its own point of view. If it made arrangements with other proposed bodies for direct access to the new international assembly, I thought the ILO would be in a very strong position.

The meeting of the governing body was called to order by the British minister of labour and national service, Ernest Bevin, on 25 January.[11] At this time, I was not overly impressed by Bevin. Although it was natural that a very important minister in the British government should pay little attention to a Canadian MP, that irritated me. Easily the most consequential person at the

11 Bevin, a former labour leader, was largely responsible for the creation of the Transport and General Workers' Union in 1922. He served, with Clement Attlee, in Churchill's war cabinet, and was soon to become an able and much admired foreign secretary.

conference, Bevin gave the image of bluff officiousness. In his opening remarks, he referred to the committee's work and noted that the question before the London gathering was the place of the ILO among newly created international organizations. The British government, he said, put the ILO "as high as possible in the scale of world organizations."[12] Bevin agreed with what I had said at Philadelphia — that the ILO should not be completely independent of the new world organization but should be a part of it. He also urged that because of the ILO's tripartite character, it must be equal in status to any other branch of the new organization. I supported these points on behalf of the Canadian government and in the report of the committee on constitutional questions submitted the following day.

In essence, our report recommended that the rules of the Organization be codified to facilitate the participation of new members. Percy Bengough suggested that we include a paragraph that would allow representatives of a state, or of the province of a federal nation, to enter into the ILO's discussions, if they were appointed by the government of an ILO member to accompany the delegation. This proposal would remove the difficulty of federal states, such as Canada, that had to find places for representatives both of federal departments and of the provinces (sometimes primarily responsible for the application of ILO decisions). I was disappointed when this suggestion was not adopted because of the pressure of time.

The committee's report contained an outline of the principles that should govern ILO dealings with the new world organization; these, it was felt, would leave the ILO delegates enough latitude to negotiate. We suggested that the ILO should strive to maintain recognition of the tripartite principle, under which the representatives of the workers and employers enjoyed equal status in the Organization with the government delegates. The constitutional decisions of the Organization should continue to be referred directly

12 ILO, *Official Bulletin*, 27(1)(1945): 23-27.

to governments. The relationship between the ILO and the proposed United Nations should be determined by agreement, although the ILO's status should not be less than previously.[13]

The only discordant note in an otherwise fruitful meeting was the inflexible opposition of the employers' spokesmen, especially the British, to the setting up of tripartite industrial committees. In spite of this, seven committees were established to exchange views on the problems of the industries in their respective countries.

This participation in planning the future of the ILO ended my formal association with the Organization. However, I have never ceased trying to find ways of bringing home to workers, employers and government the objectives of the ILO. It gives me considerable satisfaction to know that the relationship of the ILO and the United Nations is still governed by the agreement, negotiated later in 1945, for which I had helped prepare the way.

While in London, it was a great honour for me to be invited to sum up my views on the new internationalism to the Empire Parliamentary Association in Westminster Hall. After praising the heroic stand of the British people and expressing justifiable pride in Canada's contribution to the war, I launched into the major theme of my address: neither the great powers nor the commonwealth could expect to defend and preserve the peace by themselves. The welfare of nations rested on their interdependence. In the Dumbarton Oaks proposals regarding the establishment of a new international organization, the security council, comprising the great powers, might prove to be the most important agency of international action. While the most powerful states must take responsibility for helping to maintain the peace, I said (mindful of the pointedness of my remarks as a Canadian in front of a British audience) that stature and status were not the same thing and that all states should have the right to share in every discussion or

13 Transcripts of Meetings, January 1945. Department of Labour records (Vol. 3,281), PAC (see particularly the "Report on the Committee on Constitutional Questions").

decision that affected the peace.[14] The most powerful nations must recognize the role of smaller and weaker states. The proposed general assembly of all member nations should have as much power and prestige as possible since it was the body that would best exemplify the new organization's character. Canada welcomed the formation of a new general international organization, I told my audience. The five principles that I believed should underlie its operation would help the new body succeed where the League of Nations had failed. The organization ought to be equipped with the necessary military force to meet its objectives. It also should involve the closest military cooperation among the great powers, which should bear the brunt of the responsibility, with other states contributing in proportion to their ability. The new organization should be able to retain a flexibility that would allow growth by practice and experience. It should not be straightjacketed by rigid codes or rules. In addition, all members of the new structure should strive for economic as well as political collaboration.

The speech appeared to be well received. In seconding the vote of thanks, Mr. Henderson Stewart, a British Liberal MP, said: "I admire Mr. Martin's technique. He could step into our House — we would all look on him as a first-class front-bencher." I replied, "I wish that were true at home."[15]

Much of my spare time in London was taken up meeting various government officials. In several chats, Vincent Massey confided his frustration with Mackenzie King who, he felt, did not trust him to express the Canadian point of view in discussions with the

14 Gallup polls had shown that the overwhelming majority of Canadians believed in the workability of an international organization. They further believed that all independent nations in the commonwealth should have a separate representation and vote in the new body and that while commonwealth members should consult to work out a foreign policy acceptable to them all, Canada should be left free to act by itself and not have to abide by the majority wish of the commonwealth.
15 Paul Martin, *The Dumbarton Oaks Conference and After* (London: The Empire Parliamentary Association, United Kingdom Branch, 1945).

British prime minister and foreign secretary. Jealousy, he thought. George Tomlinson, Bevin's parliamentary secretary, saw to it that I met his colleagues in the ministry of labour; and I made a quick visit to Cambridge to see my former supervisor, J. R. M. Butler, hard at work editing Britain's official war history.

But most of my free time was spent visiting Canadian servicemen. Seeing the effect that the struggle was having on their lives depressed me quite a bit and reaffirmed my determination to do whatever I possibly could to prevent wars like this from ever happening again. I kept a notebook that contained hundreds of addresses of those whom I met and of their relatives at home. When I arrived back in Ottawa, I sat down and wrote short notes to them all — it was the least that I could do. I was cheered by my talks with the two chief chaplains in the Canadian army — Mike O'Neil (later the Roman Catholic archbishop of Regina) and Ross Flemington (who became president of Mount Allison University).

Immediately after my speech to the Empire Parliamentary Association, I prepared to visit General H. D. G. Crerar in the Netherlands to deliver an important letter in person. At the same time, I hoped to see men from the Windsor area and to pay my respects to the memory of those who would not return.

I left London on 3 February 1945 for Brussels, where I called on General Tommy Burns.[16] As his guest at the mess at the Château de Belle Vue, I saw the house that had served as headquarters of Hitler's two Gauleiters, Generals Gröhe and von Falkenhausen. The latter, a lover of books, had assembled a fine library, housed in a reception room. Among the works on philosophy, I noticed an elaborately bound selection of writings by Immanuel Kant, including his *Critique of Pure Reason*. Jokingly, I said to Tommy Burns that I was of a mind to take it as a souvenir. The general immediately autographed it, "with the compliments of Canadian Section 1st Echelon HQ 2 Army Group," and gave it to me. All the

---

16 General Burns had served in the Italian campaign. Later he became a deputy minister and a diplomat, and then served as commander of the first United Nations peace-keeping force in the Middle East.

officers present also signed the "stolen" book that now lies next to
John Locke's *Essay Concerning Human Understanding* on my library
shelves.

Afterwards I flew in a small plane, General Crerar's own, to his
headquarters outside Tilburg. As we came over Holland, I could
follow the never-ending line of military carriers advancing with
the equipment the Canadian forces would soon need for a major
battle. I was whisked into a jeep and driven past a big iron gate
into a compound of brick buildings, the headquarters of the
commander of the First Canadian Army. From there, I was shown
to a richly furnished railway carriage on wheels, panelled in
mahogany, where I would spend the night. It was known as "the
Viper's Den" and had been used as a brothel by Hitler's high
command before the Royal Canadian Engineers are said to have
found it buried in straw north of Caen in 1944.

When I was eventually taken along to meet General Crerar, I
suddenly seemed to freeze up. Here I was in the presence of the
commander of the Canadian forces, which were preparing for
battle in one of the most decisive wars in human history. I gave the
general the letter that had been entrusted to my care, the contents
of which I do not know to this day. He was full of questions. How
was Massey? How were things in London? Had I seen Ralston
before I left Canada? What did I think of General McNaughton's
surprising defeat in the byelection in Grey North?[17] I answered as
best I could. But what I had seen and heard of the horrors of war
since leaving Canada made our domestic political problems seem
Lilliputian, and I was more interested in what Harry Crerar could
tell me about things at the front.

After our pleasantries, we had dinner with a dozen or more of
his ranking officers. Being with men so near the line of battle made
me extremely sensitive; most were of my generation and ready to

17 The byelection to get the new minister of national defence into the House of Commons was held on 5 February. It was won by the Conservative candidate, Garfield
Case, the mayor of Owen Sound.

risk their lives in war. In response to a brief speech of welcome by General Crerar, I made some awkward remarks about my physical disability and self-consciousness about my secure position compared to theirs.

After dinner, I went back to the Viper's Den. About ten o'clock General Crerar sent for me. "Well," he said, "I must tell you that you've come at a very critical time. This could perhaps be the last push in the war. Tomorrow we shall take the offensive." The Canadians were to clear the Reichswald Forest and would try to break through the German lines at the Hochwald Forest. I asked if it would be feasible for me to go and see men in the Essex Scottish Regiment, which was camped less than ten miles away; but it was impossible because the regiment would be in the thick of battle by the following morning. However, General Crerar arranged for me to speak on the field telephone to Larry Deziel, a lieutenant in the regiment and a student of mine at Assumption. Larry was stunned to hear my voice and assured me that he would pass on the greetings I sent with such feeling from everyone at home.

At about three o'clock in the morning I was awakened by the frightening noises of war. Opening the door of the Viper's Den, I saw a soldier on guard, who said, "Well, it's started." The sky was bright with the reflection of exploding shells; trucks were rumbling by in the darkness. It was a terrifying experience for one who did not know what war was like, and sleep was banished for the rest of the night. I had my breakfast alone in the mess — everyone else was busy.

It had been suggested that I might want to see something of military government; the officer in charge of the civilian administration, Brigadier Basil Wedd,[18] showed me around. On our brief tour, we visited Canadian officers who were helping the local authorities restore some semblance of order to this recently liberated area. We walked into one of the local "town halls," and to my amazement, I came face to face with David Croll, now the military

---

18 He was formerly an executive with Massey Ferguson.

administrator, and in effect the "mayor" of a small town in Holland. After a short chat with Dave, I arranged to leave and took off for Brussels and then Paris.

Nothing could have deterred me from visiting the graves of those who had fallen at Dieppe. The effect of the seaborne raid on occupied France on 19 August 1942 was indelibly engraved on my mind. Canadians had composed the bulk of the Allied forces, and one of the chief regiments was the Essex Scottish, which had suffered terrible casualties. Very few officers — one was Captain D. F. MacRae — returned to Britain, and close to one hundred men in the regiment died on that beach. (On the morning after the raid, the people of Windsor were aghast at the first indications of what had transpired. I called on the wives and mothers of those who I knew were in the battle and spent the rest of the day letting them know that we were on their side. There was so little that one could do.)[19]

On a dull and chilly February day, I was driven from Paris to pay my respects to the Essex Scottish and other Canadians in the military cemetery at Dieppe. There were crosses marking some of the graves; the final tombstones had not been erected. I could see the names of the lads from my county who had died at Dieppe. The racial origins of the dead were so varied: Anglo-Saxon, French, and yet other backgrounds. It struck me that herein lay the character of Canada, a land of diverse national groupings. I walked among the graves, noting the names, so many of which I had known back home. I saw the grave of one young fellow whose father was violently against Canadian participation in the war. This had not stopped the young man who gave his life on the Dieppe beach. Nothing has since epitomized the concept of our nation more poignantly for me than that cemetery. Of whatever origin, these men were all members of the Canadian family.

19 There were thirty-two officers and 521 other ranks who embarked from England and five officers and forty-nine other ranks who returned. The rest were either fatal casualties or non-fatal casualties who spent the rest of the war in prisoner-of-war camps. (See C. P. Stacey, *Official History of the Canadian Army in the Second World War*, Vol. I, *Six Years of War: The Army in Canada, Britain and the Pacific* (Ottawa: Queen's Printer, 1966), p. 389.)

I arrived back in Montreal on 11 February after a flight that was broken by an unscheduled stopover in the Azores. We had engine trouble and had to wait for a couple of days to resume our journey. Percy Bengough was with me, and our standing joke was that he used this time to help organize the Azores workers into labour unions.

While I was gone, Nell had defiantly endured the eccentricities of Wyndham Lewis, whom I had commissioned to paint her portrait. The circumstances are curious. Marshall McLuhan, at that time a professor of English in Cincinnati, had called to tell me that Lewis was in Windsor, had been in touch with Assumption College and wished to see me. I knew neither McLuhan nor Lewis. In the autumn of 1943, I met Lewis over tea at the home of Miss Pauline Bondy. Father Stan Murphy, another guest, told me that Lewis was a distinguished painter and celebrated writer and that he and his wife were occupying rooms at the Prince Edward Hotel. Lewis had become associated with Assumption and had painted a series of portraits from photographs of the college superiors.

Soon after this, I acted for Lewis in collecting money for a painting he had done. In such cases the cheque is usually made out to the lawyer, so that there is no problem deducting the legal fees, but in Lewis's case it was not. Lewis suggested painting Nell's portrait as a means of paying my fee. This was to be done while I was away in Europe.

Nell and Lewis did not get along. He was a very odd fellow, coming to the house every day but keeping on his galoshes, overcoat and hat while he sketched. His reactionary ideas did not endear him to my wife, and she resented his expressing such a rabid hatred of Canada, where he was marooned throughout much of the war.

When I went to the hotel to see the painting, it was propped up against a wall. I did not like the portrait at all. The expression on Nell's face showed defiance, not the vivaciousness and warmth I always saw. But over the years, the portrait has grown on me. Lewis wanted more money and would not sign the painting without it. It is still unsigned. Only later did I learn that Nell had given him more money than he and I had agreed to. Years afterwards, when I was in Britain as high commissioner, I was pleased to be able to help Mrs. Lewis, then a widow, who was living in Liverpool in straitened circumstances.

During the time that I was at the ILO, Nell had had a more pleasant experience in some light-hearted correspondence with the prime minister. "At long last," wrote Nell to King, "the audaciousness of my unreserved Irish ancestors has overcome the reserve of my English antecedents, and as it takes courage to write to your Prime Minister, I am calling on all the nerve of the Irish. . . ." Nell had come to admire Mackenzie King as a truly great man under duress, "with an appreciation of the right time and the right place." She forthrightly told him so and added "if Paul knew I was writing this note . . . it would be so carefully edited that it would not be mine — so I shall not tell him until later."

Mackenzie King showed a side of himself to women that those of us in the party seldom, if ever, saw. His reply reveals that he appreciated Nell's freedom from the stuffy sophistication of a political zealot and he took up her breezy tone. "Please," he replied, "at all times allow your Irish ancestors to get the better of your English antecedents, especially where you are sticking up for me. Don't allow Paul to tamper with any of our correspondence."[20]

The few months after my return provided me with a satisfying mixture of high-flown idealism and practical politics. My European visit had given me ample grist for promoting the work of the ILO and for championing the exploits of the Canadian forces at the front. The visit confirmed for me the need for international cooperation to avoid such dreadful waste in the future.

This was the message I brought back home. The job that Canada's armed forces was doing, I told the press, dwarfed to

20 Eleanor Martin to King, 5 January 1945; W. L. Mackenzie King Papers (J1 series, pp. 347, 525-26), PAC; King to E. Martin, 13 January 1945, ibid., (p. 347, 527).

insignificance all petty domestic squabbles. Canadians could not really appreciate what our men were fighting for in the mud of the western front.[21] The men serving overseas exemplified a unity of purpose and action that those of us at home should try to emulate. This unity was illustrated not only by the burial at Dieppe of Major Tom Hayhurst, my wife's cousin's husband, beside men named Gelinas and Racicot but also by my visits to the military hospitals with the Protestant and Roman Catholic chaplains. What the army could do overseas, we could and must do at home.[22]

As for the ILO, I insisted that it formed the "social conscience of mankind", and although it represented a rather intangible organization as far as the average person was concerned, it deserved all our support. The industrial councils that the ILO had endorsed would provide representation for workers, employers and government in various industries — for example, the automotive, steel and textile industries — and could be a forum for the discussion of common issues. These councils would not only interest themselves in wages and working conditions in industry but also make recommendations on problems of competition, raw materials and suchlike. They could, I believed, provide an effective agency for thwarting cartels and monopolies.[23]

The resumption of parliament on 19 March presented me with an opportunity to put forth my views on the importance of international cooperation and organization. We began the session with a debate on a resolution supporting the Canadian delegation to the San Francisco conference that would establish the new world organization. Earlier, Mackenzie King had asked me to speak in the debate; he gave me a place on the roster as the first Liberal speaker after him.[24] Endorsing this resolution was one of my great moments in parliament. Its commitment to establish a system of international order embodied much of my political philosophy.

21 *WDS*, 19 February 1945; ibid.,20 February 1945.
22 *WDS*, 12 February 1945; 19 February 1945.
23 *The Globe and Mail*, 12 February 1945.
24 King to Martin, 8 March 1945, King Papers (J2 series, volume 304, file P-659),PAC.

Canada was among the first nations both to welcome the formation of a general international organization in 1943 and to discuss and approve the Dumbarton Oaks proposals. The new body would lay great stress on how to use force to maintain peace. This would be done, I said, by combining the principle of the concert of nations and the balance of power to create a stronger power bloc — the permanent members — within the security council. In previous years, I had in fact opposed this idea of the balance of power but told the House that

> . . . in this very practical world one must consider what can be done. The League failed because Russia earlier and the US through its whole history were not members. The peace of the world cannot be maintained unless the great powers, those which have the greatest forces, are prepared to use it and the mechanism [of instituting a security council] is designed to call upon them to use force on occasions of serious aggression.

If there was a distinction between the great and middle powers, one should also distinguish between some of the middle powers and certain of the lesser ones. I believed that agreement might be reached for a country to have temporary membership when the council was discussing matters that involved the ultimate use of that nation's resources in a field in which the country was particularly strong. For example, Norway could not expect representation, but when the question of shipping was discussed, it should have an important voice. This is a manifestation of the functional principle.

In addition, I argued for a more powerful general assembly — one that would be more than a talking shop. In particular circumstances, the assembly should be able, by a two-thirds majority, to express approval or disapproval of security council action. In concluding, I harked back to the war and to the failure of the League: it had displayed responsibility without power, but "power without responsibility is just as mischievous."

I had done my best and was glad that my speech was generally well received in the House, particularly by the prime minister and Brooke Claxton, the two members of the government who knew most about the subject. My fellow lodgers, Gillis and Castleden, could not resist teasing me. "Your speech," they jibed,

> shows that you are developing rapidly. Our opinion is that your new associations with Moscow's representatives (at home and abroad) should make you a real reformer some day (if Mitch Hepburn doesn't beat you to it).
> Frankly, you stole a march on us on the ILO. We both will concur fully in any move to send you to the next Teheran or Yalta conference — conditionally, of course, on the stipulation that you be allowed to remain there permanently.

This session of parliament was fuelled by rumours of an impending election and ever more intense speculation about who would be included in the cabinet changes that probably would precede it. Many of the stories mentioned my name, for there would be a cabinet vacancy in southwestern Ontario. The day after I returned from Britain, Norman McLarty had announced to his riding executive that he would not be running in the next election. The strain of office had taken its toll, and I had known for a long time that Norman intended to leave politics. Immediately, the geographical barrier to my entering the cabinet was removed, and Windsor Liberals began to put my name forward as McLarty's successor.[25] The *Globe and Mail* commented that my selection was "almost assured."[26]

That newspaper expressed a certainty that I did not feel. By this time, I knew that many considerations went into the making of a cabinet. In those days, a minister was not chosen on the basis of his education, experience and skills but for what he could contribute to the party, all things considered. Mackenzie King would look at

25 *WDS*, 14 February 1945.
26 *The Globe and Mail*, 12 February 1945.

equally qualified MPs and then at their importance to him as leader. To be sure, a minister had to be capable of running a department, but he also had to add stature and support to the party. When Pierre Trudeau picks a cabinet — and this is perhaps where he makes his mistake — he too often thinks of people like himself, so-called intellectuals with ideas. But pure ideas are not always relevant to the problems facing a government or even a political party.

I knew the difficulties that lay in the path of my appointment. King rightly looked upon me as a Franco-Ontarian, and he had never appointed a member of that community to his cabinet. Besides, there were fewer French-speaking Catholics than Irish Catholics in Ontario, and in King's mind that counted in determining the worth of a particular appointment. What would be the value of a French-speaking minister in southwestern Ontario compared, for example, with the weight of an Irish Catholic from the Ottawa Valley? There was, of course, the question of other claims to any seat allotted to a Franco-Ontarian, and Lionel Chevrier had a very strong case. I think it safe to say that the prime minister was attracted more to Lionel's personality than to mine.[27] In his diary at the time, King wrote that while I was very good with labour, I was "somewhat ponderous" — as if anybody could be more ponderous than King in full flight.

The prime minister did not have a mind that brought him into easy intimacy with French-speaking people. Of course, he could not deny the importance of Québec to the Liberal Party, but he dealt with it through surrogates — notably Ernest Lapointe and Louis St. Laurent. I had not forgotten the strength of his Presbyterian fervour when we both stood in front of the monument to the Protestant reformers in Geneva in 1936. I know that King had confidence in me, in the strength of my liberalism and (although I was not one of his white-haired boys) in my future. For some other

27 J. W. Pickersgill and D. F. Forster, *The Mackenzie King Record*, Vol. II, *1944-1945* (Toronto: University of Toronto Press, 1968), pp. 370-71. King wrote: "I saw no escape from bringing in Martin from western Ontario ."

ministers who could influence his choice of cabinet members, I likely was not high on their list as a result of my continuous agitation for reform. But King could not divorce himself easily from the illiberal view that race and religion mattered. This was especially the case with Catholics of French origin outside Québec. King did not have the same difficulty in appointing two English-speaking members from Québec, Brooke Claxton and Douglas Abbott.

As soon as the prime minister announced in the House of Commons in mid-April that a general election would take place on 11 June, we all knew that the cabinet appointments would be made within a few days. On the evening of 17 April, I was staying in Ottawa at the Lord Elgin Hotel and received a call from the prime minister. Dr. J. J. McCann, from Renfrew, another aspirant, was sitting in my room chatting. Would I see him tomorrow? King asked. He said that he might have "something helpful" to say to me. Not wanting to let Jim McCann know what the conversation was about or who was calling, I merely thanked the prime minister for thinking of me. I was sure he meant the shuffle and hoped that I had made it.

The long-awaited cabinet changes took place the following morning. I went to the prime minister's office and was received quickly. Outside, Chevrier and McCann waited their turns (Dr. McCann, it turned out, had received a call from the prime minister earlier the previous day and, I suppose, had come around to see me the night before to find out whether I too had made the grade). Mackenzie King was very gracious and said how pleased he was that he had been able to arrange things. When I saw McCann and Chevrier in the waiting room, I wondered whether I was going to be taken in, for I could hardly believe that King had reconciled himself to having three Ontario Catholics in his cabinet. When King told me that he was going to recommend my appointment as secretary of state, I was naturally very pleased. He said it was a great portfolio, one of the oldest portfolios in the government. I assured him that I would apply myself to my work as much as anyone could.

The new cabinet met that afternoon. With great euphoria I walked into the cabinet room in the East Block and took my seat at the big round table. Pictures of Canada's prime ministers looked down at us from the walls. The newly sworn members were all there: Lionel Chevrier, minister of transport; Joseph Jean, solicitor general; J. J. McCann, minister of national war services; Douglas Abbott, minister of national defence for naval services; J. A. Glen, minister of mines and resources, and me. Lionel and I sat almost across the table from King. Cabinet places were not assigned, but new ministers accepted seats farthest from the prime minister, in accordance with rank and precedence. Mackenzie King welcomed his new colleagues warmly, but to my recollection, not one of us said a word.

My Windsor colleague, Norman McLarty, completed the transfer to me of the department of the secretary of state with his characteristic warmth and style. It must have been a particularly difficult moment for him. Because he had always enjoyed a good personal relationship with the prime minister, I found it difficult to understand why King did not offer Norman a Senate seat. Norman retired voluntarily from politics. His years in office had exacted a tremendous personal toll on McLarty that none of his friends knew of. We were shocked when he died a few months later, within hours of his daughter's wedding.

At our meeting on 18 April, Norman introduced me to Dr. E. H. Coleman, the undersecretary of state, and left me to his capable briefing. We spoke generally about the department, but even this short chat made me realize that I did not know much about its workings. I would have to wait to find out more because Canada was in the middle of a general election campaign.

XII

It was a Famous Victory

O NCE THE CABINET had been announced in Ottawa, I returned home to Windsor as secretary of state and also as a candidate in the forthcoming June election. Although Mackenzie King had just set the date, the political parties had been preparing for an election for many months. My former boss, C. P. McTague, had become the national chairman of the Conservative Party in April 1944, a month after his resignation from the labour relations board.[1] This was one sign that the Conservatives under Bracken had been busy organizing — even in the midst of war.

It was to be expected that Essex East would respond to the pressures of the Conservative workers who had been stimulated by Bracken's call to arms. James E. Byrne of Woodslee, a farmer who held a master of arts degree and who also taught school, shortly declared that he intended to contest the Progressive Conservative nomination in the constituency. Jim, a bright and dedicated

---

1 While not seeking to restrain McTague from his decision, I did tell him that electioneering and public speaking were not his line of country. The election result bore out of my view. His party lost, and Charlie was trounced in his home city of Guelph.

young man, was the type of person I would have liked to have on my own team. But as Tom Fitzgerald told me, "Paul, you can't get them all." When the Conservative meeting was held — the day after my elevation to cabinet — Byrne did get the nomination, but it was nip and tuck.

Despite the resurgence of the CCF in the 1943 provincial election and the growth of popular support for that party, the Essex East branch of the party still had not nominated a federal candidate in January 1945. In fact, it appeared as though my campaigning at plant gates and my progressive labour outlook had managed to prevent a solid bloc of labour support from going to the CCF.

There was really quite a debate going on at this time in the Windsor locals of the autoworkers over the course the union should follow in pursuing its political aims. Naturally, those who held closely to the position of the Canadian Congress of Labour wanted to carry through with the CCL's endorsement of the CCF as the political arm of labour. Liberals who were active in the UAW, such as Michael McClosky, Henry Renaud and Joe Delaney, wanted the union to take an independent stand; they were dead set against the union being tied to the apronstrings of any political party.

In supporting those who wanted the UAW to retain an independent position, our party found itself with unlikely political allies. The Labour Progressive Party — the communists — also believed that the union should be unfettered. In this party's view, any other course would split labour, would weaken it in negotiations with the automakers, and would jeopardize the communists' own position in the union. This schism between the CCF and the communists came to the fore when Nelson Alles, the CCF provincial member for Essex North, resigned from the party in December 1944. Alles claimed that the CCF had veered away from the interests of the trade union movement and that its political manoeuvring had caused disunity.[2] However, it is my belief that Alles resigned because the local CCF executive would not support

2 *WDS*, 12 December 1944.

the nomination of labour lawyer J. L. Cohen as its standard-bearer in Essex East or Essex West. The local CCF leaders regarded Cohen's views as too left-wing for their comfort and were very concerned about being chummy with anyone suspected of communist leanings.

I had been keeping a close eye on the situation for some time. My links with the labour movement made it inevitable that I had gotten to know some of the communists in Windsor. One of the local organizers, Oscar Kogan, used to come to my office once in a while for a chat; he was a gregarious fellow, and I never hesitated to see him to explain the government's war policy. As a member of the House of Commons committee on the defence of Canada regulations, I favoured lifting the wartime ban on the Communist Party and releasing its leaders from the camps where they had been interned since 1939. Their right to freedom of speech and association, I argued, should not be abrogated, particularly after the Soviet Union had joined the Allies in June 1941.[3]

Since this alliance with the Soviets, and especially after my appointment as parliamentary secretary, I realized more than ever how advantageous for industrial relations it would be to secure the support of the communists in the trade unions. They had become the most committed supporters of a total war effort and were dead set against anything that might disrupt it. Sometimes they would warn the government of potential trouble in the trade unions so that steps could be taken to avert it. I remember going to Toronto once to seek the help of Sam Carr in stemming a strike that might have hampered production in an important war plant there. Sam, one of Canada's leading communists, intervened directly and the strike was called off.

By 1945, however, non-communist members of the trade unions were beginning to be concerned about cleaning house. This was no

3 In this, I found myself much closer to the CCF position against the ban than to my own party's. On 2 June, a full-page, open letter to me signed by the CCF executive, the CIO group and other prominent Windsor citizens was published in the *Star*. Subsequently, it was mailed to all MPs and led to a lot of ribbing. It contained a horrible photograph of myself. I sent a copy to Nell with an arrow to the photo with the comment, "And you married this!"

less true of the UAW in Windsor, and Charlie Millard pushed the
union's regional director, George Burt, and his friends to get rid of
the communist influence. The more opportunistic Burt, and Roy
England, however, were not as responsible as Millard, and tolerated the Marxist penetration of the union to a greater extent.

Of course, I did not support any of the communists' ideas or
practices and knew that some members of the party in Windsor
loathed me and what I stood for. Once I ventured into forbidden
territory — a Ukrainian Labour Temple in Windsor where some
CPers used to meet — thinking I could find out what made them
tick. I heard voices in the basement and went down to see what was
going on. All of a sudden, I was surrounded by half-a-dozen husky
fellows. One of them grabbed my hand. "Look at this. Lily-white!
He hasn't worked a day in his life, the son of a bitch!" Snatching
away my hand, I dashed up the stairs as fast as I could and made
myself scarce. It was a good lesson.

While the CCF and labour were trying to get their house in
order, some, including people in the prime minister's office, were
predicting my defeat. As usual, I was running scared but was
determined to keep up my supporters' morale and to create as
well-drilled an organization as possible. In March 1944 we set up
the Essex County Liberal Association; Keith Laird became provi-
sional president and Donald Emerson secretary. Brooke Claxton
came down to Windsor to add his voice to my call for liberal
reform.[4] By this time, Don Emerson had taken over as my chief
organizer in Windsor. I had known him for about ten years by then.
His mother, Beatrice, had volunteered his services as my driver
during the 1935 election campaign. I really think she did this as
much to provide a measure of safety to others on the road as to
furnish a convenience to me. Don's no-nonsense approach served
both me and the campaign well. He had helped establish the
UAW local that organized the office workers at the Ford Motor
Company, and he knew the problems of Essex East and of the
autoworkers as intimately as anyone could.

4 *WDS*, 31 March 1944; ibid., 15 April 1944; ibid., 24 January 1945.

Even before the election was announced, Don was hard at work. He had planned a public dinner to welcome me home from the ILO meeting in London and had even managed to get George Burt not only to attend but to speak. This marked the end of the period when I could count on George's support, although we always remained friends.[5] On 2 March, I met the Walkerville Liberal Association, which that night elected as its president Joe Delaney of UAW local 195. As the *Windsor Daily Star* noted, the CCF had been counting on a solid vote from the industrial unions to carry them through the forthcoming election with flying colours. It was encouraging to me to see that this was not likely to happen.[6]

My nomination meeting was set for 29 April in the St. Jean Baptiste Hall in Tecumseh. Don Emerson promised a good turn-out for the brand-new secretary of state, and he certainly delivered. For the first time, the meeting was preceded by a parade; loudspeakers had to be set up in the street outside the hall for the hundreds of people who could not get in. Ozias Dupuis, vice-president of UAW local 195, proposed my name, and Charles O'Brien, president of the Essex-Kent Corn Growers' Association, seconded the motion. I was nominated unopposed. In my acceptance speech, I spoke of the San Francisco conference to establish the United Nations and my efforts to give the International Labour Organization the highest place possible in relation to the UN. But, conscious of the fact that the average voter is curious to know what a candidate thinks of bread-and-butter issues, I acknowledged Charlie O'Brien's appraisal of my efforts to get the Ontario Seed Corn Marketing Board established. After the meeting, I walked out into the street and greeted those who had been waiting there patiently; the band struck up "Happy Days Are Here Again."

Throughout the campaign, I made a point of emphasizing that the Liberal government had established and was continuing programs for reconstruction. The government would do everything

5 When I joined the cabinet, I received congratulations from all three Windsor locals of the UAW.
6 *WDS*, 3 March 1945.

necessary to end the war, would treat our returning servicemen fairly and generously, would work for the highest possible level of employment and income — including fair wages and social welfare measures — would assure fair prices and the most equitable distribution of the national income, and would work with other countries to stimulate trade. "I support and am a member of a government," I affirmed, "that believes industry should have full opportunity for expansion, but that [it] should be regarded as providing a social [obligation] as well . . . as [serving] the needs of individuals." The partnership with industry had proven itself in war and should be carried on into the peace.[7]

At the time of the promulgation of the labour code, P.C. 1003, the trade union movement generally accepted this extension of collective bargaining and tried to make it work rather than comment on its limitations. The union leaders abandoned this attitude in late 1944, and the executive of the Canadian Congress of Labour launched a national campaign to secure amendments that would extend the enforcement of collective bargaining guarantees. There was little doubt that the union leaders who sympathized with the CCF were trying to make the weaknesses of P.C. 1003 and the government's labour policies an issue in the forthcoming general election.

Needless to say, the unions in Windsor took part in this campaign, fuelled locally by the trouble between the Ford Company and the UAW. I received many letters as part of this agitation and replied by thanking my correspondents for "strengthening my hand" in advocating labour's cause. While I wholeheartedly supported the idea of a labour code, it had become clear to me that P.C. 1003 had worked where employers accepted its intent, but the provisions of the order were rendered inoperable when management organized resistance.

In order to head off a growing polarization of opinion, which I believed would hinder the unions' achievement of their legitimate ends, I wrote a pamphlet that outlined the growth of the labour

7 *WDS*, 3 June 1945.

movement and the legitimate demands of the workers.[8] In essence, the pamphlet was a non-political document written for the Canadian Association for Adult Education. When he received his copy, however, Mackenzie King realized that the identification of a Liberal MP with progressive labour policies could help the government; he wrote to say that the pamphlet "should be timely and useful in the forthcoming political campaign."[9]

Throughout the contest, I continued to put forward the Liberals' case regarding working people. Labour's recent advances, I pointed out, were due, at least in part, to the fact that those who wished to see social reform would have a say in the government. There was great danger, however, not in a socialist victory but in the election results splitting the progressive elements and allowing reactionary Toryism to take control and to sabotage labour's gains. If I made any national contribution in this campaign, it was in providing some credibility to the party's labour policy.

The Conservatives, I told my audiences, were not the party to finish the job of reconstruction and the development of social security programs, as they made clear when they spoke against family allowances. Although the measure had been enacted by parliament, it had not been proclaimed before the House was dissolved; Mackenzie King had delayed making payments in order to dispel charges that the allowances were merely a bribe to the electorate. This deferral left me a little uneasy; it might be charged that the government had not committed itself one hundred percent to its own social program.

The Conservative leader, John Bracken, spoke against the postponement, and I spent a considerable amount of energy in Essex East defending the government's action and asking what the Progressive Conservatives would do with the family allowance legislation if they were in power. The men who were paying for the Tory election campaign, I reminded people, had always opposed social reforms. "The Progressive Conservatives are progressive

8 Paul Martin, *Labour's Postwar World*, Behind the Headlines, Vol. I, 1945.
9 King to Martin, 15 February 1945, King Papers (J4 series, p. C347488), PAC.

before an election and conservative after one."[10] As for John Bracken, he had not spent five minutes on the floor of the House of Commons since he was made leader of the party,[11] I said, but had been travelling around the country for two years urging conscription, instead of sitting in parliament and working constructively for a better post-war world.[12]

As for the CCF, I tried to give them some of their own medicine. In one advertisement, I used a laudatory statement by Clarie Gillis about my record as a champion of social reform and the rights of labour. Two days before the election, at a jammed meeting at Holy Rosary School, I repeated my message to the working people of Windsor: a strong trade union organization, I told them, is a good thing for the country. "I have urged legislation by which the right of labour to organize is guaranteed . . . . That is only common decency . . . so long as I have any strength to fight, none will interfere [with this right]." The first objective of the government was to ensure maximum employment. The drive for tanks in war could be translated into a drive for houses in peace, and the government's social legislation was intended to keep the national income near its highest level. "I've grown sick and tired of people," I said, "who think that when you take an interest in the working man you are doing something dangerous."[13]

The minister of reconstruction, C. D. Howe, came to Windsor to speak on my behalf on 21 May. It is to Howe's credit that, notwithstanding his notoriously unsympathetic attitude to trade unionists, he was refreshingly down-to-earth and was perhaps the most popular minister I could have invited to my constituency. As George Burt noted: "Howe keeps the production line going and we know just where he stands." While C. D. spoke of me as "a friend of the toilers" who had contributed to the new labour code, I

10 *WDS*, 2 June 1945.
11 Bracken had given no indication of wishing to contest a byelection that might give him a seat in the House.
12 *WDS*, 23 May 1945.
13 *WDS*, 10 June 1945.

knew he did not really share my views. His address dealt principally with post-war planning for jobs and the fear that unemployment would begin to reappear once the servicemen returned
home. He assured the largely trade union audience that this would
not happen. Howe confronted a very unpopular topic and
explained that rationing would be maintained as long as it was
necessary to supply Europe. Then he turned to the more positive
subject of planning for public works in the Windsor area if unemployment rose.

My own speeches and Howe's appearance were designed to
counter charges by the CCF candidate, W. C. MacDonald, himself an autoworker, that the government was insincere in its reconstruction policies. I was especially concerned about MacDonald's
charge that the government was not doing all it could to ensure full
employment and that it had suppressed a gloomy survey of
employment prospects prepared by the department of labour.
This latter charge I ignored. Things were well in hand, I assured
the voters. The reconversion of industry and the expansion of
consumer demand and exports would provide jobs for Canadians.
Control over scarce materials would have to be maintained to
ensure a fair distribution. We were not relying on "pious promises" but on the past performance of a government that delivered.
My advertisements in the *Windsor Daily Star* asserted that "a stable
government is a vital necessity" and that the Liberals should be
given a working majority (the prospect of a minority government
worried me, mainly because of the situation in Ontario). I was
convinced that a sane, responsible Liberal government in Ottawa
would steer the middle course and would enact legislation in the
interests of the majority, rather than of the few.

I did not downplay Mackenzie King's importance and pointed
out in most of my speeches that Canada needed his experience
nationally and in the international arena. When the party was
gearing up for the vote, my defence of Mackenzie King led to a
curious situation. I was called to the prime minister's office; when I
got there, Jack Pickersgill, fairly bouncing with excitement, said,
"This is going to be an interesting session, Paul." I asked why, and

he mysteriously replied, "You are going to become an author." Then I went in to see the prime minister. King was ensconced at the end of a long table; Ray Lawson, a prominent Liberal from London, was seated at his left. Making no bones about it, King began: "Martin, Mr. Lawson has prepared a book on me. I think that it would be an advantage if *you* were the author." I knew that King regarded me as a serious-minded man ("lugubrious" is the word he is reported to have used). He probably felt that it would be to his political advantage for the book, eulogizing the prime minister as a great social reformer, to appear with my name on it. I was flabbergasted but when I finally found my tongue, I hesitatingly asked if I could at least read the manuscript. King gave the distinct impression that he did not like my delay in giving an affirmative answer. To satisfy my conscience, I took the manuscript and made some changes in it before it appeared as an election document.[14]

On 30 May I welcomed the prime minister when he arrived in London in his private car. We drove together to the London Arena, where a large crowd had assembled for my first appearance with him as his minister in southwestern Ontario. King's address — broadcast nationally — emphasized the need to look to the future and not to dwell on the errors of the past.

After the London meeting, I went on the stump in southwestern Ontario, speaking on platforms with both federal and provincial candidates. I was not a bit confident of the Liberal prospects in the provincial election. George Drew had originally called an election for 11 June, but when King had cannily picked the same date — so that federal results would not be affected by a Conservative or a CCF win in Ontario — Drew had moved the provincial election forward a week. His Conservatives swept the province on 4 June.[15] Both the Liberal leader, a resurrected Mitch Hepburn, and the

14 I managed to get myself listed only as the editor, but the book appeared with my name as publisher as well (Paul Martin, *A Lifetime of Public Service: A Brief Biographical Sketch of Mackenzie King* (Ottawa: Paul Martin, 1945)).
15 The Conservatives won 66 seats, the Liberals 11 and the CCF 8.

CCF chieftain, E. B. Jolliffe, lost their seats. The provincial Tories also did well in Essex County and displaced the CCF as the largest group, winning three out of four seats there.

What did this mean for the federal Liberals, who would face the voters a week later? Actually, the provincial vote in Essex North bucked me up a little bit. In that constituency, part of the federal riding of Essex East, the Conservative candidate lost to Alex Parent, the president of local 195 of the UAW. Parent was elected as Liberal-Labour candidate with the backing of my supporters. Several factors had contributed to his victory, including Hepburn's incredible attempt to form an alliance with the Labour Progressive Party, a communist front. Parent had not been active in our party but was always regarded as a Liberal supporter. His status in the union had boosted his campaign greatly, and his victory indicated that the union vote had been split to the detriment of the CCF. Strong Liberal supporters in Essex East derived considerable satisfaction from an accord that had brought victory, and I took Parent's win as a good omen.

The results of the provincial vote, however, prompted my Conservative opponent, Jim Byrne, to charge that the "Oscar Kogan-Paul Martin-communist machine" had crucified the provincial Conservative candidate in Essex North, Harry Drouillard, and that there was an unholy alliance to deliver 2,000 communist votes to me in East Windsor.

In response, I noted that Byrne's fiery remarks were calculated to stir prejudice against immigrants and generally to foment dissension. I was very careful in dealing with the communists; I always had to keep in mind that most of the voters with eastern European origins remained violently anti-communist. "My record in office and my social beliefs are known to every voter in the riding," I said. "Those beliefs are based on the principles of Christian justice and charity, and they are principles enunciated by men of far greater vision than Karl Marx." Byrne's smear did, I suppose, have some foundation in fact, for the Labour Progressive Party had repudiated the CCF, and undoubtedly some of Windsor's little band of communists would vote for me — as was their right in a democratic election. As for my so-called political "machine," there were many people willing to work to help elect me because they believed in the things I believed in. "In all my public life, my door has been open to constituents. I'm not afraid to be called a politician. Next to preaching the works of God, there is nothing nobler than to serve one's fellow countrymen in government. . . . I hope God will give me the strength to serve them well."

On election day, with the faithful Buster Riberdy at the wheel, I made a tour of polling stations and then waited outside in the car for the Monmouth Road polls to report. My spirits rose when it became clear that I had won these stations for the third time. As I reached our headquarters, further returns indicated that I would have a more substantial win than in 1940. My workers, such as the indefatigable Ray Quenneville from Sandwich East, kept saying, "You're in," but to their exasperation, I told them that we had to wait for the service vote before we could be sure. Only when the other candidates had conceded — Macdonald generously, Byrne gracelessly — did I begin my traditional election night rounds. First to the *Windsor Daily Star* and the radio station to publicly express my appreciation to those who had voted and worked for me. Then, as in previous elections, on to the committee rooms and a six-hour tour of the riding, during which time newsmen estimated that I shook a couple of thousand hands. At Belle River, the crowd hoisted me into a stagecoach, and we made a victory drive up Main Street. In Riverside, Nell cheered on a group of women who wanted to kiss the victor. As the cavalcade went from village to village, the car radio kept reporting the course of the national results. It was clear that the government had done well in the Maritimes and Québec. From Raoul Chauvin's farmhouse in Stoney Point, I phoned the prime minister to tell him of my own win and about some of the more disappointing losses in my region, particularly in London and St. Thomas. King himself had been beaten in Prince Albert, the radio blared, but then the reporter corrected himself and said that the prime minister was in front by 300 votes. When we reached the Shanahan farm in Maidstone, it was certain that I would continue my brief ministerial career. The government had been given a slim majority; the Conservatives had gained twenty seats for a total of sixty-seven, and the CCF took eight more for a total of twenty-eight.[16]

I awoke on the morning of 12 June to review the unofficial returns. We had carried Essex East by a plurality of 7,197 and an absolute majority — my first — of 3,427.[17] I had won every district of the riding except Walkerville — still a Tory bastion. My overall margin of victory was five times greater than in 1940.

The results reflected the hard work I had performed for ten years on behalf of my constituents and their trust that I would carry on. Byrne's mudslinging of a few days before the election seemed to have turned voters my way. For Nell, however, the chief joy was that I could now duff my campaign clothes — a grey suit that I had worn from the time the election was called. There was a hole in one of the elbows, and the pants were so baggy that they looked as though I was permanently flexing my knees. Although I am not ordinarily superstitious, I would not wear anything but that suit; this was the most strenuous campaign I have ever undertaken and I needed all the help I could get. Apparently, some friends thought that at one stage I might have worked myself to exhaustion, but Nell and I weathered the storm side by side.

The 1945 election heralded the post-war period for Canada. True, the war against Japan was still going on, but most Canadians felt that the German surrender on 8 May had signalled the close of the war. That day, I was in Ottawa for a cabinet meeting, where it was decided to make the next day a holiday. The mood was one of great relief and jubilation. For a lark, Brooke Claxton and I rented a cab and horses; we drove about Ottawa's downtown, whooping and hollering. In the early hours of the morning we ended up in

16 King ultimately lost his seat when the soldiers' vote was tallied a week later. The Liberals won 125 or 127, depending on the leanings of two independents.
17 The result was Martin 15,099; Byrne, 7,902; MacDonald, 3,770.

Confederation Square as part of the spontaneous celebration of that historic occasion.

At one o'clock on 6 August, the first day of the Dominion-Provincial Conference on Reconstruction, the prime minister made a dramatic announcement. It had to do with a matter known to only two members of the cabinet — C. D. Howe and himself. Howe passed Mackenzie King a note, and the prime minister rose and said that an atomic bomb had been dropped on Hiroshima. A little over a week later and after another bomb had demolished Nagasaki, the war ended with Japan's unconditional surrender. As I write, I wonder how wise it was to have dropped those bombs.

The coming of peace preoccupied me greatly that summer and fall — as secretary of state, I was the minister responsible for the many government functions to commemorate the Allied victory. These began in June with the visit of Field Marshal Jan Smuts, the South African prime minister, and continued with the welcome of General Harry Crerar on Parliament Hill on 7 August. Eight days later, my department took charge of the military march-past that marked VJ Day.

The most moving moments for me, though, were greeting the soldiers as they returned to Canada from the theatre of war. On 22 June, I boarded the troop train at Lévis on the south shore of the St. Lawrence. On it were some five hundred returning soldiers, most of whom had been prisoners-of-war, including many of my friends from the Essex Scottish. I was overjoyed to see Walter McGregor, Fred Jasperson, the officer who had commanded the regiment at Dieppe, and Russell Turnbull, whom I had taught at Assumption College. Walter was my guide as I went through the train welcoming each man home.

On a similar excursion, I encountered more than I had bargained for. In mid-November, I flew to Nova Scotia with Colin Gibson, the minister for air, to greet Canadian service personnel returning on board the *Queen Elizabeth*. We could not land at Dartmouth RCAF base because of driving rain and snow but were diverted to Greenwood, another base in Nova Scotia. Our pilot, Flight Lieutenant George Wright, handled the Liberator skilfully, although the base was in darkness because of a power failure that was also hindering communication between the control tower and the aircraft. Emergency lighting was broken out and flares shot skywards, warning our pilot not to land until the flight path was ready; I later learned that personnel had been summoned to crash positions. The pilot brought in his plane, skimming some unseen hills, but missing the runway. To my great relief, he succeeded on the second approach.

My Irish-Canadian wife is not always free of premonitions. On her way overnight to Ottawa from Windsor by train, she had mentioned to a friend that she had a feeling that someone in her family was in danger. The morning after her night's journey, a fellow traveller showed her the morning paper, which carried a story about our near-miss. When Nell told me about her presentiment, I asked, "What did you do about it?" "I prayed," she said simply.

As a new member of the cabinet, I found out that I had a considerable amount to learn about the art of government. Life on the front benches was different. Most items in cabinet were discussed in the fullest detail, and any proposition presented by a minister had to be well argued. Within a week of my appointment as a member of the inner circle of government, I learned what a difficult and critical body the cabinet could be. I had a small submission to make on a question of company law and was to follow a presentation by Lionel Chevrier, another new minister. As soon as Lionel had finished saying his piece, the minister of finance, Jim Ilsley, began to put him through his paces, asking a series of questions about the cost of the submission. Such was the grilling, I decided to hold over my proposition until the next time cabinet met. When the meeting was adjourned, Ilsley turned to me and asked, "Why didn't you go ahead?" "Because of the way you devoured my colleague," I countered. He then told me that he was not just getting at Chevrier but was trying to teach all the new ministers a lesson.

As I was finding out about my fellow cabinet members, I discovered that there are times when it is best to keep silent. At a cabinet in mid-June, the prime minister mentioned that he would be sending names to the king as recommendations for a successor to the governor general, the Earl of Athlone. I assumed that this was a veiled invitation to cabinet to proffer suggestions. None was made — except by me. As a greenhorn, I had not caught on to the prime minister's moods and methods; he was not, in fact, asking cabinet to suggest who should be the next governor general. When I said that I had a name to propose, I noticed Mackenzie King glower. Could he and I have a chat about the matter? he enquired. The older members of the cabinet must have been amused, expecting that the "new boy" would be put in his place. In the outer room, next to the cabinet chamber, King told me that I had intervened in his plans for choosing the next governor general. This I acknowledged; I ventured to put forward the name of George Macaulay Trevelyan, the eminent historian in the Whig tradition, and master of Trinity College, Cambridge. Suddenly, King brightened and pronounced my suggestion splendid. But when the matter was pursued, Trevelyan declined the post, citing his age as a disadvantage.

Mackenzie King could be generous to his colleagues. He always appreciated their good work but at the same time did not hesitate to criticize them if they did not deliver as he expected. This attitude was understandable, but I could never fathom King's pleasure in pointing out his ministers' deficiencies. Hardly a colleague escaped his criticisms, not even Louis St. Laurent.

I soon began to get a better look at the business of government. In cabinet, I discovered that a good prime minister had to be a manager — a chairman rather than a chief. Much of government is a day-to-day operation. A prime minister has to deal with hundreds of decisions, each of which has to be juggled and put into place.

All the prime ministers under whom I served developed an individual style of chairing the cabinet. My earliest impression was that Mackenzie King had not read the cabinet documents — at least not with sufficient care to discuss them comprehensively. He would go around the table asking his ministers' views on any particular matter. When his time came to speak, he had absorbed enough to be able to pronounce with some conviction.

Louis St. Laurent, on the other hand, knew more about what was in a cabinet document than the minister who presented it. His technique at the cabinet table reflected his professional skill as a great lawyer. From the document, he gleaned an appreciation of what was involved and frequently would outline the proposal before the minister had spoken. Stealing the show in this way irritated me. I greatly admired St. Laurent's capacity, but I wanted to state my own case. Often, in his recital of "the facts," St. Laurent revealed his own reaction to the proposals and this had the effect of encouraging many ministers to agree with him.

Pearson's *modus operandi* was much more informal. I am certain that he always did his homework and he encouraged the fullest discussion — sometimes unnecessarily so. The pace with Mike was always easy, if, on occasion, less orderly.

No one liked discussion more than Pierre Trudeau. He is a born seminar leader. Sometimes I felt that, as in Pearson's time, there was too much discussion in Trudeau's cabinet. A lot of time was spent on cabinet committee work that often duplicated the work of the full cabinet or vice versa. No one was more tolerant of the right of discussion than Trudeau, but nobody was less sympathetic to ideas that he thought irrelevant, unsound or unintelligible. When I compare the different styles of each prime minister, the most satisfactory results were those that issued from the skilful management of Louis St. Laurent.

As well as setting up a good relationship with the prime minister, a new minister, naturally, must establish himself with the rest of the cabinet. Of those at this time, I felt particularly close to Jim Ilsley. He did not share my views, but we were friends and I probably visited his home more than any other minister's. He got along like a house on fire with Nell. An essentially serious man, always preoccupied, Ilsley was attracted by my wife's *joie de vivre*. The two of them would go to an occasional film together, not because Ilsley was particularly fond of movies but because he loved to hear the way Nell laughed in the theatre. He would forget his cares for a minute and laugh along with her. In cabinet, Ilsley would speak his mind firmly and would be absolutely unsusceptible to any influence. Sometimes I felt that this led to friction between him and Mackenzie King. No leader likes his colleagues to always speak frankly, and King in particular wanted a certain obeisance.

Many people do not realize that the discussions in cabinet are often more vigorous and difficult than those fought out in public on the floor of the House of Commons. In all my years in government, no one battled more valiantly in this forum than Jimmy Gardiner, the minister of agriculture. He was always taking on the minister of finance or the prime minister, who opposed Gardiner's projects in order to save money. Some argued that Jimmy was getting everything for those beloved farmers of his in western Canada. My earlier impressions of him, gained from gossip while I was a backbencher, were confirmed. He was a lonely figure and I tried to support him on some of his pet projects, largely because I felt sorry for him, and often because he spoke for the prairie provinces, whose problems he knew so well.

One individual whose force in the cabinet could not be denied was C. D. Howe. A complex man, Howe could not speak with the traditional command of parliamentary rhetoric, but his contributions were always telling. His interventions had authority and knowledge, particularly in matters of business, and he would express considerable impatience with those who disagreed with him. I was one of them, particularly when labour questions were discussed. A party cannot run on prayers, and Howe would often find the resources to pay the bills. He had such a respected position in the business community and with his colleagues that no one ever queried the fact that he was acting on occasion as a bagman. It is to

Howe's credit that supporter and foe alike had absolute faith in his integrity.

Louis St. Laurent was another leading member of the government that I joined. He, too, had the reputation of absolute honesty, and yet I do not know of anyone who could be more resourceful in explaining inconsistencies in his position than St. Laurent, whose keen mind enabled him to extricate himself from embarrassing situations for the most plausible of reasons. After listening to him deliver one of his long, tortuous explanations, I quietly said, "You have the reputation of being one of the most honourable men in the cabinet. But the reason you have just given seems to be as unfounded as any reason could possibly be. Yet it is so hard to put a finger on its immorality." St. Laurent laughed.

When I left the backbenches, I made it a point to handle my potential critics with kid gloves. I even used this technique on members of my own party. I would invite backbenchers who I knew were by nature opposed to my programs to come and have a chat with me. Sometimes I would invite them down to Windsor to speak for me at a meeting. This was one means of tempering their criticism while keeping them within range. By these means, for example, I avoided the consequences of having to endure the barbs of Jean François Pouliot.

As the cabinet minister for southwestern Ontario, I found there were a few "political" duties to perform, apart from administering my department. I never felt that a minister's job should involve a great amount of political organization. He must make certain that his own constituency is in good shape and maintain a supervisory interest in his region. It was proper that someone in the cabinet ought to act as a liaison between the party and the government; for my first years in government, this job fell to Brooke Claxton, who managed it better than anyone could. C.D. Howe took a measured interest, but Brooke did most of the work. Of course, this situation did not please Mackenzie King, who would blame his ministers for a lack of initiative in organization whenever anything went wrong — losses in byelections, for example.

In my part of the country, I made certain that the Western Ontario Liberal Association was operating smoothly and that candidates were properly slated in time for elections. The minister for a region was also consulted about making appointments for prosecutors in narcotics cases and for judges. This could cause problems for everyone in the cabinet. During that period, the practice of consulting the legal profession regarding prospective appointments had not been established. Currently, the pendulum has swung in the other direction. While a recommendation of a minister or an MP regarding a candidate is often politically partisan, a judge or a lawyer who is consulted about a legal appointment might make a biased recommendation based on personal friendship or on a candidate's attitude towards the law and not necessarily on his or her ability to sit on the bench.

As a minister, I found that in 1945 it was difficult to get nominees for the bench because judges were not paid well enough for some good lawyers to be attracted to the position. I remember raising the devil with Louis St. Laurent when he was minister of justice over an appointment that he had in mind. It seemed to me that every vacancy on the Ontario bench was filled by a Toronto lawyer. "I'm getting fed up with it," I told him. Peeved, St. Laurent replied that if I knew anyone better qualified from southwestern Ontario, the job was his. I named a competent lawyer, and St. Laurent told me to call him immediately. I complied, but the offer was refused because the salary was not high enough. "There's a vacancy on the Ontario Court of Appeal; give him that," responded the minister of justice. The second offer was turned down for the same reason.

At St. Laurent's insistence, I called a second lawyer. As a personality, he was not as agreeable as my first choice and had done little for the Liberal Party. "Would you like a judicial appointment?" I asked him over the phone. "Yes, I'll take it," he replied and then hung up. He never even thanked me for calling.

About this time, I had a difference of opinion with my parliamentary colleagues from Essex County over the appointment of a county court judge to replace the able Judge J. J. Coughlin.

Murray Clark and Don Brown favoured the crown attorney from
the neighbouring county. But since the two sitting judges were
English-speaking, it seemed to me that in a county with so
many French-speaking residents, there should be one judge
who could speak their language. Despite my colleagues' recommendations to the contrary, I insisted that my view should
prevail.

The cabinet's major post-election item of business did not involve
my department but rather concerned the government's reconstruction program and the Dominion-Provincial Conference that
was to open in early August. Before my appointment to the
cabinet, I had worked with Eric Stangroom on certain labour
issues that might be raised at this conference and I was aware of the
careful relaxation in wage controls that the department of labour
was proposing. I also knew that this might increase union demands
for higher wage settlements in future collective bargaining; little
did I realize that this would concern me directly in the great Ford
strike that fall. The federal government naturally wanted to retain
its wartime emergency powers over industrial disputes in order to
make the transition to peace smoother. Yet the issue at stake was
the long-term balance on labour questions between the federal
government and the provinces. The department of labour eventually decided to propose that if the provinces wished to transfer
certain aspects of industrial relations to the federal government,
amendments to the BNA Act would be considered to enable this
change to take place.

The most important set of considerations presented to the conference concerned the government's social security proposals.
They were Brooke Claxton's responsibility as minister of national
health and welfare, and he relied on my support in getting them
through the federal cabinet before they were presented to the
provinces. I agreed with him that the government must implement the promises that had been made during the war and in the

recent campaign. By 1945, nearly all industrialized countries except Canada, Australia and the United States had adopted health insurance in one form or another. Leonard Marsh's recommendations stirred interest in the proposal that was to be put before the conference. The government agreed to propose a mandatory nationwide contributory health insurance scheme to make funds available for upgrading hospitals and medical services.

The health proposals had obviously been worked out with great care, as had the briefs on old-age pensions and unemployment assistance. The rationale of the pension program, however, was different, because pensions based on a means test had been in existence since 1927 for those over seventy. One of the 1945 proposals was to institute universal pensions for anyone over seventy and to eliminate the means test. The pensionable age would be reduced to sixty-five with a test, and the level of monthly payments would be increased.[18] Brooke Claxton also proposed a measure of unemployment assistance to the provinces. This would enable the federal government to take over responsibility for the financial relief of able-bodied unemployed who had exhausted their unemployment insurance benefits or who did not qualify under the present act.

In the discussion on federal-provincial financial arrangements, Jim Ilsley said that he would urge provincial governments to vacate in perpetuity personal income and corporation taxes as well as succession duties, as they had done during the war. The federal government proposed to continue its annual rental payments with a guaranteed minimum and would increase them with the rising population of a province and the per capita gross national product. This scheme was based on provincial receipts at least fifty percent higher than those under the wartime tax agreements.

It was an exciting program, and I took an active part in the cabinet's five-day review of what came to be called the Green Book

18 Dominion-Provincial Conference on Reconstruction, *Proposals of the Government of Canada* (Ottawa: King's printer, August 1945, pp. 36-39.

proposals; these were plans not merely for the transition to peace but for years to come. They were designed to place a floor under the living standards of all Canadians — not just those with secure incomes. The social security proposals provided me with the tools for some of the important reforms I introduced later as minister of national health and welfare. At the pre-conference cabinet meetings on 30 July, I asked how much emphasis the government presentation placed on the phrase "private enterprise." Should we not think as well of public enterprise? I asked, looking directly at Louis St. Laurent, who just shrugged his shoulders. Alphonse Fournier, the minister of public works, and C.D. Howe did not think much of my question, but the prime minister did. Mackenzie King fully agreed with my comment, for he was too good a politician to allow the phrase "private enterprise" to be included on its own. The presentation was changed to meet this deficiency. This was the first time in cabinet that King indicated his general agreement with my political philosophy.

As with items that arose in the future, I found that the discussions concerned the proper presentation of the policy. Most of the important issues in the Green Book proposals had been drawn up in advance by the responsible ministers and their civil servants. Questions not only were hashed over in the cabinet as part of the agenda but also were constantly before us. At lunch or dinner when I was sitting next to a colleague, conversation would inevitably shift to an issue being looked at in the formal meetings.

The cabinet approved the proposals, and they were presented to the conference on 6 August. In his opening statement, the prime minister asked provincial governments to join in partnership with Ottawa to promote the welfare of all citizens. "We believe," he told the provincial delegations,

> that the state . . . should design programs of public development and conservation which can be readily expanded or contracted to help in balancing the rise and fall of other sources of employment. We also believe that . . . the state has an inescapable responsibility to provide, through unemployment insurance and assistance, a minimum

livelihood to those who, through no fault of their own, find themselves without work.

The federal government did not expect the provinces to
approve its agenda without some disagreement, but no one fore-
saw that the conference would become so bogged down at the
beginning. George Drew wasted little time in joining a resuscitated
Maurice Duplessis[19] to obstruct the discussion by indulging in
procedural objections to Mackenzie King's handling of the conference. As secretary of state, I was not a member of the federal
delegation, but I sat close by and listened eagerly to all that went
on. It was a very disheartening exercise for those of us avid for
change. All I could find to say in the House of Commons some
weeks later was that the conference had been remarkable and had
set the "preparatory stage" for later resolution and implementation of the Green Book proposals.[20]

Despite the government's work on reconstruction, the weeks following the general election had fuelled labour's restlessness. Don
Emerson, himself a member of local 240, had kept me well briefed
on labour issues throughout the campaign and after he became my
private secretary in July. Although I did not have any direct
responsibility for labour matters, I was caught up in it all. This was
still the formative stage of union mass organization; the "jurisprudence" of union negotiation had not yet been settled. It was
practically impossible for an MP representing an industrial constituency not to be involved. (Now that the labour scene has settled into
a pattern, it is normally much easier for an MP to remain on the
sidelines.) My riding was one of the most heavily unionized in the

19 Duplessis had defeated the Liberal government of Adelard Godbout on 8 August
   1944.
20 House of Commons, *Debates*, 10 September 1945, p. 62.

country; along with the steelworkers, and the aircraft and textile workers, the autoworkers were taking strike votes.

The unions were disturbed about the government's decision essentially to leave matters of reconversion to the large corporations. They also did not like what they considered to be the lack of effort by employers to integrate war veterans into the labour market, and the fact that servicemen were being used by industry to hold down wages. The unions rightly felt that the post-war labour problem should not be solved by using surplus manpower to depress wages.

At the end of the war, the communists had stopped actively promoting labour peace, and the UAW leadership had begun to espouse a more militant point of view. They associated less and less with the moderates in the CCL, like Pat Conroy. Despite the role of the communists in agitating for a strike, it is important to remember that there would have been no strikes if the vast non-communist majority had not favoured one.

The situation grew very tense in Windsor during the first week of September. A report submitted by Mr. Justice S. E. Richards calling for a cooling-off period was rejected by local 200 of the UAW, then in negotiations with Ford. So Humphrey Mitchell appointed a conciliation board, consisting of Mr. Justice G. B. O'Connor, Stanley Springsteen — the Ford nominee and a former law associate of mine — and Bora Laskin, a professor at the University of Toronto law school, who was representing the union. But the day after the announcement of the board's appointment, the workers in Windsor's four Ford plants voted in overwhelming numbers to strike. On 12 September, the first major post-war struggle for union security began when 10,000 workers went out on strike at the Ford Motor Company in Windsor.

In my speech on the address in reply to the speech from the throne two days earlier, I set down my general view of post-war labour problems. It would, I contended, serve the most useful purpose if I reminded both business and labour that the government had pledged that the wartime gains that had accrued to working men and women would not now be whittled away.

During the war, the government had demonstrated its determination to ensure that good relations between itself and labour were maintained. The proposals that had been placed before the Dominion-Provincial Conference the month before had included a statement by Humphrey Mitchell that labour would not be compelled to give up either its right to collective bargaining or its right to organize for that purpose.[21] I was very pleased when, during a cabinet discussion on the day the men walked off the job, the prime minister appeared to support my point of view and blamed Ford for trying to undermine the collective bargaining agreement.

It was a shame that the union had to strike in 1945 over the same issues for which it had fought earlier. While the workers wanted veterans' seniority, proper grievance procedures, two weeks' vacation with pay and a guaranteed minimum wage,[22] above all they wanted the same recognition for the union that was accorded to Ford workers in the United States. This request brought the strikers into direct conflict with Ford's president, Wallace Campbell — never personally favourable to unions — who maintained that his company could not accept a union shop. The Ford Company of Canada assumed that once the war was over, it could revert to pre-war procedures as though P.C. 1003 had never existed. This only intensified the workers' and the union's determination to gain a union shop and "checkoff."

As September passed, the signs of impending trouble grew more evident. On the seventeenth, the company announced that picketing members of local 200 would be charged under the criminal code for "besetting and watching." Judge Coughlin, the chairman of the police commission, agreed that the police should prosecute anyone who contravened the code. On 19 September, one feeder plant employing 480 men — which depended on the Ford Motor Company — closed down; other plants soon followed. Three days later, Mayor Art Reaume wrote letters to Mackenzie King and

21 House of Commons, *Debates*, 10 September 1945, pp. 59-64.
22 These were not at all unreasonable demands, considering that Ford's wartime profits had increased by tens of millions of dollars.

George Drew, pointing out that Windsor had become the testing ground for the new national labour code and urging that it was in the interest of the country and the province, as well as of the strikers and the company, to break the deadlock. I returned to Windsor on 24 September to assure him, the company and the union that I would leave no stone unturned in a search for a settlement. I strove hard to arrange a meeting between Humphrey Mitchell and his Ontario counterpart, Charles Daley. They agreed, but then called off the meeting when, at the last moment, Wallace Campbell refused to attend. By the end of the first week in October, things were getting desperate: the powerhouse employees joined the striking workers and deprived the company's buildings and property of heat and electricity. They also prevented Ford's security police from entering the plant. Families of the striking workers had begun to suffer and were granted municipal relief.

The House of Commons debated the issue on 9 October; Clarie Gillis raised the matter after the minister of finance had moved that the House go into committee of supply. Parliament showed little sympathy for the company, and I knew I would have to tread carefully. I had a double interest: as a member of the government, I must defer to its policy as enuciated by the minister of labour; but, as the member of parliament for Essex East, I must represent my constituents. I was not happy with my speech, but I did not want to say anything that would impede efforts to get the parties around the bargaining table. I pointed out that the country was going through a period of transition and that this had been one cause of labour unrest. But the Ford Motor Company had a history of poor industrial relations; yearly wages were low, and working conditions were bad. I urged the automobile industry to carry out its social responsibilities towards its employees. The solution to the present strike, I told the House, was not to be found in removing the right to collective bargaining; good faith had to be restored between the parties.[23]

23 House of Commons, *Debates*, 9 October 1945, pp. 871-73.

The government worked throughout October to devise formulas that would satisfy both parties. At one point, I flew to Windsor twice in a day to try to work out a settlement. Roy England, the president of UAW local 200, demanded my resignation from the cabinet because of the government's failure to resolve the conflict, but I was quick to let him know that he was barking up the wrong tree. The mayor, the citizens of Windsor and the parties to the dispute were becoming impatient. There was a simmering hostility in the air, and Nell received some threatening phone calls at our home on Roselawn Drive. Clearly, some irresponsible unionists were trying to intimidate me. The irony of it was that I worked as hard as anyone to protect the union.

On 3 and 4 November, the situation became more gloomy still. Local 195 of the UAW had decided to go out on strike in support of the Ford workers; now 20,000 workers were idle in the city. The police chief, Claude Renaud, appealed for assistance to the provincial attorney general, Leslie Blackwell, when the strikers prevented Ford security guards from entering the plant under the protection of the Windsor police. Blackwell agreed to send in the Ontario provincial police and, in turn, asked the federal government to supplement them with RCMP officers.

When I learned that Jim Ilsley, the acting prime minister,[24] had agreed to Blackwell's request after talking it over with Louis St. Laurent, I was fit to be tied. They had not consulted me. Ilsley did not have the background in these matters that Mackenzie King had, and the very fact that there was a challenge to the established order and to government was enough to hurry the minister of justice into a rash decision. The situation had begun to resemble the Oshawa strike; the clock was being turned back. I phoned Ilsley from Windsor to tell him that I took exception to the decision and to urge caution. He said that the RCMP would leave their guns on the plane in Windsor; the Mounties would not, he assured me, be used to break the strike.

24 Mackenzie King was out of the country at the commonwealth prime ministers'
     meeting in London. If he had been in Ottawa, this confrontation would probably
     not have happened.

The following day, 5 November, trouble broke out. The workers had seized cars and buses and had blockaded the plant. It looked as though violence might destroy all our efforts. When I went to the House of Commons that evening, I took part in a debate on the Windsor situation precipitated by a motion of Clarie Gillis on a matter of urgent public importance. Speaking in this debate was one of the hardest things I have ever had to do. I expressed my feelings about the people of Windsor and the troubles they had endured. They were, I told the House, as law-abiding and as good citizens as one would find anywhere,

> ... people who ... have as deep a respect for agencies of authority and of law as any other community in Canada. But I would not be doing my duty if I did not say that no one ... has touched upon ... the provocations and the historical situations that have led to the present difficulties. I have said that my constituents are law-abiding people; they are. They belong to a union community. That does not make them less lawful or less respectful of the agencies of authority; but the vast majority of them work in an industry whose ... annual wage output is wholly inadequate, as every person in that community knows.

I tried to praise the men on the assembly line for their wartime service, and reminded the House that

> ... when tempers are hot, when the emotions of the people are stirred, they are apt to pass judgment on a community when they are not fully aware of all the implications.

In conclusion, I mentioned Ilsley's earlier statement that there would be no effort by the police to break the strike. If they tried, I added, I could not support them.[25]

The five-day visit to Windsor of Humphrey Mitchell immediately afterwards made a settlement seem a little closer. The barricades were removed, and Mitchell went over to Detroit to meet Henry Ford, whose more conciliatory attitude would, he

25 House of Commons, *Debates*, 5 November 1945, pp. 1,841-45.

hoped, influence Ford of Canada. He also met the workers, the mayor and George Burt. But the company refused to budge.

Something had to be done. I went to see Pat Conroy, the secretary-treasurer of the Canadian Congress of Labour, in the hope that he might have a way of breaking the impasse. His office was in Ottawa, so it was easy for us to talk. Pat was a remarkable fellow and, in my judgment, easily the most perceptive and outstanding labour leader at the time. (Aaron Mosher, the president of the CCL, was also a powerful figure but did not carry the same weight with the government.) Pat suggested that it might be worthwhile to enlist the services of an influential UAW officer from international headquarters in Detroit, who would have more experience in tough negotiations than either George Burt or Roy England. He never really approved of the UAW's tactics, particularly Burt's tolerance towards the communist element in the union. I flew back and forth to Windsor twice in one day, trying to find a mediator.

It took me some time to find a labour leader willing to take on the task. Roland J. Thomas, the international president of the UAW, declined my telephone solicitation. Pat and I came up with another name, Philip Murray, the great US labour leader and head of the CIO. Murray had come to Windsor two years earlier when he received Assumption College's Christian Culture Award from Monsignor Fulton Sheen of New York. Afraid of another rebuff, I asked Monsignor Sheen to prepare the way for me. When I phoned Murray, I received an attentive reception. I reviewed events, not omitting to mention my futile efforts with UAW headquarters in Detroit. I pointed out that should the union lose in its efforts to gain its demands, there would be a serious setback in union organization in Canada. Murray called the UAW headquarters and then told me to get in touch with George Addes, the UAW's secretary-treasurer.[26]

---

26 George Addes was Walker Reuther's chief opponent in the UAW and the man Reuther had to depose to gain full power.

When I tried to set up meetings with Addes in Ottawa, I was warned against him — people claimed he was a communist, or at least a fellow traveller. Nonetheless, I thought the risk was worth it. Addes made his way to Ottawa in a government plane I had laid on; in that then-badly congested city, I could find space for him only by arranging for him to bunk with me in my room at the Lord Elgin Hotel. I will always remember George Addes that first night: before going to bed, he knelt to say his prayers — hardly the mark of a communist.

Intermittent and intense discussions followed Addes's arrival. I had felt somewhat uneasy about bringing him in on my own initiative, and soon acquainted my colleague, the minister of labour, of what I had done. The union allowed Ford's power plant to reopen and gave an assurance that these men would not be called out again. This was the first step. George Addes, Pat Conroy and I quickly realized that we would not ourselves be able to bring the strike to a speedy end. It would be calamitous if it was left to drag on into the new year, and we began to discuss the desirability and possibility of arbitration. The union, however, had developed a reluctance to rely on some of the local provincial judiciary; they believed that they were too sympathetic to the company. Pat Conroy suggested that we should look for a judge of the Supreme Court of Canada. I accepted this idea right away. No such a judge had heretofore participated in matters of this sort. Louis St. Laurent quite independently thought that a Supreme Court of Canada judge would be ideal. It was a fortuitous coincidence: St. Laurent knew Ivan Rand to be a great judge with a liberal conscience.

Although I knew that Rand's views on the rights of labour were encompassed within a progressive social outlook, I wondered whether I could convince the cabinet to appoint him. This involved a wrangle with my colleague C. D. Howe, who believed that employer and employees should be allowed to work out their own problems without government intervention. I knew that this might be fine in principle but told the cabinet that we had been involved almost from the beginning of the strike. Privately, I knew that the workers were getting fed up and might revolt against the strike leaders if a settlement was not found soon. This I wanted to avoid, for it would set the cause of unionism in Canada back ten years.

On 14 December, local 200 offered to support the appointment of an arbitrator, whose decision would be rendered within five days of the completion of his hearings on all those matters not agreed to by the two parties. The Ford management went along with this, and I learned with relief that, subject to a vote (almost certainly approving this decision), the workers would return to the assembly lines. I encouraged Pat Conroy and George Addes to urge the mass meeting on 14 December to vote for a new ballot. Conroy knew, because I had told him confidentially, that Mr. Justice Rand would be the arbitrator. Finally, six days later, the strikers voted by a three-to-one majority to return to work.

At the end of January 1946, Mr. Justice Rand announced his decision on those matters that had not been settled between the union and Ford. The union shop was denied, but the checkoff of dues for all employees of Ford, union members or not, was granted. He believed the union shop to be a denial of the individual's right to work independently of persons associated with any organized group, but "all employees should be required to . . . shoulder their burden along with [reaping] the benefit." In addition, the union was charged with the responsibility for repudiating strikes not authorized by it, and no strike was to be called until a majority vote had approved it. Any employee taking part in an unauthorized strike became liable to a fine of three dollars a day for each day's absence from work and a loss of a year's seniority for every week's continuous absence. The underlying principle of Mr. Justice Rand's report was that "unions should be made stronger but at the same time they must become responsible and more democratic."

The parties accepted the Rand formula with a minimum of objection. It was then, and remains today, a cornerstone of Canadian labour-management relations. The unions interpreted the checkoff as the same thing as a union shop. If there was the obligation to pay dues, it followed that little would be served by an individual not becoming a member with a voice in union affairs. Ten days after the announcement of Rand's decision, the secretary of district council 26 of the UAW wrote to me that following a unanimous resolution, the council wanted

> . . . to thank you for your active participation on behalf of the Ford workers during the trying days of their recent struggle.
>
> Labour appreciates those who stand firm in their knowledge of their objectives, when the struggle is enjoined; we can depend on your fullest support.

XIII

Ordering the Peace

W HEN THE PRIME MINISTER of Britain, Clement Attlee, paid an official visit to Ottawa in mid-November 1945, I set aside for an evening the problems of the Ford strike to attend the Country Club dinner in his honour. Both Attlee and his host, Mackenzie King, made amusing speeches, giving us their general impressions of their private talks.

The Canadian prime minister, in rare form, embarked on one of his most effective after-dinner speeches. King peppered his address with a number of humorous comments on Attlee's political role as the leader of a Labour government that had set out to achieve "socialism in our time." Never had I heard King so lighthearted as in this gentle satire on state socialism. When he had finished, I wondered how the restrained Attlee would respond to such a double-pronged welcome.

Attlee expressed his pleasure at visiting Canada. Because his duties as Britain's prime minister could take him more often to the remoter corners of the world, this gave him an advantage over King and other commonwealth leaders. These trips allowed him time to indulge in his favourite pastime — ornithology — and he had seen all kinds of birds in Africa, Asia and North America.

Imagine, Attlee exhorted us, his great satisfaction at finding in Canada that rare bird — a Liberal Party in office! The quip brought the house down.

Two days later, when Attlee addressed a joint session of parliament, his remarks had a graver tone. He emphasized the paramount importance of making the United Nations an effective instrument for peace. The atom bomb, he told us, was not a matter to be dealt with only by the superpowers and should be subject to the kind of controls that only the United Nations could establish. Attlee concluded by quoting Rabelais: "Conscienceless science is but the ruin of my soul."

A little over a month later, I found that I would have something to do with helping to make the new international organization, the United Nations, into a functioning instrument for peace. Almost at the last minute, an official of the department of external affairs asked me if I would be willing to go to the first meetings of the United Nations General Assembly in London in January and February 1946. Along with Louis St. Laurent, Mackenzie King had selected me, as a delegate.

My interest in the establishment of an effective world organization had never slackened. Even though the League of Nations had failed to prevent the war that had just ended, I firmly maintained my belief that international order could and must be established. Apart from my efforts at the International Labour Organization and countless speeches to every imaginable type of audience, I had participated in a series of meetings that began in 1943, to promote an international body like the United Nations. These gatherings, inspired by my former professor, Manley Hudson, brought together a group of people to work out what we called "the postulates and principles" of the international law of the future. To have the chance to apply some of these tenets at the first meetings of the United Nations was for me a great challenge.

The signing of the charter of the new organization at San Francisco in June 1945 had concluded only the first stage in the establishment of the UN. The next phase, to take place in London, would create a functioning organism. At San Francisco, the agreement on interim arrangements established the machinery to bring the charter into effective operation, set up a preparatory commission, consisting of all members of the organization, and named an executive committee of fourteen. This commission recommended that the first session of the General Assembly be divided into two parts: the first to take place in London early in 1946 to complete the organizational work and to approve the report of the preparatory commission, which became the rules and regulations of the United Nations; the second to be held in New York in the autumn to deal with problems of policy.

We knew that the charter was not a perfect document; there could not be a single nation that would agree wholeheartedly with every line of its contents. It bore the mark of many minds, but that too was something of a virtue. By combining differing conceptions of international security, it had, to some extent, reconciled them.

After taking the train to New York, I embarked on the *Queen Elizabeth* on the last day of 1945, along with Louis St. Laurent, John Read, the legal adviser to the department of external affairs, and Lou Rasminsky of the Bank of Canada (the rest of the Canadian delegation — about fifty in all — sailed on the *Duchess of Bedford*). Our liner carried most of the American delegation. St. Laurent and I had quarters on the sun deck, along with Mrs. Eleanor Roosevelt, whose room was opposite mine. Mrs. Roosevelt impressed me, but I thought she was too much of a generalist. At the second part of the first Assembly, held six months later in New York, I revised my opinion when she tackled the human rights issue with great skill and resolve. Senators Connally and Vandenberg were also on board, as well as Sol Bloom, who was chairman of the foreign relations committee of the House of Representatives.[1] John Foster Dulles, a well-known figure in the field of

---

1 Senator Tom Connally was chairman of the senate foreign relations committee. Senator Arthur Vandenberg, an eminent Republican senator who could have been president, came from Grand Rapids, Michigan. At this time, it was he, more than any other, who gave US foreign policy its bipartisan character.

foreign affairs and advisor to the 1944 Republican presidential candidate, Thomas E. Dewey, accompanied them. (I had met Foster Dulles about fifteen years before. When I was a junior lawyer in Charlie McTague's firm, we had undertaken some legal work regarding the construction of the Ambassador Bridge across the Detroit River. Dulles had represented another party in the bridge deal. I found him then to be a cold fish, always very demanding.)

The voyage provided a relaxing prologue to the hectic days that I knew lay ahead. At our dinner table, we were joined by Admiral R. Kelly Turner, who had been a naval advisor to President Roosevelt, and Page Wadsworth, the American ambassador to Lebanon and Syria.[2] Mealtimes became the focus for spirited discussions on the future of aviation, atomic energy and the Palestine question. Two days out of port, I had a small party in my cabin to celebrate the elevation of Louis St. Laurent to the British Privy Council; it had been announced in the king's New Year's honours list. During the voyage, I first broached the question of the Liberal leadership with St. Laurent. It looked as though Mackenzie King would step down in the not-too-distant future, and I told the minister of justice that he was the most likely successor. Characteristically, he was non-committal, but I am sure he had his own quiet plans.

We arrived at Southampton to a greeting from the city's mayor, and were whisked off to London in a Canadian army car. It was a pleasant drive; England was at last at peace, and the contrast with my previous trip to London could not have been more marked. Our suites at the Dorchester were palatial: I had a sitting room, a large bedroom, and a bathtub so big it reminded me of the Hart House swimming pool. Before the conference opened, I spent a great deal of time with St. Laurent and the Masseys. St. Laurent and I went to Sunday mass at the Brompton Oratory, identified in my mind with John Henry Newman. St. Laurent was a grand

2 Later, Page Wadsworth was a colleague of mine at the United Nations during the disarmament talks in 1954-55.

travelling companion and on our frequent walks showed that he knew every nook and cranny of the city, pointing out things that I had passed by. Then the two of us dined with the Masseys in their cosy penthouse above the Dorchester Hotel. Later on the trip, Massey invited Sir Harold Alexander in to meet us; he was soon to take up his post as Canada's governor general.

Before we left Ottawa, Mackenzie King had asked St. Laurent and me to carry out a special mission: to view the painting of him by the British artist Frank Salisbury that King himself had commissioned. The portrait impressed me as being that of a younger man, and I found it difficult to consider it a likeness of the King I knew, who was older, heavier and balder. Louis St. Laurent shared my view, although neither of us ever cared to tell the prime minister of our reaction. But strangely enough, whenever I think of Mackenzie King, I see him not as he was, but as he is in Salisbury's portrait, now hanging at the entrance to the Commons chamber in Ottawa.

One morning soon after my arrival in London, I visited the office of the Canadian Custodian of Enemy Alien Property. As I told Nell in a letter, I was really visiting myself, since I was the Custodian! I met the staff, talked with them generally about their work, and made the acquaintance of Margaret Guthrie, who acted as my secretary while I was in England. At lunch shortly afterwards, Margaret told me that she was getting married and asked me to give her away. It was a gesture that touched me greatly.

On 10 January 1946, twenty-five years to the day after the ratification of the Treaty of Versailles, the representatives of the fifty-one member nations gathered in Central Hall, Westminster to a welcome from Clement Attlee. This first meeting of the General Assembly of the United Nations opened under the chairmanship of the president of the preparatory commission, Dr. Eduardo Zuleta Angel of Colombia. After the opening meeting, I reported

to Nell, "Let us hope that this time we have begun well. There is much doubt . . . [among the delegates]. This may be a good thing. It may help us [proceed] in a realistic vein. Much better this than . . . over-optimism followed by another world cataclysm. We must make this attempt at ordering the peace worthwhile." Canada's stature had grown enormously since the establishment of the League of Nations; our country had played a great role in shaping the new organization. The war had changed everything; its effects were inescapable as we walked the streets of London. Speaker after speaker at the Assembly reiterated that this time we must not fail — the alternative was too appalling to consider. The very name, United Nations, recalled the sacrifice and agony of the fighting alliance born during the war years.

The delegates proceeded to elect Paul-Henri Spaak, Belgium's foreign minister, as the UN's first president. Gladwyn Jebb, the executive secretary of the preparatory commission, carried on as interim secretary general until the election of Trygve Lie, Norway's foreign minister, three weeks later. Many felt that if Spaak had waited, he would have become the first secretary general; he was the best possible choice as president, and guided that first General Assembly as no other could have. Yet I know that he would have liked to be secretary general — he told me so. But, in fact, he did not stand a chance. The Soviet Union had made it clear from the outset that they did not want to have anyone from the West in that all-important position.

Mike Pearson's name was also frequently mentioned, but he suffered from the same disability as Spaak. After the voting, I sent Pearson a telegram, expressing my disappointment that he was not chosen. In his reply, Mike said that he "viewed the results with mixed feelings — that of relief . . . predominating," since, "on personal grounds," he wanted to stay where he was. I did not know that he had already spoken to Mackenzie King about entering public life. Because of his war record, Dwight Eisenhower might have been more acceptable to the Russians, but he had no interest in the job. Perhaps this was an early indication that he, like Mike, had "other" ambitions.

The question of who would be the UN's first secretary general was settled at the beginning of February. Under article 97 of the charter, the secretary general is appointed by the General Assembly upon the recommendation of the Security Council. While discussions were underway, I went with Vincent Massey to a splendid dinner at Greenwich, hosted by Clement Attlee. Sitting beside me was a man I did not know. The topic uppermost in most delegates' minds was the secretary generalship and before we had introduced ourselves, my dinner companion turned and asked me what I thought of Trygve Lie. "I don't know him." "Well," came the reply, "I think he is likely to be the secretary general. Of course *I* am prejudiced. By the way, my name is Trygve Lie." Support for Lie had been growing, and after a meeting on 29 January, the council put forward his name to the Assembly. Two days later, his appointment was confirmed. As Mike Pearson wrote to me afterwards, none of us were quite certain how much freedom the secretary general would be given. Lie knew he was taking on a challenging assignment.

Throughout the historic conference, I served as Louis St. Laurent's deputy in his capacity as leader of Canada's delegation. This arrangement had been confirmed before we left New York. He told me then that the minister of agriculture, Jimmy Gardiner — another delegate — was unlikely to spend much time in London; he had some departmental business to attend to and would take advantage of his trip to Europe to visit the grave of his son who had been killed in France. St. Laurent mentioned that he might not remain in London for the full Assembly; in that event, I would lead the delegation. When St. Laurent did leave for home towards the end of January, I presided as we arduously ploughed through the discussion of the lengthy agenda of the day's Assembly and its committees.[3] The work was all the heavier at this meeting because the

3 On the first, the political and security questions committee, Louis St. Laurent was the delegate, assisted by Hume Wrong, Escott Reid, Charles Ritchie and John Holmes. On the second, the economic and financial questions committee, there were Gordon Graydon and me, assisted by Louis Rasminsky, Alfred Rive and D. V. Lepan. On the third committee — social, humanitarian and cultural questions — were Jimmy Gardiner and Stanley Knowles, assisted by Alfred Rive,

delegation had more latitude than it would later. Since we were feeling our way on many contentious questions, our stand depended on the situation that developed in the Assembly itself, although we were constantly in touch with Ottawa.

The increased responsibility meant, in effect, that as acting head, I had to spend much of my time explaining Canada's position to the other delegations, particularly the Americans. In addition to those I had already met on board the *Queen Elizabeth*, there were James Byrnes, the secretary of state, and, among the alternate delegates, Adlai Stevenson, whom I was meeting for the first time. Stevenson had become a great friend of Escott Reid of the Canadian group, and Escott invited me to his room in the Dorchester and introduced me to Adlai. Alger Hiss, my classmate from the Harvard Law School, took an active role as secretary of the US delegation. During our numerous meetings with the Americans, Hiss normally took notes and frequently carried messages to us from the US delegation. I admired his capacities as an efficient diplomat but, as during my time at Harvard, could still not bring myself to warm to him.

Naturally, the delegates socialized with each other a great deal at luncheons, cocktail parties and dinners. Gordon Graydon, the Conservative House leader, who formed part of our delegation, came up to me at one of these functions and presented a Russian delegate — Andrei Gromyko. "Paul" he began, "I want you to meet Mr. Gromyko, who is going to join the Conservative Party." "Is that so?" I replied. "Of course," said Gromyko, "when Canadian Conservatives become Communist." Molotov and

G. C. Andrew, R. A. D. Ford and T. L. Carter. The fourth committee, on trusteeship, had Vincent Massey as the Canadian delegate, assisted by Pierre Dupuy, John Holmes and E. A. Côté. On the fifth committee, which dealt with the United Nations administrative and bugetary questions, were Dana Wilgress and Louis Rasminsky, assisted by Escott Reid, J. B. Jones, Leo Malania and R. A. D. Ford. The sixth committee, the legal committee, had John Read as the Canadian delegate, assisted by Dupuy, Côté and Carter. Two additional committees were established for this first session only. The first was the League of Nations committee, on which Hume Wrong was assisted by Rive and Jones; the second was the headquarters committee, and Dana Wilgress and Charles Ritchie represented Canada.

Vishinsky were harder nuts to crack and grew far less friendly after the Gouzenko affair.

The Lord Mayor of London gave a glittering banquet for the delegates at the Guildhall, its roof a canvas one because of the damage by heavy German bombing. As I wrote to Nell afterwards, it was the most impressive affair I had ever been to. First of all, as each delegate arrived, he was escorted to the reception hall by a medievally dressed attendant, with an accompanying flourish of trumpets. Then the name would be called out. When my turn came, it was "My Lord Mayor, the Secretary of State of Canada." Whereupon, quite embarrassed, I walked the length of a long blue carpet flanked by ambassadors and others, at the end of which, in resplendent robes of office, was the Lord Mayor, backed by the High Sheriffs. The whole shindig, part of an ancient liturgy, should have impressed "the colonials." It did.

As representative of the senior Dominion, I sat at the head table next to Ernest Bevin, Britain's foreign secretary, to whom I passed the silver loving-cup. "Ah," said Bevin, "I love this type of ritual and tradition." It astonished me that Bevin, a former leader of the 1926 general strike, saw no inconsistency between championing such a custom and his battles on behalf of the working man. "You're acting like a real Tory," I joked. "But in this I *am* a Tory, my boy," was Bevin's condescending rejoinder. The simple fact was that Bevin was a true Britisher, as loyal to his country's institutions and traditions as he was to the cause of working people.

Among the first items of business before St. Laurent's departure was the election of the six non-permanent members of the Security Council. Under article 23 of the United Nations charter, three such members were to be chosen for a term of one year and three for a two-year term. The first ballot gave seats to Brazil, Egypt, Mexico, Poland and the Netherlands. Canada missed the required two-thirds majority by one vote but was just ahead of Australia. This necessitated a run-off, and Australia jumped ahead of us but did not receive a sufficient tally. After a third ballot, instead of forcing the Assembly to vote yet again, Louis St. Laurent moved that no further votes be taken and that Australia's election to the Security Council be made unanimous.

We had hoped to have a seat on the Security Council, but two factors mitigated against it. First, practical considerations and the charter itself required that weight be given to the equitable geographical distribution in the election of members. North America was already represented on the Security Council by Mexico and the USA, and it was expected that Canada would be appointed to the eighteen-member Economic and Social Council and to an atomic energy commission. This council was established with the express purpose of creating fairer conditions for all citizens of the world; Canada was elected to it by a large vote because the other nations felt that our country could greatly contribute to the body, by virtue of its world trade, its stable economy and its advanced social legislation. To my mind, progress on these questions was as important as the political work of the Security Council in trying to eliminate the causes of war. It pleased me greatly to cast Canada's vote for John Read, who was elected one of the judges on the International Court of Justice.

The Economic and Social Council began its work right away.[4] I was appointed Canadian representative and Louis Rasminsky acted as my alternate during this first session and provided invaluable advice. Voting for officers took place at the initial meeting. The delegate for India, Sir Ramaswami Mudaliar, was elected president, with Dr. Andrija Stampar of Yugoslavia as first vice-president. The council set up five commissions: on human rights, economics and employment, statistics, narcotic drugs, and a temporary social commission. It then appointed a committee of twelve, including Canada, which would be immediately empowered to negotiate provisions for the exchange of representatives between various specialized agencies, and the United Nations. We discussed the means of bringing these agencies (the Food and Agriculture Organization, the International Monetary Fund, the

4 The inaugural session took place at Church House, London, from 23 January to 18 February. China, Peru, Chile, Canada and Belgium were elected for three-year terms. The Soviet Union, Britain, India, Norway, Cuba and Czechoslovakia were selected for two years. Those with a seat for one year were the Ukraine, Greece, Lebanon, the United States, Colombia and Yugoslavia.

International Bank for Reconstruction and Development, and the ILO) into association with the United Nations.

Commenting on the work of the council, I emphasized that, from the beginning, we ought to "keep a sense of proportion and not promise ourselves or others more than we are able to perform." The primary responsibility for the pursuit of policies that the council must observe rested on national governments, which could not divest themselves of this obligation or use the existence of the council as an excuse for inaction. Yet the real danger did not lie in this, but in the likelihood that countries would be so intent on accomplishing their own purpose that they would adopt national positions in relative isolation, oblivious of the effect these policies would have on other nations and peoples. In my view, it was vital for the council to harmonize the policies of the member countries to ensure that prosperity and well-being in one country were not achieved at the cost of depression and poverty in others. Drawing on my work at the ILO meeting in Philadelphia, I urged that the members of the five commissions function as experts and not as representatives of their particular governments. Individuals and not states should be selected for membership, although, naturally, each sovereign government would have to be consulted.[5]

On the question of the relationship between the specialized agencies and the United Nations, I pointed out that the council faced two potential pitfalls: the danger that agencies would proliferate chaotically, each going its own way, and the risk of excessive centralization. While it was essential for the council to avoid the duplication of work, the confusion of conflicting recommendations, and the strain on the supply of qualified personnel that would result from decentralization, we had to remember that a more independent body would be a stronger and more vital one. The United Nations must, therefore, neither attempt to absorb the five agencies nor give these specialized bodies policy directives on matters that lay within their own sphere of competence. The Economic and Social Council, however, should still maintain its

5 Economic and Social Council, *Verbatim Proceedings*, first session, first meeting (1946), p. 17.

coordinating function. The cooperation between the council and the agencies would depend greatly on the selection of men of good will and commonsense as the administrative heads of the agencies. In my summing up, I pointed out that we were

> . . . opening up a new chapter in the long struggle of mankind to master his environment to the end that the material and economic resources of the world are used for the enrichment and not the destruction of humanity.
>
> Our task is not an easy one. We shall have to overcome not only the internal forces in various countries which resist change, but also the scepticism that we encounter in many parts of the world regarding the possibility of success in a cooperative effort of this sort. There are those who, notwithstanding the grim experience of the inter-war period, which should have shown that no nation can achieve prosperity in isolation, are still prepared to repeat the old errors. We must turn deaf ears to the false counsels that reach us from such groups. There are those who will maintain that it is unrealistic, idealistic, to strive for a common solution to our problems, that the only realistic course is to recognize that each country will go its own way, carry out its own policies without regard to their effect on others. This, I submit, is a false realism.
>
> . . . the genuinely realistic course for the world to pursue at the present time is to recognize that it is only through cooperation, through mutual understanding and mutual aid that all countries can in fact achieve their maximum potential in economic and social well-being.[6]

On 11 February, I seconded a resolution proposed by John Winant of the United States, calling for an international conference on trade and employment. The government authorized me to act on this matter because Canada believed that the council ought to take the initiative on matters within its jurisdiction. The 1930s, I pointed out, had shown the need to prevent tariffs from breaking down the world trade system and, in the long run, deepening the Depression. Furthermore, the world economic

6 Economic and Social Council, *Verbatim Proceedings*, first session, first meeting (1946), p. 19 ff.

system could only reorganize itself after the war given a degree of international collaboration.[7]

The next day, the council acted on the recommendation of the General Assembly and set up a committee on refugees and displaced persons. This led to an examination of the nature and scope of the problem of providing finances for an international refugee organization. I was to chair the committee that worked on the constitution of this body and our work extended into the third session of the Economic and Social Council. The obstructionist tactics of the communist countries — the Ukraine and Yugoslavia in particular — severely hindered our work. The able Leo Mates of Yugoslavia was the archetypal spoiler; the Iron Curtain countries were past masters of this stonewall technique, which became a factor in the cold war.

While I was in London, the Gouzenko espionage case came to the public's view and also focussed attention on the deteriorating relations between East and West. Unknown to us all, the cipher clerk from the Soviet Union's Ottawa embassy, who defected in September 1945, had provided the Canadian government with names of agents operating in the country as part of a Soviet spy network. Before Louis St. Laurent left London on 25 January, he intimated that something important was afoot and that I might receive one or two rather peculiar requests. I had no idea what he was talking about. After the American journalist Drew Pearson had revealed (somewhat cryptically) in early February that a Russian espionage ring was operating in North America, the cabinet was informed. I received orders to make sure that a member of our delegation in London, Gordon Lunan, who worked with us as an information officer, returned home at once. Ostensibly, he was being recalled for another assignment; to ensure that he got home, his superior, Geoffrey Andrew, was to

7 Economic and Social Council, *Verbatim Proceedings*, first session, first meeting (1946), p. 66 ff.

return with him. Lunan was arrested with the other alleged spies on 15 February, the day he landed in Canada.

The whole incident nonplussed me, for I had come to know Lunan fairly well. Sitting behind me at our morning delegation meetings, he impressed me as an outgoing fellow who performed his work very capably. He had written some speeches for me that were broadcast back to Canada. At his invitation, I had even visited his parents' home for an evening meal (Lunan had originally come to Canada from Britain). On the day of his departure — and eve of his arrest — Lunan wrote me a farewell note that mentioned that he had used my name as a reference for a position for which he had applied at the United Nations' secretariat.

A month later, Fred Rose, the Labour Progressive Party MP for Cartier, was arrested for spying as he left the grounds of the Parliament Buildings in Ottawa. About the same time, Sam Carr, the secretary of the Labour Progressive Party, was revealed as a spy, but he fled the country to escape arrest. I had known Rose ever since he won the Montreal seat at a byelection in August 1943; in fact, I had spoken at the nomination meeting of his Liberal opponent in the contest, my friend Lazarus Phillips. In the House, Rose was like a fish out of water. He appeared never to have adapted to life in Canada. Like Sam Carr, he would come to my office, when I was parliamentary assistant to the minister of labour, to discuss the best means of maintaining industrial peace during the war.

Although I have never read the evidence of the Kellock-Taschereau royal commission which investigated the spy-ring, nor that of the trials that followed, the government's case appeared to be devastating. During the period, there was some criticism of the government's holding suspects incommunicado; questions were even asked in cabinet. At lunch one day, St. Laurent admitted to me that the methods were unfortunate, but pointed out that this espionage case was unique in our experience. The government, he said, could not afford to make any mistakes and he certainly did not apologize for the course that he had taken as the minister of justice.

In any event, Gordon Lunan, Fred Rose and Sam Carr — once he was apprehended in the United States in 1949 — were all convicted and sentenced to prison terms.

In addition to my duties at the United Nations in London, I had a hectic schedule. When I reread my letters to Nell, its pace astounds me. I would scribble notes to her during voting in the Assembly, or late at night before I dragged myself off to bed. During the time that St. Laurent spent in London, he asked me to join him at 10 Downing Street to discuss with Clement Attlee and Ernest Bevin, the question of Canadian troops in Europe. The Attlee government, besieged with post-war problems including rising costs, had urged on Mackenzie King that our soldiers should stay on indefinitely in the occupation zone in Germany. This matter had come before our cabinet, which had decided that we would insist on an early return of our troops to Canada. We felt that the country could not be charged with not having made its contribution. Moreover, our consideration of Britain's immense role had been made clear in our post-war loan arrangements and other efforts to ease her great burden. In his submission to us, Attlee outlined the heavy obligations that faced his country and its people. St. Laurent replied that Canada had not shirked its responsibilities and had its own priorities to meet. We had our own contribution to make as a nation.

Apart from official discussions, we were inundated with requests for interviews and general congratulatory letters that all had to be answered. Various groups, feeling that they had a grievance that might come within the purview of the United Nations, sent out mountains of propaganda. In the last week of January, I went to Manchester, Liverpool and Edinburgh, where I spoke to large audiences about the United Nations and about Canada's desire to liberalize trading conditions throughout the world.

On 1 February, an RCAF plane took me to France and landed at Le Bourget, outside Paris. I wanted to see for myself something of how people on the continent were coping with the aftermath of a long war. Inflation had bumped up prices to five hundred times their level in 1938. The winter was particularly cold and most Parisians were suffering; a doctor showed me photographs of undernourished French children. What a contrast it was to go to the Opera with Georges and Pauline Vanier to see "Faust". I also went to mass at Notre Dame and was seated near the celebrant, the cardinal archbishop of Paris. When he lifted the wine vessel up to the altar before the Eucharist, I noticed that even he was not immune from the hard times. Underneath his elaborately embroidered vestments, he was wearing several well-used sweaters.

During the first week of the Assembly, Louis St. Laurent and I joined the representatives of other countries at a reception at Buckingham Palace given by King George VI and Queen Elizabeth. Many times, in earlier years, I had looked through the tall iron gates, wondering what it would be like to be invited inside. After we had assembled in one of the palace's beautiful halls, footmen flung open the doors at the end of the room and there stood the whole royal family as in a tableau. They moved into the room and began to mingle with their guests. We were presented to the king and queen (both slightly more full-figured than when I met them in 1939) and then to Princesses Elizabeth and Margaret Rose. As I wrote to Nell, Princess Elizabeth "made a tremendous impression on me. She has a great sense of humour and is quick as a trigger."

My conversation with their majesties was brief, but on 14 February I was asked back and spent about half-an-hour with the king. His diffident manner really impressed me. Wearing a naval uniform, he received me and then took me to the room where he had made his famous wartime broadcasts. We discussed the use of the radio; I suppose I had mentioned at some point that I was broadcasting regularly to Canada to keep our citizens informed of progress at this important international gathering. Was I impressed with the foreign secretary, Ernest Bevin? the king asked. Before I could express a view, he went on, "They wanted to make him chancellor of the exchequer. I wouldn't have it. I wanted him as foreign secretary." According to his biographer, Attlee did not recollect that George VI had even expressed a preference,[8] but to my ears the king's wish sounded more emphatic than a hint.[9]

The king and I discussed the meetings of the Security Council, where Bevin and Andrei Vishinsky of the Soviet Union had already engaged in some vigorous polemics. Vishinsky had been the prosecutor in Stalin's wicked purge trials of the 1930s and I saw his skills as an advocate at a dinner given by the lord chancellor, Lord Jowitt, for the lawyers on the United Nations' delegations. Asked to speak, Vishinsky referred to the duty of lawyers to help secure peace in the world. Men trained in the law, he said, had a special opportunity to contribute by giving it meaning through their various legal systems. The rule of law, Vishinsky concluded, would guarantee the peace of the world if we could only impress on the governments and citizens of the world that by its very nature it helped eliminate injustice. It was a good and learned speech, but as Vishinsky had and would demonstrate, its sentiments were far from his own diabolical practice.

It was inevitable that, despite its infancy, the United Nations, and particularly the Security Council, would be subjected to the strained relationship between the western powers and the Soviet Union. The most divisive issue concerned the presence of British troops in Greece to prevent the communists from taking over that country. At one point in his gladiatorial confrontation with Vishinsky, Bevin stated that the British government would not permit the Soviet Union to interfere in the Greek civil war. While their exchanges took me somewhat aback, Bevin said what he

---

8 Kenneth Harris, *Attlee* (London: Weidenfeld & Nicolson, 1982), p. 264.
9 Mackenzie King had much the same conversation when he lunched with King George VI in the fall of 1945. (J. W. Pickersgill and D. F. Forster, *The Mackenzie King Record*, Vol. III, *1945-46* (London: University of Toronto Press, 1970), p. 76). John Colville, the secretary to three prime ministers and Princess Elizabeth, also concurs that the king was responsible for persuading Clement Attlee to reverse his original intention of appointing Bevin as chancellor and Hugh Dalton as foreign secretary (John Colville, *The New Elizabethans: 1952-1977* (London: Collins, 1977), p. 76).

thought and, upon reflection, I welcomed his frankness. Bevin's forthright defiance of the Russians had been one of the opening salvos of the cold war but, nonetheless, it set a realistic basis in the initial stages of the United Nations' debates.

At one point during his verbal duel, Bevin implied that the commonwealth would somehow become involved in any military intervention. Mackenzie King, on hearing this, made it very plain that Canada would determine its own foreign policy. On the day after Bevin made this statement, the Canadian high commissioner received a message telling Vincent Massey and me that, although our government approved of Britain's resistance to communism, Ernest Bevin was not authorized to speak for Canada. Massey and I duly went to the Foreign Office to register King's objections. For a moment, I'm not certain that Bevin understood what we were getting at, but the foreign secretary listened to us politely without comment.

Although the split between the West and the East was upsetting, on the whole it was perhaps best that contentious questions were not held back. If the issues had been dodged, the UN would have taken on the undesirable characteristics of the League of Nations, putting off unpleasant things and sidestepping the controversial issues. As I sat in at the sessions of the Security Council, it dawned on me that progress was being made after all. At least we were discussing the real issues; controversy *was* a fact of life. These early debates, disturbing as they were, showed the value of a forum in which the issues that divided East and West could be discussed. The mere fact of the establishment of the Security Council recognized that the duty of maintaining peace and security rested with the great nations, all the more so since the whole membership of the UN could not act with necessary speed. Louis St. Laurent told the plenary session of the Assembly that sovereignty must not mean liberty to defeat the purposes of international peace and security. He urged the Security Council to eliminate suspicion and fear, "those evil legacies of war."

The proceedings of the Economic and Social Council reassured me that it would play an important role in international affairs.

My hope and belief was that, in time, it might even prove as important a body as the Security Council in preventing conditions that could menace international peace. Had I been asked, I would have said that the political aspects of the United Nations could not be downplayed and that the interests of economic and social stability represented by the second body should be more strongly emphasized. The decision of the Economic and Social Council on 15 February to hold a conference on world health, which eventually would lead to the formation of a World Health Organization, provided one example of what I very much wanted. But despite my hopes for the council, I was wrong. Time has shown that since 1946, the nations of the world have sought to solve problems not by pursuing the struggle for social and economic equality, but by power politics. This has considerably weakened the United Nations.

I had attended international conferences before — notably the League of Nations Assembly in 1938. It had been a failure. I left Geneva that year disturbed about the prospects of international cooperation for peace. The old organization was perfect in theory, but my hope in 1945 was that we would be realistic; we should create the United Nations in as best a form as could be, but in the light of contemporary conditions. It was important that no country either minimize or overestimate the capacity of the UN to maintain peace. Nearly eight years after my trip to Geneva, I left London feeling that the United Nations was going to work. I still believe it will.

At the first part of the inaugural session of the General Assembly, we had carried the work of the new body a step further than in San Francisco, and I looked forward to the opening of the second part in New York on 23 October. Besides, I also had my responsibilities as Canada's representative to the third meeting of the Economic and Social Council, which began its sessions on 11 September, in advance of the General Assembly.[10] This meant that during the autumn, I divided my time between Ottawa and the site of the 1939 world's fair — Flushing Meadow, the temporary seat of the UN until 1950. On weekends, I flew from New York to Detroit and then crossed the river to Windsor. As I look back on those periods of frenzied activity, I admire my wife's devotion to, and endurance of, a husband who resembled a whirling dervish. Now and then, Nell would come and spend a few days with me at the Biltmore Hotel, where the Canadian delegation lodged.

This time, my alternate on the council was Dr. W. A. Mackintosh, formerly of the department of finance. Although he was an able practical economist, his work reminded me that, at one time, economics was considered a branch of philosophy. My main advisors were two remarkable men, R. G. Riddell of the department of external affairs, and George Davidson, the newly appointed deputy minister of national health and welfare. Among the British participants were Philip Noel-Baker, a minister of state, and Hector McNeil, Bevin's alter ego. Noel-Baker quickly revealed himself as perhaps the best-informed man in foreign affairs that I have ever known. He was a scholar-statesman, and few in this century have worked harder for peace; he justly deserved the Nobel Peace Prize that he was awarded in 1957. I reminded Hector McNeil that at international conferences Bevin was too prone to attempt to speak for the commonwealth as well as his own government. John Winant, the American representative, was a rather shy speaker but a brilliant man. A former director of the International Labour Office and the US ambassador to Britain during the war, Winant was an outstanding internationalist. His suicide shortly after this session of the council shocked all those who had worked with him.

During these meetings of the Economic and Social Council, I came better to know and respect Adlai Stevenson. By this time, he

---

10 Brooke Claxton attended the second meeting of the council, which began in New York on 25 May 1946.

had become an official representative on the American delegation, headed in the autumn of 1946 by Senator Connally and including Eleanor Roosevelt and Helen Gahagan Douglas, a member of the US House of Representatives from California. Her husband, actor Melvyn Douglas, was then appearing in a play on Broadway and we all went to see his performance. Mrs. Douglas, a progressive-minded person, was a strong supporter of industrial unions and the CIO. Stevenson asked me at one point to help her prepare a speech that she was to give to the council. I went over to her hotel room and ended up drafting almost the entire statement. It was a very odd position for me to be in.

The speech dealt with a problem familiar to me. The Economic and Social Council had already decided on the form of the relationship that would obtain between it and certain international bodies, such as the International Chamber of Commerce and the World Federation of Trade Unions. The CIO, the largest trade union organization in the United States, wanted its own separate association with the United Nations. This, however, had been denied to it, for the CIO and its "international" components, like the United Auto Workers, were not truly international bodies. That these unions had some members in Canada as well as in the United States was not thought to be a sufficiently strong argument to admit them to special standing. This was an important political issue for Helen Douglas. Not only did the CIO want her to protest its rejection by the United Nations; she also faced an election in her home state and needed the support of labour. Despite her care and concern, however, Helen Douglas lost her seat in the House to Richard M. Nixon — it was the beginning of his national political career, originally based on the unjustified accusation that, as a "liberal," Mrs. Douglas was soft on communism.

In the Economic and Social Council, the vice-president, Dr. Stampar of Yugoslavia, took the chair and called upon Fiorello La

11 The Council session began without Sir Ramaswami Mudaliar.

Guardia, the colourful former mayor of New York and director general of the United Nations Relief and Rehabilitation Administration (UNRRA), to report on conditions in the areas devastated by the war. La Guardia's report precipitated the most serious and divisive issue before the council — framing a response to the problems of refugees and of relief to devastated countries, which would take effect when UNRRA was dissolved at the end of 1946.

At the London session of the General Assembly, the refugee question became linked with the UNRRA debate, and occasioned long and vigorous argument that revealed the wide differences of opinion regarding the kind and amount of aid to be given to the homeless, and especially to those refugees who refused repatriation to eastern Europe. The Yugoslavs argued that the refugee question was political and that there was no reason why the United Nations, through UNRRA, should become responsible for perpetuating the presence outside their own countries of those hostile to the governments of their native land. Others, particularly Mrs. Roosevelt, argued that the refugee issue should be responded to in a humanitarian way, and that political dissenters should not be forced to return home or be left to starve without UNRRA assistance. Furthermore, the western nations did not like providing relief to eastern European countries whose persecution of dissent was intolerable.

Britain drew the attention of the General Assembly to the urgent need to extend relief beyond the term of UNRRA. Speaking on the issue, I argued that all peace-loving states, whether they were members of the United Nations or not, should be invited to contribute to UNRRA (this proposal was opposed by the Soviet Union and, therefore, was not adopted). A committee, including Canada, was established to consider additional contributions to UNRRA.

In London, the Assembly had agreed on the four principles: that the problem was an international responsibility; that refugees should, as much as possible, be returned to their country of origin; that force should not be used to repatriate refugees against their will; and that no aid would be given to war criminals or traitors. Those who refused to return to their homelands should become the responsibility of an international body established by the Economic and Social Council.

But the resolution that the General Assembly approved in January 1946 did not end the affair; the political issue remained. The Economic and Social Council did establish a special committee on refugees and displaced persons that subsequently estimated the human dimensions of the problem. Fiorello La Guardia sat on this committee in a consultative capacity as the director general of UNRRA. I told the council on 17 September that Canada supported the four principles that had been set out in London as the underpinning of an international refugee policy. In my view, the Soviet Union was right to say that repatriation should be the primary objective of the proposed interim refugee commission, but I opposed the proposal of the Russian delegate, Nicolai Feonov, for enforced repatriation; under no circumstances must compulsion be permitted. UNRRA's plan for interim measures of an elaborate kind would be too costly, I said, and would duplicate the work of the proposed International Refugee Organization (IRO) during the hiatus between the end of UNRRA and the functioning of the IRO. Instead, Canada favoured a small, flexible body that could deal quickly with the problem of resettlement — perhaps within three years.

The following day, I was elected chairman of the refugee subcommittee of the Economic and Social Council and set out immediately to rework the draft constitution for the International Refugee Organization. I knew we must agree quickly, for we were dealing with the largest group of homeless people the world had ever known. In Europe, the Middle East and Africa, there were some 1,675,000 refugees who were being helped by UNRRA. There were another two million homeless in the Far East. Provision had to be made for them when the United Nations took over responsibility after UNRRA's mandate expired. Nations such as Canada had to be given some time to devise an immigration policy that would take into account the magnitude of the problem affecting the world's refugees. Neither one country nor even several countries could solve the problem, but each nation had to contribute to the fullest extent possible. The committee recommended against enforced repatriation.

With the newly appointed minister of external affairs, Louis St. Laurent,[12] I returned to New York City a few days before the General Assembly began on 23 October. The two of us were members of a large delegation, which included Senator Wishart Robertson, John Bracken, the leader of the opposition, and M. J. Coldwell. St. Laurent presided over a strong group, but in many ways the strongest of us all was the new minister himself. Mackenzie King had decided to relinquish the external affairs portfolio and had given it to a man who had much greater faith in the United Nations. King's reaction to the first sessions of the new body was that they had served the purposes of the Soviet Union; the Security Council functioned under the threat of Russian veto and the Assembly was a springboard of propaganda to serve Soviet ends. St. Laurent understood the pitfalls, but he also knew that the evolutionary process would result in the United Nations gaining practicability and authority. Canada had made a commitment when it signed the UN charter, and St. Laurent was going to ensure that we would live up to it.

Almost at the last minute, the prime minister decided to come to the opening of the Assembly. St. Laurent and I met him at New York's Grand Central Station a little after seven in the morning on opening day. King, I remember, was particularly annoyed because we presented ourselves on the platform and he was forced to greet us even before he had shaved. The prime minister displayed his pique further when we arrived at the hotel and were waiting for an elevator. Earlier, St. Laurent had told me that since he had matters to discuss with the prime minister, I should withdraw discreetly once we reached the hotel. King obviously wanted to get caught up on his ablutions and at the elevator he dismissed

12 He was appointed on 4 September 1946.

his senior lieutenant as well as his junior minister. Remembering his earlier admonition, St. Laurent winked at me and shrugged as King turned his back to go up to his room.

The Assembly met at Flushing Meadow, a tedious drive from congested Manhattan. In the following few weeks, we drove hundreds of miles back and forth to the world's fair buildings as well as to the committee headquarters at Great Neck, Long Island. It was tiresome; we would leave the hotel at 8:30 in the morning and yet could not begin our meetings before 10 o'clock. Sometimes we did not get back to the hotel until 10 at night, and before we went to bed, often worked on reports to Ottawa.

At its first meeting, the Assembly was welcomed by President Harry S. Truman, who reaffirmed his country's support for the United Nations. The acting mayor of New York, Vincent R. Impelleteri, also greeted the delegates and invited the United Nations to make New York its permanent home. Paul-Henri Spaak noted that the United States and the Soviet Union had both taken a place at the UN and had expressed their intention to be active participants. He saw the presence of the two superpowers as a good omen, especially when compared to the circumstances at the League of Nations in 1919; when it began its sessions, neither country was a member.

After the opening ceremonies, we drove all the way back to Manhattan for President Truman's reception at the Waldorf Astoria. Since King was a head of government, protocol dictated that his delegation should be among the first to be received by the president. Most of the delegates were pleased to talk with King, but one was not: Vyacheslav Mikhailovich Molotov, the foreign minister of the Soviet Union. Yet this was the man that Canada's prime minister chose to seek out. King asked me to approach Molotov and steer him over. I never saw anyone avoid an encounter with such dexterity — he bobbed quickly from person to person, making certain that I did not catch his eye. King's reason for so eagerly seeking a chat with Molotov was not clear to me. After all, Canada had just exposed a Soviet spy ring and had expelled high-ranking Soviet diplomats. If the prime minister had wanted to indicate that the Gouzenko incident did not disturb our desire for cordial relations with the USSR, there were better methods than this.

After the opening festivities and Mackenzie King's departure, we quickly established a routine. The Canadian delegation met in its lounge in the hotel each morning to plan the day's work. St. Laurent presided, as I did in his absences. Our delegation was an impressive one largely because of its non-partisan character. M. J. Coldwell had been at San Francisco, and both he and John Bracken seemed pleased to participate in the first meetings of the United Nations.[13] I suggested to the delegation that in view of the many Canadian newsmen covering the meeting, each delegate should take a turn at holding a morning press briefing. It was, I believed, important that Canadians get useful impressions from their own news sources and not have to rely on the foreign press for an interpretation of events.

At the delegation's meetings, there was pessimism about the relations between the communist bloc and western democracies. We argued, however, that we had to treat the Soviet proposals on their merits in order to avoid the appearance of not taking the United Nations seriously. We knew that the Russians were trying to appeal to all those with progressive views by championing desirable causes, such as disarmament, and the defence of small nations and colonial peoples. Even though we knew that this was done purely for propaganda purposes, our stature would suffer in international public opinion if we appeared to disagree. We had to take the initiative.

Louis St. Laurent took part in the general debate on 30 October. He pointed out the shortcomings, notably the failure of the Security Council and the military staff committee to make progress in implementing article 43 of the charter. This lacuna meant that armed forces and other facilities to maintain peace

13 Gordon Graydon had gone to London as the Conservative representative; Stanley Knowles was there on behalf of the CCF. Previously, Graydon and Coldwell had gone to San Francisco. King was pleased that the general election campaign had precluded Bracken's attendance there.

were still not available to the UN. Without the means to enforce the provision, it could hardly be said that the Security Council could actively promote the settlement of disputes. St. Laurent also proposed that the judicial functions of the organization be strengthened, and pressed for the acceptance of the compulsory jurisdiction of the International Court of Justice. As the fall meeting of the Economic and Social Council had foreshadowed, one of the major issues before the United Nations that session was the over-powering refugee question. The third committee — that on social, humanitarian and cultural questions — began to consider the report of the council on the question of refugees and the constitution of the International Refugee Organization. Vishinsky, the Soviet delegate on this committee, still argued that the problem could be solved by enforced repatriation. Mrs. Eleanor Roosevelt took strong exception to this. I agreed with her, both in my capacity as chairman of the council's committee and as the representative of the government of Canada. On 9 November, I told the committee that Canada would cooperate with an international refugee or-ganization. Months had passed since the issue was first debated; I hoped that enough states would shortly ratify the IRO charter to bring the organization into being. At the same time, UNRRA had to be given the wherewithal to continue its functions until the new organization was established. In order to prevent the Russians from appearing as the sole defenders of the cause of the underdog, it was good to press them on this issue and to underline their unwillingness to grant their own citizens human rights — includ-ing freedom from want and fear. Our arguments on refugees were part of this strategy.

If past discussions on the issue had been heated, the debate on the draft constitution of the International Refugee Organization proved to be even more contentious. Every one of the rejected arguments was hauled out again. Finally, the committee members defeated the attempts by the eastern European countries to exclude resettlement operations from the IRO's functions. One clause, however, passed despite Canada's objection, and put all financial contributions for large-scale resettlement on a purely voluntary basis. It removed the obligation for eastern European countries to contribute to the financial re-establishment of the refugees. This omission violated the very principle of international cooperation which the United Nations should strive to attain. The previous month, I had stated in the constitutional committee of the Economic and Social Council that the new refugee organization could not carry out its functions unless all countries helped, and that each state that approved and signed the constitution should do so only if it was prepared to contribute fully — financially and otherwise.

This was the state of things when the matter came up before the third committee. The members of this body rejected a Canadian amendment proposing compulsory financial contributions, despite our best efforts to convince them to the contrary. Nevertheless, we voted in favour of the constitution as it stood; individual countries had to concede on specific points to make any overall progress. Despite our reservations, we thought that the constitution of the IRO, as considered by the third committee, provided the necessary machinery.

The debate in the third committee ran concurrently with discussions on the demise of the United Nations Relief and Rehabilitation Administration, which still had more than 800,000 people, all in Europe, under its care. The members of the General Assembly were worried that UNRRA would cease to function on 31 December 1946 without leaving arrangements for these hapless thousands. Led by Fiorello La Guardia, a number of European countries had tried to secure an acknowledgment that some international agency would continue the services that UNRRA had performed. La Guardia appealed for an emergency fund of $400,000,000 to ease the situation.

By its very nature, the United Nations Relief and Rehabilitation Administration was a vast affair. Yet it had continued to grow, in order first to procure relief supplies, and then to arrange for shipment overseas and their eventual distribution. Britain, for example, wanted to spend the costs incurred by UNRRA's administration, on needy people in the UK. The United States joined the

British and this indicated that the two largest UNRRA contributors were not prepared to accept the burden of continuing this heavy financial responsibility. Supported by Brazil, they had brought forward a resolution that would have placed the granting of relief on a straight two-way basis — donors would deal with recipients directly instead of through a relief organization such as UNRRA. Fiorello La Guardia forthrightly challenged his own government.

Canada, the third-largest contributor to UNRRA, had had ample opportunity to consider the stalemate. As Canada's representative on the second committee, I thought that the nub of the problem lay in the method of meeting the expected relief needs in 1947 and not in the amount of money *per se*. We believed that the central question remained: should the problem be met by the United Nations acting in concert, or by some other arrangement between the granting and the receiving nations?

While Canada understood and supported this position — UNRRA was indeed turning into something of an octopus — we believed that the purposes for which it had been established remained the responsibility of the United Nations. Our delegation felt that the number of countries that funded and supplied UNRRA should be extended in order to lift some of the burden from the very few nations that had contributed the bulk of the relief supplies to date. Every member of the United Nations should be able to make some contribution, however minimal, to the projected relief needs for 1947. Contributing countries often had not proceeded as quickly as they might have done to speed their own recovery.

Mayor La Guardia had often told delegates to the UN that he wanted to speak of tomorrow, not of yesterday. A nice sentiment, I thought to myself, but too simple. I knew that Canada had played an important role in supplying the immediate post-war relief. The extent of that contribution had been made possible by our accumulated agricultural surpluses. For example, Canada's wheat exports in 1943-44 were some sixty million bushels more than that particular year's crop (our reserves of wheat had supplied the rest).

In making our wartime relief effort, we had reduced our reserves to the point where, at the end of the crop year in 1946, they were below the minimum needed to assure a domestic supply of wheat. Canada had increased its agricultural production in order to meet the demands for relief and rehabilitation. Despite this, Canadians still had to endure rationed butter and meat — a sensitive issue for the King government. The department of finance was arguing that our proposed contribution was still too high. In stating our country's position at the United Nations, I had to take into account popular feeling in Canada, which was not unanimously in favour of UNRRA. The country was split between those who felt that we had done all that we could to meet the international relief emergency[14] and those who maintained that we could supply more food and take in more refugees.[15]

In efforts to work out a solution, La Guardia withdrew his proposals for continuing a grandiose relief organization and put forward to the second committee a scheme for an international board with recommendatory powers regarding relief. His statement had great importance for the Canadian delegation; in introducing his own proposal, La Guardia also offered to jettison his plan and accept, "sight unseen," any Canadian solution. Even for those accustomed to the flamboyant Fiorello, this was quite a show, and underlined the impasse that the committee had reached.

Those of us at that early December meeting were sincerely trying to find a means of giving relief to individuals and countries that would require assistance when UNRRA closed up shop. We carried out our discussions in good faith and with a humanitarian regard — most members of the economic committee favoured some form of international relief plan. In order to pave the way to a solution, I repeated that, two weeks earlier, at the outset of the

14 The Gallup Poll (as reported in *The Ottawa Evening Citizen*, 3 November 1946) showed that 64 percent thought we were doing all we could; in Québec, 26 percent felt we were doing too much.
15 Regina, *The Leader Post*, 12 November 1946.

debate on post-UNRRA relief, Canada had not hesitated to express its attitude: our country would participate in any plan that could be agreed upon. In the best of faith, the United States and Britain had decided that they could no longer carry the burden. Canada, Denmark and a few other countries did not wish to see them withdraw; no organization could be international in scope without their support and action. The committee, therefore, had to acknowledge the deadlock and work around it to find a solution.

Once La Guardia had issued his challenge to Canada, our delegation, in consultation with the department of external affairs, worked feverishly to find a solution. We came to the conclusion that we could support the resolution that stood in the name of the United States, the United Kingdom and Brazil, adding a compromise amendment that would, we hoped, provide an interim solution acceptable to both sides. The Canadian government pressed on with its commitment to create an international agency and recognized that this agency would be dangerous to our interest as well as international goals without the membership of the United Kingdom and the United States. If they did not join, the largest contributor would be Canada, and the agency would probably be dominated by the USSR, which would use our resources almost exclusively for relief in eastern Europe.

The Americans originally proposed a resolution recommending that relief supplied by individual countries should be cleared through the United Nations secretary general, but this was not considered adequate to fit in with our belief that aid should be international. Quietly, the Americans indicated that they would support the appointment of a committee of technical experts to investigate and make recommendations. They asked Canada to put this position forward in our amendment to the original American resolution. The amendment empowered the Assembly to establish a technical committee of experts to study the requirements for the essentials of life in countries that needed relief, and to report not later than 15 January 1947 on the amount of financial assistance required in each country, according to the means available in each for financing contributions. Our amendment was accepted by the economic committee, and an accommodation reached. This had the effect of maintaining an international façade after the closing down of UNRRA. Even La Guardia recognized that it was the most that could be obtained under the circumstances.

One of the most sensitive issues of the Assembly concerned the treatment of East Indians settled in the Union of South Africa. The question was brought forward by the government of India, and this began debate on a subject that was to come before the United Nations time and again. Louis St. Laurent was concerned that the UN might be acting beyond its jurisdiction; at a meeting of our delegation, he reminded us that the United Nations was an organization of sovereign states, and their domestic jurisdiction must be respected. Mrs. Pandit, the Indian delegate,[16] indicated her resolve to have the question discussed. I will never forget the support given to her in the General Assembly; as her graceful figure made its way back to her seat, the delegates erupted with applause. It was a sad day for the distinguished South African prime minister, Jan Smuts, when the Assembly clearly expressed its growing resentment of racial discrimination by its cold reception of him and his government's policy, a political creed that we all agreed had no place in the modern world.

In participating in these opening sessions of the United Nations, I was aware that the international climate was one of contest. This mood, however, did not deflect Canada's support from the new international organization. I felt privileged to be the country's

16 Vijaya Pandit, Nehru's sister, was later India's ambassador to both the USSR and the USA. She was president of the UN General Assembly 1953-54.

voice as the organization took up its essential task of building and maintaining peace. The founding nations had established a structure for international collaboration within a year of ending a world war. Problems posed by the vast number of refugees and the millions of people in need of food presented the nations of the world with a challenge that had to be met. Today, it is hard to imagine the significance that issues like this had at the time. Canada's role in these two matters was as great as any that we had ever been called on to assume.

As we left New York, representatives of three parties assessed the scene. John Bracken described the Assembly as "staggering along slowly."[17] M. J. Coldwell thought that the session had yielded a surprising amount of unanimity and gave cause for optimism. I was the most sanguine of all, saying that more progress was made than I had expected.[18] This was not idealism on my part; I knew that the years ahead would test the will to succeed of member nations. We were, after all, groping our way out of the wilderness of unrestricted national sovereignty and of the chaos left by war. The beginning of the cold war — the split between East and West— would, we all knew, make the task even more difficult. We may have been moving slowly but this was preferable to rushing headlong into inevitable disaster.

17 *The Globe and Mail*, 15 November 1946.
18 *Winnipeg Free Press*, 16 December 1946.

XIV

Sitting in State

F ROM THE DESK OF the secretary of state — once used, rumour had it, by John A. Macdonald — I carried out my ministerial duties. My office, an enormous one on the west side of the West Block, dwarfed the furniture as well as the occupant.[1] From the window, I could look out at the Gatineau Hills, and sometimes would imagine that I could even see the clock tower at St. Alexandre.

Certain governments and parliamentarians stand out at particular times and the cabinet that I joined in 1945 is acknowledged to be one of the best in Canadian history. The impression a government makes on a generation depends on many factors; leadership is perhaps paramount. For all his deficiencies, Mackenzie King was a great prime minister. He knew how to direct his cabinet and

---

1 The department's staff were in various buildings on both sides of the Ottawa River. The West Block housed three branches: corporations, naturalization and honours; the King's Printer was in Hull, while the Custodian of Enemy Alien Property, the Civil Service Commission, and the Registrar of Bankruptcy were in downtown Ottawa office buildings.

how to delegate responsibility. The four prime ministers in whose cabinets I was privileged to serve were able and dedicated men, but the strength of their respective governments often depended on the public's impression of individual ministers. Prime ministers rarely interfere in departmental operations. King's ministers were supreme in their departments; the public servants occupied an important but secondary role and acted accordingly. This created the impression that the cabinet was comprised of individuals chosen for their experience and presumed competence.

Successful government should highlight the role of ministers selected democratically by the people. It is my belief that an administration should reflect the lead given by all ministers, supported by strong public servants whose advisory role is to supplement the efforts of those elected to govern. If some ministers lose much of their influence and create bad impressions, it is because their role has so often been assumed by bureaucrats — specialists in particular fields. I have seen many ministers lose rank in cabinet committees because of the over-participation of some of their senior public servants. It is not for the public servant to govern or to appear to govern. *That* is the job of those chosen by the people.

Right after taking over as secretary of state, I lost no time in learning about the department and its functions. Because cabinet met only once a week, ministers were not saddled with committee meetings and were, therefore, able to spend a lot of time in their departments, mastering their portfolios. The secretary of state held responsibility for the Civil Service Commission, the Custodian of Enemy Property and the Registrar of Bankruptcy. I was not the Civil Service Commission's administrative chief but its channel for reporting to cabinet and to parliament on policies and functions, such as wage and salary levels, and hours of work. The King's Printer and the Public Archives reported to the secretary of state as did the branch which looked after the incorporation of companies under Dominion charter. In addition to this, at the end of the war, the department acquired the naturalization branch of the department of national war services.

I soon became familiar with most of the staff in the department and knew many of them by their first names. Although I was close to all senior civil servants, I did not hesitate to bypass heads of divisions and occasionally would phone the junior officers responsible for doing the legwork on a particular issue that had caught my attention. Sometimes the top bureaucrats, particularly when I was secretary of state for external affairs in the 1960s, feeling that I was undermining their position, would express their displeasure; but I always insisted that it was the minister's privilege to consult any of his officers, at any time. I think that my rapport with all the departments in which I served was in large measure due to an effort to make all those under me feel that they were part of a team. The chain of command is an important principle to observe, but a department of government is not a military or an episcopal organization. Valuable opinions can come from the bottom as well as from the top. Too great a reliance on rank and proper channels can hinder a minister — or a bureaucrat — from getting to the heart of an issue.

In order to function effectively, a minister has to learn to organize his time. The first thing I did when I got to my office in the morning was to call in my private secretary and a stenographer. The three of us would then plan the day. Naturally, most of my time had been allocated well in advance, but I would fit in extra appointments between those already set up for me. As we went through the letters, I would say yes or no to particular ones and leave my staff with the responsibility of drafting the replies, which I would read and sign later. I saw the deputy minister at ten o'clock as the first formal business of the day. There was a regular cabinet meeting on Thursdays, and the caucus met on Wednesday. As a junior minister, I was asked to sit on what was called "the council"; every week, with the other five or so members, I tediously passed routine orders-in-council that were not always put before the full cabinet.[2]

The members of the House of Commons are quick to test a neophyte cabinet member, and I quickly learned the need to be fast on my feet. The first time I shepherded some minor matters through the House and was discussing the increases required by the King's Printer, I had made my presentation, but the opposition, anxiously trying to rattle me, vigorously contradicted my statement. To my horror, Ian Mackenzie, the minister of veterans' affairs and acting House leader, stood up, took issue with what I said, and proceeded to give an explanation which was perfectly ridiculous. Obviously, he had been lifting a few glasses with his friends. With a great sense of fair play, the members of the House of Commons understood the difficulty of my position and passed the item quickly.[3]

Besides my ministerial duties and work on the Hill, I was called upon to make speeches and attend functions away from the capital. Much of my activity outside Ottawa, particularly on public platforms, not only provided information about the work of the department; it also helped to form opinion and to arouse public interest in matters that I hoped the cabinet would adopt. This proselytizing proved particularly necessary when I was minister of national health and welfare. Despite my schedule, it was a rare weekend that I did not get back to the constituency.

The first of July 1946 marked the end of one of the most unenviable tasks that I had to carry out as secretary of state. Cabinet had decided that, on that day, the king would announce the civilian

2 This was in the days before a fully-developed committee system took over the functions of this smaller committee. In May 1946, I was also made convenor of the cabinet committee of advertising.
3 The Hansard account of this has been edited (House of Commons, *Debates*, 5 July 1946, p. 3187).

honours list granting various British awards to those who had contributed significantly to Canada's war effort. It was impossible to satisfy everyone who felt that he or she deserved an award. To try to extricate myself, if only partially, from this delicate position, I had insisted that the cabinet should decide on the basic principle of selection — no exception permitted. The matter was reviewed several times in late March and early April 1945, and my colleagues agreed to supply me with lists of recommendations.

An awards coordination committee, headed by Dr. E. H. Coleman, the undersecretary of state, examined the names to avoid disparities in the method of selection and to enforce standards; preference was given to voluntary unpaid service. Dr. Coleman knew how sensitive this subject could be and, therefore, we laid down criteria and a committee of civil servants prepared the recommendations. Coleman further warned me about accepting any suggestions from my colleagues in the House. All proposals were to be sent to him; they were then considered at a special cabinet meeting on 13 June.[4]

Since no civilian honours had been conferred since 1943 (the United Kingdom had been asked not to include Canadians on its honours lists), the task was herculean. We also decided to supplement the ministerial list with names provided by other agencies, such as the Wartime Prices and Trade Board, the National War Finance Committee, the National Research Council, and voluntary agencies recommended by the minister of national war services. Something in the neighbourhood of 1100 names were to go forward.

Although my colleagues had accepted the guidelines, a few appeared to honour the criteria more in the breach than in the observance when it came to enforcing them. Even the prime minister urged me to add a name to the list; it did not conform to the accepted categories, and I reminded him of this.

---

4 Cabinet Conclusions, 21 March 1946, W. L. Mackenzie King Papers (J4 series, vol. 419), PAC.

Vincent Massey had often spoken regretfully to me about the non-existence of a system of Canadian honours; he wanted to emulate the British honours list. Now that I was secretary of state, Massey was eager to convert me to his opinion and when I was in London at the United Nations General Assembly, he took the matter in hand and arranged for me to accompany him to the College of Heralds and to the office where all orders, decorations and medals were on display. I recognized that there might be a place for honours, but our course of action since 1919, when titles were abolished in Canada, caused me to believe that it would be a mistake to revert to granting them and other lofty British honours to Canadians.[5] However, I felt that investitures for members of the military services deserved to be continued.

The question was intensely personal for Massey. On 22 May, the acting prime minister, J. L. Ilsley, received word from Mackenzie King in London, asking him to approve George VI's request to confer the Companion of Honour on Vincent Massey, who was retiring as high commissioner to the Court of St. James. This would be an exception to the normal rule of not allowing public servants to accept such high honours from the monarch. Knowing that it was very important to Massey, I facilitated government approval and he gained his coveted award.

The honours question has always been a contentious one in Canada. Mackenzie King was so bothered by the issue that he refused to proceed with the creation of a Canadian system of awards. When John Diefenbaker was visiting me in London in the 1970s to receive the Companion of Honour from Queen Elizabeth II, he referred to the Companion of the Order of Canada as the "Cuckoo" award, compared to his C.H. A reporter overheard his comment and exclaimed, "Oh, Mr. Diefenbaker! How can you say that when Paul Martin received that recognition only a few

5 R. B. Bennett revived the practice of granting titles during his term as prime minister from 1930 to 1935. Mackenzie King reverted to the abolition when he gained office in 1935.

days ago?" Thinking quickly, Diefenbaker retorted, "*He* is the only one to have deserved it."

Although I was pleased to receive the Order of Canada, I have always been proud of not having any other personal honours. My unembellished suit distinguished me on most formal occasions. Once, at dinner at the Soviet Embassy in London, I was taken for a waiter — the only other formally dressed man in the room who was not sporting a chestful of medals.

During the time that I was enmeshed in the working out of the honours list, I was also preparing the first piece of legislation I would introduce as a minister — a Citizenship Act. The drafting of this bill made me aware for the first time as a minister of the need to establish my independence from bureaucratic advisors. My deputy, Dr. E. H. Coleman, belonged to the old school of empire and was opposed in principle to the enactment of such a measure. Although he helped me as best he could, I went elsewhere to find the support and knowledge I needed to draw up the legislation. One of the most helpful individuals to new ministers was Arnold Heeney, the clerk of the privy council. Often, I would go to him if I were making a submission to cabinet and discuss the best means of bringing it forward. This was particularly the case at the beginning, until I got used to the routine.

Immediately after my appointment, I set the wheels in motion on a project that had come to mind when I was visiting the military cemetery at Dieppe. There, pondering the status of those who had served their country and had died overseas, the desirability of establishing a separate Canadian citizenship took hold of me. During the war, I had mentioned the need of such legislation,[6] but my visit to Normandy turned this thought into a crusade.

6 On 4 May 1942, I mentioned in the committee on the defence of Canada regulations that Canada's naturalization laws were in a deplorable state.

Mackenzie King had demonstrated considerable enthusiasm for a citizenship act when I first mentioned it to him during the election campaign. I could see that I had struck a sympathetic chord, as I talked to him about my experiences at Dieppe and my conviction that it was essential to incorporate into law a definition of what constituted a Canadian. In my own mind, and I am certain in the prime minister's, this piece of legislation fitted in with Laurier's vision of a separate Canadian nation. At the end of the war, the best sort of nationalist feeling pressed us forward. King forthrightly referred to citizenship in a speech from Winnipeg and I brought the subject up again shortly after the votes had been counted. Once I had explained to him that the features I proposed required a knowledge of nationality laws that was beyond the experience of my departmental officials, the prime minister offered to provide whatever assistance I needed. It was no reflection on them; naturalization practice was based on the jurisprudence (with which they were unfamiliar) of long-established procedures applicable to the dominions and to the United Kingdom.

I discovered that while he had been at Oxford, Gordon Robertson, of the prime minister's office — later an outstanding clerk of the privy council and secretary to the cabinet — had studied the whole range of nationality laws in and outside the commonwealth and empire. I had already talked to him and found his knowledge of the greatest value in helping me develop my plan. In spite of King's offer to help me, he replied to my request for Robertson's services by expostulating, "Robertson! *He* won't be able to help you." This, I knew was a device to discourage my temporary use of one of the most intelligent men on King's staff. In the end, however, the prime minister consented and Gordon was grudgingly lent to me. Thus it was that Robertson and David Mundell of the department of justice, as well as representatives from external affairs, the department of immigration and the privy council, set up a committee to study the question of citizenship throughout the summer of 1945.

Many years later, in 1963-64, Gordon helped me during the very difficult Columbia River negotiations with Premier

W. A. C. Bennett. He displayed an amazing grasp of extremely complicated matters and impressed the unsmiling and frustrated premier. At one point, when Bennett was particularly hostile because he had not fully understood the federal government's position, I asked Gordon to intervene. This he did at great length and with his customary erudition. When he had finished, I repeated Mackenzie King's deliberately ridiculous remark to the effect that Robertson would be of no help. It broke the ice; Bennett laughed, and we soon reached a settlement.

There was no such thing in law as a Canadian citizen; the terms then most frequently in use were "Canadian national" and "British subject." For some time, ambiguities in the three acts that dealt with citizenship caused trouble. The Naturalization Act of 1914 sought to provide for the application of extra-territorial powers in order to give naturalized British subjects in Canada the right to be designated Canadians abroad as well as at home. It followed earlier acts that had existed since shortly after 1867. In 1921, C. J. Doherty, the secretary of state, introduced the Canadian Nationals Act that met Canada's commitments to the League of Nations in order to permit Canada to become eligible for election to the International Court of Justice — admirable but very limited purposes. Furthermore, this act defined Canadian citizenship only by reference. There was an unrelated but existing definition in the Immigration Act of 1910 which set out who was permitted to enter and to live in Canada. Few countries established citizenship by an immigration act; and even the definition in this act was circumscribed and determined citizenship only for immigration purposes. The complications of the three statutes left some individuals who lived in Canada without any nationality or with a nationality in one part of the commonwealth but not according to Canadian law. This should have been remedied years before.

Throughout World War II, the adult education movement in Canada had sponsored various programs to make Canadians aware of their distinctive identity. These courses had been devised mainly for immigrants, but there was a great general interest in "citizenship education," not just for those who had moved to Canada but also for the millions who had been born here. The wartime Bureau of Public Information had established the Canadian Council of Education for Citizenship, which eventually led to the formation of the citizenship branch of the department of national war services.

Those interested in citizenship education, as well as nationalists who wanted to remove the vestiges of the colonial past, provided public backing for my proposal. Late in August, T. S. Ewart, a lawyer, supported the case for action, in an impassioned letter published in the *Ottawa Citizen*. He deplored the fact that Canadians lived under statutes that provided for the designation "British" on registration of births, marriages and deaths; and were described as "British subjects" on their passports. "These stupid regulations," Ewart fulminated, "are caused by the inability to recognize the change in status of our country from that of a colony. . . . [to an independent nation]." I agreed and was determined that there should no longer be any question of divided allegiance.

On 4 September 1945, cabinet considered draft legislation that would repeal the Canadian Nationals Act and certain provisions of the Immigration Act under a new bill that would also redefine the status of Canadian citizens, British subjects in Canada, and aliens. One provision would give a married woman the same right to choose her nationality as her husband and, when adopted, this made Canada the first nation in the commonwealth to recognize the separate and independent status of women.[7]

After I had made my presentation, King remarked that an act based on these proposals would remove any apparent lack of equal status Canada might have had when compared to other independent nations. While I agreed with King's desire, I could not support his conclusions at all; in my view it was juridically incorrect. After all, Britain and other sovereign commonwealth states, with the exception of the Irish republic, had no separate citizenship status. Canadians were, and under the bill would continue to be, British

7 Cabinet Conclusions, 5 April 1945, King Papers (J4 series, vol. 419), PAC.

subjects. Citizenship, as I saw it, would give all Canadians a common status. The cabinet accepted the report, and later that day I drafted a paragraph for inclusion in the speech from the throne that would proclaim the government's intention to proceed with the bill.[8]

Four days after the opening of parliament on 6 September, I gave the legislation advance publicity in my speech on the address. Symbols, I told the House, were important to a nation, and the government's decision to clarify and regularize the status of Canadian citizenship constituted a major feat. Our membership in the family of nations had been recognized; we had won our certificate of nationhood; it now remained to designate ourselves citizens of our country, not only in fact but in legal enactment.[9]

For a time in early October, it looked as though the introduction of the bill might be delayed; cabinet decided on 10 October to defer placing the new bill on the order paper.[10] It was obvious that many of my colleagues had other priorities. As in my very first years in parliament, those from prairie constituencies were preoccupied with wheat sales and price stability. I, too, was so caught up with other things — especially the strike of the Ford workers in Windsor — that I may not have been as forceful in promoting the measure as I could have been.

However, the same day that cabinet decided to defer the bill, the CCF's G. H. Castleden prodded the government by moving that the House of Commons should express its favourable view of measures to establish citizenship legislation. Nevertheless, he indicated that he would not proceed with his motion if I gave an assurance that my proposals would be put before the House. When I gave this undertaking, Castleden dropped his motion and, a week later, cabinet approved the bill for introduction.

I unveiled my most important initiative as secretary of state on 22 October when I moved for leave to present bill 20, respecting

---

8 I spoke immediately after Mackenzie King.
9 House of Commons, *Debates*, 10 September 1945, pp. 59-64.
10 Cabinet Conclusions, 10 October 1945, King Papers (J4 series, vol. 419), PAC.

citizenship, naturalization and the status of aliens. The purpose of the bill, I told the House, was to remove the anomalies and confusions that had surrounded the old legislation and to create a new status of Canadian citizen that would neither take away from anyone who now had it nor eliminate for persons born or naturalized in the future, the status of British subject. It was "of the utmost importance that all of us, new Canadians or old, have a consciousness of a common purpose and common interests as Canadians."[11]

To my disappointment, the bill was allowed to die on the order paper at the end of the session and had to be reintroduced in 1946. The opposition reasonably requested time to digest the complicated provisions affecting Canada's relations with the commonwealth. The whole government legislative program had bogged down, and the House was very far behind in discussing government business. Another reason was that Mackenzie King was in Britain at the prime ministers' conference, and I wanted him to be in the House when the bill was debated.

The bill's postponement gave me time to speak extensively on the subject and to promote it through newspaper articles. Grant Dexter of the *Winnipeg Free Press* published a series of five articles outlining the benefits of the legislation and generally educating the public about its scope and intent. "The old order," wrote Dexter, "has been allowed to drag along until the present time."[12]

A considerable amount of time and energy in my department was taken up with the question of a new Canadian flag to replace the Union Jack. Originally, Jack Pickersgill had prophesied that the adoption of a new flag, if it were the Red Ensign, would unite the Liberals and divide the Tories.[13] The announcement in the speech from the throne that the government wished to pursue the issue

11 House of Commons, *Debates*, 22 October 1945, pp. 1,335-37.
12 *Winnipeg Free Press*, 22 March 1946; ibid., 23 March 1946; ibid., 25 March 1946; 26 March 1946; 27 March 1946.
13 Pickersgill to King, 7 August 1945, ibid. (J4 series, p. C1612047) PAC.
     to fly a distinctive Canadian flag."

opened the floodgates.[14] There was considerable support, however grudging, even from such groups as the Imperial Order of the Daughters of the Empire, who basically opposed any change from the Union Jack. Some Toronto MPs, however, went to considerable lengths to stir up the holy war to "Stand by the Flag," that *The Sentinel*, the newspaper of the Orange Order, proclaimed. My department was deluged with flag designs by the thousand sent from across the country. Some designs were very strange: one showed a staring eye on a yellow star with a background of purple; another depicted stampeding black buffalo. The colour combinations startled the eye — even those that portrayed more traditional symbols, such as coats of arms, beavers, crowns or maple leaves.

Interest and emotions ran so high that Mackenzie King decided to appoint a joint committee of the Senate and of the House of Commons to study the question and to make recommendations. The debate that followed the motion of acting prime minister, Jim Ilsley, to appoint the committee, showed how strongly everyone felt about the flag. Ian Mackenzie, the minister of veterans' affairs, spoke of the need for a Canadian flag; it was, he declared, a debt to our soldiers in two world wars as well as a symbol of our status. G. R. Pearkes, the Conservative member for Nanaimo and a former army general, agreed that the Union Jack had not met all Canadian requirements and argued that the flag to adopt was the Red Ensign that had been carried in both world wars. M. J. Coldwell urged the committee to take its time so that the most distinctive design would be chosen, while T. L. Church, the Tory member for Toronto Broadview, did not want to abandon the Union Jack.[15] On 14 November, the House overwhelmingly agreed to establish the committee; Senator Norman Lambert and

14 P. C. 5888, 5 September 1945, had authorized that "until such time as action is taken by parliament for the formal adoption of a national flag, it is desirable to authorize the flying of the Canadian Red Ensign on Federal government buildings within as well as without Canada, and to remove any doubt as to the propriety of flying the Canadian Red Ensign wherever place or occasion may make it desirable to fly a distinctive Canadian flag.

15 House of Commons, *Debates*, 13 November 1945, pp. 2,084 ff.

Walter Harris, MP for Gray-Bruce, were made joint chairmen. We all knew that the issue had become so controversial that the real task of the joint committee was to allow the situation to cool down.

The promotion of a new flag and the citizenship legislation were not expressions of a narrow nationalism but were understandable demonstrations of pride in Canada and its growing autonomy. Nationalism as an expression of communal bonds I did not feel was a danger, but I did fear the exaggeration of that consciousness; the recent memory of Nazism was a great corrective to chauvinism. It was my belief that there had been too little and not too much national pride. By working to strengthen it further, we were not weakening our ties with the commonwealth or with Britain. In fact, compared to the pre-war years, I thought that Canada was becoming more outward-looking and would be better fitted to play its full part in the world if Canadians had a sense of community expressed by appropriate symbols.

These were the ideas in my mind when I appeared before the committee in early December. Tracing the history of flags in Canada, I noted that the Red Ensign — which had the Union Jack in the upper left-hand corner and the shield of Canada in its centre — had been authorized for use in 1869 for Canadian ships other than naval and government vessels. For lack of another flag, it had been flown from many official buildings and had always indicated the presence of the prime minister at international gatherings. The campaign for a distinctive Canadian flag, I noted, had begun after the Great War and had resulted in various efforts by the government to select a design. Privately, I realized quickly that there was little likelihood of success this time around. Little did I foresee that it would be two decades before the debate would be over — and that it would be conducted in almost as acrimonious a manner as in 1945.

Of course, my work on the flag and on citizenship legislation did not mean that the department's other responsibilities looked after themselves. Items that came before me as secretary of state ranged from state visits to recommending the reversion to standard time. As the guns boomed and the bells peeled out, I handed the Great Seal of Canada to the new governor general, Lord Alexander of Tunis, at his installation on 12 April 1946. Very concerned about the proper preservation of government records, I put forward proposals for their conservation. As the Custodian of Enemy Alien Property, I found myself in a rather peculiar situation. Diverse types of assets seized from enemy aliens came into my hands, including a circus in the Maritimes. For several months, the department operated it at a profit and, when winter came along, sold off the animals.

My responsibilities for "working conditions" for the public service also included those for lieutenant governors, who generally felt they were underpaid. On a less exalted level, I made myself a popular man with public servants by lopping off their day the extra half-hour added throughout the war, and by making certain that no political appointees served on the Civil Service Commission, which for the first time was composed only of public servants.[16] One noon hour, I ambled along to a government cafeteria, looked around and sat down with two junior stenographers while I ate my lunch. Overhearing the chatter about grievances and working conditions in the government, I explained that my observations in Windsor had shown me the importance of good employer-employee relations.

The parliamentary session that opened in the middle of March 1946 provided an opportunity to expand upon the importance of citizenship as an expression of the Canadian ideal for which Laurier had striven. Using this theme in moving second reading of the citizenship bill, reintroduced early in the session,[17] I told the House

16 Cabinet Conclusions, 19 September 1945, King Papers (J4 series, vol. 419), PAC; Cabinet Conclusions, 14 April 1946, ibid.; Ottawa, *The Evening Citizen*, 5 October 1945; ibid., 8 October 1945.
17 House of Commons, *Debates*, 20 March 1946, p. 131, for the introduction of the bill for first reading. The motion for second reading was made on 2 April (ibid., pp.

of Commons that the measure demonstrated the maturing of Canada as a nation. In two world wars, we had borne our full and serious responsibility; our fighting men had brought honour to their country. For the unity of the country and for the fulfilment of its potential, it was of the utmost importance that Canada should give its people the right to designate themselves Canadian citizens in law as well as in fact. Previous efforts had not been successful — notably the citizenship bill introduced in 1931 by C. H. Cahan, the secretary of state in R. B. Bennett's government; I was determined to rectify that failure. It was not to our credit that Canadians could not address one another with the full sanction of the law as citizens of our country.

The citizenship bill would eliminate difficult personal situations where the wife of a Canadian citizen or a person born out of Canada whose father was a national at the time of birth had trouble entering the country. There was also the problem of the prohibited immigrant to Canada; a person who could not enter Canada under the Immigration Act, yet was entitled to a Canadian passport. It would remove the vagueness and, in some instances, the lack of a legal basis for determining nationality. The proposed act also would get rid of difficulties encountered by the department of external affairs arising out of the need for diplomatic protection for Canadians and Canadian interests abroad.

One of the bill's major aims was to provide for "a more effective and impressive ceremony of admission into the Canadian family." Our citizens, I reminded the House, were made up not only of those who were familiar with British institutions but also

> . . . of many thousands of new Canadians living in all parts of the country who have a notable contribution to the development of Canada. There are people who came from many parts of Central Europe and who are now living and working as Canadians on our farms and in our factories. Many of those people came here without

---

502-17) and the House went into committee to study the bill on 29 April (ibid., pp. 1,015-39; ibid.,2 May, pp. 1,114-64; ibid., 3 May, pp. 1,198-1,214; ibid., 7 May, pp. 1,309-14; ibid., 13 May, pp. 1,470-91, and ibid., 14 May, 1,499-1,509). The motion for third reading was introduced on 15-16 May (ibid., pp. 1,575-91).

being able to speak the two languages of the country and without being accustomed to its traditions. Most of them have rendered notable service to Canada. We should not lose the opportunity of . . . reminding them that just as we are glad to welcome them to our shore, now that they are here they should enjoy with us the full measure of partnership in the Canadian community.

An appropriate ceremony would make the adoption of citizenship more than an ordinary procedure.

The act had seven sections. The first dealt with those who were born in Canada, on Canadian ships or to Canadian parents domiciled abroad; it defined them as Canadian citizens by right of birth. Part II of the bill concerned those who were not born Canadian but who acquired citizenship at a later stage; it provided that people who had been naturalized in Canada, non-Canadian British subjects who had lived in Canada for five years or more, and non-Canadian women who had married citizens and come to live in Canada — all would become citizens forthwith. It also set out the qualifications for those who would acquire citizenship in the future under conditions that resembled those in the Naturalization Act, except that non-nationals who served abroad in the armed forces would require only one year of residence in the country instead of five. Those who wanted citizenship would have to file a declaration of intention not less than one year and not more than five years before naturalization. The bill also substituted twenty years of residence for a knowledge of English or French (this would allow many long-time residents — from eastern Europe, for example — to gain citizenship). British subjects, who hitherto had been able to become Canadian citizens simply after five years' residence, would still have that privilege but would have to take out papers to prove it (This was a change more in procedure than in substance, since non-Canadian British subjects had no right of entry under the old act until they had been domiciled in Canada for five years). Married women would have the right to choose their own citizenship.

The rest of the bill dealt with various other proposals, such as loss of citizenship, that might occur after the acquisition of a foreign nationality. Canadian citizens would retain their status as British subjects. Under the new act, those who were British subjects in other parts of the commonwealth would be recognized as British subjects in Canada. The act, in short, was designed to guarantee that no one would lose any rights or status he or she already possessed.

In summary, I pointed out that "for a young nation, Canada has done great things and Canadians have derived a growing national pride from what Canada has accomplished. We feel that . . . we can afford to hold our heads high and be proud of the fact that we are Canadians." If there was:

> . . . one thing from which we in Canada have suffered, to the detriment of this magnificent country, it is from a feeling of divisiveness — lack of that fervent and urgent unity that can make a people work together as a great community with conviction that the welfare of all is the goal of their effort. It is not good enough to be a good "Bluenose" or a good Ontarian or a good Albertan. Sectional differences and sectional interests must be overcome if we are to do our best for Canada. The only way this can be done is through encouraging a feeling of legitimate Canadianism . . .
>
> Citizenship means more than the right to vote; more than the right to hold and transfer property; more than the right to move freely under the protection of the state; citizenship is the right to full partnership in the fortunes and in the future of the nation.[18]

John Diefenbaker, the first speaker for the Conservative Party, agreed with what I had said, particularly with my claim that the bill symbolized our aspirations as a nation. He added that it had achieved a lifelong dream of his. However, he proposed that, a citizenship act should be followed by a bill of rights. Diefenbaker criticized that section of the bill requiring a British subject from commonwealth countries to file a notice of intention with the citizenship court in the same way as others before becoming a citizen. Would, he asked, this provision not strike at the unity of British citizenship? I said that it would not.

18 House of Commons, *Debates*, 2 April 1946, pp. 502-10.

The House divided on the bill much as I had expected. A substantial number of members worried that commonwealth relationships would deteriorate in the wake of the act. Diefenbaker's unjustified objection that it would split the commonwealth was taken even further by his colleagues such as Tommy Church, an old-style imperialist, who took a determined stand against it. On the other hand, Liguori Lacombe, MP for Laval-Deux-Montagnes, expressed the French nationalist position that urged the elimination of Canadians' status as British subjects in order to eradicate all evidence of inferiority.

The reaction of these two extremes proved beyond a doubt that the bill was a careful balance of opinion expressed in terms that accommodated the general wish for a separate Canadian citizenship. For my part, I would have preferred to leave out the section of the bill that stated that Canadians remained British subjects[19] — it left Canada with a mark of inferiority. However, I recognized that if Canadians' status as British subjects had been done away with, the bill would not have passed. The compromise in the bill was a very wise one and ensured the passage of a measure that could not and did not seek to placate the extremists.

We thrashed out this compromise in cabinet because my colleagues themselves were of two minds about including the provision regarding British subjects. Finally, it was left for Mackenzie King and me to decide. The prime minister agreed with my political instincts when I said that if we omitted mention of the question of British subjects entirely, and just created Canadian citizenship, we would not avoid the issue. Someone, I argued, would be bound to ask about the legislation's effect on Canadians' status as British subjects. An offhand response to this question, saying that the bill left us British subjects by default, would not satisfy anyone. We could, I thought, take the wind out of the Tories' sails by including a bold statement in the bill itself. And this is what we did.

---

19 In subsequent legislation, this was corrected when the status "British subjects" was removed from the enactment.

The Globe and Mail still complained that it was unreasonable to force a British subject to live in Canada for five years before taking out citizenship. I had already bowed to the opposition and removed the bill's provision that like everyone else British subjects had to be examined before a citizenship court. Instead, they were allowed to apply to the secretary of state for a certificate after fulfiling their residence requirement. Almost without exception, French-language newspapers supported the bill and severely castigated the Tories' carping attitude. My compromise, however, gave me the general support of Conservative papers like *The Globe and Mail*.[20] There was, I realized, little to be done about the hidebound opposition from true-blue imperialists who objected to classing "Britons" with "Slavs" and who railed against the bill as another example of French Canada forcing its will upon the rest of the country.[21] Equally adamant, *Le Devoir* claimed that "la double allégeance que ça soit envers le Canada et l'Empire, . . . c'est la négation même de la citoyenneté canadienne et encore plus du patriotisme canadien."[22]

During the debate on second reading,[23] Diefenbaker reopened the question of a bill of rights and offered an amendment to the effect that a certificate of citizenship should be deemed to include certain rights (freedom of religion, freedom of speech, and the right to peaceable assembly; no suspension of *habeas corpus* except by parliament, and no compulsion to give evidence before any tribunal in the absence of counsel or other safeguards). This amendment, I argued, was unacceptable, since already the law of the land included these rights in the common law, the Magna Carta, and the legal system. No act of one parliament could limit the freedom of action of its successors, and infringements of rights could be taken pursuant to the authority of any parliament. Therefore, the only means of providing greater guarantees than

20 *The Globe and Mail*, 5 April 1946.
21 *Toronto Telegram*, 6 April 1946.
22 *Le Devoir*, 7 December 1945.
23 The discussion on second reading continued in the House from 2 April until the end of the month. See footnote 18 for all reference to the debate.

currently existed would be to enact an organic law that could not be changed by the Canadian parliament; this type of law did not exist in the British system of government. In the American constitution, there is a declaration of rights that arose as the testament of revolution, but a bill of rights for Canadians must differ widely in concept and implementation. The British system, as Tennyson said, was that for:

> *A land of settled government,*
> *A land of just and old renown,*
> *Where freedom slowly broadens down*
> *From precedent to precedent.*

A fundamental constitutional departure, I contended, should not be taken in a section of an act that prescribes conditions for the issuance of citizenship certificates; if anywhere, it should be in a bill by itself.

Diefenbaker's argument, however, gained considerable public support. *The Globe and Mail* claimed that, "parliament has permitted, without any serious protests, the steady infringement of the rights which belong to all Canadians."[24]

On 14 May, when this historic bill was reported back to the House from the comittee of the whole, I thanked the members for their contributions and cooperation. The CCF leader, M. J. Coldwell, spoke appreciatively of my handling of a difficult measure. I also thanked Mackenzie King for the assistance of Gordon Robertson, who had continued as my chief assistant during the bill's passage through the House. It became an act by royal assent on 27 June and was proclaimed by the govenor general on 1 July 1946.

Despite the new ground broken for the commonwealth countries by the Canadian Citizenship Act — except for the Republic of Ireland, they had scant legislation on the subject — those who believed that the act conferred little benefit reacted adversely.

---

24 *The Globe and Mail*, 10 May 1946. The *Winnipeg Free Press*, 20 May 1946, supported this argument.

Some argued that my French-Canadian outlook had provoked me into introducing a bill that would divide Canada completely from Britain. This argument even made its way into the New Zealand parliament, where the attorney general, H. R. G. Mason, concluded that the act was an indication of a spirit of separateness by the French-speaking Canadian population that could not be controlled. He and others who felt this way totally misinterpreted my motives.

With great pride, I took part in the ceremonies in the august chambers of the Supreme Court of Canada to mark the new status of Canadians. These took place during Citizenship Week on the night of 3 January 1947, two days after the new act had come into force. Under the solemn eyes of the chief justice and his brother judges, resplendent in their ermine-trimmed robes, people from various parts of Canada received the first citizenship certificates. After my opening remarks about the significance of the act as a symbol of the achievement of nationhood, Mackenzie King received the very first certificate. It pleased the prime minister greatly when the audience applauded as he began, "I speak as a citizen of Canada."[25] Wasyl Elnyiak, the first Ukrainian to farm in western Canada, received his certificate immediately after the prime minister. Elnyiak was a very old man and came to the ceremony only after a great deal of arm-twisting. We had discovered him after a long search through the immigration department's records. Only once during the ceremony did the applause equal that given to the prime minister. The audience was acknowledging Mrs. Stanley Mynarski of Winnipeg who went forward with the Victoria Cross of her son pinned to her dress. King stood up and bowed to her as she passed near his chair.[26] The presence of

25 J. W. Pickersgill and D. F. Forster, *The Mackenzie King Record*, IV, *1947-1948* (Toronto: University of Toronto Press, 1970), pp. 5-6.
26 The others were Giuseppe Agostini, a conductor for the CBC; Kjeld Beichman, a Danish-born potter from New Brunswick; Maurice Labrosse of Ottawa and his Aberdeenshire bride; Yousuf Karsh, the famous photographer; Mrs. R. P. Steeves of Vancouver; Gerhard Ens of Rosthern, Saskatchewan, and Andrew B.MacRae, a descendant of one of the oldest families in Prince Edward Island.

the recipients of the certificates brought home the symbolism of the ceremony to those in the room, as well as to those listening in on the national broadcast of the proceedings.

Another major ceremony took place in the large rotunda of Montreal's Hôtel de Ville on 8 January 1946. Mayor Camilien Houde had gone out of his way to cooperate, and what he organized was impressive. Over a thousand citizens assembled to witness the chief justice of the Québec Superior court present certificates to the mayor and to others who represented the city of Montreal and the province of Québec. My speech tried to answer those who did not like the provision that Canadians would remain British subjects, and I spoke positively about national pride while deprecating fanatical racism and nationalism.

There was an unfortunate side effect to the Montreal ceremony. Because he had stirred up illegal opposition to the registration of manpower in 1940, Mayor Houde had spent most of the war in an internment camp, and some individuals and newspapers, questioned his receiving the first certificate handed out in Québec. The man who was the most upset, however, was Louis St. Laurent, who felt that he ought to have been given the first certificate. St. Laurent was very hurt about it and he told me so in no uncertian manner. I agreed with him and told him I regretted the choice but there was little that could be done; no other federal politician had received the first certificate in his home province. Although Louis St. Laurent and I often disagreed on policy matters, this was the only time we had any incident that bordered on the personal. It upset me quite a bit.

Two days later, I received my own certificate of citizenship from Judge Albert Gordon at a gathering in Patterson Collegiate in Windsor. I recalled in my remarks that during my visit to the cemetery at Dieppe, I had formulated a desire to recognize the common sacrifice of those who lay there. The lads from the Essex Scottish who rest in the cemetery at Dieppe and the thousands of others who sleep in military cemeteries on several continents symbolize Canada, and this legislation, which affirms our common national condition, was enacted to honour their memory.

XV

Far From Home

MY PARTICIPATION IN the various citizenship ceremonies was something of an anomaly, for I was no longer secretary of state.[1] But the prime minister had asked me to look after these functions because I had been committed to a citizenship act since my pilgrimage to Dieppe.

After the 1945 election, the prime minister had begun to consider shuffling his cabinet. In many ways, the cabinet changes made over the next eighteen months were the most important of King's prime ministerial career. Everyone knew that they would confirm the direction that the Liberal Party would take after the war and would also influence the succession to the prime ministership; King was growing old and was feeling increasingly unwell. C. D. Howe, one of the ministers with whom King discussed his cabinet shuffle, suggested promoting the more right-wing members of the party and shifting Brooke Claxton and me, who represented the progressive side of liberalism, into junior

---

1 Colin Gibson, the minister of national defence for air, became the new secretary of state on 11 December 1946. Mackenzie King had given me a new job as minister of national health and welfare.

portfolios.[2] I discovered later that the prime minister considered either leaving me as secretary of state, or moving me to external affairs, national health and welfare, or to the post office.[3]

In his calculations, Mackenzie King had to take into account that the party could not afford to move too far to the right. Fully realizing that liberalism was a political faith that concerned itself with the welfare of ordinary people, King knew that its policies and programs had to be tailored to ensure security for the individual. On 16 September 1946, the Social Credit candidate had won a byelection in Pontiac, Québec. Although Alphonse Fournier, the minister of public works, was in charge of the organization of the campaign, and I had emphasized progressive liberalism in a speech there — it was right across the Ottawa River from my old Pembroke stamping-ground — the Liberal candidate went down to defeat. Similar byelection losses on 21 October in Toronto Parkdale and in Portage La Prairie were directly attributable to a strong CCF showing; that party was obviously attracting disaffected Liberal voters. The electorate had made clear its desire for reform by defeating Liberal candidates in the first three byelections following VJ Day. Howe's proposals for cabinet changes would have been a defiance of these expressions of the public will for policies directed towards aiding the ordinary man and woman.

As a means of holding the CCF in check, Brooke Claxton and I had continued to argue for an enlightened and reformist liberalism. In my speeches during the byelection campaigns, I pointed out that the besetting evils remained the same after the war as they had always been — poverty, insecurity and fear. The two of us argued in cabinet, with some support, that the Liberal program

2 In a list of prospective ministers that Howe sent to King, he suggested that Claxton be given the department of veterans' affairs and that I be moved to the department of national war services. He further proposed that the department of national health and welfare be entrusted to Dr. J. J. McCann of Renfrew (Memo by C.D. Howe, July 1945, King Papers (J4 series, p. C161,252)) PAC. When I discovered this note in Mackenzie King's papers, I could not help but think that, in 1935, I urged Vincent Massey to impress on King the desirability of the early inclusion in the cabinet of C. D. Howe, the engineer from Port Arthur.
3 Typewritten note, August 1945, King Papers, (J4 series, p. C161,285) PAC.

would use the best of both public and private initiative to raise living standards and to give people more opportunities: in short, that liberalism must steer its reform course between the extremes of right and left.

With his customary caution, Mackenzie King undertook the reassignment of his ministers in several stages. The first step took place on 4 September, when the prime minister resigned his external affairs portfolio and appointed Louis St. Laurent to the post. For the time being, the new external affairs minister also retained responsibility for the department of justice, but we knew that this situation could not last very long and that more changes were in the wind.

During the second stage of the cabinet shuffle, I was in New York at the United Nations General Assembly. When St. Laurent resigned from the justice department on 9 December, he was immediately succeeded by the finance minister, Jim Ilsley. Ilsley had tired himself out during the war, and Mackenzie King, concerned about his mental fatigue, thought that he would enjoy a lighter workload in justice. The nation owed Ilsley a great debt. To replace him in the department of finance, King chose Doug Abbott, who had been minister of national defence. An able man, Abbott breezed through life, but I could not help wondering how he would manage to confront the issues that had worn down his predecessor.

These changes affected the various players' hopes of succeeding to the prime ministership. By this time, Mackenzie King had begun to push St. Laurent more into the public eye in the hope of persuading him to stay in politics and to "inherit" the leader's mantle. Ilsley, one of the few ministers who was not afraid to stand up to King, received a position that removed him from the spotlight. For the younger ministers like Claxton, Abbott and myself, the changes confirmed that the leadership of the party would continue to rest firmly in the hands of its elder statesmen. Claxton and I had a quiet rivalry in seeking out assignments that related to international affairs — he had gone to the Paris peace conference in the summer of 1946, while I had been at the UN — and the appointment of a separate minister of external affairs meant that our opportunities in that field would be more limited. Doug Abbott's appointment to finance put him in the forefront of the younger ministers, but that department was known to take its toll.

In New York, Brooke Claxton phoned me several times; he had kept his ear to the ground and informed me of what was going on. He called me during the contentious debate on the United Nations Relief and Rehabilitation Administration to tell me that I too would shortly be hearing from the prime minister. On one of my quick trips to Ottawa, Ian Mackenzie had suggested that I might be moved to the department of immigration. That would have been fine with me. The only department to which I had any objection was labour; the Ford strike had made it obvious that as minister of labour I would be extremely vulnerable to the pressures that inevitably weigh heavily on MPs who represent industrial ridings. When Claxton next phoned, his news took me aback. He told me that I would be asked to assume his job in health and welfare. "Be prepared," Brooke advised.

After his call, I pondered alone about what the change would mean. The department of the secretary of state — a basically legal ministry concerned with long-standing matters and services — was certainly a different kettle of fish from health and welfare, which was in the forefront of the Liberal party's post-war reform program. The change would provide an opportunity to accomplish what I had always wanted to do; but still I was worried. Although my enthusiasm was great, I also worried because I knew that I would run into all kinds of opposition from within the cabinet, starting with Mackenzie King himself. Health and welfare programs cost money, and King always considered himself the guardian of the privy purse. My wish would be to expand health and welfare programs and force the government to catch up on some of its promises. A commitment to health insurance, for example, had been part of the party platform in 1919, when Mackenzie King was chosen to lead the Liberals. I did not want to go into health and welfare unless I could be sure of enacting these desirable and much-needed measures. I knew what Brooke's problems had been; he had spoken to me about them. When he chose the first deputy minister of welfare, Dr. Brock Chisholm, a psychologist who had been in the army, Claxton was sure that Chisholm's advanced social views would not go down well in Ottawa. Moreover, federal-provincial battling over the federal government's Green Book proposals had effectively scuttled the immediate implementation of the health and welfare reforms that they contained.

The next day, the prime minister's phone call indicated that his plans were, in fact, as Claxton had predicted. I told King that I could not return to Ottawa because of the urgency of my work at the UN on the refugee question. However, I immediately sent him a telegram, formally submitting my resignation so that he would have a free hand. Before he telephoned me back the following morning to confirm my new job, I had already read about it in the newspapers.

The Christmas holidays gave me some time away from my hectic life to reflect on the past and the future. It seemed to me that I had moved very far away from Pembroke and St. Alexandre — and yet I knew that in many ways I could never leave them behind. The past spring, just after my trip from London, I had returned to Pembroke; early in March, the town's citizens gave a banquet for me. Political affiliations were forgotten and some of those who had called me a young rabble-rouser in 1928 now came along to shake my hand (I'm not so sure that they had entirely changed their minds). The Mayor of Windsor, Art Reaume, brought greetings and sat near Jim Reynolds, my former boss at the Colonial Lumber Company. No one was happier than my mother — she needed no convincing of her son's virtues. Yet the reception, I explained to the audience, was really a tribute to my parents, brother and sisters to whom I owed so much. Not many days later, I was greatly touched by the welcome of the students and faculty when I paid a short visit to St. Alexandre.

These two gatherings linked the past with the present and brought home to me the continuity of the two themes that had dominated my life so far. Trust, I reminded the citizens of Pembroke, not only formed the basis of friendship in small Ontario towns, but was also the key constituent in harmonious international relations. The United Nations, an example of this trust, was to ensure progress and stability throughout the world. At St. Alexandre, I expressed my admiration for some of the college's staff, who had taught us to have faith in Canada. The students presented me with an address that I have kept as a treasured possession. It spoke of the impression that Laurier had made on me when I was a student at the college, and linked my work with his.

More recent personal experiences also directed my thoughts as I deliberated about the future. A tornado had struck Windsor on the night of 17 June. In Ottawa, the only news I could obtain was that it had inflicted its heaviest damage near my home. Greatly concerned, I tried phoning my wife, and grew even more agitated when I could not reach her. Early the next morning, I flew home and found that Nell was fine. She had seen the furious spiral during the evening as she was hanging out the washing, but she went to bed, unaware that the telephone lines near our house had been knocked out.

As I visited the victims of the tornado, the generosity of the community became manifest, and the municipality was given the authority to allocate temporary housing and supplies. The incident brought home to me all the more clearly that government must find a means of supplementing private charity by organized welfare programs.

Just two months later, during a cabinet meeting that approved my appointment to the second part of the UN General Assembly in New York, I was called outside by a message: Nell insisted on speaking with me on the telephone. When I took the call in an outer office, she was beside herself. "Come home, come home, our son has polio." At that instant, I knew just how my parents must have felt when I was taken ill as a boy. I went back to the cabinet room and passed Louis St. Laurent a note explaining the situation.

He interrupted the agenda to inform my colleagues, before he turned to me and said, "Paul, you had better be with your wife." Ignoring my protests that I would wait until the end of the meeting, C. D. Howe insisted that I go immediately and promised a government plane for the trip — a scarce and carefully husbanded resource in those days.

In no time, I was in Windsor airport, from where I was rushed to the isolation ward. There he was, our handsome eight-year-old son, paralyzed in the throat and unable to speak. Despite our great consternation, Paul appeared to take it all as something of a joke; he was smiling and wriggling around in the bed. Mercifully, the crisis passed fairly quickly and Paul began to mend, even though it took almost a year before he recovered fully.

During the summer of 1946, Canada suffered from the most severe epidemic of poliomyelitis in the country's history. Thousands of children suffered from this crippling disease and many died. We were very lucky that our son was not left with any disability. The similar experiences of father and son could not but lead me to draw comparisons with the past medical science had indeed progressed since the turn of the century — but, as in my youth, I knew that advanced treatment was still not available to all, even though over forty years had elapsed since I had contracted spinal meningitis.

It was clear that my personal values and background would dictate the goals that I must strive for in my newest assignment. The benefits of medical science should be made universally accessible; families must be protected against unemployment, the elderly must be given adequate old-age pensions; children should receive the assurance of at least the basic necessities of life and an education that did not come from the beneficence of others. The path was clear and the test was plain.

Index